Dr. S.E. Stoven
307 Hills Rd
Cambridge

£7.50

*Psychosexual Problems:
Psychotherapy,
Counselling and
Behavioural Modification*

Psychosexual Problems: Psychotherapy, Counselling and Behavioural Modification

Edited by

SIDNEY CROWN

Consultant Psychiatrist,
The London Hospital, Whitechapel,
London, England

1976

ACADEMIC PRESS · London
and
GRUNE & STRATTON · New York

U.K. edition published and distributed by
ACADEMIC PRESS INC. (LONDON) LTD.
24/28 Oval Road
London NW1

United States Edition published and distributed by
GRUNE & STRATTON INC.
111 Fifth Avenue
New York, New York 10003

Library of Congress Catalog Card Number: 76 1075
ISBN (Academic Press): 0 12 199350 7
ISBN (Grune & Stratton): 0 8089 0953 3

Text set in 11/12 pt IBM Baskerville Roman, printed by photolithography,
and bound in Great Britain at The Pitman Press, Bath

Contributors

GEORGE BEAUMONT   *Neuropsychiatric Clinical Research Group, Medical Department, Ciba-Geigy, UK, Ltd., Macclesfield, Cheshire, England*

JOHN BLANDY   *Professor of Urology, The London Hospital Medical College, University of London; Consultant Surgeon, St Peter's Hospital, London, England*

IRENE BLOOMFIELD   *Principal Clinical Psychologist and Psychotherapist, Department of Psychological Medicine, University College Hospital, London, England*

H. A. BRANT   *Professor of Clinical Obstetrics and Gynaecology University College Hospital and Medical School, London, England*

FRED H. BURBANK   *Clinical Instructor of Psychiatry, Department of Psychiatry and Behavioural Sciences, Stanford University, California, USA*

H. C. CAMERON   *Consultant Child Psychiatrist, St. George's Hospital, London, England. Sometime Honorary Consultant Child Psychiatrist, Leon Gillis Unit, Queen Mary's Hospital, Roehampton, London, England*

PHILIP CAUTHERY   *Physician in Charge of Student Health Service, University of Aston in Birmingham, Birmingham, England*

MARTIN COLE   *Director, Institute for Sex Education and Research, Birmingham, England; Lecturer, Department of Biological Sciences, University of Aston in Birmingham, Birmingham, England*

DAVID GOLDMEIER *Research Registrar, Whitechapel Clinic, The London Hospital, Whitechapel, London, England*

DUNCAN GUTHRIE *Chairman, Committee on Sexual Problems of the Disabled, Horsham, Sussex, England*

PREBEN HERTOFT *Head of the Psychiatric Out-patient Clinic, Director of the Sex Research Unit, The University Clinic of Psychiatry, Rigshospitalet, Copenhagen, Denmark.*

C. J. LUCAS *Director and Psychiatric Adviser, University College, London Health Centre, London, England*

DOUGAL MACKAY *Principal Clinical Psychologist, St Mary's Hospital, London, England*

LOUIS MARTEAU *Roman Catholic Priest; Director of the Dympna Centre; Lecturer in Pastoral Psychology and Psychotherapist, Department of Psychiatry, The London Hospital, Whitechapel, London, England*

AUDREY NEWSOME *Head of the Appointments and Counselling Service, The University of Keele, Keele, Staffordshire, England*

J. S. NORELL *Dean of Studies, The Royal College of General Practitioners, London, England*

BRICE PITT *Consultant Psychiatrist, The London Hospital, Whitechapel, London, England*

P. RODIN *Consultant Venereologist, Whitechapel Clinic, The London Hospital, Whitechapel, London, England*

S. J. STEELE *Director of the Academic Department of Obstetrics and Gynaecology; Reader, The Middlesex Hospital Medical School, London, England. Honorary Consultant The Middlesex Hospital, The Hospital for Women, Soho; Honorary Consultant Gynaecologist to the Margaret Pyke Centre for the Study of Family Planning, London, England*

G. T. WATTS *Consultant Surgeon, General Hospital and Hospital for Women, Birmingham, England*

Foreword

I am in no sense an expert on the subject matter of this book. Paradoxically, that may be an advantage, since the layman comes to it without any professional or ideological preconceptions.

Three things strike me about it. First, it is remarkably comprehensive in its scope, and the powerful team of contributors covers a vast range of problems. Secondly, it sets out to be sober, modest and responsible; the rights of the patient are fully recognized, there is no arrogant assumption of omniscience or omnipotence, and with one or two exceptions, there is very little yielding to the temptation to go "way out". Thirdly, there is a healthy recognition that most of these problems need more than one adviser for their solution; the interdisciplinary approach is a salutary safeguard against exclusive and proprietary specialization.

Inevitably, on such matters as these, some of the statements and the views expressed will be controversial, in circles both lay and professional. Not everybody will agree with all of them — I am not sure that I do myself, in so far as I have any right to an opinion. But far more important than any of that is the fact that this sort of problem can nowadays be frankly discussed in the open air, as it were, and not behind the bushes. Nobody can be in any doubt that there are psychosexual problems in the lives of many people. Whether there are more of them than there used to be, or whether it is simply that they are now more openly acknowledged, is anybody's guess. What is clear is that responsible and authoritative examination of them can do nothing but good to unhappy and distressed sufferers. That is why I welcome this book.

Wolfenden   *March 1976*

Preface

The aims of this book were set out in a letter sent to contributors. Would they discuss psychosexual problems as these presented within their area of special interest? It went on

> ... "the book could be unusual in covering psychosexual problems in groups of people several of which, to judge from the neglect of them, are not expected to have any. The aim of the early chapters is to outline major current approaches to the treatment of psychosexual problems; and of the later chapters to show how these approaches are applied to specified groups."

What, then, are the main points? First, psychosexual problems present in persons and groups whose needs are not catered for adequately either by recognition of the problems or by the provision of appropriate help. Secondly, there are a number of different therapies now available for psychosexual problems; the uses and limitations of these need to be made explicit. Thirdly, persons attempting to help with psychosexual problems come from a wide variety of backgrounds, medical and non-medical; this book should cater for their different needs. Fourthly,

> ... "Although contributions may be as technical as authors think appropriate they should concentrate on clarity so as to appeal to those whose job it is to advise on psychosexual problems from a variety of technical backgrounds: psychiatrists, psychologists, social workers, general practitioners, counsellors, welfare officers, physicians, clergy doing pastoral work, etc."

These aims are ambitious and it is for the reader to judge how far we have been successful. If an editor is permitted one personal observation, I felt pleased and proud, as chapters arrived, that contributors had taken such trouble with their preparation. Above all they showed human concern and involvement with the subject.

Acknowledgements

It has been a particular pleasure to work with Anthony Watkinson and Jane Duncan of Academic Press. Their interest, friendliness and efficiency made editing both painless and exciting.

Involvement with the psychosexual problems of others would, for me, be impossible without the backing of my wife, June, and our children, Anna, David and Giles.

Sidney Crown   *March, 1976*

Contents

ɪ | Sex Therapies

ii | Psychosexual Problems and the Life Cycle

iii | Psychosexual Problems in Medicine and Surgery

iv | Sex Education

Introduction

SIDNEY CROWN

This book is about psychosexual problems; the contexts in which they occur, many of them unusual; about their treatment; and about their prevention — or at least reduction — through appropriate sex education.

Psychosexual Problems

Sexual or psychosexual? There is an immediate problem in terminology. Both terms are used by different contributors to this book. For many the terms are interchangeable but psychiatrists, particularly those in the psychodynamic tradition, prefer "psychosexual" because it emphasizes that sexual problems are only rarely — although they are sometimes — limited to sexuality. The whole personality is usually involved, inner life and outer life particularly relationships.

Research into sexuality has passed through a number of phases (Brecher, 1970), the contributions of Freud, Kinsey and Masters and Johnson being outstanding. The writings of the pioneers of sex research, Havelock Ellis, Kraft-Ebing, van de Velde and others range from the description of clinical sexual abnormalities through to the pattern and variation of sexuality within marriage. The early psychoanalysts, particularly Freud, Abraham and Stekel, were concerned to understand sexual phenomena within the background of the systematic theory of psychosexual development outlined particularly by Freud himself. An early paper "Three Essays on the Theory of

Sexuality" (Freud, 1905) still seems a masterpiece, and remains alive
and helpful in understanding sexual dysfunction and sexual deviance.
Hertoft (Chapter 7) for example notes its current relevance.

Psychoanalytic theorizing, while remaining firmly developmental
in its orientation, has, through what is known as ego psychology,
become also concerned with man's personality as it copes with the
demands of the basic drives and the conscience as well as the demands
of the external world, particularly of relationships. A bio-psycho-
social approach is embedded in the writings of Anna Freud (1965)
and of Erikson (1965). The coherent theorizing of these writers is
helpful in conceiving psychosexual problems. It is used by several
contributors in this book to understand the problems of adolescent
sexuality (Chapter 5), sexuality in young adults (Chapter 6), the
problems of sexual deviance (Chapters 7, 8), as well as underpinning
the psychodynamic psychotherapies, individual (Chapter 1), group
(Chapter 3) and marital (Chapter 8).

The characteristic of modern studies in sexuality is their objec-
tivity. The survey researches of Kinsey *et al.* (1948, 1953) were a land-
mark. Meaningful questions were asked of defined samples of ordinary people to find out about sexual behaviour in general rather than
those "presenting" with sexual problems to psychiatrists or to counselling services. Survey research was later aimed at special groups
such as young people (Schofield, 1968) or women (Fisher, 1973).

At the level of basic science physiological research into human
sexuality has been immeasurably advanced by the study of Masters
and Johnson (1966). These investigators bought human sexuality
into the laboratory and made meticulous observations and measure-
ments. Their later attempt to apply some of their findings to the
treatment of human sexual inadequacy (Masters and Johnson, 1970),
while only loosely attached to fundamental research, has nevertheless been an influential book therapeutically.

From these and other studies has emerged an acceptable classification of psychosexual problems which will be used throughout this
book. These may be classified as sexual inadequacy and sexual
deviance. Sexual inadequacy includes male impotency, a term that
is now restricted to erectile difficulties; secondly ejaculation problems,
premature, delayed or absent. Sexual deviance consists in acts or
fantasies which are a partial or complete substitution for heterosexuality. These used to be called by the perjorative term "perversion", a term which has been replaced by the more acceptable
"deviance". It is interesting that Hertoft (Chapter 7) uses another

term "sexual minorities". This might prove more generally acceptable to the general public and the deviant alike.

Public response to the advances in sexual understanding has itself catalysed other significant developments especially attitude-change relating both to the range of normal sexuality and to sexual deviance. Homophile organizations have fought successfully to remove shame and stigma from sexual minorities. The term "gay" for homosexual has passed into most of our vocabularies. Female sexuality has come under scrutiny in the light of recent advances in knowledge and changes in attitudes to traditional womens' "roles". The work of Masters and Johnson has helped to change preoccupation and value judgments about, for example, the "vaginal" versus the "clitoral" orgasm. In the public context the Womens' Movement has emphasized the sexual rights and expectations of women and drawn attention to the social—cultural definition and limitation of the womans' "role" in our society. The effect of this has been positive on the whole but there may follow problems relating to these modifications in the traditional female role which will only become manifest during the next decade.

Concern with valid and fulfilling relationships has influenced marriage and the family in their traditional form which have been attacked and defended with equal vehemence. Permanent or semi-permanent relationships have been modified in various ways. There has never been a greater variety of accepted, acceptable or experimented-with relationships. This must have an effect, yet to be evaluated, on child-upbringing e.g. the psychological problems of one-parent families. Despite the generally greater prevalence of marital dissolution this may reflect changes in social attitudes as well as legislation (Divorce Reform Act, 1969) so that people have higher aims for personal fulfilment and feel that a mutually destructuve relationship is better ended — both for the adults and any children involved.

Presentation and Context of Psychosexual Problems

We are concerned in this book to show how sexual problems occur at various points in life. Also psychosexual problems present differently to general practitioners, community-based counselling services and to specialised departments within a hospital.

Within the life-cycle, persons with psychosexual problems other than young adults are neglected, sometimes totally. To be under twenty or over thirty is to be a sexual outsider. But sexual problems occur in adolescence, or in middle-age or in the elderly and are of relevance and importance.

Complex medical, psychological and social factors lead patients to ask advice on sexual problems initially from their general practitioner, from a hospital or from the various social and community services helping with special problems e.g. The National Marriage Guidance Council. Sometimes the decision seems arbitrary. Thus a young woman, a virgin after six years of marriage, presented to a gynaeco-logical department asking for artificial insemination (AIH) and was referred to me. The patient's general practitioner might have conceived the problem differently and referred the husband, known to suffer from a serious mental illness, directly to a psychiatrist. Provided all concerned are aware of the problems the end result should be the same; otherwise chaos may result.

I hope that specialists reading this book will not only become more sensitized to the detection of sexual problems presenting in unusual ways within their own speciality but will also, from the therapies discussed, get some idea of those therapies or combination of therapies likely to be helpful in the particular case.

Sex Therapies

If forms of marriage and other ongoing relationship have proliferated the multiplicity of sex therapies is bewildering to the potential client and to the potential referrer. The general public recognize, somewhat uneasily, that choice of sex therapy might be crucial for their personal happiness. They recognize that while doctors tend to agree about the treatment of physical conditions they often, in good faith, disagree fundamentally about the appropriate management of a psychosexual problem. The proposed treatment of impotency might vary from an anti-depressant drug to psychoanalysis.

Even among psychotherapists there may be basic differences in formulating sex problems and their management, for example, by someone whose particular interest is in dynamic psychotherapy or behavioural psychotherapy.

It is impossible to deal with all the psychotherapies which might be appropriate for a psychosexual problem. Our aim is conservative: to restrict ourselves to orthodox counselling, psychotherapy and behavioural modification techniques. These include the psychotherapies derived broadly from psychodynamic understanding and including individual psychotherapy, group and marital psychotherapy. From clinical psychology counselling is represented and from learning theory and applied social psychology techniques of behavioural psychotherapy.

A number of evolving psychotherapies, sometimes called the "new therapies" have been omitted. Persons with sexual problems can and do benefit from these therapy situations which have a variety of names: basic encounter groups (Rogers, 1969), consciousness-raising groups, Gestalt therapy (Perls *et al.*, 1973), marathons and others. At present however these therapeutic techniques are often unsystematic, training for them is not yet clearly formulated and there may be danger to clients in terms of possible psychological damage although the prevalence of this is difficult to assess (Lieberman, *et al.*, 1973). The "new" therapies are represented by the school of psychology called Humanistic Psychology and the interested reader is referred to their journal: "Self and Society".

Prevention of Sex Problems Through Education

We are concerned with preventive medicine. It is almost certainly impossible to prevent sex problems from emerging in our complex society. Their prevalence and severity however may be reduced and the most positive suggestion is through sex education. The school child and the young adult seem obvious initial targets. In the interim however sex education may also be aimed at adults, particularly parents or potential parents. The parallel here is the education for pregnancy and delivery that enlightened departments of gynaecology offer the pregnant woman and her husband.

Sex education faces difficulties of public acceptance, of adaptation to different age-groups and different social backgrounds (e.g. see Cole p. 449) as well as in developing the most effective methods of teaching and content of such courses. In this book Cole details the argument in a healthily controversial way bound to stimulate interest and thought. Beckmann *et al.* (1975) have provided details of a sex education course suitable for medical students.

Plan of this Book

In Part I therapies relevant to psychosexual problems are described. In Part II psychosexual problems are described in approximately the order they may occur during life — in the adolescent and physically handicapped adolescent; the young adult; in marriage; in relation to sexual deviance; in a religious setting; and in the elderly. Part III discusses psychosocial problems as these present in a variety of medical and surgical situations including general practice; in the physically handicapped; in gynaecology and obstetrics; in relation to family planning; in urology; in venereology; following major abdominal surgery; and as an untoward effect of drugs. In Part IV a new approach to sex education is outlined. Finally in the Conclusion I have tried to bring together what seemed to be some of the general findings of the book.

References

Beckmann, J., Hertoft, P., Larsen, J. F., Laursen, A. M. and Wagner, G. (1975). Course in basic sexology for medical students. *British Journal of Medical Education*, 9, 114–124.

Brecher, E. M. (1970). "The Sex Researchers." Andre Deutsch: London.

Divorce Reform Act (1969). HMSO, London.

Erikson, E. H. (1965). "Childhood and Society." Penguin Books: Middlesex.

Fisher, S. (1973). "Understanding the Female Orgasm." Penguin Books: Harmondsworth.

Freud, A. (1965). "Normality and Pathology in Childhood." International Universities Press Inc: New York.

Freud, S. (1905). "Three Essays on the Theory of Sexuality." The Hogarth Press: London.

Kinsey, A. C., Pomeroy, W. B. and Martin, C. E. (1948). "Sexual Behaviour in the Human Male." W. B. Saunders Co: London.

Kinsey, A. C., Pomeroy, W. B., Martin, C. E. and Gebhard, P. H. (1953). "Sexual Behaviour in the Human Female." W. B. Saunders Co: London.

Lieberman, M. A., Yalom, I. D. and Miles, M. B. (1973). "Encounter Groups: First Facts." Basic Books, Inc: New York.

Masters, W. H. and Johnson, V. E. (1966). "Human Sexual Response." Little, Brown and Co: Boston, Mass., USA.

Masters, W. H. and Johnson, V. E. (1970). "Human Sexual Inadequacy." Churchill Livingstone: Edinburgh.

Perls, F. S., Hefferline, R. F. and Goodman, P. (1973). "Gestalt Therapy." Penguin Books: Middlesex.

Rogers, C. R. (1969). "Encounter Groups." Penguin Books: Harmondsworth.

Schofield, M. (1968). "The Sexual Behaviour of Young People." Penguin Books: Harmondsworth.

Sex Therapies

1 | *Individual Psychotherapy*

SIDNEY CROWN and C. J. LUCAS

The aim of this chapter is to give an account of individual psychotherapy with special reference to individuals with psychosexual
difficulties. More general discussion of individual psychodynamic
psychotherapy is provided in other easily available texts, as for
example those of Malan (1963, 1975) and in a forthcoming contribution by one of us (Crown, 1977). In the present context, therapy
will usually be within the framework of once-weekly sessions, face to
face, and lasting three quarters of an hour. Although techniques of
exploration, ventilation and interpretation form the basis of our
approach, we suggest that it may be useful to complement or combine these techniques with other approaches.

Contemporary Sexuality and Sex Therapies

The sexual scene has probably never been more complex whether
from the point of view of a young person faced with it, or the middle-
aged and elderly looking, possibly enviously, upon it. Also the scene
shifts making both the problems of growing into it and the problems
of deciding the aims and therapeutic methods for those who are
casualties complex and difficult. These problems are often heightened for those moving from one culture to another such as immigrants or students studying overseas. Sexual experimentation is
probably less restricted than at any previous time; contraceptive
techniques are easily available in most of the developed countries

and abortion is more available than ever before. Permanent living arrangements, including marriage, are undergoing change and development (see Chapter 8); sexual education despite the need for greater dissemination (see Chapter 19) is probably reaching a wider and younger audience than previously; and attitudes to sexual deviance, particularly homosexuality, are becoming more liberal and accepting. Living as we are through these changes it is impossible to know what problems may replace the problems of the repressive attitude to sexuality of previous generations such as excessive guilt over masturbation, unsatisfied sexual curiosity, sexual fear and ignorance.

In view of all this the sex therapist needs to allow himself flexible aims for his treatment, aims which are fully discussed with the patient or client, and he should be aware of the multiplicity of helping techniques available. This book aims to deal with the major contemporary sex therapies. Psychodynamic individual psychotherapy is discussed below and psychodynamic marital therapy in Chapter 8. Other major approaches are group psychotherapy (Chapter 3), counselling (Chapter 2), and the behavioural psychotherapies including the behavioural marital therapies and social skills training (Chapter 4).

Surface and Depth

One of the most basic ways in which therapies differ is in whether the mainsprings of human motivation are seen as below conscious awareness as in the psychodynamic therapies, or on the surface and available to consciousness as in the learning therapies; or whether this does not matter because what is used therapeutically is what is actually in the patient's mind at the time, as in counselling. While to the theoretician the above questions are fundamental, to the pragmatic therapist, doing whatever seems likely to prove therapeutically effective, the problem of conscious or unconscious motives seems irrelevant except to the preliminary choice of treatment. Thus a basic reason for suggesting a psychodynamic approach may be if it is felt that not only are the motives guiding the patient beyond the threshold of conscious awareness but that it is important to uncover these motives if a true resolution of the conflict is to be achieved. Thus, when an individual seeks help with a psychosexual problem the following questions must be asked: First, does the problem

appear to be "normal", in the sense of a usual or average, problem
of a developing individual? If so, then a counselling technique is
likely to be relevant. Second, does the sexual problem appear to
stem from deep conflicts whose non-resolution is expressed in symptoms such as depression and anxiety? If so, a psychodynamic
approach is likely to be relevant. Third, do the roots of the problem
appear to be far in the past and the patient's responses over-learned
so that they appear habitual and repetitive? If so, then one of the
behavioural psychotherapies may be the most appropriate approach
to treatment.

The remainder of this chapter will be devoted to psychodynamic
individual psychotherapy. The principles of therapy will be outlined
and their application to psychosexual problems will be discussed.
Where the question of combined treatments arises cross-reference
should be made to relevant chapters of this book.

Assessing the Patient

Descriptive Assessment

It is important that a detailed account of the problem complained of
is obtained together with detail of the patient's family history and
his personal history. It should be borne in mind that psychosexual
problems may present as a "cover" for other difficulties, and vice
versa. In addition it is important to note the severity of psychiatric
symptoms especially anxiety or depression, and to make some assessment of the underlying personality. A useful clinical classification
of personality is that of Shapiro (1965) who differentiates the hysterical, obsessional, paranoid and impulsive personality types. The
obsessional is a rather rigid and meticulous person, preoccupied
with punctuality, obstinate, parsimonious with money and affection,
controlling of others, his assertive or aggressive feelings kept mostly
below the surface although these powerful feelings may occasionally
escape in outbursts of loss of control. The hysterical personality is
the converse, being extroverted, shallow in emotion and relatively
unworried about the sort of things that worry an obsessional. While
the hysterical or obsessional personality does not, of itself, form a
barrier to psychotherapeutic treatment, the other personality types,
the impulsive and the paranoid, carry warning signs. An impulsive

person is one who cannot tolerate inner stresses or anxieties and tends to do something to express these tensions, to "act-out" in behaviour rather than to suffer. Important examples of such persons are those who are drug dependent as on heroin, cannabis, cigarette smoking, food or gambling. All these dependencies tend to have an impulsive component in their personality make-up which is extremely difficult to manage in psychotherapy. The paranoid personality, characterized by hostility, resentment and the feeling that the environment including the human environment is hostile is difficult to treat because it is hard to establish a viable therapeutic alliance characterized by sufficient mutual trust. Though a convenient framework, the traits are often mixed. In adolescence and late adolescence it is particularly difficult to "type" personalities.

Psychodynamic Assessment

In this section the aim is to state rather simply the principles of a systematic dynamic assessment of a patient or client. Being "systematic" is the essence of this appraisal. It is necessary to look serially and separately at the various aspects of a person and his relationships and to bring the totality together when this has been done. The case history in clinical medicine forms a close analogy. Symptoms and signs are examined in the different bodily systems (cardiovascular, respiratory, etc.) and the findings brought together at the conclusion in the form of a differential diagnosis. These diagnoses are essentially clinical hypotheses for further testing in therapy. Equally the implications of a psychodynamic assessment are systematically tested in psychotherapy.

   A psychodynamic appraisal should look at four fundamental aspects of the person: psychosexual development, the ego defence structure, the superego or conscience and interpersonal relationships.

Psychosexual Development

A clear account of psychosexual development is that of Erikson (1965). Erikson's viewpoint is bio-psycho-social, attaching importance to all three of these basic aspects of human personality and its development. In espousing this tripartite viewpoint Eriksonian ego psychology extends classical psychoanalysis which has tended to ignore social factors or at best to underestimate their importance (Crown, 1975). Erikson's is also an extremely practical viewpoint in clinical psychotherapeutic practice.

The two earliest phases of development are the oral phase and the anal phase. By *oral phase* is meant the development during the first year or eighteen months of life in which feeding, sucking and biting activities are of great importance and the mouth is the main organ for the early expression of sexuality and anger. From a psychosocial point of view this is the phase in which the baby establishes or fails to establish basic trust with the parent or caretaking figure the importance of which is fundamental to all subsequent development.

The *anal phase* of development refers biologically to the ability of the child to control bladder and bowel sphincter functioning, and to gain pleasure from this control. In Erikson's phrase there is a battle for autonomy. Psychosocially this phase is one of control of, and often conflict with, the caretaking figure, by holding back or expelling faeces and urine. Psychosocially, if the baby has a good relationship with the parent this control is achieved smoothly during the anal phase between the ages of eighteen months and three years; if not problems and conflicts between parent and child are likely and these may be reflected in the development in the adult of an obsessional personality structure.

The third phase of psychosexual development is the *phallic-oedipal* (from about three to six years) in which the major problem and conflict is that the child becomes attracted to the parent of the opposite sex and feels itself to be in a rivalrous relationship with the parent of the same sex. The psychological conflict of this stage is one of initiative versus guilt. The phallic-oedipal phase is of great practical importance in psychotherapy because human relationships are so fundamental to happiness and fulfilment, and for the first time the child is experiencing the frustration relating to a human triangle. This period is also of practical clinical importance because cognitive development has been progressing apace so that learning, memory and speech are adult in form and complexity. Also the child is old enough so that, even as an adult without great practise, memories relevant to this time can be retrieved.

It is usually felt in psychoanalytic thinking that these three phases, together called *infantile sexuality,* allow the laying down of basic personality structure. This is not to say that further important episodes and sensitive developmental periods do not happen later during the primary school period, during adolescence and adulthood. Relatively speaking, however, psychoanalysis shares with ethology (the study of complex animal behaviour) the basic assumption that early experience is more important for personality development than later.

Two other concepts must be briefly mentioned: *fixation* and *regression.* Relating either to biological factors or to psychosocial factors a child can linger too long at one phase of development, becoming "fixated" at this, so that if there is a conflict in later life then there will be a tendency to go back, to "regress" to this phase of development.

For practical clinical purposes the therapist needs to be able to get some idea of basic psychosexual development and, from the consideration of symptoms and personality, to see which phase of development is likely to have been of particular importance for a given patient. This includes not only how far a given person has progressed psychosexually but whether they have gone back (regressed) to a given phase. The therapist can then go on to a consideration of ego structure and defence mechanisms.

Ego Structure and Defence Mechanisms

The concept of the ego and mechanisms of defence, originally developed by S. Freud, was systematized by Anna Freud (1961). It is assumed that one part of the personality, the "ego", uses various coping or defence mechanisms in order to control anxiety and these coping or defence mechanisms are characteristic of a given person. There are two simple models to be considered here: the sources of anxiety and the description and classification of basic defence mechanisms.

The *sources of anxiety* are assumed to be three: the external or real world, the basic drives and the conscience or superego. Anxiety coming from the real world is self-explanatory. Anxiety coming from the drives is activated when either sexuality or aggressiveness is aroused giving a "signal" so that, if this anxiety is not coped with, the personality may be threatened or even overwhelmed. The characteristic anxiety of the conscience or superego is that of guilt. It is surprising how helpful this simple model is if the therapist will ask him or herself what is the likely source (or sources) of anxiety being experienced by a given patient.

Defence mechanisms are hypothetical mechanisms that help to cope with anxiety from these three sources. It is assumed that all human beings share certain defence mechanisms, that particular clinical sub-groupings are characterized by particular defences and that particular individuals have their own unique pattern. Thus anxiety may be *repressed* by which is meant that it is held down although not by a conscious effort of will; it may be *projected* i.e. disowned and felt to be coming from an outside source as in the paranoid personality and paranoid illnesses. It may be *denied* meaning that anxiety in the real world is not acknowledged; this defence is characteristic of the hysterical personality. Or intellect and emotion (affect) may be separated one from the other by the process of *isolation of affect* as in the obsessional personality. In the impulsive personality the basic problem is the inadequacy of the defence mechanisms so that anxiety aroused from any source tends to be expressed in action which may, from a growth and developmental viewpoint, be counter-productive. There are defences other than those included in this simplified account. A more detailed account of defence theory is that of Brenner (1957).

It is useful for the therapist to assess the defence structure characteristic of the patient, which defences are involved, what is their balance and, more important, whether the defence structure is effective in dealing with anxiety. Effectiveness is judged by whether or not the patient is relatively symptom-free or whether he shows psychoneurotic symptoms such as free-floating anxiety, phobic anxiety (fixed specific fear), obsessive-compulsive phenomena (rituals of thought or action which possess an impelling force but are felt by the patient to be absurd), depression (sadness) or hysterical symptoms which "convert" anxiety into physical complaints which do not have an organic basis and which seem often to produce some "pay off" in the patient's life (secondary gain). In thinking of "symptoms" it is important to stress that a capacity to experience psychological pain is part of normal psychological life.

Psychosexual problems are unique in that relatively severe sexual difficulties such as sado-masochism or homosexuality or sexual attraction to children or exhibitionism are all compatible not only with a good adjustment in important areas of functioning such as work and social relationships, but also the patient frequently does not suffer from psychoneurotic symptoms. Thus psychosexual problems are more of a personality disturbance than a psychoneurosis.

Conscience and Guilt

That particular emotion which relates to an action or fantasy
"disapproved" by the person's conscience or superego is termed
guilt. It is convenient to differentiate "appropriate" guilt — when a
person infringes his own (and usually society's) moral precepts, and
neurotic guilt in which a person experiences the emotion with the
absence of any real infringement of his conscious values. In psychodynamic terms, the conscience is regarded as originating from an
internalized version of parental values; but in the neurotic individual
it is apt to be far harsher than the real-life parents, and may impose
a crippling inhibition on the patient's capacity for enjoyment.
Defences as described in relation to anxiety also operate in relation
to guilt. In addition the restoration of imagined damage (reparation)
may be used to reduce the sense of guilt; a scrupulous over-conscien-
tiousness is a common feature of the obsessional personality.

It is clear that an assessment of this area is of crucial importance
in relation to psychosexual problems, in which guilt feelings may
be excessive, deficient, oscillating in capricious ways or inappropriate.
Guilt may be partly or wholly unconscious and expressed in disguised
forms as, for example, in self-punishing behaviour.

Interpersonal Relationships

Finally the form and quality of interpersonal, including sexual,
relationships should be assessed. This includes discussion of relationships with the same and the opposite sex. It should also include
early relationships to significant figures (parents, sibs), as well as to
persons outside the family — older, younger; peer and occupational
groups.

Summarizing, the patient's history has been taken, his symptomatology noted and his basic personality assessed. A psychodynamic
appraisal has been made so that some idea is gained of his level of
psychosexual development and whether he has fixations at any particular phase, or whether it seems likely that he has regressed to a
particular phase. The ego structure has been assessed and observations
made through personality traits, symptoms and type of defence,
about how the patient deals with anxiety and also the major sources
of this anxiety (external world, drives and the conscience). The
structure of the conscience or superego has been considered and a

decision made whether this is basically normal and healthy or whether the presence of inappropriate guilt feelings, or of acts which seem to be prompted by guilt and the need for punishment, are in evidence. Finally the form and quality of interpersonal, including sexual, relationships has been considered. Given this comprehensive combined appraisal it is now possible to outline the technique of psychodynamic individual psychotherapy.

Technique of Psychodynamic Individual Psychotherapy

The aim in this section is to outline the principles of this type of treatment so that their application to psychosexual problems can be discussed in the final section. The basic principles of psychotherapeutic technique can be most helpfully summarized in terms of the continuity of the psychotherapeutic relationship. Thus the therapeutic alliance is established at the beginning of therapy; then follows the main period of psychotherapeutic interaction with interventions; lastly comes the termination of therapy.

Therapeutic Alliance

This is discussed in detail by Sandler *et al.* (1973). What is involved is that the patient and the therapist should both know what they are about, in terms of the aims, methods and practicalities of therapy; the basic parameters of therapy should be established particularly frequency and times of sessions, length of sessions and fee if treatment is outside the NHS. The most usual frequency of psychodynamic individual psychotherapy is once-weekly, the session length forty-five minutes and therapy can often be relatively brief varying probably between three months and one year. This upper time limit needs particular consideration. There may be entirely appropriate and justifiable reasons why therapy should continue for longer than one year. In these circumstances group therapy may be useful. In terms of practical clinical experience we suggest that there should be carefully thought-out reasons for going on longer than one year; therapists should be self-critical before they decide, together with the patient, to continue. If a fee is appropriate it should be set at a level which

does not in itself create a new anxiety by forming an undue drag
on individual or family finances. In contemporary times, with a
range of alleviative approaches available, it is necessary to discuss
the type of therapy felt to be appropriate and this will include,
where relevant, the combination of psychodynamic individual
psychotherapy with other therapies discussed elsewhere in this
book; for example group therapy, behavioural or marital therapy.
Within reason during the establishment of the therapeutic alliance
a patient's questions should be answered about the therapist's background and in particular his training. It is difficult to lay down
rules, but our practise is to answer questions which seem to have a
largely factual basis but where a question involves obvious curiosity
as for example whether the therapist is married, number of children,
political views, etc., then these can be put back to the patient as
being questions about which more will be gained by discussion with
him as to why he wishes to know rather than by a simple answer.

Free-association

The psychiatric history-taking and the additional questions needed
to make a psychodynamic appraisal both involve the therapist in
direct questioning. Classical psychoanalysis then turns to the technique of free association whereby the patient reports everything that
comes into his mind. It is now realized that in techniques other than
classical psychoanalysis such freedom of association is not possible.
What is encouraged however is that the patient should, so far as is
possible, say everything that comes into his mind and that he should
try not consciously to choose or censor the topics as these occur to
him. The idea of associating freely should be explained in a way that
is suited to the individual patient's personality, needs and anxieties
and social background. Some patients simply need an explanation
as bald as the previous sentence. Others want reassurance that they
will be helped if they get "stuck", or further guidance as to what
is wanted. It may be necessary for the therapist to use terminology
suitable for a given age group as, for example, to an adolescent the
suggestion that a topic might be "kicked around between us". The
therapist needs to become aware of different patient's personal
modes of speech, characteristic use of pauses between sentences, and
the amount of guidance they need so that on the whole topics come

from the patient and are not constantly supplied by an over-impatient therapist. In psychotherapy, in contrast to psychoanalysis, the therapist is likely to be more active, and to show and use his personality more than in the classical situation which aims at the crystallization of a transference neurosis around the person of the mainly passive psychoanalyst.

Psychotherapeutic Interventions

Linking Comments

By linking comments is meant that the psychotherapist brings together facets of the patient's experience which at the time of their presentation the patient may not have been aware. Thus important aspects of past experience may be linked with experience in the present; experience in the present in one area or sector of a patient's life may be linked with experience in other current areas; or, problems and experiences in the past and present may be linked with attitudes and feelings towards the future. Linking consists essentially in seeing things in a manner which is different from that in which the patient up to that time has seen them although all items are in a sense within conscious awareness and available.

Interpretation

It is in the area of "interpretation" that psychodynamic psychotherapy finds one of its unique features differentiating it from the other therapies discussed in this book especially counselling and the behavioural psychotherapies. The uniqueness lies in the fact that interpretation makes the explicit assumption that some of the mainsprings of our actions and feelings lie below the threshold of awareness yet exert a powerful influence upon our behaviour. Interpretation makes particular use of the relationship between the therapist and patient. This is in comparison to the behavioural psychotherapies which minimize this relationship or regard it as a "nonspecific" factor; and counselling which works not with the relationship as such but with the thoughts and feelings of the client as these become available to consciousness.

Interpretations are of four main kinds: interpretation of transference, interpretation of defences against anxiety, interpretation of
dreams and interpretation of the "negative therapeutic reaction".

Interpretation of Transference

A major psychodynamic aspect of the relationship between patient
and therapist is described in terms of the "transferring" on to the
person of the therapist feelings and attitudes felt towards important
figures, from an earlier period of the person's life. It is a basic principle of psychodynamic individual psychotherapy that through the
further understanding of these transferred attitudes and feelings the
patient is able to understand many of his current problems in connection with interpersonal relationships particularly close relationships.
In this sense the transference relationship of patient to therapist is
particularly apposite to the understanding of psychosexual problems.
Ideally what is attempted is to try and find a link between feelings
the patient has had towards important figures in the past, feelings
that he has of a similar type to important figures in his present life
which are then linked with feelings that the patient may be experiencing towards the therapist. This combination cannot always be
achieved, but when it is, can produce immensely increased understanding and insight on the part of the patient. A therapist should always,
if an attitude or feeling on the part of a patient towards him seems
inappropriate to the situation, suggest to the patient that what he is
experiencing may be derived from worries and anxieties in relation
to significant figures in his earlier life.

Interpretation of Defences Against Anxiety

Characteristic defences against anxiety, for example regression,
denial, projection, isolation of affect have been mentioned earlier.
It is usually clear from the psychodynamic appraisal of the patient
the sort of defences he or she is likely to use according to the phase
of psychosexual development that seems of particular importance
to that patient. Thus the patient who seems to have problems in the
earlier stages of his development (basic trust) will be likely to be
non-trusting towards everyone including the therapist and to use
particularly the mechanism of projection; the patient who has been

fixated at the anal phase of development is likely to use intellectual-
ization or isolation of affect; the patient who has difficulties mainly
in interpersonal relationships and particularly with persons of the
opposite sex is more likely to use the mechanisms of repression and
denial relating to the phallic-oedipal stage of development. One of
the aims of psychotherapy is to allow the patient to understand any
marked imbalance in his defence mechanisms, their relative ineffec-
tiveness or inappropriateness, or the way characteristic defences
dominate his perception of himself or others. It is necessary therefore
to interpret to the patient when defences seem illustrated in his
life and in the therapy situation so that he can come to terms with
his underlying difficulties and make a more appropriate adjustment
to anxiety.

Interpretation of Dreams

While dream interpretation played an important part in the early
development of psychoanalysis and is still of importance in formal
psychoanalysis, in psychodynamic psychotherapy it is useful to
deal with the dream in the same way as any other material, (thoughts,
feelings, ideas, memories, fantasies) that is produced by the patient.
In other words it is one route to understanding the patient's unconscious mind but not the only or, as Freud called it, the "royal road"
to this. In psychodynamic psychotherapy it is also helpful to give
the patient some instruction in the use of dreams. It can be shown
that a dream or even a dream fragment represents something in his
current life and at the same time reflects wishes, fears and anxieties
from an earlier phase of his life. Thus the dream is cast, so to speak,
in the costume of the present but expresses in coded form important
events of the past and therefore often provides useful material for
therapy.

Negative Therapeutic Reaction

The negative therapeutic reaction describes the situation where a
patient, apparently progressing in psychotherapy, seems to get worse
again by developing other symptoms or behaving in a regressive way;
in other words to go back one step for every two steps forward. From
a psychodynamic point of view this is considered to reflect unconscious

guilt so that any pleasure including the pleasure of making gains in psychotherapy arouses guilt feelings which in turn lead to a loss of what has been gained in therapy — hence the name negative therapeutic reaction. When it is observed, the negative therapeutic reaction should be interpreted to the patient so that he is made aware not only of what is happening but of the significance of this in relation to his conscience or superego and paradoxical expression of guilt.

In conclusion, the use of these various interpretations, when appropriate, should lead to increased *insight* for the patient into the roots of his psychosexual problem. It seems likely that insight is one of the basic mechanisms leading to improvement in all psychotherapies although by itself it is almost certainly not enough. It must be combined with working-through.

Working-through

It is seldom that insight alone produces change in experience and behaviour. Working-through takes place both inside and outside the therapy session. In therapy it consists of the further cognitive and emotional understanding and generalizing of the insights of therapy. In formal psychoanalysis it refers to the integration of a piece of insight by "working-through" the defences repeatedly (Sandler *et al.*, 1973). In psychodynamic psychotherapy it is useful to extend this concept to include the practise of actual behaviour outside the psychotherapy session the experience of which is in turn fed back to therapy leading to further insights. As an example a patient may understand his basic mistrust of people by experiencing negative attitudes to the therapist in his therapy sessions. He must in addition be able to see, through his relationships with people in the outside world, how unjustified and based in fantasy is this basic mistrust. This combination of cognitive change within therapy and behavioural change outside therapy are two important factors producing change in psychotherapy.

Termination of Therapy

The important points about terminating therapy are first to decide when it should happen and secondly to decide how. When therapy should be terminated depends mainly, of course, upon the patient's complaints and their amelioration or resolution. It is, however, also related to the aims and philosophy of the therapist. Some therapists have an idealized concept of normality; others accept more limited goals, such as improving the patient's life situation including his psychosexual problem. The technique described in this chapter is appropriate to the second of these aims rather than the first. Either the patient or the therapist may suggest enough has been achieved. If this is agreed it is necessary to decide how slowly or quickly therapy should be terminated. This depends on the temperament of the patient; some like to stop almost immediately within one or two sessions; others like to fix a date several weeks in advance. It is important that the patient discusses in detail his or her feelings about terminating therapy so that this is seen as a break with someone who has helped and is of importance to them but not as an unresolved dependency. It is useful to many patients to be told that, while the therapist is making no pre-judgments of the future, if things go badly or if minor problems come up they can always return for further psychotherapy if appropriate.

Psychosexual Problems

There is an almost infinite number of ways in which psychosexual problems present clinically. This book is therapy-orientated and the various chapters show how psychosexual problems present at different times of life or to different specialized medical and surgical services. In the remainder of this chapter we wish to discuss the general management of psychosexual problems by psychodynamic individual psychotherapy, the principles of which have been outlined.

Psychosexual Problems Secondary to Psychiatric and/or Personality Disorder

It is not uncommon for someone to attain heterosexual satisfaction and adequacy despite profound psychiatric and personality problems; in contrast other people appear psychiatrically stable yet they have

profound sexual difficulties. Thirdly there may be the combination
of personality and/or psychiatric problems and psychosexual problems. These possibilities will be considered in turn.

Sexual Adequacy with Personality Problems

Problems may arise when such a person having perhaps for a number
of years had casual relationships including casual sexual relationships wishes to make a more permanent or "significant" relationship
and finds these repeatedly go wrong. He may become disturbed, feel
inadequate, develop minor psychosomatic complaints such as headache, abdominal pain, etc., and possibly ask for psychotherapeutic
help. This type of patient is often well suited to psychodynamic
individual psychotherapy if their need has become obvious to them
because their functioning may be adequate and appropriate in other
fields. Depending upon the severity of the personality problem they
may be easy to help or extremely difficult. If the personality difficulties reflect early development, for example, excessive egocentricity
(narcissistic personality disorder), or paranoid mistrust of deep relationships they can prove extremely resistant to treatment. On the
other hand if the personality problems stem from a relatively late
stage in psychosexual development, the phallic-oedipal phase, memories and insight may be readily available and behavioural modification
more likely.

Sexual Inadequacy and Normal Personality

This second group can be remarkably difficult to help with dynamic
psychotherapy because, as they themselves tend to point out,
there are no major areas of stress or disturbance to analyse and understand, only a sexual problem. It is well worth establishing, by a trial
of psychotherapy, that the initial impression of "normality" is
correct but, if this is so, then such patients may be more effectively
treated by behavioural modification techniques (Chapter 4). When
a learned habit such as sexuality becomes disturbed over a long
period, it is extremely difficult with exploratory or ventilative psychotherapy alone to promote change. Some more direct form of
intervention such as behavioural modification will usually be required.

Combined Personality and Sexual Problems

The third group, in which there are both personality and sexual disorders may, again, be suitable for psychodynamic individual psychotherapy alone or for a combination of this with behavioural psychotherapy. It is usually sensible to work with the personality problem using dynamic psychotherapy initially. If there is personality improvement the sexual problems not infrequently also improve. On the other hand a number of patients show remarkable improvement in terms of personality functioning and yet sexuality lags behind. Again this group may need the opportunity of a combined behavioural modification technique.

Sexual Inadequacy

Male Sexual Inadequacy

A useful method of clarifying the problem is to take the sex act as a sequence from before it starts to after it finishes and to localize the problem in this sequence. Thus the sexually inadequate man must be asked about his sexual drive, whether he has felt this to be "average", low or excessive according to his own standards and whether it is easier or more difficult for him to express it in autosexuality (masturbation), with his wife or other permanent or semi-permanent attachment or with casual girlfriends. This allows some assessment of basic sexual arousal and sexual expression. He can then be assessed on the next major division which is related to erection or ejaculation. Erectile inadequacy (impotency) must in turn be sub-divided into whether or not the man can get an erection, whether he can maintain it until penetration, or whether he loses it after penetration and before ejaculation. Ejaculatory inadequacy consists either in premature ejaculation or, much rarer, ejaculatory incompetence (Bancroft, 1971). Ejaculatory incompetence can then be broken down into whether ejaculate is produced during masturbation and not during sexual intercourse or not produced during either. Orgasmic capacity must also be assessed in the male, divided into psychic orgasm which is total loss of control, the ability to merge body images with the partner, and a feeling of complete release; and physical orgasm which relates to the production of sperm. One may next enquire whether after the actual sex act the man experiences loving feelings towards his partner or whether there are negative feelings such as rejection, disgust or, in some cases, a feeling of being unclean and the need to wash or bath.

Female Sexual Inadequacy

Sexual inadequacy in the female can be assessed along the same sequence starting with sexual arousal. It is useful to consider separately sexual foreplay and sexual orgasm. So far as foreplay is concerned sexually inadequate women can be sub-divided into those who do not get full pleasure but do not actively object to foreplay; and those who find this actively displeasurable. This may lead to a specific fear of being touched or the threat of being touched so intense as to be classified as phobic anxiety. Or these negative feelings may lead to spasm of muscular groups leading to difficulty in penetration (vaginismus) or deep pain after penetration (dyspareunia). The sexual orgasm in women is a problematic area psycho-physiologically. Fisher (1973) in his book on the female orgasm estimates that approximately 60% of women do not consistently experience sexual orgasm. Another problem about the sexual orgasm in women is that, due to the influence of Masters and Johnson (1970) undue emphasis has been attached to it, including the possibility of multiple orgasm, as if pleasure is limited to this. This is not always the case. Further, a psychologically sophisticated woman may be concerned with the psychoanalytic controversy about whether the female orgasm should be primarily clitoral, vaginal or both. Finally it is important to ask about feelings following the sex act especially whether she feels rejected or unloved, whether the man leaves her or stays; and the use of a double or single bed especially any disagreement about this.

Miscellaneous Heterosexual Problems

This is a group of sexual problems many of which are dealt with in other chapters of this book. Thus sexual problems may arise due to inexperience on the part of the man or woman. It is often forgotten in an age which is generally regarded as liberated and "permissive" that there is still much ignorance about sex. It is important, therefore, that there should be considerable extension of sex education (Chapter 19). It is not infrequent for a couple to present with one or both in a state of remarkable sexual ignorance. This may include ignorance of the anatomical parts taking part in the sexual act, ignorance of positions in intercourse, fear about adventurous sexual play, uncertainty, ignorance and fear about contraception (e.g. a number of women are still not absolutely certain that the contraceptive pill is "safe" if taken as prescribed). These are the sort of problems that respond well to sexual counselling techniques (Chapter 2). Other miscellaneous heterosexual problems may arise through physical handicap (Chapter 13), problems of religious attitudes, scruples and fears (Chapter 9), problems of ageing (Chapter 10) and a number of others which individually appear relatively rarely in the clinical practice of the individual psychiatrist or psychotherapist but together add up to a significant area of sexual misery, doubt and non-satisfaction.

Sexual Deviance

This problem is dealt with in detail in Chapter 7. From the point of view of the psychodynamic psychotherapist the problem can be divided into homosexuality and other problems of sexual deviance which will not be further discussed here. Homosexuality is however the most prevalent sexual deviance. It is essential to decide whether the primary focus of treatment is the homosexuality as such or related problems such as anxiety, depression, feelings of inadequacy or feelings of sadness and longing about marriage and children. This of course largely depends on how the patient expresses his need. He may himself say that he wishes his sexual orientation to be changed or, more frequently, that he has no desire for this but would like to come more to terms with himself in relation to other areas of his life. In our opinion it would be a rash therapist who offers to change a long-standing, solely homosexual orientation; on the other hand if a homosexual of either sex has shown definite evidence of heterosexual interest in fantasy or reality and even more of heterosexual performance even if only on one or two occasions the prospects are much brighter. Following Kinsey *et al.* (1948) it is helpful to think of homosexuality on a continuous spectrum of behaviour and fantasy from the exclusively homosexual to the exclusively heterosexual. It is always important to enquire not only into actual behaviour but

also fantasy in terms of daydreams, sexual wishes, etc., and in particular masturbation fantasies and whether these are homosexual or
heterosexual

On the basis of these enquiries the decision can be made and discussed with the patient as to whether or not change in sexual orientation is an appropriate aim of treatment or other related psychological
problems noted above. If the homosexual orientation is the aim of
treatment then a decision must be made whether this should be done
by a psychodynamic individual psychotherapeutic approach, by
group therapy, by a behavioural approach or a combination of these.
If the problem is to deal with related difficulties such as depression,
anxiety, identity problems or sadness about non-fulfilment as a
family man then psychodynamic individual or group psychotherapy
is likely to be appropriate.

Summary

In modern society there is a changing attitude to sexuality and a
multiplicity of sexual aims and sexual adjustments. There are also
many therapies. The importance attached to unconscious factors
differentiates the psychodynamic psychotherapies from all others.
The psychodynamic appraisal of the individual includes appraisal
of psychosexual development; the characteristic pattern of coping
or defence mechanisms against anxiety; the structure of the conscience or superego and interpersonal, including sexual, relationships.
The technique of psychodynamic, individual, once-weekly psychotherapy starts with the establishment of the therapeutic alliance in
which the basic parameters of therapy (frequency, length of treatment, etc.) are decided. The major psychotherapeutic interaction
consists of various interventions (e.g. linking aspects of the patient's
life; or "interpreting" aspects of his experience which are not at
the time of the interpretation within conscious awareness). Use may
be made of the relationship between patient and therapist (transference) and interpretations made of characteristic defences against
anxiety. The achievement of change in psychotherapy is through
insight or personal understanding and the opportunity to practise
what is learned. The termination of treatment is discussed; particularly the need to agree with the patient the time over which termination should take place. Psychosexual problems appropriate for

treatment with psychodynamic individual psychotherapy are discussed and some guidance is given to the assessment and management of these problems.

References

Bancroft, J. (1971). Sexual inadequacy in the male. *Postgraduate Medical Journal*, 47, 562–571.

Brenner, C. (1957). "An Elementary Textbook of Psychoanalysis." International Universities Press, Inc: New York.

Crown, S. (1975). Psychoanalytic psychotherapy. *In* "Issues and Approaches in the Psychological Therapies."(Bannister, D. Ed.), pp. 187–200. John Wiley and Sons: Chichester.

Crown, S. (1977). "Dynamic Individual Psychotherapy: Concepts and Technique." Academic Press: London. (To appear.)

Erikson, E. H. (1965). "Childhood and Society." Penguin Books: Harmondsworth.

Fisher, S. (1973). "Understanding the Female Orgasm." Penguin Books: Harmondsworth.

Freud, A. (1961). "The Ego and the Mechanisms of Defence." The Hogarth Press: London.

Kinsey, A. C., Pomeroy, W. B. and Martin, C. E. (1948). "Sexual Behaviour in the Human Male." W. B. Saunders Co: London.

Malan, D. H. (1963). "A Study of Brief Psychotherapy." Tavistock Publications: London.

Malan, D. H. (1975). Psychoanalytic brief psychotherapy and scientific method. *In* "Issues and Approaches in the Psychological Therapies. (Bannister, D. Ed.), pp. 201–222. John Wiley and Sons: Chichester.

Masters, W. H. and Johnson, V. E. (1970). "Human Sexual Inadequacy." Churchill Livingstone: Edinburgh.

Sandler, J., Dare, C. and Holder, A. (1973). "The Patient and the Analyst." George Allen and Unwin: London.

Shapiro, D. (1965). "Neurotic Styles." Basic Books, Inc: New York.

2 The Treatment of Sexual Problems by Group Therapy

FRED BURBANK

Seen in isolation, current theories and practices regarding the uses of group therapy for the treatment of sexual problems present a bewildering array of points of view, sharing many elements with the parable of the blind men seeking to determine the shape of an elephant (Shah, 1970).

> "As they did not even know the form or shape of the elephant they groped sightlessly, gathering information by touching some part of it . . . The man whose hand had reached an ear was asked about the elephant's nature. He said: 'It is a large, round thing, wide and broad, like a rug.' And the one who had felt the trunk said 'I have the real facts about it. It is like a straight and hollow pipe, awful and destructive.' The one who had felt its feet and legs said: 'It is mighty and firm, like a pillar.' Each had felt one part out of many. Each had perceived it wrongly."

Similarly, focus only upon isolated, superficial differences in technique between groups that treat sexual problems obscures similarities that are more basic to them. Perceived in a more integrated fashion, the curative factors common to most group therapies emerge and indicate that the basic processes of group therapy are effective for the treatment of a wide variety of sexual problems.

General Therapeutic Principle of Group Therapy

Because there can be wide variation in the characteristics of group therapists, in the characteristics of group members, and the book-

keeping or administrative aspects of a therapy group, it may appear
as though there are a multitude of group therapies. Group therapists'
characteristics include the theoretical orientation of the therapist
(psychoanalytic, process, educational, behavioural, etc.) and the
behaviour characteristics of the therapist (directive, confrontive,
supportive, interpretive, interactive, etc.) (Shaffer and Galinsky,
1974). Member characteristics can likewise vary widely from group
to group. Groups can be constructed to be homogeneous or heterogeneous with respect to a wide variety of demographic variables
including age, sex, sexual orientation, and diagnostic category. Members can be related, as with couples groups, or unrelated, as in
mixed groups. Similarly, administrative aspects of a group, the size
of the group, where the group meets, when it meets, whether the
group membership is open or closed, whether the number of sessions
are fixed or indefinite, whether or not information about the group
is transmitted prior to the beginning of the group, the length of
sessions, the frequency of meetings, whether meetings are held
while the leader is gone, whether member interactions are allowed
outside the group, and more, increase the superficial differences between
groups to an enormous size. However, as Yalom (1970) and others
(Corsini and Rosenberg, 1955) point out, there are a limited number
of factors that affect therapeutic change in the group setting.

Although the relative importance of therapeutic factors may vary
from one group setting to another and may vary from early phases
of group therapy to late phases of group therapy, the basic mechanisms
which effect change in the group setting operate across groups which
appear quite dissimilar. In general, groups which focus specifically on the treatment of a sexual problem and which exist for a short
period of time (weeks or months) help members to make changes
through the following mechanisms:

1. Ventilation — the open expression of feelings and thoughts
   that are associated with the sexual problems. For example,
   "It feels good to get my problems off my chest, to tell someone else what I've been thinking."
2. Instillation of Hope — the process of seeing others struggle
   and cope with a sexual problem in an effective manner. For
   example, "If he can make changes, maybe I can too."
3. Universality — the realization that the sexual problem is
   experienced by others. For example, "We're all in the same
   boat, I'm not the only one with this problem."

4. Education — the process of gathering information from the therapist or other patients about human sexuality, about sexual relationships, about psychodynamics, about methods of relaxation, about methods of augmenting sexual responsiveness, and more. For example, "I never knew that was how it worked, I always thought that sort of thing was abnormal."

5. Altruism — the feeling that even though you have a problem you can still be of benefit to other patients, that you are important in relation to other people in the group. For example, "I didn't realize that with all my problems I could be of help to anyone."

6. Improving Socializing Techniques — the development of more effective modes of interacting with other individuals, practiced either in the group or outside the group. For example, "I thought I had to act that way when I wanted attention."

7. Imitative Behaviour — modelling oneself after someone in the group or using someone else's methods of dealing with a problem. For example, "That seemed to work well for him so I tried it too."

Groups which run for longer periods of time (years), are less structured, and aim at basic changes in character structure, tend to also incorporate:

8. Group Cohesiveness — a feeling that you are part of a group, that you are accepted, appreciated, and liked in the group despite self-disclosure and the expression and display of a wide range of thoughts and feelings towards other group members. For example, "Even when I get angry, I feel as though I am a member of the group."

9. Recapitulation of the Primary Family Group — the ability of the group to stimulate conflicts present in early family relationships with, hopefully, more effective resolution of these conflicts in the group. For example, "The way you relate to me makes me feel just like I did when my mother got angry at me."

10. Interpersonal Learning — the ability to use the here-and-now interactions in the group to correct distortions in relationships (similar to transference distortions) and to understand the dynamics that led to maladaptive types of relationships with other people. This factor is of such complexity that it

is very difficult, if not impossible, to attempt to capture it
with a single, typical quote.

Group Therapy for the Treatment of Sexual Deviations

In general, complaints regarding sexual deviations originate from
outside the person who is performing the sexual deviation and are
brought forward by the social structure surrounding that individual.
Consequently, most of the literature describing the use of group
process to treat sexual deviance reports experience with patients who
are, to one degree or another, involuntarily in treatment.

By and large, either the object choice or the type of interpersonal
sexual behaviour brings public attention to the sexual deviant.
Although most investigations lead to intrapsychic origins to these
problems (Stoler, 1972 and Bemporad, 1975), initially the complaints are not expressed in terms of intrapsychic distress by the
patient. The patient usually perceives his primary problem as a
difficulty with legal authorities. Group therapy of sexual deviation
must, in addition to the usual task of therapy, take into account
that patients often do not want treatment and that treatment is at
the request of an outside social agency.

Mathis and Cullens (1971) report the use of group therapy for
males apprehended for exhibitionism and referred to treatment by
the police department, by the district attorney's office, or through
the court. Patients in these groups had their length of treatment
determined by a judicial sentence. The authors found that without
a sentence for a minimum of six months the success of treatment was
small. The groups were all homogeneous, all members were apprehended for exhibitionism. Hence, within these groups there was an
immediate sense of universality to the problem, i.e., all "being in the
same boat."

These groups were created with male and female co-therapists in
order to stimulate a family setting somewhat the reverse of childhood patterns. The male therapist assumed the role of leader and
organizer with the female therapist being an equal but relatively
passive. In short, there was an attempt to recapitulate the primary
family group in a more therapeutic way.

Forty-five men were admitted to the programme over a period of
three years. Their ages ranged from eighteen to fifty years and

many patients in this setting had multiple convictions for exhibitionism. It appeared to the authors that the impulse to exhibit was
predictable following some situation that lowered the self-esteem
of the patient. This pattern was interpreted to the group on repeated
occasions. In addition to uncovering unconscious, repetitive patterns,
didactic teaching was used extensively throughout the groups to
increase the members understanding of the interpersonal aspects of
sexuality. According to the authors, sex was discussed:

> "As a method of communication between man and woman, and we saw
> exhibitionistic episodes as a breakdown of this communication whether the
> female was wife, mother, or girlfriend."

Issues of termination from these groups were heavily weighed by
the opinions of other group members. Group members tended to be
more harsh and more conservative than leaders at the time that
termination was brought up. Termination from the group was on a
gradual basis. Once terminated, members could return to the group
at monthly intervals or at other times when life situations seemed
stressful. For those exhibitionists who were able to remain in the
group longer than six months, the results of the treatment were good.
The authors were left with the feeling that group therapy was an
effective treatment for otherwise healthy men arrested for exhibitionism.

Other workers have also reported on the use of group therapy for
the treatment of criminal sex offenders. Attempts have been made
to develop clinical measurement instruments in this setting by
Sadoff *et al.* (1971). Research attempts to define what aspects of
group therapy are most helpful to the treatment of sex offenders
have led to somewhat variable results. The meaning of such terms
as "cohesiveness" and "hostility" within a group have proven to be
difficult to measure (Roether and Peters, 1972). Doubt concerning
the understanding of these terms has been raised by Guttmacher
(1972). Sufficient interest exists in the group treatment of sexual
deviation to attempt to further understand the variables in group
process which lead to change for the sexual deviant.

Costel and Yalom (1971) describe the use of group therapy for the
treatment of institutionalized sex offenders at the Patuxent State
Hospital in Maryland and the Atascadero State Hospital in California.
In these settings, patients were detained for an indeterminate period
of time for their sex offence. From these two treatment settings, the
authors determined those factors which were necessary to establish
effective group treatment programmes. For the paedophile, group

process is best directed toward control or sublimation of sexual
impulses rather than towards total rehabilitation of the offender
with adult females as the object of choice. Where the character of
the sexual activity has caught the attention of the legal authorities,
in the form of exhibitionism or aggressive sexual behaviour, group
therapy is best directed at alteration of the basic character structure
through long-term intensive group therapy. Awareness of factors
operating outside the group treatment setting were also stressed.
Differences between norms of a group and the norms of the outside
institutions may represent particular problems towards effective
group therapy. Treatment of sex offenders within an institutional
setting may take much of the selection of the patients away from
the control of the group therapist. Particularly disruptive to the
therapeutic effectiveness were changeovers or losses of therapists due
to institutional needs which were at odds with patient or group
therapy needs. Prolonged contract with the therapist appeared to be
very important; also, the inclusion of a female as co-therapist
appeared to be of particular value.

Peters and Roether (1971) describe the use of group therapy for
probationed sex offenders. These authors report the use of small
group processes to treat sexual deviants in the outpatient clinic of
the Philadelphia General Hospital. To these authors, group therapy
is the treatment modality of choice for sex offenders. In addition
to the therapeutic effect of group cohesiveness, the authors reason
that the social factors relevant to the anti-social acts could perhaps
be best understood and integrated within the setting of the small
group. Based upon detailed individual histories, social interviews,
and psychological testing, homogeneous groups of exhibitionists,
paedophiles, homosexuals, and assaultive sex offenders were created.
Heterogeneous groups, mixtures of these four categories, were also
created. The group process drew new members into the group and
helped elicit open discussions of sexual behaviour, anti-social and
otherwise. Universality also played an important part helping to
break down the isolation which is common to sexual deviants. Members were relieved to realize, "Everyone here does it." The authors
describe how long-term members were more able to confront denial
in new members than therapists could.

Once group cohesiveness was established, members sensed support
from one another. This, in turn, led to increased group interaction
and participation. With increased group participation came increased

awareness of the interpersonal styles of each group member. Quite accurately, the authors point out that group acceptance is not necessarily group approval of the sex offence. The patient learns:

> ". . . his feelings are understandable and that he personally is acceptable, while his anti-social behaviour is rejected."

In addition, group members learned simple social rules of interpersonal interaction such as one person speaking at a time. As the group progresses, more complex social interactions occurred and more complicated social skills were acquired. As is often the case with group therapy, it was hoped that the self-understanding learned in the group would extend to interpersonal relationships outside the group. Over and over again, Peters and Roether (1971) point out that many factors of group therapy are at work at one time during the course of a well-functioning group. They report that treatment occurred in three phases: an initial phase characterized by high level participation with the group, a middle phase characterized by levelling off of participation, and a final phase with involvement even greater than the involvement during the first phase.

Follow up studies were conducted. In a retrospective analysis of matched sex offenders, the untreated comparison group had a higher percentage of re-arrests. Before therapy, those individuals included in the group therapy programme were convicted of more crimes than the comparison group. However, once the treatment procedure was completed, they showed fewer arrests for sex offences and for non-sex offences. The authors conclude that the programme was effective in changing the rate of all anti-social behaviour, not only anti-social sexual behaviour.

Group Therapy for the Treatment of Gender Identity and Homosexual Problems

In an attempt to use group therapy to prevent future gender confusion and future homosexual interpersonal problems, Green and Fuller (1973) attempt to identify and treat "feminine boys" in a group setting, at the same time creating separate groups to treat the mothers and fathers. Seven boys were identified and constituted the feminine boy's group, ages ranging from four to nine years. They defined "feminine boys" as those boys who:

"showed an enduring interest in dressing in women's clothes or improvising
them if unavailable; they strongly preferred girls as playmates; in fantasy
games such as 'house' and 'mother and father' they invariably portray a
female; they select girls' toys over those typically preferred by boys; they
display feminine gestures; and they may overtly confide their wishes to be
girls."

The boy's group met weekly for one hour with a male therapist in
a recreational area. The recreational area included slides, swings,
monkey bars, basketball and hoop, kickballs, and ample space for
running and tag games. The mothers' group met bi-weekly with
male and female co-therapists for one hour. The fathers' group also
met bi-weekly with a male therapist. Bi-monthly, the parents met
together with both therapists in a single group. The group therapy
of the boys stressed verbal reinforcement of masculine behaviour
and the use of masculine nouns whenever possible. For example,
"That's a good boy," and "Come on guys," and "You're getting
taller, you're going to be a big man when you grow up," were
typical therapist-boy interactions. The boys were encouraged to
perform activities involving large muscles and were encouraged to
perform acts of bravery such as climbing high on the monkey bars,
plunging head first down the slide, running, or kicking a ball. Similarly, the boys were discouraged from performing feminine gestures.
For example, a therapist might comment, "Hey, don't run like that,"
when a boy ran in a particularly feminine way.

The mothers' group, on the other hand, tended to rely more
heavily on factors of group process. The mothers were able to
share their common concerns over the feminine behaviour of their
boys. Apparently for many mothers it was the first time that they
had expressed their concerns over this worrisome behaviour. Also,
since there were age differentials in the children involved in the play
group, mothers who tended to deny the significance of early feminine
behaviour had a chance to speak with mothers whose sons were
older and had exhibited similar behaviour at an earlier age. In addition
to generating a sense of universality to their problems, the groups
also encouraged the mothers to exchange information. For example,
one mother's successful handling of a feminine behaviour trait was
picked up by another mother. Similarly, a sense of hope was also
instilled in the group. One mother's pessimism about her son's
behaviour was often changed by another mother's optimism that
success could be obtained. In addition, interpersonal learning also

occurred in the group for the mothers. Unconscious elements in each mother which encouraged feminine behaviour were uncovered during the group therapy sessions. Finally, therapists often employed didactic education regarding the normal development of childhood play as a means of therapy.

In the fathers' group, the authors described a common expression of guilt. The fathers were remorseful that they had not involved themselves more heavily in father—son activities. Each father was relieved to hear that there were other fathers who felt similarly. Many felt that after a hard day's work there was little extra energy to engage in activities with their sons. However, when one father, though reluctantly, joined the Indian Guides with his son and was able to relate its beneficial effects, another father followed suit and also was able to increase his father—son activity. In addition to describing their own feelings regarding being the father of a feminine son, the fathers explored some of their own historical material. One father described how during his childhood he saw very little of his own father, and consequently had concluded that his son would need little of his time. However, after the interactions in the group setting, this father decided that whatever his own developmental needs had been, his son currently needed his time and that he would make more time available.

The outcome of this creative, tri-part group therapy approach to early feminine behaviour in boys was examined. The authors felt that there was a reduction in cross-dressing in actual or improvised women's clothing, in feminine gestures and speech, in feminine role taking, and in statements expressing a desire to be a girl. The authors believed that even though their study was in the preliminary stage, the clinical experience was encouraging and the three-fold approach appeared to be helpful in changing feminine behaviour in boys.

Transsexualism, an extreme form of feminine identity in a male, has been considered very resistant, if not entirely resistant, to successful psychotherapy. Forrester and Swiller (1972) report a male who was identified while in the Navy as a transsexual and who apparently was able to orient to a male role following the use of group therapy. The authors postulate that transsexuals do not lack motivation for change but have intense fear of authority figures leading to massive resistance to individual psychotherapy. Those authors believe that group therapy might be particularly helpful for the treatment of transsexuals.

Homosexuality has been extensively treated with group psychotherapy. Haden (1972) has worked widely with the treatment of homosexuals in the group setting. He describes the current conceptual confusion that exists regarding basic ways in which homosexuals are viewed. On the one extreme are those who classify homosexuality as a sexual deviation. On the other extreme are those who wish to consider homosexual behaviour as a normal sexual orientation. Distinctions are also made, by Haden, between those homosexuals who are a public nuisance, performing sexual activity in parks, public toilets, and other gathering places, versus those who consider their homosexuality to be a private matter and seldom come to the attention of legal authorities. He points out that although homosexuality may appear to be a homogeneous concept, it is really no more homogeneous than any concept of heterosexuality. In his words:

> "Each individual is different, and to each his homosexual orientation has different meaning."

That author believes that group therapy is actually a more effective approach to the treatment of homosexuality than individual therapy and identifies in his discussions many curative and corrective factors.

In addition to group processes, counter-transference feelings by a group therapist also affect the therapeutic outcome of group therapy. Haden feels that the group therapists' therapeutic objectives and optimism towards change must be clearly and unequivocally stated to the group. In his own words:

> "I feel that limited objectives stated by the therapist are handicapping. With homosexuals I make it clear that my objective is complete reversal of their sexual orientation and the initiation of a growth potential that will help them to move constantly toward greater maturity and a more productive and enjoyable life."

He begins the process of therapy for potential group members by individual psychotherapeutic sessions and only when he believes that there is a positive transference to him as a therapist does he progress to the level of group therapy for that individual. He informs the individual about the general operations of group process before the individual enters the group. He openly presents his theoretical orientation to the patient, stating that homosexuality is brought about by early life experiences and that he believes that these maladaptive experiences can be corrected through the process of group therapy. Because the group members have similar life problems oriented around homosexuality, they are able to actively confront new members with a great deal of knowledge about homosexuality. In addition to the here-and-now aspects of group process, Haden also recommends examining, in the group, autobiographical or historical information in order to allow other group members to know the new member more fully. Through this process of autobiographical review, the author believes that the homosexual individual begins to recognize the patterns of his early life which led him to avoid close intimate relationships with peers. Similarly, developmental abnormalities in the homosexual male to his mother and father are examined.

In order to deal with highly anxiety provoking material, Haden describes the use of "group suggestibility" to allow group members to enter into deep relaxation and to experience their anxiety provoking situations in the presence of the group. In addition, photographs depicting homosexual acts are presented in the group in order to elicit strong feelings concerning explicit homosexual activities. The reactions of the group members are then dealt with in the here-and-now interactions of the group. In sum, Haden incorporates a wide variety of treatment techniques into the setting of group therapy, incorporating historical material, here-and-now group process analysis, as well as specific experiential material such as group suggestibility and group responses to erotic homosexual photographs.

Haden believes that of those homosexual males who enter his groups, approximately one-third are able to lead permanent heterosexual lives. A third of the males become bisexual while one-third continue a homosexual life pattern. It is interesting to note that the length of treatment described is from two to three years, a period of time to allow significant change in characterological structure from the group process in addition to dealing with the more circumscribed problems of homosexuality.

Another long-term approach to the treatment of homosexuality through group therapy is described by Gershman (1975). Unlike Haden's groups, Gershman's groups include homosexual females. Also unlike Haden, Gershman describes the use of group process to treat the characterological problems and neurotic symptoms of the homosexual without great emphasis on changing the sexual orientation of the patient. His experiences indicate that only a small minority of homosexuals seeking treatment desire to change their sexual orientation. Virtually all homosexual patients, however, wish relief from their neurotic symptoms. Supporting the notions of Green and Fuller (1973), Gershman feels that is is very unlikely that sexual orientation will change if the symptoms of homosexuality begin at early ages, between five and six. Adversely, it appears to

him that there is a much greater chance of reorientation of sexual
object choice if homosexual symptoms begin during adolescence.
In addition to describing the administrative aspects of his group
therapy setting, Gershman describes at length those therapeutic
features of group therapy which allow change. He points out the
importance of dealing with genuine emotional responses in the
group, as opposed to intellectual discussions. Here-and-now group
interactions are analysed and appropriately interpreted in relation
to the entire fabric of the homosexuals' life experience. As with
Haden, group therapy described by Gershman is a long-term process.
The maximum length of involvement in any group has been arbi-
trarily set at five years. As groups mature, the subject matter and
emphasis of the group moves away from the presenting sexual complaint toward the basic character neurosis of each member.

Truax and Tourney (1971) attempt to perform a controlled
investigation upon the effectiveness of group psychotherapy for
the treatment of homosexuality. The treatment group consisted of
six sub-groups with five members each for a total of thirty subjects.
The control group consisted of twenty untreated subjects. Most of
the subjects were undergraduate or graduate university students of
high educational attainment. The ages were all under thirty-five and
all appeared to the authors to have substantial motivation for treatment. Group treatment was for a relatively short period of time,
seven months. The group process was begun with an initial discussion
of mistaken concepts concerning homosexuality, using the group
setting for didactic education. In addition, historical information
about each member was actively elicited by the group leaders. The
members readily identified with and empathized with problems
expressed by others. As similarities between them emerged, many
homosexual men described anxiety over assertiveness and ability to
participate in aggressive competitive activities when young. Common
childhood memories described in the group setting were those of
feminine interests at a time when their peers were identified with
one another through masculine activities. Behaviours and attitudes
common to the mothers of the group members included: shielding
the homosexual from his peers at early ages, discouraging masculine
interests, encouraging narcissistic behaviour, and portraying of the
world as hostile and untrusting.

Outcome surveys indicated that compared to the control group,
the treatment group had more heterosexual dating and greater

decrease in homosexual behaviour. Some members of both the treatment and control groups, however, showed increases in homosexual behaviour with the increase somewhat less in the treated group than in the control group. In addition to improvement centered around homosexual behaviour, the improvement was also noted in neurotic symptoms with a reduction of anxiety and depression. Finally, as the authors point out, seven months is a short time span for treatment. However, a follow up study indicated that some subjects were able to consolidate gains made during the group therapy and that improvements continued after therapy had ceased. These authors believe that the group setting, in addition to providing a wide variety of mechanisms for therapeutic change, was more engaging to the homosexual and allowed him to remain in therapy when he might otherwise have run from therapy in the individual setting.

Stemming from difficulties reported in the individual psychotherapy of homosexual patients, Covi (1972) points out that group therapy creates a group pressure that helps prevent early departure from therapy. In addition, unproductively intense transference reactions are not often experienced during group therapy with the diffusion of transference feelings into the group. Group pressure to help the homosexual enter therapy and to lessen unproductive transference reactions led the author to conclude that group therapy may be the most helpful means of dealing with homosexuality. Also, whereas mixing homosexuals and non-homosexuals in the same group is usually considered to be a difficult process, to Covi the use of male and female homosexuals in the same group allows the introduction of female points of view at the same time keeping the group sufficiently homogeneous with respect to the homosexual orientation. Covi, like Gershman (1975), does not attempt to direct therapy towards a change of sexual object choice, but instead directs energies towards the relief of neurotic symptoms. Included in Covi's groups were patients who were referred as a requirement for probation or parole. Of the thirty patients treated in this group therapy setting, twenty-two were males and eight were females. To Covi, sexual material seemed to play a rather disproportionate role in each patient's life. In addition, loneliness and lack of close friends were common elements among the members.

In general, across many different theoretical orientations and in many different therapeutic settings, group therapy has proven to be an effective method of treatment for problems associated with homosexuality.

Group Therapy for the Treatment of Sexual Arousal Problems

Unlike the patient either referred to therapy for sexual deviation or the patient complaining of difficulties related to homosexuality, there exists a wide variety of patients who suffer from inability to become sexually aroused in situations in which they want to become aroused. There has been a tendency to classify these problems according to physiologically defined syndromes, e.g. premature ejaculation, anorgasmus, impotence. However, just as homosexuals do not comprise a homogeneous group neither do, for example, males who ejaculate rapidly. In general, individuals who are having difficulty with sexual arousal complain of intrapsychic distress, concern over their lack of physiological sexual arousal, and problems with the quality of their interpersonal relationships. Often, the quality of interpersonal relationships is such that the person has no sexual partner. When there are profoundly disturbing intrapsychic elements to the problem of sexual arousal, individual or group therapy which is not primarily focused on sexual arousal or upon the current sexual partner is generally best pursued. However, when the intrapsychic elements are not pronounced, the focus of therapy can be directed toward the problem of sexual arousal, loosely referred to as "Sex Therapy" (Masters and Johnson, 1970; Kaplan, 1974; Lobitz and LoPiccolo, 1972). Also when intrapsychic elements are not too pronounced, problems with the relationship with the sexual partner can be addressed directly, referred to loosely as "Couples Therapy" (Bermann and Lief, 1975; Hollander, 1971).

Couple Therapy Groups

While the treatment of couples is now commonplace, the initial decision to treat couples, let alone couples in groups, was a bold one in the face of psychoanalytic prohibitions against seeing the relative of a patient. Perelman (1960) describes many of the problems encountered when one therapist attempts to deal with a couple. He points out that many couples come to treatment as a "court of last resort" often before seeing a judge for divorce, and not infrequently after seeing one. Often there is considerable motivation within the couple for separation, much more so than towards continuing the relationship. A second difficulty encountered with treating a couple stems from one individual thinking that the other needs to be overhauled. As Perelman states it, "Straighten him out and the marriage will be o.k." In addition, when neurotic interactions within the couple become repetitive and bitter, the working through of deeper psychological elements becomes very difficult. In this setting, it is commonly felt that therapist interventions either favour one side or the other. Such a triangular situation almost always leads to a multitude of difficulties. Finally, the therapist can develop "double counter-transference" feelings, developing feelings towards each member of the marital unit which may be more than the therapist can cope with.

Consequently, Perelman moved the treatment of couples into the group setting and ameliorated some of the difficulties of seeing couples alone. Characteristics of the initial phase of a couples' group are described. The author points out that initially couples tend to sit together indicating that the couples respond to the group not as individuals but as a unit. Couples present mutual defences and common actions which would not occur as readily if the group were mixed in composition. In addition, sex differences appeared in the groups. Wives were described as being more vocal, more productive and more aggressive while the men, by and large, were more passive and defensive. When fantasies involving other members of the group appeared, hostilities and anger towards members flourished. Because of the amount of disruption that occurred with the introduction of fantasy material, it was the author's opinion that preparation of group members should be made prior to their entry into the group in order to allow such material to emerge without being threatening to the couple's relationship. Another characteristic of the married couples group was the feeling that disclosure of deeper psychological material would, in some way, also endanger the marital relationship. Such a fear acted as a restraint to active group participation. Also, the problem of one couple getting "better" before others did represent an additional difficulty. Finally, one member of a couple left the group raising the dilemma as to what to do with the remaining member. All in all, however, even though many problems existed within the couples' group, it was Perelman's opinion that after the initial difficulties, the group tended to respond in similar fashion to mixed groups.

Van Emde Boas (1962), growing out of an investigation of "failure" in the treatment of problems of sexual arousal found that the treatment of one member of a couple in what he terms a "zipper" relationship failed because "fundamental mechanisms involved in the zipper relationship remained untouched, as, indeed, did the marital conflicts themselves." The treatment of the partner in isolation from the initially treated patient was also unsuccessful. Consequently, he decided to treat both partners in the same setting, in a group composed of "zipper" relationships.

Van Emde Boas (1962), like Perelman (1960), points out that in the treatment of a couple in the individual setting, non-therapeutic triangles can be formed. However, in the group setting, the therapist does not find himself in an uncomfortable set of counter-transference entanglements. He can function with less feelings directed towards him since the transference is split up or diluted in the group setting.

To Leichter (1962) having the partner in the group allowed the group to put the patient's behaviour into better perspective and allow for greater understanding. However, as seen by Perelman (1960) married couples fear change in the partner for fear that this will change their relationship. Such changes are seen as threats to the equilibrium of the relationship and lead to increased anxiety in one of the partners. If, however, the symbiotic nature of the relationship can be treated, individuals can emerge rather than stereotyped husbands and wives. As this married couples' group matured, each marital partner moved in the direction of diminished unhealthy ties with the spouse.

Gottlieb and Pattison (1966) describe group dynamics which are characteristic of married couples' groups. Such groups provide support and acceptance for patients and couples through difficult times, they simulate typical interactions which the couple experiences and which can be observed and changed in the group setting, and they allow couples to see their partners in a more realistic light with less projective distortions. The authors point out that even though there are theoretical considerations which would lead away from the treatment of couples in the group setting, those theoretical objections are overweighed by the practical success of such a format of treatment. Similar conclusions are reached by Blinder and Kirschenbaum (1967), Framo (1973), and Reckless *et al.* (1973).

Sex Therapy Groups

Although the use of group process for the treatment of problems

of sexual arousal is often considered quite new, the first report of
the use of group treatment for sexual arousal difficulties was
published twenty-five years ago. Van Emde Boas (1950) reported
on the treatment of anorgasmic women, and it was out of this
experience that he developed the format of treating marital couples
in groups. By "anorgasmic" he referred to those females who
complained that they could not reach vaginal orgasm. As the author
states:

> ". . . it would be quite wrong to put these patients off with a few words
> of comfort . . . or the kind of advice favoured by Helena Wright, who is
> content with the always achievable clitoral orgasm which she holds — in
> my opinion quite wrongly — to be of equal value as an orgasm felt in the
> vagina."

Responding to transference and counter-transference difficulties
which arose during the individual therapy of a female trying to deal
with problems of sexual arousal, the author shifted to group therapy
to make treatment available to a wider number of females and to
dilute transference and counter-transference difficulties.

The first group was created in 1948 and consisted of eight females
between the ages of twenty and thirty. No special screening of
patients was performed. All females entering the clinic complaining
of the inability to reach vaginal orgasm were accepted into the group.
Interestingly, females who were better known to the therapist at that
time, those already under treatment, were excluded from the group
for various reasons. One female was excluded because she had a
husband she clearly disliked. In addition:

> "Others again, women who, after a single discussion, were quite content
> to put up with only a clitoral type of orgasm, were found ineligible for
> this elaborate type of treatment."

All members of the group who were accepted had previously failed
through individual psychotherapy to relieve their inability to
achieve vaginal orgasm.

Sessions were forty-five minutes in length and were held weekly.
The author reports a twenty-month period during which the group
operated. Interestingly, the author describes an "observer-assistant"
who was a female who was:

> "psychologically trained, able to take down notes in shorthand and to
> take part in discussions when necessity arose. Her presence produced no
> difficulties. She was accepted as a member of the group and intermediary
> between the patients and the leader. Furthermore, being a women she
> was accepted as a 'fellow sufferer', someone like a sister or mother to

other women who could take over when the need arose, temporarily
taking over the leadership of the group herself."

By modern terminology, she would probably be considered a
female co-therapist and from current experience, the addition of
this female might have added substantially to the success of this
group.

The group was open, new members could join when older members graduated or dropped out. Consequently, the group leader attempted to keep one or two more advanced members of the group in the
group in order to help set the pace and to carry some of the culture
of the group. Although the leader describes being initially quite
active, he states that his role became more passive as time progressed
and the group matured.

In addition to dealing with explicit sexual material, the group
explored other areas in the lives of the group members. The author
reports that many of the women felt less nervous and less emotionally tense as a consequence of group therapy. They also reported
improved relationships with their husbands, fewer feelings of
inferiority, and fewer depressive moods. It was the author's opinion
that significant characterological changes had occurred as a result
of the group therapy.

Therapeutic change came from a variety of elements within the
group. Didactic education regarding the social role for men and
women occurred. Members emotionally supported each other and
were able to relate emotionally charged experiences to one another.
Interestingly, although this report is very early in the history of group
therapy, the group process is clearly identified as being more important than the relationship of the individual group members to the
leader.

Additional mechanisms of change included identification with
other members in the group, re-creation of the family setting with
the male group leader identified as the father and the female group
assistant identified as the mother, and learning through observation
by passive members of the group. The dilution of the transference
through the group setting, the significance of the seating arrangement of the group and the recapitulation of characterological styles
within the group were also identified as curative factors. Although
Van Emde Boas relates that little is understood of the mechanisms
of recovery, throughout his report he describes many mechanisms
which are now identified as common to group therapy. Of the

fourteen members who could be considered regular attenders of the group, six were able to obtain vaginal orgasm. Those patients did not obtain vaginal orgasm expressed a desire to include their husbands in further therapeutic work.

Growing out of quite a different tradition than Van Emde Boas, Barbach (1974) states that:

> "Laboratory studies by Masters and Johnson of human subjects participating in various forms of sexual activity have exposed the vaginal orgasm to by a myth."*

Barbach directs therapeutic attention towards females who have never achieved orgasm by any means. Due to the high probability that a female will be able to learn to reach orgasm, in isolation, through masturbation, she designates these females as "preorgasmic." Reasons given for the treatment of these women by group therapy include the lack of a partner, which would exclude them from couple therapy, and the prohibitive expense of seeking therapy individually or as a couple.

Two female therapists led the groups which met one and one-half hours twice a week for a period of five weeks, or ten sessions. The women were encouraged to describe their feelings regarding sex and masturbation, and, in addition, the group leaders expressed positive attitudes towards masturbation and sexual pleasure. In addition to work within the group, sexual activity outside the group was prescribed. The results of the sexual activity assigned in the group and carried out outside the group were brought back into the group and analysed. For example, prior to the assignment of the self-exploration of each female's genitals, the leader gave a didactic description of the anatomy and function of female sexual genitals. Prior to the assignment of masturbation, a film showing a female in the process of masturbation was shown to the group. As the females progressed in therapy and were able to reach orgasm through masturbation, the assignments included sexual activity with partners. Genital self-stimulation was then incorporated into sexual activity with the partner, first by having the partner observe the female stimulate herself to orgasm, next having the female direct her partner's manual stimulation to her genitals, and finally having the female stimulate her own genitals with the penis contained in the

---

* Whereas Barbach quite accurately reports Masters and Johnson (1970) finding that from an anatomical point of view there are no differences in pelvic responses to sexual stimulation, she overlooks possible intrapsychic differences in the manifestations of sexual arousal and orgasm (Fisher, 1973; Shainess, 1975; Clower, 1975; Hollender, 1975).

vagina. Barbach reports that of the first eighty-three women who
participated in the groups, 91% were able to achieve orgasm through
masturbation within ten sessions.

A follow up study (Wallace and Barbach, 1974) of seventeen of
the eighty-three women was undertaken. All seventeen of these
women had become orgasmic during the five week course of treatment. These seventeen women had been treated in three groups.
Since the use of non-manual masturbation techniques was part of
the treatment programme, one of the early findings of the follow-
up study was that of the nine women who first experienced orgasm
through the use of a vibrator or by running water over the clitoris,
eight were able to reach orgasms by manual stimulation. Interestingly,
the one woman who could not reach orgasm by manual stimulation
was, nontheless, able to experience orgasm with her partner one
year after treatment. This was interpreted by the authors to indicate
that women do not become fixed on their initial method of achieving orgasm.

In a similar report, Zilbergeld (1975) describes four groups
composed of six to seven men each. Two males led three of the
groups while the fourth group had a female as the co-therapist.
Although partners were not directly treated in this group, some of
the men were in long-term relationships, some were in dating relationships, and some dated little or not at all. Three of the groups included
both premature ejaculation and erectile problems while the fourth
contained men complaining of premature ejaculation only. Although
a considerable portion of the report makes reference to group process
phenomena and its curative effects upon the patients, the groups
are described as having minimal spontaneous member interactions
with most interactions directed between leader and members. The
goals of the groups were to correct specific problems with sexual
functioning, to allow clients to develop social skills necessary to
deal with a variety of sexual situations, and to help the clients
to cope with new sexual partners. The author believes that approximately two-thirds of the clients were able to achieve the goals of
reversal of their specific sexual malfunction.

As with the groups reported by Barbach (1974), isolatory sexual
activity in the form of masturbation was identified as one of the
primary techniques which allowed change to occur. For premature
ejaculation, masturbation was used to teach the client to focus on
his penile sensations and to stop stimulation just prior to ejaculation.
For erectile difficulties, masturbation exercises were also used.

This time the major learning experience included directing the client to stop stimulation at some point during self-stimulation and lose the erection. Then, stimulation was continued and the erection regained. Repeating the cycle of gaining and losing erections was designed to teach the men that erections come and go, that a lost erection is not a catastrophe, and that once an erection is lost it may be regained with proper stimulation.

Elements of group process which were either explicitly or implicitly identified include the use of the group to provide the opportunity for vicarious learning. Another group process phenomena which appeared to be curative was the effect of self-disclosure in the group. Also, the process of sharing feelings regarding sexual problems was encouraged in the group. The group leaders hoped that sharing and openness would transfer to the client's future interactions with his sexual partner. Termed "assertive training", group members were explicitly taught that they have the right to refuse sexual advances just as females have the right to refuse sexual advances. In addition, since anxiety and sexual arousal are poor bedfellows, the clients were taught to recognise anxiety and not to expect sexual responsiveness when they were anxious. Finally, a large amount of group time was spent imparting attitudinal information by the group leaders under the notion of "debunking male sexual mythology."

One of the most interesting findings of this study was that men who are in long-term relationships and whose partners would not come to treatment were the most resistant to change. It was Zilbergeld's opinion that the treatment would have to focus on the interpersonal aspects of the relationship before specific improvements in the area of sexual arousal could occur. Another interesting finding from this report was that the inclusion of the female co-therapist was thought highly desirable. The female co-leader provided clients direct experience with a female in the group. Interpersonal learning appeared to occur more readily because the female's opinion was regarded quite highly by the males in the group and hence she was taken very seriously when she expressed beliefs concerning female points of view.

Drawing from the traditions of treating couples for sexual problems and from the traditions of treating marital problems in the group setting, Kaplan et al. (1974) describe the treatment of four heterosexual couples complaining of premature ejaculation. Group sessions described were forty-five minutes in length and were held weekly over a six-week period. Exercises were carried out by the

husband and wife in the privacy of their home. The results of these
exercises were then brought back in to the group setting. In addition, .
in the group setting, group dynamics were employed in the service
of revealing and resolving couple conflicts. As a result of their pilot
study, it appeared to the authors that assigned sessions at home
could be successfully incorporated into the group setting. In addition, the group process was helpful in dealing with obstacles and
resistances which were motivated by maladaptive interpersonal
dynamics. At the end of the group sessions, two of the couples were
successful in relieving the symptom of premature ejaculation. At
the end of two months following the end of the group, the other
two couples also reported that ejaculatory control had been regained.

Unlike Barbach (1974), Zilbergeld (1975) and Kaplan *et al.*
(1974), Kaufman and Krupka (1973) rely exclusively on group
process for the treatment of sexual problems and work over a longer
period of time within the group setting. They describe the use of
group therapy in a university counselling programme for individuals
experiencing sexual problems and conflicts. Individuals and couples
were included in their groups. Although initially all applicants were
included in their programme, a procedure for screening members
who were more appropriate for the group was finally employed.
A helpful description of the characteristics of group drop outs
is given. The first general characteristic includes those patients who
tend to lack internalization of their problem. These patients see the
problem as outside of themselves and do not see it as part of their
own character structure or makeup. The second characteristic of
group members who do not remain in their group is withdrawn interactions while in the group. These members were never able to
become active participants in the groups. In addition, they tended to
alienate more active group members and were unable to recognize
their alienating forms of interaction. The groups were non-structured
and experiential with no set programme brought forward by the
therapist. In general, the characteristics of the groups tended to be
like those of out-patient groups which deal with general neurotic
and general characterological problems. However, even though the
format was that of general group therapy, the identification of the
groups as "sex therapy" allowed members to talk more freely and
openly about their sexual lives.

In the opinion of the authors, the use of male and female co-
therapists created a structure similar to the family. The presence
of the male and female therapists who at times disagreed allowed

the group to learn new methods of dealing with conflicts. In addition, members were able to model after the group therapist. Another curative factor identified in these groups was the learning of how other people think in addition to how they feel. In the author's words:

> "Since most of the people coming to the group have mixed up notions of what others think, we can begin to let them in on the real world."

The authors conducted two groups which they later characterised as the "younger group" and the "older group" based upon the psychological development of the group members, rather than on their chronological ages. Eight out of the ten members of the younger group reported subjective satisfaction with changes in their sexual problems. According to the authors, all of the members of the older group noted "positive changes." In general, impotency and premature ejaculation appear to be most amenable to this type of treatment. They concluded that their results with anorgasmic females were less clear-cut and felt that feminine orgasmic response was influenced heavily by the particular relationships in which the woman was involved. Homosexuals did poorly in their groups. Half of the homosexuals dropped out within a few meetings, which was attributed by the authors to the heterogeneous composition of the group.

Two reports, growing out of the tradition of behaviour therapy, also indicate the importance of group process for the treatment of sexual problems. In a report by Lazarus (1961) in which systematic desensitization was used in the group setting, the treatment of "five impotent men" is described. The study compared the use of systematic desensitization to treat two impotent men in a group setting to the treatment of three impotent men by a process identified as "group interpretation." The two males treated by group desensitization were reported as recovered. Although none of the men in the interpretive group were recovered during the same time period, those men, nonetheless, elected to continue the interpretive group even when group desensitization was offered. Although not explored further, it appears that there were benefits which those members were receiving from that group process. Even though the interpretive group was not highly successful in helping the men achieve erections, in the opinion of the author, those groups enabled many to achieve:

"constructive modification of their self-evaluation, often clarified their
evaluation of others, and enhanced their potentials of interpersonal
integration."

Lazarus (1968) later reports two other groups specifically constructed to treat sexual problems. The first group treated three
"impotent" males. Unlike his previous groups, before the group
began the use of the desensitization procedure, Lazarus gave extensive instructions concerning manual and oral sexual stimulation
techniques. Quite clearly, the group was used to impart information.
Next, the partner of each of the males was seen and interviewed.
The author was able to convince the female partner to accept a
range of non-coital sexual activity which had been previously rejected as part of the sexual repertoire. The next step in the group
treatment process involved the use of "sexual prescriptions." The
patients were directed to focus attention on pleasuring their partners by skillful oral and manual stimulation. Hence, before the
process of group desensitization had even begun, the authors were
able to facilitate intrapsychic attitudinal changes in the male's partners, to expand the range of mutually agreed sexual repertoire, and
to increase the importance of non-coital activity. In sessions three,
four and five of the five stage group process, group desensitization
treatments using traditional hierarchies were employed. Following
treatment, the impressions of the three men as to what factors were
most important in their cure revealed that one man thought the
desensitization process effected the most change in him. However,
two of the men stated that the most important element was the
change in the wife's willingness to engage in sexual activity other
than intercourse. It would appear that the author was able to effect
a change in the attitudes of wives, emphasizing the importance of
interpersonal factors in sexual functioning (Freidman, 1973).

In the same report, Lazarus (1968) describes the treatment of
four "frigid women." In this group setting, a wide variety of group
techniques were used. To begin with, sessions were divided into
four parts with the first part being devoted to discussions of
sexual attitudes. The second part in the procedure included didactic lectures about sexual functioning. The third and fourth elements
involve more classical behavioural techniques including relaxation
training and the use of imaginal desensitization hierarchy. Treatment
of these females continued for fourteen sessions. One of the patients
was able to state that she "always achieved satisfactory climax."
Two of the patients reported achieving orgasmic satisfaction on 50%

of their sexual encounters. One patient was unable to continue
treatment in the group. It was reported that "a complex marital
situation proved to be responsible for her sustained asexual reaction."
This female was referred to couple therapy with her husband.

Advantages of the Treatment of Sexual Problems by Group Therapy

In settings where cost may exclude some patients from therapy, the
use of group treatment may allow service to be provided to more
than one patient or more than one couple at a time. As pointed out
by Van Emde Boas (1950), and Barbach (1974) to many people
suffering from problems with sexual functioning, group treatment
may be the only financially feasible method of delivering services.
In institutional settings for the treatment of sex offenders, group
psychotherapy may be the only form of treatment available given
the staffing abilities of the institution.

Beyond the parsimony of treating many people at one time, there
are features unique to group therapy which are not observed in the
treatment of individuals. When couples are brought into a group
treatment setting, as in couples' groups, the dynamics of the relationship can be seen in the here-and-now interactions of the group and
examined (Perelman, 1960; Leichter, 1962). Also, in the group
setting, triangular therapist — couple interactions are lessened. The
dilution of transference and counter transference reactions also allow
individuals to explore explicit sexual material more readily in the
group setting (Van Emde Boas, 1950, 1962).

For patients who relate poorly to persons in authority or to
persons who are perceived as very different from themselves, group
therapy may be the most suitable form of treatment. Group support
can help such patients enter therapy and remain in therapy during
uncomfortable early periods. Homosexual problems (Gershman,
1975; Haden, 1972) and problems of sexual deviation (Peters and
Roether, 1971; Mathis and Cullens, 1971) appear to benefit particularly from the sense of homogeneity which groups can create. Also,
when a high degree of sociopathy exists in patients, group support
can be changed to group pressure to help keep particularly difficult
patients in treatment.

For boys at risk of becoming homosexual (Green and Fuller, 1973)
group experience can stimulate the normal group play of boys, hence

facilitating more adaptive child—child interactions. Finally, the successful treatment of many problems with sexual arousal can also occur in the group setting. Group process techniques can focus on here-and-now member interactions, while sexual assignments or homework performed outside the group can be brought back into the group for analysis.

Limitations to the Treatment of Sexual Problems by Group Therapy

A feature common to most group interaction, competition, can at times work to spur on new attempts at success by lagging group members. However, the opposite can also occur. If a group member sees others progressing much faster, discouragement may occur. In individual therapy, the patient's progress can be measured without reference to the rate of progress of others. However, in a group, progress, or lack of progress, is at all times compared from member to member. Such comparisons may occasionally work to discourage further effort at therapy by a particularly slow moving patient.

Another problem of the treatment of sexual problems in a group setting is also common to all group therapies. If groups are composed such that one or two members are markedly different from other members, group work may not be sufficiently relevant to the minority to allow therapeutic change to occur. Hence, although it is not innately a problem of the group treatment of sexual disorders, marked heterogeneity of groups may work at times to inhibit therapeutic change. Also, interactions of group members outside of the group may create problems. Sub-grouping, secrets held between group members, and other hidden processes tend to inhibit therapeutic interactions in a group. In the special case of a couples' group, members of the couple may not freely interact in the group, they may protect one another, or they may overly expose one another as the group progresses. Whereas such couple dynamics may at times be observed and interpreted, at other times they may inhibit therapy and be destructive to the process of therapy in a group. Finally, as with any form of therapy, lack of training and experience or lack of understanding of countertransference feelings by the group therapist can limit the effectiveness of group therapy for the treatment of any sexual problem.

References

Barbach, L. G. (1974). *Journal of Sex and Marital Therapy*, 1, 139–145.
Bemporad, J. (1975). *In* "Sexuality and Psychoanalysis." (Adelson, E. Ed.), pp. 267–290. Brunner/Mazel: New York.
Berman, E. M. and Lief, H. I. (1975). *American Journal of Psychiatry*, 132, 583–592.
Blinder, M. G. and Kirschenbaum, M. (1967). *Archives of General Psychiatry*, 17, 44–52.
Clower, V. L. (1975). *In* "Masturbation from Infancy to Senescence." (Marcus, I. M. and Francis, J. J. Eds), pp. 107–143. International Universities Press, Inc: New York.
Corsini, R. and Rosenberg, B. (1955). *Journal of Abnormal Psychology*, 51, 406–411.
Costel, R. and Yalom, I. (1971). *International Psychiatric Clinics*, 8, 119–144.
Covi, L. (1972). *Psychotherapy and Psychosomatics*, 20, 176–180.
Fisher, S. (1973). "Understanding the Female Orgasm." Penguin Books: Harmondsworth.
Forrester, B. M. and Swiller, H. (1972). *International Journal of Group Psychotherapy*, 22, 343–351.
Framo, J. L. (1973). *Seminars in Psychiatry*, 5, 207–216.
Freidman, H. (1973). *American Journal of Psychotherapy*, 27, 421–429.
Gershman, H. (1975). "Effect of Group Therapy on Compulsive Homosexuality." Audio-Digest Foundation: Los Angeles.
Gottlieb, A. and Pattision, E. M. (1966) *Archives of General Psychiatry*, 14, 143–152.
Green, R. and Fuller, M. (1973). *International Journal of Group Psychotherapy*, 23, 54–68.
Guttmacher, J. (1972). *American Journal of Psychiatry*, 129, 361–362.
Haden, S. B. (1972). *International Psychiatric Clinics*, 8, 81–94.
Hollender, M. H. (1971). *Current Psychiatric Therapies*, 11, 119–128.
Hollender, M. H. (1975). *In* "Masturbation from Infancy to Senescence" (Marcus, I. M. and Francis, J. H. Eds), pp. 315–328. International Universities Press, Inc: New York.
Kaplan, H. S. (1974). "The New Sex Therapy." Brunner/Mazel: New York.
Kaplan, H. S., Kohl, R. N., Pomeroy, W. B., Offit, A. K. and Hogan, B. (1974). *Archives of Sexual Behaviour*, 3, 443–452.
Kaufman, G. and Krupka, J. (1973). *International Journal of Group Psychotherapy*, 23, 445–464.
Lazarus, A. (1961). *Journal of Abnormal and Social Psychology*, 63, 504–510.
Lazarus, A. (1968). *In* "Basic Approaches to Group Psychotherapy and Group Counselling." (Gazda, G. M. Ed.), pp. 149–175. Charles C. Thomas, Springfield, Ill., USA.
Leichter, E. (1962). *International Journal of Group Psychotherapy*, 12, 154–163.
Lobitz, W. and LoPiccolo, J. (1972). *Journal of Behaviour Therapy and Experimental Psychiatry*, 3, 265–71.
Masters, W. H. and Johnson, V. E. (1970). "Human Sexual Inadequacy." Little, Brown, and Co: Boston, Mass., USA.

Mathis, J. L. and Cullens, M. (1971). *Current Psychiatric Therapies*, 11, 139—145.

Perelman, J. S. (1960). *International Journal of Group Psychotherapy*, 10, 136—142.

Peters, J. J. and Roether, H. A. (1971). *International Psychiatric Clinics*, 8, 69—80.

Reckless, J., Hawkins, D. and Fauntleroy, A. (1973). *American Journal of Psychiatry*, 130, 1024—1026.

Roether, H. and Peters, J. (1972). *American Journal of Psychiatry*, 128, 1014—1017.

Sadoff, R. L., Roether, H. A. and Peters, J. J. (1971). *American Journal of Psychiatry*, 128, 224—227.

Shaffer, J. and Galinsky, M. (1974). "Models of Group Therapy and Sensitivity Training." Prentice-Hall, Inc: New Jersey, USA.

Shah, I. (1970). "Tales of the Dervishes. Teaching Stores of the Sufi Masters over the Past Thousand Years." E. P. Dutton and Co: New York.

Shainess, N. (1975). *In* "Sexuality and Psychoanalysis." (Adelson, E. Ed.), pp. 145—156. Brunner/Mazel: New York.

Stoler, R. (1972). *Danish Medical Bulletin*, 19, 287—301.

Truax, R. and Tourney, G. (1971). *Diseases of the Nervous System*, 32, 707—711.

Van Emde Boas, C. (1950). *International Journal of Sexology*, 4, 1—6.

Van Emde Boas, C. (1962). *International Journal of Group Psychotherapy*, 12, 142—153.

Wallace, D. H. and Barbach, L. G. (1974). *Journal of Sex and Marital Therapy*, 1, 146—154.

Yalom, I. D. (1970). "The Theory and Practice of Group Psychotherapy." Basic Books, Inc: New York.

Zilbergeld, B. (1975). *Journal of Sex and Marital Therapy*, 1, 204—214.

3 Counselling

AUDREY NEWSOME

Change and transition are two of the most overworked words in general use today. Those of us who attend professional conferences and meetings tend to cringe a little when yet again these words introduce a paper on almost any subject of a professional and contemporary nature. People have always complained about change, but at no time in history have they been so affected by the speed of change as those who live in the Western world and in some of the rapidly developing countries.

Whether, as a reader of this book, you are engaged in education, the medical profession, social work, any other occupation, or simply alive to the world around you, changes which have occurred in your lifetime are likely to have excited, amazed and possibly overwhelmed you. You are likely to agree that this generation is one which has experienced an unprecedented rate of change in scientific and technological development, but also most profoundly in attitudes, beliefs and values which have brought freedom and satisfaction to many, but at the same time increasing confusion and insecurity. Toffler (1970) illustrates the dramatic changes which are now taking place by defining the present as the 800th lifetime, the one at which we have arrived having divided the whole of man's existence into lifetimes of 62 years. This lifetime, he says, makes a sharp break with all past human experience because in this lifetime man's relationship to resources has reversed itself, causing nation after nation to face crises of an economic and social kind never before experienced on such a scale. The increased speed of communication has brought these crises to our attention not only more quickly but

in a more graphic form which, unless we become emotionally satu-
rated by the experience, increases our awareness of others. Now we
not only hear of disasters in the press and on radio, we actually see
live on television the tears of bereaved relatives at the graveside, or
the pathetic lifelessness of a starving child. Perhaps it is not surprising that it is within this generation that the counselling movement
itself, both professionally and in the application of its skills by those
whose principal occupation is as a practitioner in some field of education, medicine, social, community or work setting reflect the
speed of change in the understanding of human behaviour. Toffler,
a journalist, sociologist and an adviser to the Institute for the Future
in considering ways of helping people to cope with tomorrow says:

> "To help tide millions of people over the difficult transitions they are
> likely to face we shall be forced to 'deputise' large numbers of non-
> professional people in the community — businessmen, students, teachers,
> workers and others — to serve as 'crisis counsellors'. Tomorrow's crisis
> counsellors will be experts not in such conventional disciplines as
> psychology or health, but in special transitions such as relocation, job
> promotion, divorce, or subcult-hopping."

When counselling is mentioned the very word itself can be relied
on to generate a wealth of response. "What's so new about it — we've
been doing it in medicine for years: if you're a doctor you're bound
to be a counsellor"; "It's far too dangerous for anyone to attempt to
do it unless they themselves have had a thoroughgoing training in
psychoanalysis"; "What's the need for it anyway — we coped with our
own problems in my day and we survived". To introduce oneself
as a counsellor is to risk either immediate rejection or a lengthy
monologue on the unique and insoluble problems of "my friend",
or a request from the intrigued stranger for an instant analysis of
their character and a prescription for the solution of difficulties.
The professional is as much to blame as the public for the confusion
presently attaching to the meaning of counselling. Any conference
on counselling will only serve to confirm the lack of precision in
the meaning and the difficulty which professionals experience in
attempting to define the difference in the goals of psychotherapy
and counselling and to answer the question "Who is a counsellor?".
In recent years other professions have faced similar problems in
defining the role and setting up standards for medicine, teaching,
psychology and social work. Now it is the turn of the counsellor to
face and begin to solve the same problem. Just as there are in the
community many individuals who would be rejected by these older

professions as insufficiently equipped to practise within their
particular profession, so there are numbers who use some of the
knowledge and skills in carrying out other professional roles or in
their everyday lives. The same is true of counselling, but the problem of defining the boundaries is more difficult. Everyone, by
virtue of being human, considers himself to be an authority on the
problems of others and entitled to proffer his counsel even if his
own life is in utter disarray.

It is easier to say what counselling is not than to give an acceptable
definition of what it is. Many attempts have been made of definition
over the past two decades, but usually fall short of gaining agreement
even from those who see themselves as counsellors, since they tend
to reflect the particular philosophical orientations of those individuals
or the settings in which they work in an occupation which, since it
is fundamentally concerned with understanding the infinite complexities of human beings in a complex and changing society, is itself in a
state of flux. In no occupation can there be greater uncertainty and
change. Attempts at definition are like those to grasp quicksilver,
for when you think you have got it suddenly it is gone — the human
conditions and its environment have changed. Perhaps that is part
of the appeal in counselling to those of us who practise it; the continuing need to acquire new knowledge and to change, adapt and
accept a state of ongoing change and uncertainty.

The Range of Counselling Services

Definitions of counselling and the setting of standards for professional
practice will depend on the setting in which counsellors work. Presently
these are many and diverse. The Church, once seen as the fount of
wisdom and concern for the human condition, in recent years has
come to appreciate that new knowledge in the fields of sociology,
psychology and education can help it to do better those things which
it has previously done in its pastoral care (Chapter 9). Many clergy
are now turning to courses on counselling theory and practice and
not only using these skills in the Church, but identifying increasingly
with the professional counselling movement and a minority are
entering full-time counselling jobs in education and other fields.
Of more contemporary institutions, the National Marriage Guidance
Council has given considerable leadership in recent years to the

counselling movement by training lay people to help others experiencing difficulties in their marital relationships and to give help to
younger people in education and the community in the broader field
of human relationships.

Although staff in all levels of the educational system in Britain
have traditionally prided themselves on their provision of pastoral
care, it is only in the past decade that there have been developments
in the appointment of staff specially designated as counsellors to
assist young people with decision-making and with the difficulties
they experience as they progress through the educational system.
For several decades there have been specialists working to provide
careers advice. Only recently have they begun to re-evaluate their
role and to identify the core of their work as counselling for which
they are seeking special preparation. Many working in this specialization have become increasingly aware of the complex nature of the
world of work and of quite dramatic changes in the place of work
in society and are seeing themselves operating more as life-style
counsellors concerned to help people with broader decisions on the
use of their lives than simply those on how to earn a living. A more
sophisticated approach of this kind demands not only the provision
of information, but a capacity on the part of the counsellor to
understand the stage of development of the person who seeks his
help and skills to assist his client to develop an awareness of his
own identity and to accept responsibility for the shaping of that
identity through the choices and decisions he makes. Such an
approach is quite different from the now outdated methods applied
by the careers adviser whose claims to professionalism rested on the
quantity of occupational information which he possessed, his capacity to "sum up" the person and select, by virtue of his personal
experience, those occupations best suited to the client. Increasingly,
we are becoming aware that "experience", a once much-prized possession for advisers in almost any field, has not simply assumed less
significance, but can even be a positive handicap in attempting to
help others to deal with contemporary concerns. Even if there was
a time when "if I were you" gave acceptable authority to the advice
which followed, it is unlikely now to be accorded very much respect,
especially if it is said by someone whose age, position in society
and behaviour are at all removed from that of the client. Unfortunately, I believe it to be true that in education generally, and more
particularly in higher education, the gap in values, in respect and
in communication appears to have widened with the provision of

more educational opportunities for more young people since the
Second World War. In partial recognition of this fact, some educational institutions are looking to the new breed of counsellor to
solve the problem and are likely to be disappointed if they rely
solely on counsellors to do the caring for them. Unless teachers and
administrators look at ways in which they can improve communication with their students, the quality of the educational experience
being provided will diminish. Communication skills are an essential
tool of the counsellor. They are capable of being learnt by very many
more teachers and by the students themselves.

In an attempt to respond to the crises in society, numbers of
movements have been established. There are organizations like
"Cruse" which set out to help the recently widowed person. There
are pregnancy advisory services which seek to help individuals who
believe that they have become accidentally pregnant. There are
groups attempting to deal with individuals who have come into
conflict with the Law or who have suddenly found themselves
evicted from housing. The Samaritans have developed a now well-
established system for responding both in crisis and in an ongoing
way to the depressed, lonely and suicidal in society.

More recent years have also seen the development of support
groups and counselling for those who see themselves as special or
a minority in society. Within these groups it is generally felt that
unless the counsellor shares the concerns and problems of that
particular group he cannot properly understand them. This appears
to be true of the homosexual groups. It is also true in the women's
liberation movement and in some of the racial minority groups,
where the behaviour of all but those of a similar sex or race lacks
credibility to many of the membership. Those who share a common
disability like multiple schlerosis or the loss of a limb often feel that
only similarly afflicted people can provide adequate counsel.

In discussing the variety of settings in which counselling is offered
and sought, it is obvious that the *perceptions* which each individual
has of the organization offering help and of the person practising
counselling will not only determine the extent to which it is used
but the *kind* of use which is made of it. The mere provision of counselling and the labelling of a door "Student Counsellor" or any other
form of counselling will not automatically assure its use in expected
ways. People will seek help where it best suits them — where their
anxieties are least aroused in doing so and where they expect to
receive help. In attempting to develop healthier and more humane

institutions we should not lose sight of that fact. We also need to
be aware of the fact that people's expectations of any one of us
will depend on a number of things not always easy to define or
fully understood. We are not always fully conscious of the many
subtle reactions which we have to a person which make him or her
acceptable and approachable or unacceptable and even forbidding.
One thing we do know is that people tend to stereotype the expectations of people in specified roles. Many people expect that the
doctor will diagnose the nature of a physical or psychiatric problem
and prescribe the cure — that he will take responsibility for the
decision on any sort of action that needs to be taken although he
will certainly not have the time to listen for more than a few minutes.
In many cases they are right and the stereotype is reinforced. The
marital counsellor, on the other hand, will be expected to give considerable time on a number of occasions to the unveiling of the
difficulties in a relationship and will help to identify possible ways
of tackling the problem. If the doctor or the marital counsellor
decides to operate outside the stereotype of the role which he recog-
nizes the client is giving him, then he will need to make this quite
explicit to the client in order to achieve the new goals.

A Definition of Counselling

Whatever the setting in which it is provided, counselling is, for me,
the application of intelligent, educated love to an individual or a
group seeking help in their personal development or in problem
solving. Such a simple definition runs the risk of being undervalued
or even ridiculed. Aren't we all intelligent, educated and loving? Of
course, very many people have the potential for becoming so and
for developing more effective relationships by the exercise of these
qualities, but not all will have the willingness, interest and capacity
to apply them to the care and development of others in this way. In
this context what I mean by love is the capacity to feel and demonstrate profound respect for another individual, his integrity and his
capacity to become self-directing. By applying this love in an intelligent and educated way I imply the willingness on the part of the
counsellor to develop and apply knowledge and skills to assist in
the growth of another individual in the clarification of his goals or
in the resolution of his concerns, to understand his, the counsellor's

own needs, and to make sure that in the satisfaction of these he is
not in any way pressurizing the client or imposing on him. The application of intelligent, educated love in the role of counsellor implies
not only sound initial training, but the need regularly to update that
training and continuously re-evaluate himself in that role as a changing
influence on others. The counsellor is the instrument of whatever is
effected in the counselling relationship and he must assume responsibility for making sure that his pitch and performance are of as
high a standard as possible. He must also be willing to seek the help
of others who are prepared to be constructively critical of his performance. The counselling relationship is an extraordinarily privi-
leged one and deserves the highest standards. I know of no other
profession the behaviour of whose members is as open to scrutiny
and criticism as is that of counsellors. Perhaps if they and their
effectiveness could be measured by their apparent skill in using a
drill or stethoscope, or their capacity to quote impressive scientific
facts about behaviour, it might be different. None of this is usually
possible or relevant to the counsellor's work and the counsellor must
be willing to take responsibility for his person and the effect he has
on others. He must, at the same time, be humble enough to seek the
counsel of others in order to keep a healthy perspective on what he
is doing.

The Counselling Setting

What actually happens between the counsellor and the person seeking
help depends on a considerable number of variables, some relating to
the counsellor and the setting in which he is working, and some to the
person seeking help. Both have preconceived notions of what they
expect of themselves and of one another, which need to be recognized
quite early in their work together. Since counselling as a professional
practice is so new, there are few people seeking the help of a counsellor
who can have any clear expectations of what will happen to them
once they have plucked up the courage to seek help. Will they be
psychoanalysed, persuaded into certain courses of action, cajoled,
interrogated, left to fill fifty minutes with embarrasing silence punc-
tuated by the revelation of foolish anxieties — just what will happen?
Similar fears confront newcomers to counselling work. Will they be
able to respond to those seeking their help in appropriately helpful
ways? Will they be able to provide the climate necessary to listen to

and accept the concerns, anxieties, problems and fears of others and
enable those seeking help to deal constructively and creatively with
their concerns in ways which allow them to develop greater self-
respect? The counsellor with a full appointments diary may easily
forget what it feels like to wait in a waiting-room rehearsing the first
few lines of the problem to present to the counsellor. He may also
fail to recognize what unfinished business he has to cope with in the
relationships the client previously formed with authority figures like
parents, doctors, teachers, priests and others who may have had significance in the earlier life of the client. Although I believe myself
to be an accepting and caring person, providing no reason for anyone
to fear me, I need constantly to remind myself that my whole persona
and the setting in which I work represent many different things to
those who come to see me. I can only be myself, but I must make
sure that the way in which I present myself is as genuinely caring as
I can make it.

The impressions which a client gains of counselling start well before
he sees a counsellor. They start with the telephone call or the meeting
with the receptionist whose manner and attention to their request
sets an expectation of what is to follow. The waiting room, too,
must provide a warm, pleasant and comfortable atmosphere which
conveys to the client the feeling that thought has been given to him
and his comfort. Unless there is good reason, which will need to be
explained, the client must not be kept waiting beyond the time of
his appointment. All this may appear to be stating the obvious, but
my own experience of quite contrary conditions in hospitals and
other institutions convinces me of the importance of paying attention
to setting the conditions as well as possible. Similarly, the counsellor's
room deserves attention. Few of us have very much choice of accommodation, but what is done with the space is important. A pleasantly
decorated and furnished room with comfortable chairs helps to create
an accepting atmosphere. For me it is important that the immediate
area in which I am counselling is uncluttered by official-looking
papers and files and that the person seeking my help and I sit in comfortable chairs near one another and away from the barrier of a desk.
The physical environment needs to convey the feeling that there is
time for the client and good conditions for sharing his concerns.
Counselling is a *shared enterprise* in which the outcomes will depend
on the willingness of both counsellor and client to apply themselves
intently to the question which needs to be solved or to the behaviour
which the client seeks to change or to develop.

The Counselling Process

It is extremely difficult to convey adequately what happens in the
counselling relationship itself without watching a number of audio-
visual tapes of actual counselling sessions or reading the scripts of
such sessions much as one would read the script of a play. It is
then necessary to analyse the kind of material presented by the client
and the nature of the counsellor's response. In attempting to help
beginning counsellors to respond selectively to clients' needs as
appropriately as possible Hackney and Nye (1973) have devoted
a book to examples and exercises designed for this purpose. It is
clearly not possible in a single chapter to offer training of the kind
which they attempt, but a modified version of the ideal model of
the counselling process offered by Newsome *et al.* (1973) may provide a simple, if over-idealized, description of what is likely to
happen.

The Person Comes for Help

He may come of his own accord or because someone else has suggested he should. In certain cases he may even have been told to come:
if this is the case the counsellor needs to be aware of the fact if he
is to cope effectively with the possible hostility which this may
have generated.

The Counsellor Attempts to Relate to the Client

The nature of the developing relationship is of crucial importance
and if it goes wrong there will be little hope of achieving anything
very constructive. The counsellor must convey, unselfconsciously,
to his client a warm regard for him as a person of real value. By
the way in which he relates to his client, by what he says, the way
he says it and the attention he gives his client, he must show that
he is willing to allow him to reveal his concerns and his feelings in
his own way. If the counsellor begins to actually like his client
and to demonstrate his respect for him in the way in which he
responds, the client is likely to begin to feel a little more comfortable
about revealing more about himself — a climate of trust will begin
to develop without which little growth is possible. The nature of

this stage will be very different from the taking of a case history in which control lies firmly with the questioner. It will demonstrate the willingness of the counsellor to listen and try to understand, not to take control.

The Helping Situation is Defined

It is necessary at an early stage to explore what kind of help may be possible and what sort of goals (however tentatively defined) may be established for the time available. This part of the process communicates to the client that there is a shared task ahead which will involve work and effort on both their parts. This kind of definition may not even be achieved at the first meeting of counsellor and client.

The Counsellor Encourages his Client to Give Free Expression to his Concerns

It is at this stage that the counsellor's ability to empathize with the client needs to be communicated if further progress is to be made. Unless the client feels that he is being received and understood he will quickly lose confidence in the process, becoming uncomfortable and reluctant to commit himself to it. The counsellor's comfort with himself, as well as his ability to reflect feeling accurately and to respond at the right level, will be important to the way in which counselling develops and the direction that counselling takes.

The Counsellor Accepts, Recognizes and Helps to Clarify Negative Feelings in the Client

It is vital that the counsellor does not seek to evade his client's expression of fear, anger, depression, doubt or whatever it may be. Negative feelings need to be faced and vague reassurance at this stage can be positively harmful. Nor must the expression of such feelings be cut short before they have been fully expressed. It is often painful to listen to a person denigrating himself or spelling out in detail the extent of his anguish or self-rejection, but this must be endured if growth is to take place later. It is usually the case that only when negative feelings have been fully explored can faint and hesitant expressions of positive feelings be voiced.

The Counsellor Accepts and Recognizes Positive Feelings

In other words, the counsellor's behaviour will indicate an understanding totally devoid of judgment. To call a person good can be just as threatening as to call him bad. It leaves the counsellor in the position of power, able to grant or withold approval as he wishes.

Development of Insight

With a lessening of fear and anxiety, insight should now be developing and the counsellor, by his responses, will try to assist the growth of self-acceptance and understanding necessary to effect change.

Establishing of New Goals

With the development of more self-acceptance there will come an increased clarification of needs which will lead to the tentative establishing of new goals and objectives. It is possible at this point that the counsellor's role may become more directive or didactic, for the client may set up for himself goals which require for their attainment certain forms of expertise or information which the counsellor possesses. He may focus on methods of developing social skills or even recommend reading or seeking materials which will help in the client's education.

Growth of Confidence and Ability to Take Decisions

At this point the client will be initiating small but significant actions and will need the counsellor's reinforcement and support. The counsellor will be alert now for the moment when counselling sessions should terminate.

No More Need for Help

Ending a counselling relationship is not always easy and the counsellor must beware of breaking off the process prematurely. Usually
the client takes the initiative quite comfortably and healthily. If
all has gone well he will leave with greater respect for himself and
an increased capacity to take responsibility for his own behaviour.

Such an analysis of what happens excludes any exposition of
the different methodologies of counselling which may be used to
assist the client. The range is now extensive of group and individual
counselling methods which may suit a particular counsellor or client
or the resolution of a particular problem. It is beyond the scope of
a single chapter to describe them in detail. The non-directive approach
used in both group and individual counselling which was developed
by Carl Rogers merits careful study, particularly by doctors and
teachers whose traditional approach to patients and pupils has
assumed that *they* must take responsibility for the person seeking
help. A non-directive approach assumes that the person seeking help
has the resources for solving his own problem and that the role of
the counsellor is to facilitate the development of those resources
so that the client does not become dependent on the advice of the
counsellor, but will emerge from the counselling process with greater
respect for himself and his own capacity to cope. However, perhaps
one of the ways in which counselling is differentiated from other
forms of psychotherapy or psychoanalysis is in the range of methodologies which may be used by one counsellor in the course of his work.
Depending on the nature of the problem, the time available and the
way in which a client is likely to respond, the counsellor and client
may agree to use behavioural methods, role-playing, group counselling, to continue in client-centred counselling if that was the orientation of the initial contact with the client, or to adopt a number of
different approaches which may seem likely to help in the resolution
of the problem. The counsellor must be able to change gear easily and
quickly when it appears to be in the interests of the client to do so.
He must be willing to enter into the world of the client and share
the feelings which the client is experiencing, whilst at the same time
monitoring his own response to the client and, on occasions, assessing the point at which it may be necessary to effect the referral of
the client to someone else more able to help. How can the counsellor
achieve all these acrobatic feats and still remain genuine in the relationship with his client? It is difficult — it demands real concentration,

extreme sensitivity and the capacity to draw on a background of extensive knowledge about behaviour. It requires the exercise of considerable self-awareness in order that the counsellor may use himself as effectively as possible and not impose on the client.

The Counsellor and his Values

Most professional counsellors and other practitioners using counselling skills are likely to have developed their values in a world outdated by a decade at the very least and, more usually, by twenty or thirty years. Any attempt on the counsellor's part to use past experience as though it has current relevance is likely to be dangerous unless it is subjected to critical re-evaluation. Those of us who work with young people may persuade ourselves that we are in touch with the contemporary world by maintaining close contact with them. To some extent this is true. If I were to discontinue counselling of young people now it would be only a very short time before I began to feel out of touch with the language and the cults favoured by the young and to lose a feeling of authenticity in relating to them or talking about them. I also recognize how frequently I look back in time to evaluate present experience. My personal base-line for measuring experience and value is certainly pre-decimalization — sixty-five pence has much less meaning than thirteen shillings. The expectations set of a girl and woman in the home, school and society in which I grew up have fleeting and sometimes more far-reaching effect on my current behaviour. What is "right" for me is often a modification of what was expected in the environment of my childhood. It was a world in which the career expectations of a woman were very different from those of today; occupational choice was considerably smaller, minority groups were Jewish rather than Asian, homosexual identification was concealed rather than revealed in the way in which it is today. The contraceptive pill was non-existent and termination of pregnancy as well as suicide treated as criminal acts. Far fewer married women were in paid work. In 1951 22% of them were in paid work; in 1971 the percentage had risen to 42% with the largest increase being in the group of women aged between 35 and 54, which contained six times as many economically active women as in 1921. It is not surprising that many adults judge the contemporary world by values established at a more impressionable period

of their lives and that many fail to recognize that their recom-
mendations for other people's behaviour are often based on this
experience. The doctor faced with a depressed young married woman
with small children may have several courses of action open to him.
He may choose to prescribe an anti-depressant drug or sleeping
tablets; he may recommend or reinforce a suggestion from her that
she should take on a job outside the home; he may make a referral
to another agency to help her, or he may see her regularly to
monitor her condition and allow her to talk about her feelings. Whatever he does, he is likely to believe that he is operating in *her* best
interests, but he may be failing to recognize that he will, in part, be
affected in his choice of treatments by his own values and attitudes
assumed in the process of his own past experience.

Similarly, the counsellor, however non-directive he may consider
himself to be, may well reinforce kinds of behaviour with which he
himself feels more comfortable and which may be more in line with
what he expects of a male or female client, or simply of what he
considers to be "healthy" behaviour. There is evidence, provided
by Broverman *et al.* (1970), to demonstrate that clinicians appear
to adopt criteria of adjustment to sex-role stereotypes as criteria
of psychological health. In vocational counselling practitioners often
actively discourage clients of the opposite sex from exploring occupations which they see as predominantly male or female.

The Sexuality of the Counsellor and His Response to It

Like the client, the counsellor is contained in a physical mould to
which he has his own idiosyncratic set of responses affecting not
only his own behaviour but his comfort or discomfort with the
behaviour of others and his response to it as a counsellor. In training
often insufficient attention is paid to the exploration of the potential
counsellor's uniqueness and his response to his sexuality, his enjoyment of it, his fulfilment, satisfaction and expectations or his fears,
apprehensions, inhibitions and rejections. The extent to which the
counsellor fits the accepted stereotype of male or female will affect
his acceptance or rejection with colleagues in the institution in
which he works, and it will affect the referrals he receives. The
extent to which the counsellor is comfortable with his own sexuality
and accepting of others will certainly affect the nature of the con-

cerns presented to him and his selective response to them. If the counsellor is unaccepting of his own sexuality and fearful of the expression of selected aspects of sexuality in his clients, his relationship with the client will be inhibited, the material presented to him will be affected and his response selective to the exclusion of those areas which evoke the counsellor's own anxieties. When the client is very self-rejecting and fearful he may well hint at behaviour which he feels to be so totally repulsive and unaccepting to himself that if he were to reveal it he would run the risk of rejection even by the counsellor. If the counsellor is comfortable enough with himself he is likely to feel free to allow the client the expression of this in his own good time. Clearly, there will be cases where the behaviour which is revealed merits the attention of a psychiatrist rather than a counsellor, but there are likely to be more occasions when the acceptance of the expression of behaviour which is causing such alarm is in itself therapeutic.

When in training, counsellors, doctors and teachers are asked to reveal in strict confidence some aspect of their behaviour which they have been too frightened or ashamed to reveal previously to anyone else: it is amazing and saddening how often mention is made of masturbation or incidents of homosexual behaviour in adolescence or some other behaviour which they consider to be deviant which has been carried as a heavy cross ever since. Potential counsellors themselves need the opportunity of counselling to explore their own needs and yet how rarely is this recognized and provided for in training.

Equally, counsellors need support after training, not only in the early stages of their work but continuously if they are to cope effectively and responsibly with the demands made upon them. In the early stages of practice many counsellors work alone and if unsupported by a psychiatrist, or similarly qualified practitioner, may either find the pressures of the job overtaxing or fail to recognize ways in which they or someone else might be more effective with the client. Although, in general, the sex of the counsellor is less important than his effectiveness to gain acceptance as a counsellor and establish rapport with his client, there are some cases in which it is particularly important to the client to be able to see a man and vice versa. The woman who lacks confidence in her capacity to sustain a relationship with a man for more than the briefest period may benefit greatly from counselling by a man who is able to allow expression of these feelings and remain available to her professionally

in an ongoing relationship until she has developed greater confidence
and self-respect. Equally, for the counsellor there may well be problems and limitations imposed by virtue of his or her sex. It is, for
example, generally more difficult for the heterosexual male counsellor to feel comfortable and understanding for the homosexual male
client and for the female counsellor to accept easily the lesbian client.
There are greater elements of threat in establishing a professional
relationship which may, in part, stem from unresolved fears of the
counsellor about his or her own sexuality, which become reactivated
by the client and his concerns. With support, the counsellor may be
enabled to work more effectively or he may find channels for referral to someone likely to be more helpful in the particular case.

Developmental Counselling and Crisis Intervention

In understanding himself, his values and his behaviour, the counsellor
himself must take account of where he is in the life span. If he is to
give help to those who seek it with decision making or with coping
more effectively with their lives, then the counsellor will need to
know more about the developmental stages through which individuals
pass and what, in general, are the normal developmental tasks with
which they are expected to deal at a particular stage. Clearly, there
are dangers in expecting individuals to conform to a uniform pattern
of development, but it is equally dangerous for the counsellor to
ignore the knowledge available to him on behaviour of people
derived from developmental studies of the human being throughout
his life. It is equally important for him to understand the nature of
crisis which usually occurs for an individual at periods of discontinuity between stages of development. Much of the stress which
people experience stems from their not having already coped with
tasks more appropriate to an earlier stage in their development. An
appreciation of what are normal developmental tasks not only for
a particular stage in development, but for individuals in particular
subgroups in society of a socio-economic, racial or occupational
kind are necessary in the establishment of a base-line of understanding. A developmental task has been defined by Havighurst (1953) as:

> "a task which arises at or about a certain period in the life of the individual,
> successful achievement of which leads to his happiness and to his success
> with later tasks, while failure leads to unhappiness in the individual, dis-
> approval by the society and difficulty with later tasks".

Many psychologists have formulated theories of life stages usually linked to an examination of careers throughout the entire course of people's lives and giving particular emphasis to preparation for and stages in their working lives. Much of this work is extremely useful, and longtitudinal studies of the kind undertaken by Dr Super and his associates help us to understand that an individual's progress in preparation for and during his working life is far less smooth and straightforward than our capacity for selective recall of our own past would delude us into believing. However, such research findings are outdated as soon as they are published and although they help us in our understanding of behaviour we need to remember that the conditions of the world in which we live and our values are in a continuous process of change.

Counsellors working in educational settings will certainly need to understand the normal behaviour of young people in the early stages of their development, whilst at the same time valuing individual differences sufficiently to resist the temptation to see as sick or disturbed, those who do not fit the stereotype of boy or girl at a particular age. Counsellors working with the late adolescent and young adult also need to understand that stage in development sufficiently well to help individuals to cope with the flood of demands made upon them. It is a stage at which people are required to make a variety of decisions of an educational and vocational kind, to behave in ways which often conflict either with their parents or with their peers, but which are crucial in their establishment of an acceptable identity. It is an age at which physical, emotional and environmental changes impinge on a person in a more concentrated form than at any other stage in the normal development of an individual and although strong arguments can be applied for the provision of counselling at various stages in life, I believe that more sensitive educational and counselling provision at this stage would do much to educate and prepare people to deal with later stages in their development in a healthier way than is presently possible. This could, at least, prevent some of the crises which occur because individuals have never learnt to develop healthy interdependent relationships, the capacity to make decisions and to live creatively in a world which is increasingly unpredictable and insecure.

In recent years some attention has also been given to the preparation of people for retirement, a time for re-evaluation of oneself in relation to the use of time, to relationships with contemporaries, learning to cope with reduced physical energy and possibly different

living conditions. With an overall increase in life expectation, it
clearly makes sense to develop methods of preventing unnecessary
physical and mental ill-health when sudden changes occur in behaviour patterns developed over a period of forty or fifty years.

Until recently, the most neglected stage in the life-span was
that of the middle years. Changes in the economy and in technology
which have rendered a significant proportion of this age group unemployed have forced us to begin to take a critical look at this stage
in development. The fact that the housewife in mid-life becomes
particularly vulnerable to mental ill-health and to alcoholism when
the family to whom she has devoted her time and energy for at
least ten or fifteen years no longer need her and leave her without
a sense of purpose and fulfilment has begun to focus attention on
the needs of this particular group (Chapter 8).

There is now considerable evidence to show that illness occurs
more frequently at periods of discontinuity between life-stages, at
points of entry into school, entry into work, into marriage, to the
stage of becoming a parent and into retirement. If the concern of
counsellors is with the promotion of health and with assisting
people to cope well with their own development, then they must
become familiar not just with the techniques of counselling, but
with understanding human growth and development and with the
nature of crisis and crisis intervention when this becomes necessary.
As defined by Erikson (1968) crisis no longer connotes impending
catastrophe, but a

> "necessary turning point, a crucial moment, when development must
> move one way or another, marshalling resources of growth, recovery and
> further differentiation".

Such a definition enables the counsellor and client to treat the
"crisis" as an opportunity, a chance to utilize the extra energy which
it produces in the client in constructive ways, enabling the client to
emerge from it with an increased sense of self-respect. Caplan (1961)
in his concern for developing models for the prevention of mental
ill-health states:

> "In order for professional workers to help a person in crisis, it is not only
> necessary for them to understand the nature of crisis reactions and to have
> the skill to influence him to adopt a healthy approach to his crisis tasks;
> they must also be available to offer him this help during the relatively
> short period of crisis disequilibrium, when his choices of coping patterns
> are being made".

Although it is sometimes administratively difficult to organize, counsellors must be flexible in their use of time if they are to respond both to the normal developmental needs of others and be available to respond to their needs in crisis.

Counselling the Adolescent and Young Adult

The period from the onset of puberty to the mid-twenties is of particular importance in the development of identity and in the establishment of patterns of behaviour for later stages in development. It is in itself a period of transition from a largely unconscious period of identity development in childhood to a more developed but still changing concept of the self in relation to others which comes through the establishment of a variety of roles and through achievements and failure in the world of education, or work and of social life. It can be a period of great richness for the individual who finds excitement and rewards in his greater freedom. It can also be deeply depressing and empty for those young people who compare themselves adversely with others around them in almost everything they do and feel trapped in a meaningless existence. In their struggle to become adult, many young people go through a period of rejecting those adults whose beliefs and attitudes they have previously taken for granted, and although this may be a necessary stage in their development, it is hard both for the young person and his parents until that stage is resolved.

Adolescence is a period when people are faced with choices to be made, some of which may have long-lasting effect. Some are choices which may crucially affect the style of life a young person will lead, the kind of people he will meet and the kind of person he will become. In the face of such important decisions, young people become confused and anxious often to the point of sickness. Parents, even if they are not rejected, are often ill-equipped to give adequate help. In understanding the crises which young people face, the counsellor has a unique opportunity not only of accepting such situations as normal at this stage of development, but of assisting in their resolution and at the same time, through his own acceptance of the young person, giving him the chance to re-evaluate his relationship with his parents. It would be folly to suggest that all young people experience serious difficulties in the process of becoming adult or that those who do require either the help of a counsellor or medical practitioner. Some most need the opportunity to "go it alone" and it may be

more therapeutic for a young person to step off the traditional
conveyor belt for a time and test his capacity to take responsibility
for himself by trying out different jobs or by travel than to receive
psychiatric help or counselling support.

With the increase in the length of full-time education young
people spend more of their adolescence in the company of their
peers and it is therefore not surprising that peer-group influences
have become stronger in recent years. The conflicting pressures to
comply with parental ambitions, to be approved of by their peers,
and at the same time to be true to themselves and establish an
acceptable image of themselves imposes strain, and understandably
results in what Erikson (1968) has described as role confusion.
Those of us who work with young people can corroborate Erikson's
theory with numerous case studies of individuals who make frequent
and often incomprehensible changes in courses of study or jobs
become promiscuous in their sexual relationships, overindulgent in
the use of drugs, or seriously depressed.

Sexual Stereotypes and the Adolescent

Masculine and feminine behaviour is no longer as clearly defined as
it was. The blurring of clearly-defined roles for men and women has
brought greater freedom for many to enjoy satisfactions from employing both masculine and feminine traits in their personalities. It
has, at the same time, brought greater confusion to those who are
struggling to identify themselves sexually and socially in relation to
their peers. The process of sexual identification is a delicate process
of matching oneself against the generally accepted image of the
Ideal man or Ideal woman in one's culture. Hunt (1974) tells us
that the *ideal woman* is seen in Western society as

> "less aggressive, less independent and dominant, less active and more
> emotional, and more reluctant to take decisions".

The ideal man is

> "less religious, less neat and gentle, less sensitive to others and less
> expressive of emotion".

If such models are accepted by young people they are likely to affect
their development, particularly at adolescence, when they are more
than usually concerned with self-examination. Ideal models of men
and women at that stage are often drawn from the world of leisure

and sport with which young people are more familiar than with the world of work. Pop stars and footballers provide some of them. At the same time, the Women's Movement and the Gay Liberation Front have impinged very considerably on attitudes in society and thrown into dispute many of the previously accepted stereotypes of male and female. Young people, who may not have seriously questioned their own sexual identification, may feel forced to do so and those who have found it difficult to establish satisfactory relationships may begin to doubt their own sexuality. Adolescence can be a very lonely time. Those who leave home for higher education or work may find it difficult to make friends, particularly of the opposite sex, and, in their loneliness and anxiety, begin to question whether they should join a homosexual group or whether they must seek heterosexual intimacy as a means of establishing at least some level of relationship. Many need the opportunity and time to explore their own feelings and attitudes in an accepting atmosphere devoid of the judgmental attitudes of both parents and peers.

In early adolescence the bodily changes which take place may have important impact on psychological development. Whilst for a boy early maturation may bring distinct advantages, the same is not true for girls whose social and intellectual development usually fails to keep pace with their early physical development (Jones, 1949). A proportion of young people find it difficult to accept their bodies as "good" male or female personifications and perceive them as unacceptable or unattractive to the opposite sex. In fear of being rejected they then withdraw from relationships and so confirm to themselves their apparent lack of attraction. Others are so keen to assert themselves as men or women that they are fiercely male or female, overplaying to an extent which ultimately worries them, and they then find it difficult to modify their behaviour. Few are so rejecting of themselves that they become anorexic or attempt suicide, but those who do draw our attention dramatically to their utter loneliness and need for help.

Sexual Identification, Achievement and Occupational Choice

Although many of the differences between the sexes are indeed self-evident, some are not and are only revealed by psychological measurement. It has been shown by Hunt (1974) that girls perform better, on average, than boys on verbal, clerical and arithmetical tasks; that boys perform better, on average, than girls on spatial, mechanical and visual tasks. There is, of course, a good deal of over-lap and many exceptions to the rule. However, those who are coun-selling adolescents on subject-choice and achievement need to explore not only the differences which occur naturally, but the subtle ways in which individuals modify their achievement in order better to fit the image of being feminine or masculine. Many studies have shown that in older adolescence in particular women students who had previously been superior in achievement to their male contem-poraries decline in achievement as their need to be seen as feminine becomes greater. The counsellor's often unacknowledged attitudes to his own sexuality and that of his client may well result in a form of collusion which prevents the individual from fulfilling himself or herself as much as is possible.

Boys who wish to enter predominantly male occupations like engineering or building may suffer feelings of personal failure as well as academic failure if they do not obtain the necessary qualifications for entry at the appropriate level to that form of work. Through compensatory activities in leisure it may be possible to enable individuals to feel more complete. There are many examples of academically very competent women occupying traditionally "male" jobs indulging their femininity in dress-making and home-making in their free time and of men in more traditionally female jobs like ladies' hairdressing enjoying horseriding or boxing in their free time.

As many women are less accepting of themselves in competitive, aggressive behaviour and, equally, as men are less approving of such behaviour, fewer women than men aspire to positions of leadership. When women do achieve such positions, not only are men disapproving, since their own dominance is thereby challenged, but many women are also disapproving of behaviour which, by implication, is not quite feminine. It takes considerable courage for most individuals to contravene the accepted norms of society and, although much of life is a compromise, counsellors must be able to assist individuals to explore the infinite range of possibilities for their clients if they are to be enabled to live with reasonable comfort and healthy respect for themselves.

Preparation for Counselling

Just as it is possible to teach first-aid to non-medically qualified people and lecturing techniques to those who are not qualified as teachers, so it is possible to teach counselling skills to those whose principal occupation is not full-time counselling. Indeed, unless well-trained counsellors concern themselves with the improvement of interpersonal relations in the institutions in which they are employed, they will make a less constructive contribution of their skills to the health of that institution. Where full-time counsellors are employed there is a danger that others may try to relegate to them their responsibilities for involving themselves in a healthy concern for others Warnath (1971). Counsellors need to be alert to this danger and to recognize that part of their responsibility should be exercised in helping others in the institution to communicate more effectively and to listen more intelligently to the needs of others. Role-playing, the use of video-tapes, group methods, seminars and individual help may all be usefully employed. Exercises in methods of responding to clients have been outlined by Hackney and Nye (1973) and prove useful to beginners in counselling.

For the person intending to practise as a counsellor there is as yet no consensus of opinion on what constitutes professional preparation. Basically, the counsellor needs to understand the society in which he lives and works, the clientele with whom he is working. He needs also to understand himself as fully as possible and his own interactions before he can effectively use the variety of counselling techniques now at his disposal. Furthermore, he will be most effective if he is trained not simply to counsel in a one-to-one setting but to engage in a number of active roles in a variety of settings. He will need a knowledge of normal developmental psychology and a sufficient knowledge of abnormal psychology to begin to recognize the borderlines of health and ill-health and the limits of his competency. He will need to understand the groups with whom he is working in relation to a wider society and he will need to appreciate the dynamics of learning and decision-making. He will certainly need to explore counselling theories and be well supervised in his initial practice with clients.

At present a number of training courses exist for practitioners of counselling in an educational setting which are usually of one year's duration. The Social Work Advisory Service publication on Counselling lists many of these. Similar, often part-time, courses exist for clergy and for counsellors working in therapeutic communities or other settings. There is at present no opportunity of formal training for those who train counsellors, and there is an obvious need to give urgent attention to this and to consolidate and strengthen

such training for counsellors as already exists. If the Departments
of Education and Health and Social Security could be persuaded
to contribute financially to such training they would be making a
small investment in the prevention of problems occurring which
ultimately cost a great deal to the country in the maintenance of
hospital beds and penal institutions for the treatment of more
seriously disturbed people.

The Counsellor's Own Needs

Opportunities for continuing professional training must be taken
if the counsellor is to keep up to date in his practice. In what is
presently an ill-defined profession such opportunities are not easy
to obtain and are sometimes found in the training and conferences
of other professions such as medicine, teaching, social work and
psychology. Proposals for the establishment of a British Association
of Counselling hold promise for the kind of opportunities which
are required — where those practising in a variety of settings and with
different age groups can share and learn from one another, where
they can learn to respect one another's skills and the contribution
each can make to a healthier society.

    Equally importantly, it is necessary to recognize that to operate
effectively in counselling and give the kind of intelligent educated
love to which I referred makes enormous demands on the counsellor.
It implies the investment of his own personal resources to the development and growth of his client. It is possible for the counsellor to
become so depleted by his work that he can no longer give the quality
of relationship which makes him effective as a counsellor. Counselling is by no means simply a one-way process, even though the
focus of attention is on the client. There are great satisfactions in
working as a counsellor which, as in other occupations, will vary
between counsellors. It is, however, important for counsellors to
recognize that they too are subject to the same stresses and strains
imposed by the rapid changes in society and by the life-stages
through which they are passing. If they are to love and respect
their clients they must love and respect themselves enough to recognize their own needs for refreshment and replenishment. The way
in which they seek renewal will again vary. It may be in seeking
relaxation through the enjoyment of music or art, through the

peace and beauty of the countryside or the anonymity and stimulation of a large city, through laughter and fun with partners and friends or in countless other ways which renew one's physical and emotional energy to continue to give of one's love and skills.

Summary

The accelerated speed of change of this lifetime has highlighted the need to help people to cope with some of the normal developmental tasks and crises which occur often at times of transition throughout life in an increasingly unpredictable world. Counselling in its many applications lays emphasis on assisting individuals or groups to use their energies to achieve healthy growth.

Attention to the setting in which counselling takes place helps in the establishment of a constructive climate in which counsellor and client can work together on the concerns of the client. An awareness of the differing values of client and counsellor and the ways in which these, and the sexuality of client and counsellor, affect the relationship are essential. Equally, an understanding of the developmental stages of life and of the nature of crisis and ways of intervening are necessary if the counsellor is to assist healthy growth. Adolescence deserves particular study, since it is at that stage that individuals are called on to make choices and decisions and to cope with accelerated changes in themselves which set the pattern for later development.

Since the counsellor is the instrument of whatever is achieved in the counselling relationship, he must make sure that he is as effective as possible. Professional training, ongoing support, instant re-examination of himself and his values, the sharing of insights with others, and professional and personal refreshment are all essential to the provision of responsible counselling.

References

Broverman, I. K., Broverman, D. M., Clarkson, F., Rosenkrantz, P. S. and Vogel, S. R. (1970). "Sex-role Stereotypes and clinical judgements of mental health." *Journal of Consulting Psychology*, 34, 11–17.

Caplan, G. (1961). "An Approach to Community Mental Health." Tavistock
    Publications Ltd: London.
Caplan, G. (1966). "Principles of Preventive Psychiatry." Tavistock Publications
    Ltd: London.
Erikson, E. H. (1968). "Identity: Youth and Crisis." Faber and Faber Ltd:
    London.
Hackney, H. and Nye, S. (1973). "Counseling Strategies and Objectives."
    Prentice-Hall, Inc: New Jersey, USA.
Havighurst, R. J. (1953). "Human Development and Education." Longman:
    London.
Hunt, S. M. (1974). "Sex Differences." Vernon Scott Associates Ltd.: Leamington
    Spa.
Hutt, C. (1972). "Males and Females." Penguin Books Ltd: Harmondsworth.
Jersild, A. T. (1963). "The Psychology of Adolescence," Macmillan: London.
Jones, H. E. (1949). "Motor Performance and Growth: A Developmental Study
    of Static Dynamometric Strength." University of California Press: Berkeley.
King, J. S. (1974). "Women and Work," Manpower Paper No. 10, Department
    of Employment, HMSO: London.
Miller, D. (1969). "The Age Between." Cornmarket/Hutchinson Ltd: London.
Newsome, A., Thorne, B. J. and Wyld, K. L. (1973). "Student Counselling in
    Practice." University of London Press Ltd: London.
Rogers, C. R. (1973). "Becoming Partners." Constable: London.
Super, D. E. and Overstreet, P. L. (1960). "The Vocational Maturity of Ninth
    Grade Boys." Career Pattern Study Monograph No. 2. Teachers College
    (Columbia University) Press: New York.
Super, D. E., Kowalski, R. S. and Gotkin, E. H. (1967). "Floundering and
    Trial After High School." Cooperative Research Project No. 1392. Teachers
    College (Columbia University) Press: New York.
Toffler, A. (1970). "Future Shock." Pan Books: London.
Tyler, L. E. (1953). "The Work of the Counsellor." Appleton-Century-Crofts:
    New York.
Warnath, C. F. (1971). "New Myths and Old Realities." Jossey-Bass Inc:
    San Francisco.
Warnath, C. F. and Associates, (1973). "New Directions for College Coun-
    sellors." Jossey-Bass Inc: San Francisco.
Wrenn, C. G. (1973). "The World of the Contemporary Counselor." Houghton
    Mifflin Co: Boston, Mass., USA.

4 | Modification of Sexual Behaviour

DOUGAL MACKAY

Introduction

Although there is some dispute as to who actually introduced the concept of "behaviour therapy", it first really emerged as a distinct psychotherapeutic school with the publication of books by Wolpe (1958) and Eysenck (1960, 1964). The fundamental postulate of this approach is that neurotic disorders are simply faulty behaviour patterns, which have arisen through traumatic or inappropriate learning experiences, and are therefore potentially modifiable through suitable retraining. This is in marked contrast to the view taken by psychodynamic psychotherapists, who typically view the superficial presenting problem as an indication of underlying personality disturbance. In view of these basic differences of opinion regarding the nature of the disturbance and the importance of "symptoms", it is not surprising that these two schools of thought should have proposed such radically different kinds of therapeutic intervention. While psychoanalytically-oriented psychotherapists are concerned to remove defences, facilitate insight development, and assist the "working-through" process, behaviour therapists attempt to modify the observable behavioural abnormalities by direct manipulation.

Following on from their belief in the prime importance of learning in both the genesis and treatment of neurotic disorders, the early practitioners turned to the experimental literature on those types of learning known as *conditioning*, in their endeavour to devise maxi-

mally effective retraining procedures. As a result, all of the techniques
which behaviour modifiers now apply clinically bear a close resemblance to the experimental procedures of Pavlov (1927) and Skinner
(1953). For a comprehensive review of the basic principles the reader
is referred to Rachlin (1970). However, despite the apparent scientific respectability of this approach, the commonly voiced assertion
that there is an intimate relationship between laboratory-derived
laws and the techniques used in the clinic has been seriously questioned (e.g. Breger and McGaugh, 1965). Such theoretical issues are
clearly outside the scope of this chapter and have, in any case, been
well discussed elsewhere (Bandura, 1969; Kanfer, 1970).

Despite its undoubted efficacy, behaviour therapy has never been
particularly popular in either psychiatric or lay circles. The reasons
for this are varied. Some of the blame must certainly lie with the
early spokesmen for the movement who sought to win support for
behavioural methods by attempting to discredit the more traditional
psychotherapeutic approaches. The futility and clumsiness of these
attacks won the new school few friends. Nowadays, however, far
from rejecting psychoanalysis out of hand, many behaviour therapists have felt it necessary to include psychodynamic formulations
into their treatment programmes for many of their more complex
cases (Lazarus, 1971; Meyer and Liddell, 1975).

Another reason for the tarnished image of behaviour therapy
concerns the over-use of crude aversion therapy techniques as practised in the 1960s. To many people, the name behaviour therapy is
still synonymous with the somewhat barbaric treatment of sexual
offenders who were referred by the courts during this period. Nowadays, few practitioners make use of primitive faradic aversion methods.
Instead they are more concerned to isolate and deal with the
behavioural problems underlying this behaviour, and make adaptive
responses more reinforcing. In those cases where it is necessary to
make the formerly pleasurable activity less attractive, it is customary
now, as will be shown later, to make use of cognitive techniques.

Perhaps the most important factor which has contributed to the
unpopularity of the behaviour therapy approach is the unpalatibility
of the mode of presentation of treatment reports in the psychotherapeutic literature. Whereas Rogerians and psychoanalysts tend to
describe, at great length, the feelings of the client and the subtleties
of the patient/therapist relationship, behaviour therapists tend to
write about disorders, techniques and significance levels. It is regret-
table, in my view, that in their endeavour to attain scientific

respectability, many of the foremost behaviour therapists have felt it necessary to design experiments which bear a closer resemblance to drug trials in clinical pharmacology than to investigations of subtle psychological changes. Research involving the uncritical use of nco-Kraepelinian diagnostic categories, together with various inflexible treatment "package deals", might permit the investigator to employ complex experimental designs and elegant statistical techniques, but has little relevance to the sensitive clinician who is faced with a client in distress.

There is a more complex issue involved here than just the popular appeal of behaviour therapy. The type of investigations which are carried out and the discussion points raised in the literature are a reflection of the whole underlying philosophy of the treatment approach. The fact that the relatively new journal *Behaviour Therapy* tends to publish more individual case reports and papers on "therapeutic issues" than the traditional publications in this field would suggest that many clinicians who use behavioural methods are now beginning to feel that the patient, rather than the disorder, should be the primary object of study. This is not to say that there is no place for the multi-group design. Indeed the fact that the tools of the trade have been tried and tested in this way is a source of great comfort to all modifiers of behaviour. Furthermore, no new advances would be made in treatment "hardware" should such macroscopic studies be discontinued. But behaviour therapy should not be regarded simply as a set of techniques which can be prescribed, like drugs or electro-convulsive therapy, according to a medical diagnosis. Rather it should be viewed as a complete approach to psychological problems in its own right.

The cornerstone of individual-oriented behavioural psychotherapy (as it shall be called here) is its assessment procedure known as the behavioural analysis.

Behavioural Analysis

The expression "behavioural analysis" tends to be bandied about in clinical psychology circles without there being any obvious general agreement as to its precise meaning. It is a sobering fact that, in view of the enormity of the behaviour therapy literature, so little has been written on the fundamental issues of assessment and treatment deci-

sion making. With the outstanding exceptions of Kanfer and Saslow
(1969) and Meyer (1973), most behaviour therapy authors have
persisted with the traditional "cook-book" mode of presentation,
with a token reference to the behavioural analysis in the opening
pages. Since there is no universally-accepted definitive statement
in the clinical literature as to what the behavioural analysis actually
involves, it will be necessary to give my own views (inspired by
Kanfer and Meyer) as to how a behavioural treatment programme
should be formulated. The various stages have been set out in a structured form in the interests of clarity, but these should be regarded
as guidelines rather than as rigid procedural directions.

Obtain a Precise Description of the Maladaptive Behaviour

Whereas most psychotherapists are prepared to start treatment with
only a general idea as to the presenting problems, the behavioural
approach requires a very detailed picture of the presenting difficulties prior to the commencement of treatment. In particular, behavioural psychotherapists find it necessary to determine whether
the problem manifests itself at a *cognitive* level (i.e. thinking), an
affective level (i.e. feeling), and/or a *behavioural* level (i.e. doing).
Thus, taking as an example the hypothetical case of a male patient
with homosexual paedophiliac inclinations, one would want to
know right away about his attitudes to boys, the emotions they
produce in him, and the way he behaves in their presence. Measures
for these three types of response can be obtained by self-rating
scales, psychophysiological devices, and naturalistic observations,
respectively. By carrying out such assessment procedures, one establishes not only the pertinent classes of response, but also a base-
line which can be re-examined at various stages through therapy
in order to estimate treatment efficacy.

It should be pointed out here that although the cognitive,
affective, and behavioural components generally co-vary, there
are many cases where this in fact is not so. Thus it is perfectly
possible for the paedophile in our example to be distressed because
he *thinks* he is attracted to young boys, whereas he may not in fact
respond to them psychophysiologically, or even approach them.
In such a case, the emphasis in treatment would be on cognitive
manipulations.

Define the Controlling Stimuli

According to Skinnerian principles, the organism does not learn to carry out a particular response in a psychological vacuum, but in the presence of certain determining stimuli. It is customary, in behavioural parlance, to turn this round and describe these stimuli as exerting influence over the response in question (i.e. "stimulus control"). In cases of human behavioural problems, there is a tremendous variety of stimuli which can set the occasion for a response. It may be found helpful here if a distinction is made between three main stimulus classes which can be loosely termed *object characteristics, situational cues,* and *life events.* In our paedophiliac example, the response may be determined by the age and/or physical appearance of young boys he encounters. It is such concrete superficial features of the stimulus class which constitute the "object characteristics". "Situational cues" refers to the fact that whereas he would approach a youth in a public lavatory or back street, he would be less likely to do so in a classroom or other public place. By "life events" is meant the more subtle factors which sometimes are found to be powerful response determinants (e.g. heavy work-load, arrival of mother-in-law). These three sets of stimuli may interact with each other. For instance, job stresses may make paedophiliac behaviour a highly probable event, but the patient will not actually engage in it in the absence of a suitably endowed sexual object, or if the situation is not appropriate. Similarly, the presence of an attractive youth in a private place, without the impingement of the more diffuse stimuli, would reduce the likelihood of a sexual response.

Whereas probably all behaviourists would accept that it is essential to determine the object characteristics and situational cues before commencing treatment, some might quarrel with the inclusion of life events in the behavioural analysis. Behavioural technologists, in particular, would tend to regard such data as being both unscientific and irrelevant. Certainly it must be conceded that there are many cases where background stimuli of this sort play a minimal role and can therefore be ignored where treatment plans are concerned. Nevertheless, broad-spectrum behavioural psychotherapists maintain that, in certain cases, these factors are at least as important as the more superficial stimuli, and must be incorporated into the therapeutic programme if any fundamental changes are to take place.

Determine the Reinforcers

In addition to setting the occasion for responses, stimuli also influence
the learning process by operating as consequences of responses.
Skinner distinguishes between three kinds of response outcome. A
positive reinforcer (reward) is the name given to a stimulus which
immediately follows a response and, by so doing, increases the
probability of the recurrence of that response. *Negative reinforcement,* which also leads to an increased response rate, involves the
removal of a noxious stimulus. It applies in those situations where
the individual carries out a response in order to *avoid* or to *escape*
from an unpleasant experience. Thus, for example, the ritualistic
hand-washing behaviour of some obsessive-compulsive patients can
be regarded as a series of avoidance responses which are negatively
reinforced by the reduction of anxiety concerning dirt and germs.
Finally, *a punishment* is the name given to a stimulus which leads
to a decrease in the probability of the occurrence of a particular
response.

   In the behavioural analysis, it is essential to determine the consequences which are maintaining the behaviour. The paedophile
may make sexual approaches to young boys because he, quite
simply, derives pleasure from so doing (positive reinforcement)
or, alternatively, because this particular activity serves to dissipate
tension (negative reinforcement). Clearly information regarding
the nature of the response consequence should have some considerable bearing on the type of treatment programme instigated.

Explore Other Problem Areas

Before beginning treatment, it is essential to unearth any other
behavioural abnormalities or sources of distress. Having done so,
an analysis along the lines described above should be carried out to
determine the relevant precipitating stimuli and reinforcers. Should
these be found to be similar to the ones already isolated, then it
can be hypothesized that these various areas of difficulty are closely
interrelated. In such a case, the therapist would be advised to treat
these problems simultaneously. Returning to the example of the
paedophile, it may be found that the life event of job stress, in
the absence of an appropriate sex object or situation, typically
gives rise to, say, excessive gambling. Under these circumstances,

the therapist would be advised to treat both disorders together otherwise the extinction of one maladaptive response would be likely to increase the strength of the other. In cases where the abnormal behaviours are not related in this way, it is customary to treat them sequentially.

Test Out the Hypothesis by Investigating Past Behaviour

Having completed the various analyses, it is advisable to test out the preliminary hypothesis by obtaining reports of the patient's past behaviour from the patient himself and/or from an informant. In particular, the behavioural psychotherapist is interested in finding out how the patient responded formerly in the presence of the isolated controlling stimuli, and how he used to behave in order to obtain the relevant reinforcers. A history of maladaptive behaviour in relation to these events would certainly be consistent with (but not necessarily confirm) the hypothesis.

Test Out the Hypothesis by Administering Techniques

Support for the hypothesis from the above sources would encourage the behavioural psychotherapist to employ one of the tools of his trade in an endeavour to put his ideas to the test. In view of his "penchant" for objective measuring devices (see first sub-heading above) he will then soon become aware as to the validity or otherwise of his hypothesis. Unlike those psychotherapists who do not clearly define their goals or obtain pre-treatment base-lines, the behavioural psychotherapist may find, after a few sessions, that his model of the patient has been quite unambiguously disconfirmed through non-response to the techniques. However, at least an erroneous analysis of the problem becomes apparent very quickly with this approach.

The proven inefficacy of various techniques with a particular patient does not of course mean that the treatment is to be terminated. On the contrary, this new experimentally-acquired data is used to help the clinician re-analyse the problem and devise a different treatment programme. The important thing to note here is that the behavioural psychotherapist always has a rationale (albeit a wrong one!) for using a particular set of techniques. This is in con-

trast to the trial-and-error mechanistic approach favoured by tech-
nique-oriented modifiers of behaviour.

Re-evaluate the Hypothesis at Intervals

The fact that the patient may respond to the adopted techniques in
the early stages of treatment does not mean that the behavioural
analysis has been completed. At any point in time, a plateau might
be reached, a new maladaptive response might appear, or the old
response might re-establish itself. The therapist has to make use of
this information by incorporating it into his ever-changing model of
the patient, and modify the programme accordingly. Thus, the
behavioural analysis is very much an on-going process rather than
just a preliminary diagnostic step.

An account of the various stages involved in the behavioural
analysis is usually followed by two questions: (a) is it really necessary
to go through such a laborious procedure before applying techniques?
and (b) is this not psychotherapy rather than behaviour therapy?
It is important to consider these two issues before examining
behavioural techniques associated with sexual problems.

So far as the first question is concerned, it must be conceded that
there is no actual evidence that behavioural psychotherapy produces
greater success rates than the "blind" application of techniques. The
main reason for this apparent gap in the experimental literature is
that individual-oriented psychotherapy cannot easily be fitted into
the multi-group factorial design so favoured by technologists. Nevertheless, many experienced practitioners of behavioural methods
have come to the conclusion that the simple application of techniques
is insufficient. Meyer and Liddell (1975), for example, state that:

> "in our experience, it (i.e. the behavioural analysis) has proved to be
> extremely useful because behaviour is complex and a complaint seldom
> appears in isolation" (p. 225).

True, in many cases the treatment programme which emerges after
several hours of analysis may turn out to be identical to the one
suggested by the elementary "cook-book" based on diagnostic
categories. In other cases, however, a rigid adherence to a symptom-
based classificatory system could lead to the utilization of a totally
inappropriate set of techniques. In such a case, the behavioural psychotherapist might be prepared to join forces with his psychoanalytic

colleagues and predict that "symptom substitution", or at least some non-fundamental change, is likely to take place. Technologists, on the other hand, would point out that if one procedure fails it can always be replaced with another one, and so on until the patient finally responds. That an appropriate treatment programme will be devised eventually is considered to be sufficient grounds for rejecting time-consuming and potentially redundant preliminaries. However, patients who have undergone an ineffective brand of therapy, are likely to reject another offer of help from the same clinician. As mentioned above, the behavioural analysis does not guarantee immediate success for the initially employed techniques, but it would seem to follow that a hypothetico-deductive approach should lead to less radical chopping and changing of methods than a purely empirical approach.

The assertion that the behavioural analysis (and therefore behavioural psychotherapy) has little resemblance to the behaviourist position can be more easily dealt with. Behavioural psychotherapists maintain that change is brought about by action rather than discussion, that the patient's current situation should be the focal point of therapy, that the patient should take responsibility for his treatment, and that insight is not essential for change (although awareness of stimulus-response connections can facilitate the learning process). Not even the most directive, pragmatic and non-interpretive psychotherapist would go along with all of these points. Thus, despite the flexible, individualistic flavour of behavioural psychotherapy, it differs from other types of psychological treatment in that its methods are deeply rooted in learning theory traditions.

Behavioural Treatments of Sexual Disorders

In this chapter, the customary distinction is made between *sexual dysfunctions,* where there is some impairment of performance, and *sexual deviations,* where the type of sexual activity the individual typically engages in is unusual and subject to censure, from others or even himself. The presentation format adopted here, for each of the two types of disorder is as follows: After a brief account of learning theory formulations of the particular disorder type, the basic techniques are described, together with all relevant research findings. Finally a case report is provided to illustrate how these and other non-sexual techniques are incorporated into the behavioural psychotherapy approach. It is hoped that this will bring about a clear understanding of what behaviour therapy actually involves, while at the same time guard against fostering the erroneous belief that all one has to do with sexual problems is to match the technique to the type of disorder.

Regrettably, some of the most naïve and mechanistic work carried out in behaviour therapy has been that concerned with sexual problems. The fact that sexual behaviour, as such, is composed of fairly discrete units which are amenable to measurement has meant that many quasi-clinical researchers have been attracted to the field. In their predictable fashion, they have produced the usual sort of findings that people with disorder X will be more likely to respond to Treatment A than to Treatment B. However the whole area of sex, as will be shown, is an exceedingly complex one. It involves a whole range of emotions and attitudes which are generally closely linked to many other areas of the individual's life. To ignore these more covert matters is to miss the whole point in many cases.

Sexual Dysfunction

Sexual dysfunction is the term used in those cases where the sexual performance of a couple is impaired in such a way as to cause distress to either one or both parties. It is certainly not uncommon. In fact Masters and Johnson, the leading authorities in this field, claim that at least 50% of all marriages in the United States are characterized by some form of sexual inadequacy (Masters and Johnson, 1970). Whether this statistic refers to the proportion of people who are *actually* distressed, or to the proportion of people Masters and Johnson feel *should* be distressed (because they do not reach the somewhat arbitrary criteria proposed by Masters and Johnson) is however not so clear. Nevertheless few would dispute that there are a great many couples whose whole relationship is adversely affected by their inability to overcome a sexual difficulty of one sort or another.

It should be noted here that it is now customary to talk about sexual dysfunction in relation to the couple as opposed to the individual. Undoubtedly one of the major contributions made by Masters and Johnson in this area was to switch the emphasis from the impotent male or "frigid" female to the disordered couple. Following on from their argument that distress experienced by one partner must inevitably affect the other partner (and even the whole family), these authorities have come to the conclusion that there is

"no such entity as an uninvolved partner contending with any form of sexual inadequacy" (Masters and Johnson, 1970).

Although taking such a position effectively eliminates the "it's all her fault, doctor" attitude, there are potential dangers here in that the relatively disorder-free partner may start to become over-anxious about his involvement in the problem, which could ultimately prove counter-productive. However, despite this very real risk, most sex therapists would now agree that it is essential to work with the problem in the context of the relationship. Certainly the bulk of the early behaviour therapy research in this area, with its emphasis on the individual who has (or at least appears to have) *the* problem, seems remarkably naive in this post-Masters and Johnson era.

Before going on to discuss learning theory models and techniques, it is important to clarify the terminology which will be used. *Impotence* can be defined as

"a man's inability to attain or maintain an erection of sufficient strength to enable him to perform the act of intercourse" (McCary, 1973).

According to Kelly (1961), three types of impotence can be distinguished. *Organic impotence* is caused by some anatomical defect, such as a lesion of the central nervous system or perhaps the posterior urethra. *Functional impotence* has, as its basis, a general disruption of bodily functioning caused by such diverse factors as spinal cord disease, drug over-use, certain endocrinopathies, ageing, excessive fatigue, and so on. *Psychogenic impotence* is the term used in those cases where the male's inability to perform is due to, what can loosely be called, psychological factors (e.g. anxiety, negative attitudes to the opposite sex, maladaptive habit patterns, etc.). It is only this latter type of impotence which concerns us here. Masters and Johnson (1970) have further sub-divided this category into *primary impotence* (where the male has never achieved coitus) and *secondary* impotence (where he has been successful on at least one occasion). Although some clinicians feel that this distinction is of value at a descriptive level only, Masters and Johnson themselves maintain that these sub-diagnoses have important implications for both treatment and prognosis.

Whereas there is general agreement as to the nature of impotence, a precise clinical definition of *premature ejaculation* has proved rather more elusive. To some sex therapists, an ejaculation is only regarded as premature if it precedes intromission. Others maintain that if emission takes place within ten seconds of penetration, then the male should be regarded as having a sexual inadequacy of this sort. Still others state that the man who cannot delay orgasm until at least one minute after entry should be referred to as a premature ejaculator. Masters and Johnson (1970) have suggested that such arbitrary time figures should be replaced by their own (equally arbitrary) percentage figures. Thus they maintain that if the female does not reach orgasm on 50% of occasions, then the male can be seen to be ejaculating prematurely. However, since it has been estimated that 75% of American males reach orgasm within two minutes (Kinsey *et al.*, 1948), and that most women require a rather longer period in order to climax (Gebhard, 1966), it would appear that, as indicated above, the majority of couples emerge as having a sexual dysfunction when the Masters and Johnson criteria are applied. Regrettably such pronouncements from the world-acknowledged experts, have not only had the effect of encouraging complacent couples to improve the quality of their sexual relationship, but have also given rise to a sort of "Masters and Johnson neurosis", whereby previously contented partners have become anxious and over-aware of the mechanics involved when having intercourse. Finally, although premature ejaculation can have a physical basis, such as an irritation affecting the glans or an infection of the prostate or urethra, it is usually caused by psychological factors.

A less common male dysfunction is *ejaculatory incompetence,* which can be defined as the inability to emit semen intra-vaginally. In most cases the man is able to ejaculate through masturbation, but in a minority only nocturnal ejaculation is possible.

With regard to female sexual inadequacies, it must be pointed out straight away that the term "frigidity" is now very much out of vogue in view of its non-specificity, its connotations of irreversibility, and the stigma associated with it. Instead, Masters and Johnson have suggested the phrase, *female orgasmic dysfunction.* This term is used in those cases where the female repeatedly fails to proceed beyond the "plateau phase" of the sexual response cycle (Masters and Johnson, 1966). Once again these authorities make a distinction between *primary orgasmic dysfunction,* where the female has never achieved orgasm, and *situational orgasmic dys-*

function where she has succeeded on at least one occasion by some
means or other. Organic impairments (e.g. central nervous system
lesions; pelvic abnormalities) or functional disorders (e.g. hormonal
imbalance; drug over-use) may be implicated. Otherwise the cause
is likely to be psychological with emotions (e.g. fear; hostility) and/or
negative attitudes towards sex or her partner, at the basis. The criteria
and incidence figures are clearly inextricably bound up with the impotence statistics cited above.

Two more specific types of female sexual inadequacy are *dyspareunia* (painful coitus) and *vaginismus* (severe contraction of vaginal
muscles prior to penetration). Although there is quite a high probability of physical abnormalities in the case of the former, vaginismus
is considered by Masters and Johnson to be predominantly a psychogenic disorder.

In the remainder of this section, the behaviourist views of human
sexual dysfunction are presented.

Learning Theory Formulations of Sexual Disorders

Behaviourally oriented clinicians regard sexual dysfunction of a
psychogenic nature as having arisen through the process of classical
conditioning. An experience of guilt, pain, or humiliation, which
accompanies sexual behaviour, is likely to lead to the building up
of a lasting, but potentially reversible, association between sexual
cues and anxiety. It is well known (e.g. Masters and Johnson, 1966)
that anxiety directly inhibits sexual performance because it has
a direct effect on some of the autonomic functions involved in the
sexual response. Since penile erection is a para-sympathetic function
and ejaculation is a sympathetic one, the presence of anxiety (which
acts sympathetically) will both inhibit erection (as in impotence)
and facilitate ejaculation (as in premature ejaculation). Anxiety
has a similar depressing effect on the responsivity of the female.
With repeated failures, the connection between sexual stimuli and
anxiety continues to strengthen until the individual feels obliged
to engage in avoidance behaviours of various sorts (e.g. going to bed
late; getting drunk; wearing hair curlers when retiring) in order to
reduce the anxiety. The assertion that classical conditioning can
account for the genesis of sexual problems whereas the operant
paradigm is required to explain its persistence is known as the two-
factor theory of learning (Mowrer, 1947).

Many contemporary behaviourists (e.g. Bandura, 1969), unlike the hard-line pioneers of this treatment approach, maintain that the individual can acquire an aversion for a particular set of stimuli without ever having suffered an unpleasant experience in their presence. It has, in fact, been experimentally demonstrated (Barber and Hahn, 1964) that imaginal aversive occurrences can bring about emotional responses in a similar manner to real-life noxious stimuli. The cognitive aversion therapy known as "covert sensitization", (Cautela, 1967), which is discussed below, is also of relevance here. Thus it is quite in keeping with a broad-spectrum behavioural position to view many of the conditioned anxiety responses to sexual cues as having arisen through listening to lurid accounts of other people's unfortunate exploits, for instance, rather than through an actual unpleasant experience at an overt behavioural level.

Masters and Johnson (1970) speculate, along quasi-behavioural lines, that engagement in various types of semi-satisfactory sexual activities can lead to the male acquiring the specific disorder of premature ejaculation. Apparently middle-aged men, who make use of the services of prostitutes, are generally pressurized by them to achieve orgasm as quickly as possible, for obvious reasons. This learned habit of rapid sexual responding is then likely to transfer to other situations involving intercourse. Similarly, many young people, due to lack of privacy in more orthodox surrounds, are obliged to copulate, cramped in the back seats of cars. The increased muscle tonus, which inevitably accompanies the acrobatics required to accomplish such a feat, leads to early ejaculation. Once again, this pattern of responding tends to generalize to all sexual situations. Finally, the constant practice of "coitus interruptus", as a method of contraception, can lead to anxiety about semen emission and the development of either premature ejaculation or ejaculatory incompetence.

Behavioural Techniques

Systematic desensitization

Long before behaviour therapy had been established as a treatment school, it was well known that one way of overcoming a specific fear was to gradually approach the object under anxiety-free conditions. In the celebrated case of "Little Albert", Watson and Rayner (1920) recommended this method as the best way of eliminating the furry animal phobia they had created in a small boy. An actual demonstration of this procedure was carried out a few years later by Jones (1924) with "Little Peter", who had also acquired a furry animal phobia through laboratory procedures of dubious ethics. Peter's fear was extinguished through a deconditioning process in which a rabbit was brought gradually closer to him while he was engaged in eating his favourite food. Eventually he developed a more positive response towards the animal, and this generalized to other previously feared creatures, without further training being required.

In his pioneering book on behaviour therapy, Wolpe (1958) developed this procedure and gave it the name "systematic desensitization". According to him, the effectiveness of this treatment method is due to the process of "reciprocal inhibition":

> "If a response antagonistic to anxiety can be made to occur in the presence of anxiety-evoking stimuli, so that is is accompanied by a complete or partial suppression of the anxiety responses, the bond between those stimuli and the anxiety responses will be weakened" (p. 71).

The first step in a systematic desensitisation programme is to obtain from the client some detailed information about the various features of the phobic stimulus which influence the anxiety response (cf. "object characteristics" above). Thus in the case of a so-called "agoraphobic", it would be important to determine the significance of such stimuli as traffic volume, street width, time of day, distance home, and so on, in relation to the patient's avoidance behaviour. When this data has been collected, a hierarchy of phobic situations can be created ranging from the least anxiety-provoking (e.g. looking out of the window at night), to the most feared (e.g. travelling in a crowded train in the rush hour). For a detailed account of the process of hierarchy building see Wolpe and Lazarus (1966).

The second step in the programme is to decide on the anti-anxiety response to be used. If necessary, the patient has to be coached in this skill until his performance has reached the required criterion. Although such potential anxiety-inhibitors as assertion and sexual arousal have been suggested by Wolpe (1958) for this purpose the majority of desensitization programmes have involved relaxation induction of one form or another. Until recently, Jacobson's somewhat long and tedious progressive muscular relaxation programme was the method of choice. Here the patient is asked to contract and then relax specific groups of muscles in order that he might learn to distinguish between the sensations of relaxation and tension.

However the degree of success obtained in studies by Lang (1968, 1969) and Migler and Wolpe (1967), which have utilized relatively brief tape-recorded relaxation instructions, would seem to indicate that complex muscular relaxation is not a *sine qua non* for desensitization. Another quick way of relaxing a patient is by means of various pharmacological agents. Friedman (1966) recommends intravenous administration of the barbiturate, methohexitone sodium (Brevital), for this purpose, because of its rapidity of action, controllability, and freedom from unwanted after-effects. Hypnotic suggestion can also be used to induce relaxation (Wolpe, 1958).

Once a hierarchy has been established, and relaxation training completed, the desensitization programme can be got under way. The patient is first of all asked to imagine a neutral scene, and then the least arousing situation at the bottom of the hierarchy. If he is able to carry this out without experiencing anxiety, the next item is presented, and so on. Should he feel distressed at any stage, he is told to raise his finger and an item lower down the scale will be presented. On no account should a session be terminated while the patient is experiencing anxiety, because the last stimulus-response connection tends to be better-learned than its predecessors. In many cases *in vivo* desensitization is conducted as well as (or instead of) imaginal desensitization. In fact Lazarus (1971) reports that, in general:

> "graded real-life exposure and modeling procedures seem to achieve better results than mere imagined exposures to hierarchy items" (p. 106).

Turning to sexual disorders, Wolpe (1958) was one of the first to demonstrate that systematic desensitization is an effective procedure in those cases where anxiety inhibits sexual performance. In this early study, males with impotence or premature ejaculation were treated with self-conducted *in vivo* programmes, based on the principles described above. They were first of all trained in progressive relaxation to enable them to overcome any anxiety they might experience during treatment sessions. They were then given instructions that, on those occasions when they felt a strong desire to do so, they should lie beside their partners in a relaxed way and to carry out preliminary foreplay exercises. If this was successful on a few occasions, they were told to engage in gradually more and more advanced sexual behaviour, but on no account to attempt intercourse until all the anxiety had been eliminated. This simple procedure has provided the basis for most currently employed behavioural treatments for sexual disorders.

Lazarus (1963) carried out a standard systematic desensitization programme with 16 women who presented with, what he termed, "chronic frigidity". The hierarchies, which were carefully tailored to suit the requirements of each patient, included a mixture of pre-coital scenes and inhibitory stimuli (e.g. sight of male genitals). Significant improvements were obtained with 9 of the 16 patients after a mean of 27.8 sessions. Of those who terminated prematurely, it was noted that most of them expressed considerable hostility to men in general or their partners in particular. This is mentioned here because of its relevance to the technology/psychotherapy issue which is so central to the theme of this chapter. A behavioural analysis of these failed cases might have revealed that assertion training or marital contract therapy (see below) would have been more appropriate than a direct attack on the presenting symptom.

One or two procedures which have departed a little from the traditional approach have proved particularly successful. Brady (1966) achieved marked improvements with four out of five "frigid" women who avoided coitus because of revulsion and/or various anxieties. He administered the drug Brevital in conjunction with relaxation instructions, and then desensitized them using their own individual sex hierarchies. After an average of only eleven sessions, the four who responded reported finding intercourse much more pleasurable and were able to become aroused sexually to a far greater degree than before. Similarly, Lazarus (1961, 1968, 1969) departed from the usual format by carrying out desensitization in a group setting with impotent men and frigid women. Judging from his results, it would appear that group methods can be at least as effective, and far more economic, than the classical Wolpeian approach.

Although by no means all workers in the sexual field have found systematic desensitization to be outstandingly successful (e.g. Cooper, 1969), recent evidence would seem to suggest that it is more effective in overcoming sexual anxieties than more traditional psychotherapeutic approaches (Obler, 1973). Its particularly significant contribution has been to concentrate on the specific sources of anxiety for each individual. Regrettably some of the much-publicized approaches which have been derived from it have tended to neglect this individualistic aspect. On the negative side, the work on desensitization can be criticized on account of the emphasis given to the dysfunctioning individual as opposed to the couple. It would seem to

most contemporary clinicians to be almost futile to attempt to
modify the behaviour of one member of a partnership in this particularly sensitive area, without involving the other. Furthermore,
by agreeing to treat just one person, the therapist is virtually collud-
ing with the spouse in labelling the person who has sought assistance
as *the* one with the problem. In conclusion, therefore, if it is used in
the context of the marital relationship, there is still a place for
systematic desensitization, particularly where the anxiety concerns
a specific aspect of the sexual situation.

Aversion relief

Aversion relief is the name given to a training procedure which involves
the presentation of a stimulus the subject has previously avoided,
immediately following the termination of a noxious event. As a result
of this, he learns to approach the previously shunned object.

Lazarus (1971) reports the successful treatment of an unmarried
female, with a strong revulsion for male genitals, who did not respond
to desensitization because of the difficulty she experienced in fan-
tasizing sexual scenes. It was decided therefore to overcome this very
specific problem by using this aversion relief procedure. As the therapist announced "shock", a current was passed to electrodes which
had been placed on her hand. She was instructed to tolerate the
pain for as long as possible. When she felt it was becoming really
unbearable, she was instructed to turn her attention to a set of
photographs of male nudes which had been placed in front of her.
As soon as she started to examine them, the shock was automatically
terminated. An additional component of the treatment programme
was the intermittent administration of shocks, contingent upon gaze
avoidance of these pictorial stimuli. After several months of therapy,
she reported that she enjoyed most aspects of sexual foreplay and
intercourse, with the particular exception of oral-genital contact.

Although it might appear from this report that the success was
primarily due to the sophisticated conditioning procedures employed,
Lazarus is less convinced:

> "It should be noted that only the very naive clinician would attribute change
> in the preceding instance to conditioning. The active variables at the very
> least involved a therapeutic relationship and an abundance of persuasion
> and suggestion. None of the foregoing may have sufficed, however, if not
> for the primary incentive derived from the patient's love for her boyfriend"
> (Lazarus, 1971, p. 158–9).

Thus aversion relief could perhaps have a role to play as just one component of a programme designed to overcome a specific repulsion of anxiety in place of systematic desensitization.

The Techniques of Masters and Johnson

Although most behaviour therapists make use of the techniques of Masters and Johnson (1970), it should be emphasized that these two celebrated workers do not regard themselves as working within a behavioural framework. While recognizing that many of their techniques are similar to those devised by early behaviourally oriented clinicians, they take pains to emphasize that the focal point of their programme is insight-development (pp. 26–7). Commentators on their work are, however, by no means so convinced that this is the case. Marmor (1971) maintains that their approach stands mid-way between psychodynamic and behavioural therapies. Murphy and Mikulas (1974) go further and claim that much of the programme consists of inefficient forms of counter-conditioning. They are also of the opinion that if the insight-development aspects were to be cut down, and more powerful behavioural methods introduced, the approach would be even more effective.

It is not the purpose of this section to attempt to summarize the whole Masters and Johnson programme for overcoming sexual inadequacy. There are many outstanding reviews of their work already available (e.g. Belliveau and Richter, 1970). Instead, those of their various patient-participative methods which can be easily construed in learning theory terminology are described and then examined from a behaviourist viewpoint.

The *sensate focus* is probably the best known of the various sexual retraining techniques introduced by Masters and Johnson. The rationale behind it is that the sexually dysfunctioning couple have lost the ability to think and feel in a fully sensual manner, due to the various stresses and pressures which they associate with intercourse. They therefore have to be taught how to engage in tactile contact, in the uninhibited way of childhood. Each partner learns not only that being touched is pleasurable, but that exploring and caressing the body of a member of the opposite sex can be exciting and stimulating in itself (i.e. "give to get"). They are encouraged to engage in the sensate focus under conditions which are dissimilar to those associated with the anxieties, frustrations, and resentments of their former love-making days. Although this is easily achieved with couples who go to St Louis, Missouri for the actual Masters and Johnson programme, those who are living at home while undergoing therapy can also modify the controlling stimuli by practising in the morning instead of the evening, or in the lounge instead of the bedroom.

Intercourse is banned throughout the early stages of treatment so that sexual communication of this sort will come to be regarded as an end in itself rather than just a means to an end. The ban itself generally has the effect of reducing tension in the relationship in both sexual and non-sexual areas. Furthermore, many couples report a dramatic increase in desire for intercourse when it has been expressly forbidden in this way. This is similar to the "paradoxical intention" method of treatment (Frankl, 1960). The lifting of the ban takes place when the couple have been able to achieve a pre-intercourse position without experiencing anxiety. Some clinicians never explicitly raise the ban on the grounds that, by so doing, the anxiety level is automatically raised at this penultimate stage of therapy. Instead they prefer to wait until the couple "break the rules" so to speak. There is no general agreement on policy here.

Looked at from the behaviourist viewpoint, the sensate focus is highly reminiscent of systematic desensitization in that it is assumed that a pleasurable response will become associated with sexual cues, in place of the formerly occurring anxiety, through a process believed to be similar to the Wolpeian notion of reciprocal inhibition. Furthermore, it is customary to create a sort of hierarchy, in that certain parts of the body are designated "out of bounds" initially, and are then gradually included as progress is made. In addition, Masters and Johnson have produced a special lotion, with a texture similar to seminal fluid and vaginal secretions, which can be applied during the sensate focus. In this way, both parties can be trained to gradually overcome any aversions they may have to bodily secretions. Thus from a strictly behaviourist position, sensate focus can be regarded as a sort of multi-purpose but unsystematic type of desensitization.

It is impossible to quote efficacy rates of the sensate focus *per se,* because there are no reports of it having been prescribed in isolation. However, Masters and Johnson (1970) claim to have treated successfully 73.8% of secondary impotence cases, and 80.7% of both types of orgasmic dysfunctionals, after five years follow-up. Since the sensate focus plays a major part in these treatment programmes, the evidence would suggest that it is an extremely effective form of treatment.

Thus while orthodox systematic desensitization would seem to be the treatment of choice for the elimination of specific anxieties (e.g. semen; sight of genitals), the more global sensate focus would appear to be best-suited for dealing with the various diffuse anxieties concerning coitus.

The Masters and Johnson *squeeze technique* for premature ejaculation is very similar to the orgasm-delaying method previously described by Semans (1956). Here the female manually stimulates the penis until the male experiences the sensations just prior to the point of "ejaculatory inevitability". When he indicates to her that this stage has in fact been reached, she immediately ceases to massage him and squeezes quite strongly the glans of the penis, by placing her thumb on the frenulum (lower surface) and second and third fingers on top of the glans. This should last for three to four seconds. As a result of this sudden pressure, the male loses his seemingly insurmountable desire to ejaculate. The whole procedure is repeated a few times for a total duration of about twenty minutes. It should be mentioned here that since the male is apparently unable to apply the technique to himself, it is probably the psychological, as opposed to the physiological, aspect of the squeeze which is effective here.

As the male becomes more adept at delaying orgasm, the couple are advised to make use of this method in the context of full sexual intercourse. Incidentally it is recommended, in cases of premature ejaculation, for the female to sit astride the male. He inserts his penis and waits until he reaches the point just prior to the loss of ejaculatory control. At this stage he withdraws rapidly, and the squeeze is applied. Through this somewhat arduous training procedure, the male eventually becomes more skilled at delaying orgasm. Masters and Johnson (1970) report a 97.8% success rate in the treatment of premature ejaculation.

From a learning theory viewpoint, it is conjectured that the effectiveness of this approach is due to the fact that conditioned anxiety to sexual cues gradually extinguishes after this series of non-reinforced trials. This reduction in anxiety in turn leads to a lessening of sympathetic discharge, and orgasm is thus delayed.

Masters and Johnson, following Shaw (1954) recommend the use of graded *vaginal dilators* in the treatment of vaginismus. The female is initially encouraged to stroke herself with the smallest of these conically shaped instruments, which has been lubricated with jelly, and then to attempt to insert it into the vagina while relaxing the various surrounding muscles. On no account must she attempt to force in the object. When she has learnt to introduce this one successfully, and keep it in for several hours, the whole procedure is repeated with the next largest, and so on. Although the male may have little to contribute directly during the early stages of this treatment, Masters and Johnson consider it necessary for him to be present throughout. Not only will this help to overcome the female's inhibitions about being aroused publicly, but it can prove a valuable learning experience for the male himself. As the female progresses, he begins to play a more active role (e.g. introducing the dilators; finger-insertion). Of the 29 cases of vaginismus treated in this manner, 20 achieved orgasm for the first time, 6 recovered the ability to do so, and the 3 who did not reach this stage at least obtained considerable relief from the symptoms.

From a behaviourist viewpoint, it would appear that the technique is basically a straightforward example of Wolpeian *in vivo* desensitization (Dengrove, 1971). Murphy and Mikulas (1974), however, point out that:

> "relatively standard hierarchies as implicitly used by Masters and Johnson may not be ideal for all clients" (pp. 225).

Thus in many cases, self-stimulation with a dilator may be found to be too difficult a starting place. Similarly the transition from dilators to finger-insertion can cause problems with some patients. Clearly, on such occasions, the more sophisticated methods for obtaining hierarchies as developed by behaviour therapists (e.g. Wolpe and Lazarus, 1966) would seem to be indicated.

To conclude, the Masters and Johnson programme has contributed considerably to the treatment of sexual inadequacies. Although these authors claim to be working from a quasi-psychodynamic basis, it would appear that most of the active ingredients are either straightforward examples of behaviour therapy, or at least are amenable to a learning theory analysis. Behavioural technologists would argue that a closer allegiance to behavioural principles would have led to the development of more effective techniques. Behavioural psychotherapists (see below) have tended to be critical of blind acceptance of this and other "package deals". Nevertheless, few would deny that the actual success rates Masters and Johnson report (*report* rather than *demonstrate*) are extremely impressive. Whether this is due to their approach *per se*, to the non-random nature of their clientele,

or to the holiday atmosphere they provide for their clients, is as yet
undetermined.

The Techniques of Lobitz and LoPiccolo

Although the Masters and Johnson approach has received the bulk
of the publicity in this area of therapy, the more recent work of
Lobitz and LoPiccolo (1972), based more closely on behaviourist
principles, would seem to have at least as much to offer. Their
various techniques are particularly well-suited to those who have
to carry out sex therapy on a once-a-week out-patient basis. Some
of the more important innovations they suggest are as follows:

In the first place, they advocate the need for systematic *data
collection.* For each type of sexual behaviour, the client is asked to
keep a record of its duration, degree of pleasure it gave to self and
partner, and any other relevant information. They reason that in
view of the impracticalities of observing the actual behaviour, detailed
behavioural reports are essential when succeeding steps in treatment
are being planned.

The perennial problem of *client motivation* is dealt with by demanding a refundable penalty at the outset of treatment. The couple get a
portion of this money back each session unless an appointment is
failed, data sheets are not completed in time, non-specified sexual
behaviour is carried out, and so on. When such a violation occurs,
the deposit for that week is not returned. Despite the authoritarian
ring to it, this strategy would seem to be a useful one to adopt in
helping clients to help themselves.

The focal point of the Lobitz and LoPiccolo approach is the *nine
point masturbatory programme.* In view of the findings of Kinsey
(1953), that more women reach orgasm through masturbation than
any other outlet, and of Masters and Johnson (1966), that female
masturbation produces a more intense orgasm than coitus, these
workers have reasoned that the most effective way of treating
orgasmic dysfunction is through self-stimulation. The various
stages involved in their highly structured masturbatory programme
for females are briefly summarized:

1. learn to appreciate own nude body; identify various parts
of the vaginal region using hand-mirror and diagrams; practice
exercises for improving pelvic musculature control;

2. touch (as well as look at) genitals, without any particular attempt at self-arousal;
3. isolate the areas which give pleasure when touched;
4. manually stimulate these areas using lubricant;
5. increase intensity and duration of stimulation;
6. if orgasm is not attained, use a vibrator;
7. male to watch female masturbating;
8. male to induce orgasm in female either manually or with vibrator;
9. engage in coitus with the male stimulating the female genitals as in step 8.

The final ingredient of this sophisticated approach involves the teaching of *interpersonal sexual skills.* While it is assumed in the Masters and Johnson programme that frequent open discussions about sexual responsivity will reduce inhibitions, the more structured methods of modelling and role playing, not only to overcome anxiety but also to improve skills in this difficult area of communication, are preferred by Lobitz and LoPiccolo. In the safety of the therapeutic situation, the couple practice how to initiate sexual activities and also how to reject such overtures without antagonizing the partner. This would seem to be an important and much-neglected aspect of sexually-related behaviour.

The success rates they achieved with this ingenious programme put them at least on a par with Masters and Johnson. Of 13 cases of primary orgasmic dysfunction, all 13 reached the 50% criterion proposed by these authorities. With male disorders, they successfully treated 6 out of 6 premature ejaculators and 4 out of 6 cases of erectile failure. Their only disappointing results were obtained with 9 cases of secondary orgasmic dysfunction, of whom only 3 improved significantly. However these authors point out that it was the last 3 treated who made progress after some changes had been made in the treatment programme.

To conclude, Lobitz and LoPiccolo have not only suggested some welcome refinements to the Masters and Johnson approach, but have also introduced some radical methods of their own for increasing heterosexual arousal. The greater degree of structure in their approach makes it particularly suitable for out-patient clinical work, where there is a high probability that less than precise instructions will be distorted and wrongly carried out.

Behavioural Psychotherapy Approach

As mentioned earlier in this chapter, behavioural psychotherapists
are more interested in tailor-making programmes to suit the requirements of the individual than in simply applying techniques. Although at least some of the above-mentioned authors might not
have intended it, their techniques have been taken out of context
and presented in introductory text books in almost statute-like
form. As a result, the premature ejaculator who consults his
well-read family doctor these days is quite likely to have "the
squeeze" prescribed during his first session. It is the purpose of this
section to caution against such practices and to demonstrate that
the powerful retraining methods outlined above are only effective
in certain cases. A fuller behavioural examination might indicate
that a non-sexually based technique would be far more appropriate.
This point is illustrated by the following brief case report.

The Case of the "Emotionally Constipated" Housewife

Mrs M presented with symptoms of chronic vaginismus. She had
been married twice and, apart from a semi-successful "rape"
carried out by her first husband, had never experienced sexual
intercourse. She would not allow herself to be touched anywhere
near the genital area, and, in fact, found it difficult to touch herself
there. A programme of desensitization, involving vaginal dilators,
was attempted initially with only limited success. After a year's
treatment by this method, she was able to introduce the largest
dilator in the presence of her husband and, in fact, managed to permit
penetration on two occasions. However, at no stage did she derive
any sensual pleasure from these activities. Thus despite the fact that
she had made some obvious progress in certain directions, her
sexual responsivity had not in any way improved as a result of
this prolonged cook-book type of treatment.

At this stage a full behavioural analysis was conducted, along the
lines suggested on p. 87, with the following results:

Step one. The problem appeared to be cognitive, affective, and
behavioural in that she did not want to have sexual intercourse, she
"froze" when it was suggested, and avoided it by consistently
delaying time of going to bed. Self-reports and behaviour ratings
were carried out.

Step two. The precipitating stimuli were purely stiuational, in
that she did not generally avoid her husband (object characteristics),
nor did the problem fluctuate from day to day (life events).

Step three. The reinforcer for avoidance behaviour was anxiety
reduction.

Step four. She also avoided situations where she was expected
to demonstrate emotions (e.g. visiting in-laws). This anxiety was
not affected by the nature of the emotion or the sex of her companion. Again negative reinforcement appeared to be maintaining
the behaviour. It was therefore suspected that the sexual anxiety
was just one aspect of a more general anxiety about demonstrating
feelings (cf. "constipation of the emotions", Salter (1949)).

Step five. Her parents had argued incessantly when she was a
child, and eventually they split up leaving her to be passed from
relative to relative. She can recall her early attempts at craving
affection from her parents had been rejected (i.e. punished). This
aspect of her conditioning history was consistent with the hypothesis
formulated in step four.

Step six. A programme designed to desensitize her to her anxiety
about showing emotions was introduced (cf. Palmer, 1973) involving
hand-holding, initiating kissing sessions, cuddling in public, etc.

Step seven. After three weeks, her husband reported that she was
more demonstrative and spontaneous than she had ever been. After
6 weeks, she began to make sexual advances. Intercourse was achieved
two weeks later during which she reached her first orgasm. The
dramatic improvements which followed this were picked up by both
the self-report inventories and behavioural ratings. She is now a
mother and is able to demonstrate affection to her baby without
difficulty. The hypothesis, that the basic anxiety concerned emotional demonstration, would thus appear to have been confirmed.

Although it is clearly not possible to mention here all the non-
sexual techniques which have been found to be relevant to these
problems, both *assertion training* and *marital contract therapy*
are of particular importance here.

In many cases the poor sexual performance of one partner is
just a reflection of the more general difficulties he is experiencing
in this interpersonal relationship. For instance the "hen-pecked"
husband, who is constantly being manipulated, is unlikely to be
confident and capable of dominance on entering the bedroom. In
such a case, an attempt to treat directly the sexual problem of
impotence or premature ejaculation would be unlikely to succeed.

One possible remedy here is to train the husband to *assert* himself
by means of Lazarus' (1966) "behavioural rehearsal" procedure. This
simply involves role playing, with the therapist modelling the
appropriate behaviour. Since unassertiveness is very often stimulus-
specific, it is usually essential to involve the spouse, and arrange
for practice sessions to be conducted at home. Clearly the wife must
be prepared to co-operate with the treatment for this to be effective.

Undoubtedly, many sexual difficulties which couples present
with are closely related to more general anxieties and resentments
in their relationship. In cases where these factors constitute the basic
problem, it would clearly be both naive and futile to prescribe, say,
the sensate focus. On the other hand, if sexual inadequacy is the
prime cause of friction between the partners, then relatively little
would be achieved by working just with these negative feelings.
Once again a full behavioural analysis should reveal the most appropriate approach to take in each individual case.

In those instances where interpersonal conflict is fundamental,
behaviourally oriented clinicians will tend to carry out *marital
contract therapy* (Stuart, 1969). Before describing this innovatory treatment method, the causes of many types of marital conflict, in learning theory terms, must first be examined. It is
conjectured that when one marital partner wishes to modify the
behaviour of his spouse, he is likely to employ "aversive control"
(i.e. coercion) rather than positive reinforcement for the desired
behaviour. In other words he uses the "If you don't . . . , then I
won't . . . " strategy. By behaving in this way, the instigator acts as
a model for the victim, and it is quite likely that the person who
has been effectively manipulated will also adopt this behaviour-
change approach. As a result, reciprocation, and eventually escala-
tion of negative reinforcers, will take place. At this stage, either
or both parties are likely to seek to escape from the relationship
by withdrawing emotionally, turning to drink, being unfaithful,
or moving out.

In marital contract therapy, the aim is to teach the couple to use
positive reinforcement in order to shape the behaviour of the other
person. This is achieved by asking each partner to draw up a list of
changes he would like to see in his partner. These requests must be
phrased in precise behavioural terms. Thus instead of suggesting
simply that the other person should help with the housework, it is
essential to state in detail the actual chores (e.g. hoovering lounge
carpet). When both partners have drawn up their lists, an agreement

is then negotiated so that individual A will receive a specified reward
for carrying out B's request, and vice versa.

A distinction must be made here between the *contingency contract*
model favoured by Stuart (1969) and the *independent consequences*
arrangement proposed by Patterson and Hops (1972). In Stuart's
model, the behavioural changes desired by both parties are inextricably bound up, in that if one fails to accomplish a task, the other,
by withdrawing the negotiated reward, is in turn similarly deprived.
For instance, if the husband fails to return home by six as requested,
his wife would not then wear his favourite clothes, and as a result
she would not be taken out to dinner by him. To prevent the whole
programme collapsing in this way, Patterson and Hops (1972) have
devised the *independent consequences* arrangement, which ensures
that the breakdown of one programme does not mean that the
other is automatically jeopardized. Thus with this method, for
instance, the husband will be allowed a Sunday morning lie-in if
he gets home every weekday by six, while his wife will be taken
out to dinner if she cleans the kitchen floor. Patterson's approach
would appear to be the more satisfactory in that here the wife
may still be able to earn her evening out, even though the husband
has been disqualified, through tardiness, from receiving his reward.
Thus some modification of behaviour will still be taking place.
Punishment can also be incorporated into the programme in that
the partner who fails may be obliged to donate a gift, for example,
to the other one.

Marital contract therapy has been attacked by many psychotherapists on the grounds that it is superficial and essentially irrelevant
to the important issues in close interpersonal relationships. There
are two points worth making here. The first is that many couples
with a potentially fulfilling relationship allow it to be seriously
damaged through non-communications and resentments concerning
relatively trivial day-to-day matters. The second is that it is not,
in this author's opinion at least, the actual content of the contracts
that is so important. Rather it is the acquisition of the knowledge
that aversive control is a highly destructive and ultimately ineffective strategy to adopt in a close interpersonal relationship.

Sexual Aids

Many of the behaviour therapy techniques for increasing sexual
arousal, which have been outlined above, involve the contrived

use of diverse forms of erotic stimuli. Since many therapists and patients have reservations about the place of artificial devices in an area which is concerned with feelings between people, it is important to consider the uses and dangers of these objects. For the sake of convenience, these sexual aids will be divided into three categories: *visual, mechanical,* and *human.*

Before examining the relevant issues here, it is important to stress that no-one could or should designate what is acceptable and what is not in this controversial field. The views expressed here should therefore be regarded as those of the author, and not of behaviour therapists or clinicians in general. It follows from this that no therapist should ever feel coerced into recommending devices which he personally would reject, just as no patient should comply with a treatment suggestion he finds repugnant. Apart from the question of individual values, the sexual aid is unlikely to prove very successful under these circumstances.

Many critics of behaviour therapy have expressed concern about the use of *visual* materials (e.g. magazine pictures, nude films) as facilitators of sexual interest. These stimuli have been attacked on both moral and practical grounds.

The moral argument centres around the potential danger that the male who learns to become sexually aroused while gazing at pin-ups is likely to become a "heterofetishist", rather than develop into a person who is capable of profound emotional involvement. In other words, he may come to regard members of the opposite sex as mere sexual objects which are there to be employed in order to gratify his own needs. This is less likely to happen if, as has been strongly recommended, the relationship is treated rather than the individual. Thus in conjoint behavioural therapy, interpersonal communication, of both the sexual and non-sexual variety, is considered to be as important a goal as autonomic responsivity. Role playing, emotional expression exercises, and tuition in cognitive restructuring are some of the treatment components which are frequently used in addition to fantasy training with pictorial stimuli. In my view, therefore, visually evocative stimuli have a useful role to play as sexual catalysts, but should always be used in conjunction with relationship-oriented techniques, to prevent the patient becoming over-concerned with the body rather than the whole person.

A criticism of a different sort is that the patient may learn to respond to the erotic females depicted in the glossy nude magazine, but fail to become excited by his less glamorous, real-life partner.

This is a potentially valid point which all therapists should be aware of. Two solutions suggest themselves. One is to use this material initially, and then advise the patient to switch gradually from fantalisizing about Playboy-type pictures to thinking about his own partner, after he has made some initial progress. The second solution is to use photographs of his partner, in various stimulating poses, throughout the programme. This latter treatment strategy, which has been employed successfully by LoPiccolo *et al.* (1972), would seem to satisfactorily answer both the practical and moral questions which have been raised here.

A number of *mechanical* devices (e.g. vaginal dilators, electric vibrators, plastic penises, artificial torsos) have been recommended by clinicians as aids to sexual arousal. As with visual stimuli, this practice has received a mixed reaction in both medical and lay circles. Since dilators and vibrators have helped a large number of previously unresponsive females to reach their first orgasms, it is not the efficacy of these instruments which is in doubt. Rather it is the belief, that the use of these gadgets actively encourages the individual to engage in self-stimulation, which has evoked criticism in certain quarters. The important issue here would therefore seem to concern not the actual objects themselves, but the ways in which they are used. In my opinion any device is perfectly acceptable, provided (a) that the patient's partner is involved at all stages of treatment, and (b) that it is to be relied upon less and less as the primary source of arousal. (Whether it should ultimately be eliminated altogether is a matter for the couple to decide themselves.) Thus the use of artificial penises and torsos is discouraged here, not because they are unsavoury objects in themselves, but because 'they tend to serve as sexual substitutes rather than as sexual aids. Equally, dilators and vibrators should never be prescribed simply as masturbatory aids by a therapist. Thus, provided they are employed in a properly supervised treatment programme, with the close involvement of the partner throughout, a strong case can be made for including mechanical devices in behavioural types of sex therapy.

Up until now in this chapter, it has been assumed that everyone who seeks help of this kind has a partner who will agree to come along and co-operate with treatment. However there are many patients who present alone. In such cases, a small minority of sex therapists have advocated the use of *human* sexual aids to get around this difficulty. The employment of *sexual surrogates,* as they are called, is undoubtedly the most controversial issue in this whole field. The arguments put forward in favour of substitute partners are that:

1. without a partner of some sort, treatment will over-emphasize pornography and self-stimulation, rather than the subtleties of sexual communication;

2. neither the therapist nor the patient will be able to assess exactly how much progress the individual has made at any point in time, unless he has the opportunity to practice with a member of the opposite sex.

Those who are opposed to the use of surrogates claim that:

1. it encourages the individual to engage in sexual relationships without emotional involvement;

2. it may lead to the patient becoming chronically over-dependent on the surrogate;

3. the motives of the surrogate are open to question.

The latter argument, which could equally well be applied to sex therapists in general, is of little relevance to the question of patient care, and can therefore be ignored for present purposes. Although this may mean that the pros and cons seem evenly matched, it is my opinion that the dangers outweigh the advantages. This is because it is difficult to imagine how a balance can be reached between indifference and deep attachment so far as the feelings of the patient for his surrogate are concerned. Thus the alternative programmes for the solitary patient might be limited in what they have to offer, but would seem to be far less hazardous for an individual, who is already distressed, to undertake.

To conclude, sexual aids have a considerable amount to offer in terms of increasing the sexual interest of the dysfunctioning male or female. They are, however, open to abuse, and the therapist must be careful to ensure that these devices do not totally dominate the treatment programme. If used carefully, and in the context of a relationship where possible, no clinician should feel reluctant to recommend sexual aids (with the possible exception of surrogate partners) in his endeavour to strengthen feelings in this most intimate area of personal relationships.

Sexual Deviations

It must be made clear from the outset that the term "deviation"
as used in this chapter refers to *statistically* abnormal sexual practices
rather than to behaviour which is considered to be unnatural or
pathological. In the view of most contemporary behaviour therapists
(e.g. Bandura, 1969), the clinician should never attempt to impose
a particular set of values on to his client, but should help to broaden
the latter's behavioural repertoire, if requested to do so, thus providing him with a greater freedom of choice of outlet. Hence, ignoring
for the present the early aversion therapy work with homosexuals
referred by the courts, few learning theory practitioners would agree
to directly alter a client's sexual orientation without his expressed
wish. Obviously the attitudes of the individual clinician are likely
to manifest themselves in a subtle fashion through his non-verbal
behaviour despite valiant attempts at concealment. All that can be
said here is that the behaviour therapist should always be aware
of this fact, and should take pains to cut down such potentially
influential cues to a minimum.

Although there is an almost endless list of unusual sexual activities,
only the ones with which behaviour therapists have attempted to
work with are mentioned here. An *exhibitionist* can be defined as
someone who obtains sexual gratification from the act of displaying
his genitals to members of the opposite sex. A *voyeur* is the name
given to a person who derives sexual gratification from observing
other people undressing or engaging in sexual activities. A *masochist*
is the term used to refer to someone who obtains sexual pleasure
from being hurt, physically or mentally, by his partner. *Fetishism*
is that form of sexual behaviour where an object serves as the stimulus
for arousal (e.g. underwear). It is closely related to *transvestism* (from
the learning theory viewpoint at least) where the individual only
obtains gratification by actually wearing some garment(s) associated
with the opposite sex. This must be distinguished from *transsexualism*
where the individual does not cross-dress for erotic purposes, but
because he wishes to become a member of the opposite sex.

Two of the more common sexual outlets in this category require a
little more elaboration at this stage. *Homosexuality,* where sexual
orientation is directed towards same-sex members, has been divided
into two types by some authors. Feldman and MacCulloch (1971)
are among those who make a distinction between *primary homosexuality* (where the individual has never had any heterosexual

interest) and *secondary homosexuality* (where he has been interested in the opposite sex at least at some stage). This proposed division will be examined further in the next section. The term *paedophilia* is used in those cases where the preferred object is a pre-pubertal individual. The paedophile is usually biassed in either a homosexual or heterosexual direction although bisexuality is not uncommon.

These then are the major types of sexual deviation which concern us here.

Learning Theory Formulations of Sexual Deviations

Behaviour therapists have employed more or less the same sort of classical conditioning paradigm to explain the genesis of the majority of the various types of deviation outlined above. The elementary version of this model states that when a particular object is presented at the same time (or preferably just before) the onset of sexual arousal, an association will be built up between the two events so that the sight of that object in the future will be likely to elicit a sexual response. Thus if a young male has his first experience with a female who had been wearing black stockings, then (according to this model), it would be likely that he would develop a fetish for these garments in the future. Similarly the youth who dresses up in his mother's clothing and achieves a strong positive erection due to the tightness and/or texture of the material will tend to engage in cross-dressing behaviour in the future in order to optimalize sexual arousal. Once again the two-factor theory of learning (see p. 97) is employed in order to explain both the origins and and persistence of conditioned autonomic responses.

The experiments of Rachman (1966) and Rachman and Hodgson (1968) certainly provide evidence to show that a learned response can be acquired in this way. In the first experiment, slides of boots were presented immediately before slides of nude females, which had been previously shown through penile plethysmography (Bancroft *et al.*, 1966) to be sexually arousing. These three subjects all reached the criteria of five successive penile responses to the conditioned stimulus (i.e. the boot slides) within 65 trials. All subjects demonstrated the phenomenon of stimulus generalization to at least one other stimulus (i.e. low-heeled black shoes) which had not been used in the experiment. Rachman and Hodgson (1968) repeated the experiment with five subjects. In this study, the importance of classical conditioning *per se* was demonstrated by including a backward conditioning procedure for each subject. One weakness of these experiments is that the conditioned stimulus employed was the sight of an object which is commonly used by fetishists. It would have been interesting to investigate whether they would have achieved similar results with, say, a woollen scarf. It is not inconceivable that certain objects, for some reason or other, are more readily conditioned in this way than others. The fact that silk, leather and rubber account for the vast majority of fetishes would certainly seem to support such a view.

Despite the success of these experiments, the fact that a sexual response can be conditioned in such a manner does not of course automatically imply that all deviations arise in this way. In fact clinical findings would suggest that it is unlikely that the process is so simple. Most sexual deviants, for instance, find it difficult to recall any one major occurrence or concentrated sequence of events which led to them suddenly becoming interested in their sexual object of choice. Instead they tend to report that the onset was gradual. Eysenck's (1968a) somewhat involved and hypothetical notion of incubation, based on Pavlov's concepts of cortical excitation and inhibition, could however conceivably account for this, thus still supporting the principal role of classical conditioning. Another difficult finding to explain is why one person will engage in sexual relations with a black-stockinged female and thereby develop a fetish, whereas another will not. Eysenck's findings that introverts tend to be more easily conditioned than extraverts (Eysenck, 1968b) is clearly relevant here but would seem to be an insufficient explanation in itself. Perhaps the greatest weakness of this simple classical conditioning hypothesis is that whereas it would lead one to expect that, as a result of their first experiences, all people would become exclusively heterosexual, fetishistic, or whatever, the evidence in fact would seem to favour the notion of dimensions of sexual orientation (Kinsey *et al.*, 1948); Feldman and MacCulloch, 1971).

Some of these difficulties have been partly answered by McGuire *et al.* (1965) who propose that masturbatory conditioning may play at least as important a part in determining sexual preference as actual events. From clinical findings, they report that a sexual experience, which is not sufficient in itself to eroticize a particular object, may become incorporated into masturbatory fantasies. If the person's only sexual outlet is to repeatedly masturbate to a particular fantasy, then, through association, this symbolic representation will become increasingly erotic. These authors give simple examples of patients who, when trying to recall an exciting sexual experience, succeeded in conjuring up a very clear picture of the apparel the young lady had been wearing, but had great difficulty in remembering much about the characteristics of that particular person. After a time, she receded almost completely from the fantasy, and the clothing image was all that remained.

This somewhat hypothetical explanation of symbolic conditioning can account for the insidious development and individual variation difficulties mentioned above but has to be stretched a little to account for the fact that many people find more than one type of sexual object sexually arousing. Presumably a particularly stimulating real-life experience might lead to the previously used fantasy being replaced for a time. As a result it would grow in strength and eventually come to co-exist with the other one in that person's fantasy life. In view of the intangibility of symbolic conditioning processes, it is possible only to speculate here.

Turning to homosexuality, it will be recalled that Feldman and MacCulloch (1971) make a distinction between the primary and secondary types. According to these authors, the aetiology and prognosis are very different in these cases. So far as secondary homosexuality is concerned, they take the usual learning theory view that it arises through conditioning procedures. If an early experience takes place in the presence of a member of the same sex, then this type of sexual object is likely to grow in strength through a process of incubation (Eysenck, 1968a) and/or masturbatory conditioning (McGuire *et al.,* 1965) and in later life become the preferred outlet. Another possibility is the occurrence of a traumatic heterosexual experience which might lead to avoidance behaviour, so far as opposite sex members are concerned, and thus to a greater likelihood that same-sex members might become erotically preferred.

With regard to primary homosexuality, Feldman and MacCulloch (1971) point to evidence (e.g. Neumann and Elgar, 1966) that adult sexual behaviour can be influenced by an imbalance of sex steroids in the developing brain. As a result, the morphological male child tends to show little aggression, prefers "feminine" toys, and seeks out the company of girls rather than boys. Although Feldman and MacCulloch do not deny that social learning can influence this behaviour, they maintain that the sexual orientation of primary homosexuals is determined predominantly by biological factors. Less controversially, they favour a similar neuroendocrinological explanation for the genesis of transsexualism as well. Since these workers minimize the causal role of the environment in these instances, it is hardly surprising that they should also feel pessimistic about the likely response of these patients to behaviour therapy. The fact that primary homosexuals, in fact, have responded poorly to their anticipatory avoidance programme (see below) is taken as supportive evidence for their hypothesis.

Not all behaviour therapists have taken such a gloomy view of prognosis, at least so far as primary homosexuality is concerned. Wilson and Davison (1974), in their excellent review of the behaviour therapy literature on homosexuality, suggest that the reson why primary homosexuals did not respond to Feldman and MacCulloch's rigid regime might have been because behavioural analyses of these cases would have perhaps revealed that their programme was a totally inappropriate method of treatment to adopt. They argue that a schedule designed to increase heterosexual arousal and improve social skills would have achieved far more with these patients than this essentially negative programme. With regard to Feldman and MacCulloch's suggested dichotomy, Wilson and Davison reach the following conclusion:

> "Drawing a fundamental and potentially far-reaching etiological distinction like this on the basis of outcome response to a fixed therapeutic regime is extremely hazardous . . . "

Clearly this issue is still to be resolved.

Lest I be accused of blatant sexism, some explanation is necessary to account for the fact that all the above examples have a distinctly male bias to them. This is simply because, as far as can be ascertained, there is a much higher incidence of deviant sexual practices in the male population than in the female one. In the case of lesbianism, the actual incidence figures are uncertain because society's relatively tolerant view of this outlet has presumably led to only a small proportion actually seeking help. Disregarding this, the reason why females are under-represented so far as the other deviations are concerned, is somewhat obscure. McCary (1973) suggested that the under-representation of females here is due to the fact that boys develop a stronger sex drive earlier than girls do, and are therefore exposed to a greater number of experiences that could lead to the emergence of variant sexual behaviour (p. 357). Certainly the fact that women, regardless of age, who masturbate to orgasm, do so once every two to four weeks (Kinsey *et al.*, 1953), whereas adolescent males do so, on average, 2.5 times per week, is consistent with McGuire's view that masturbatory fantasies are largely responsible for the origins of sexual deviations. No other learning theory explanation has been put forward to account for this discrepancy.

Basic Techniques

Aversion Therapy

Although there are reports of aversion therapy techniques having been used with fetishists (e.g. Clarke, 1963), transvestites (e.g. Morgenstern *et al.*, 1965), exhibitionists (e.g. Evans, 1968) and assorted deviations (Thorpe *et al.*, 1964), most of the systematic work in this area has been carried out with homosexuals. The reason for this is presumably that these subjects are more freely available. The following discussion will therefore be limited to two of the more important studies using this particular group of patients.

By far the most impressive results in this area have been those obtained by Feldman and MacCulloch (1971), using their own anticipatory avoidance programme. Nearly 60% of the unselected patients who underwent their programme were considered to have responded successfully after at least a year's follow-up. Male slides were projected on to a screen for eight seconds during which the patient had the option of pressing a switch or not. If he did not do so, then he received an electric shock after eight seconds when the slide was automatically removed. If the switch was pressed, then, on certain occasions at least, the slide would be removed and no shock administered. The patients were asked to look at the slide as long as they found it attractive, rather than to approach the whole task as a sort of reaction time experiment. There are various other intricacies in their design, all apparently based on sound learning theory principles. The crucial component of this treatment, at least so far as its authors are concerned, is the anticipatory avoidance aspect. Others, however are not so convinced of this. Rachman and Teasdale (1969) maintain that the effectiveness of this approach is due to the classical conditioning features of the design. Wilson and Davison (1974), on the other hand, state that:

"it is reasonable to suggest that aversion-relief is the critical ingredient in

the Feldman and MacCulloch package and that the presumed importance
of conditioned aversion to homosexual stimuli is irrelevant" (p. 18).

Such a parochial controversy however need not concern us over-
much here.

A recent study which should be included here is that reported by
Bancroft (1970) into the relative effectiveness of aversion therapy
and desensitization with homosexuals. The interesting point about
this study is that although the aversion therapy condition failed to
bring about a diminution in homosexual responsivity, a significant
increase in heterosexual arousal took place. Bancroft has given the
name "paradoxical facilitation" to this totally unexpected finding
(at least from the learning theory viewpoint) whereby unsuccessful
aversion therapy to homosexual stimuli led to heterosexual adjustment. This result raises the possibility that much of the reported
success in this area is in fact unrelated to the basic principles thought
to be underlying aversion therapy, and is suggestive of the involvement of cognitive factors.

Covert Sensitization

In recent years, behaviour therapists have, in general, become more
aware of the importance of cognitions in both the genesis and treatment of behaviour disorders (e.g. Meichenbaum, 1973). One innova-
tive cognitive technique, which has been used successfully with
sexual deviations, is *covert sensitization* (Cautela and Wisocki, 1971).
These authors claim that an aversive treatment which is cognitively
based has many advantages over the faradic type. For a start, it is
far less unpleasant for both patient and therapist, and is therefore
likely to reduce the drop-out rate (of both parties!). In the second
place, cognitive techniques have potentially a wider range of applicability than overt techniques. A third advantage is that the patient
can employ the procedure in a self-control fashion when necessary.
Finally, following the work of McGuire *et al.* (1965), fantasy retraining should be at least as effective as real-life conditioning.

The major steps in a covert sensitization programme, as suggested
by Cautela and Wisocki (1971) are as follows:

1. the subject is asked to think about approaching the deviant
object of his choice;
2. he is instructed to imagine that he is actually approaching it;

3. he is requested to fantasize that he is in the process of reaching
out for it;
4. he is immediately told to imagine a horrible event (e.g. that he
is covered in vomit, maggots, manure, etc.) while the therapist
helps by providing lurid details;
5. he is finally instructed to leave the object, and as he does so,
it is suggested that the noxious stimulus will gradually disappear.

Cautela and Wisocki (1971) provide follow-up data on eight homosexuals who had been treated by this method a few years previously
(Cautela and Wisocki, 1968). Three were happily married and were
exclusively heterosexual, two had some residual homosexual urges
but were adapting to heterosexuality, and three remained exclusively
homosexual.

Despite these encouraging results, regrettably little further research
has been carried out in this area.

Systematic Desensitization

As suggested above, many people who engage in unusual sexual practices do so because of the anxiety they experience in the presence
of women, or at least in the presence of women in sexual situations.
It is therefore hardly surprising that systematic desensitization has
been employed quite widely in this field. Since the basic technique
has previously been described in the section on sexual disorders,
just a brief mention of some work in this area shall be provided here.

LoPiccolo *et al.* (1972) give an account of the treatment of a
homosexual who was treated by a programme which was principally
one of *in vivo* desensitization, although it included some additional
components. The patient and his wife were asked to work through a
behaviour hierarchy ranging from hugging, kissing and massage,
through penis stimulation, to mutual thrusting during intercourse
leading to ejaculation. Although homosexual fantasies had to be
employed at the beginning of the programme, by the end of it,
heterosexual fantasies were being employed exclusively.

Of the other work in this area, the study by Stevenson and
Wolpe (1960) in which three homosexuals were desensitized to
their social anxieties concerning women, and the case report of
an exhibitionist who was desensitized to three separate hierarchies
(Bond and Hutchison, 1964) are particularly noteworthy.

Masturbatory Retraining

If masturbatory fantasies can help to strengthen a sexual deviation (McGuire *et al.*, 1965), then it would seem to follow that they could be used in order to increase heterosexual interest, with individuals who do not find this type of stimulus attractive. A considerable amount of work has been carried out in this area.

Davison (1968) has described a sexual reorientation technique along these lines which he used in the treatment of a client with sadistic fantasies. The procedure involved requesting the client to masturbate, using his usual fantasies, and then to switch to pictures from *Playboy* magazine as soon as possible. When he was able to do this more or less successfully, real-life photographs of scantily-clad females were substituted for the glossy pin-up stimuli. This technique was only partially successful however. At this stage, therefore, it was decided to introduce a covert sensitization approach to eliminate the sadistic fantasies while the patient persevered with his heterosexual fantasy programme at home. After a few weeks of this combined approach, the client reported that he was no longer employing sadistic fantasies and was using exclusively heterosexual stimuli of the pictorial and imaginal kind.

Jackson (1969) successfully treated a voyeur by requesting that he masturbate, using the most exciting pornographic pictures he could find, whenever he felt a desire to peep. When he became quite adept at this, *Playboy* pictures were introduced. As a result of treatment, he lost his voyeuristic desires and, in fact, formed two satisfactory relationships following the termination of treatment.

The most systematic work in this area has been that of Marquis (1970). In this approach the client is instructed to masturbate using his usual fantasy and then to switch to a heterosexual one at the point of orgasm. After he has achieved success on several occasions, he is requested to introduce the heterosexual fantasy at increasingly earlier stages until it is being used at the outset. If, at any stage, the client becomes aware that his sexual arousal level is diminishing, he is advised to switch back to the original fantasy and change once again when he is more highly aroused. Marquis (1970) provides reports of 14 assorted sexual deviants, including a fetishist and a masochist, who were treated by this method. This technique was also incorporated into the treatment programme of LoPiccolo *et al.* (1972) which was described above.

Although few behaviour therapists would attempt to treat a sexual deviation using just one of the methods described above, one of these fantasy retraining techniques should be included in any sexual reorientation programme.

Classically Conditioned Heterosexual Arousal

One way of training clients to respond heterosexually is to adopt
the learning paradigm employed by Rachman (1966) in his fetishistic
induction experiment, but using a female slide as the conditioned
stimulus and the hitherto preferred object as the unconditioned
stimulus. Beech *et al.* (1971) report having successfuly treated a
homosexual paedophile in this way. Pictures of pre-pubertal girls
were paired with gradually more mature girls. As the latter became
more arousing, so they were used in turn as the unconditioned
stimuli for still more mature girls, and so on. Eventually the client
was able to respond sexually to girls of the appropriate age group.
Herman *et al.* (1974) used a classical conditioning approach in
the treatment of three homosexuals, two of whom responded successfully to this method. Slides of nude females served as the conditioned
stimuli and excerpts from homosexual films were used as the unconditioned stimuli. Systematic variations in the procedure for each
subject demonstrated that, with the two who responded, classical
conditioning *per se* was responsible for the change.

Instrumentally Conditioned Heterosexual Arousal

From a technological viewpoint at least, one of the most ingenious
methods for increasing heterosexual arousal is that described by
Quinn *et al.* (1970). They employed a positive reinforcement procedure in order to shape directly penile responses in the presence
of heterosexual stimuli. They report the case of a young homosexual
(Kinsey rating 5) whose homosexual interest diminished somewhat
following 35 sessions of anticipatory avoidance conditioning along
the lines suggested by Feldman and MacCulloch (1971). However
he experienced feelings of anxiety and depression when imagining
or carrying out heterosexual behaviour. It was decided therefore to
train him to become more sexually aroused in the presence of
heterosexual stimuli.

Prior to treatment, he was deprived of water for 18 hours, and
given salt and an oral diuretic to ingest, in order to sensitize him
to liquid reinforcers. He was then presented with a female slide he
found attractive and was encouraged to fantasize to it. An increase
in his phallic blood flow, as measured by the penile plethysmograph,
was reinforced by a drink of chilled lime juice. This had the effect

of increasing the amplitude of the penis in the presence of hetero-sexual stimuli. However, although it was found to be possible to directly condition this physiological response, at no time did he attain a full erection during treatment.

In the absence of any controlled experimentation with this procedure, one can only conclude that it is certainly an interesting departure from mainstream research in this field, but clearly further investigations are required before it can be properly evaluated and considered for clinical use.

Behavioural Psychotherapy Approach

The assorted procedures described above have proved successful in inducing sexual reorientation. However, once again, it must be emphasized that behaviour modification should not be regarded as a mindless technology based on a questionable assumption of homogeneity regarding diagnostic groups, but as a therapeutic approach which can be adapted to the requirements of the individual. Thus in the case of the Feldman and MacCulloch (1971) study, the fact that 40% of the clients did not respond to that approach does not necessarily mean, as the authors suggest, that these treatment failures are to be dismissed as being biologically different and therefore unsusceptible to behavioural methods. It could also be argued that these people engage in homosexual behaviour for different reasons than those who responded, and that a more subtle and psychologically (as opposed to technologically) sophisticated approach should have been taken.

The aim throughout this chapter has been to emphasize that while the behaviour modifier must be able to master the basic techniques in order to practice, he is unlikely to prove very effective unless he masters the skills common to all psychotherapists. That is he should learn how to explore all the factors relevant to the problem in each individual case, and devise his treatment on the basis of this. Once again a case illustration is provided to demonstrate how the behavioural analysis can be used in order to design a treatment programme.

The Case of the Easily Harrassed Exhibitionist

Mr R., married with two children, was referred by the courts for psychiatric treatment for indecent exposure to young girls. He was initially given faradic aversion therapy which, although initially effective, did not produce any lasting change. A behavioural analysis (see p. 87) was carried out with the following results:

Step 1. The actual behaviour problem was that he would occasionally expose himself and masturbate publicly in a certain wood which schoolgirls passed through each day.

Step 2. A close analysis of the situation revealed that he was more likely to carry out this behaviour when he and his wife were not on speaking terms (i.e. "life events"). He would feel both frustrated and depressed by their failure to communicate, and, at this point, would be considered to be "at risk".

Step 3. The reinforcer in this case was thought to be the reduction of tension following engagement in this activity. The response of the girls seemed to be irrelevant.

Step 4. On those occasions when he felt upset but could or would not expose himself, he would drink heavily for a short period (e.g. one bottle of spirits in an evening). This would calm him down.

Step 5. Information gleaned from his mother revealed that he had always had a low tolerance level of frustration. (e.g. he would get physically violent if he did not get his own way).

Step 6. It was decided therefore to carry out (a) marital contract therapy to reduce the tension in the relationship, (b) behaviour rehearsal aimed at teaching the couple how to argue properly instead of withdrawing, (c) anxiety management training to help him cope with frustration, and (d) covert sensitization to eliminate his drinking and deviant sexual behaviour.

Step 7. After 12 weeks of intensive therapy along these lines, the marital relationship had improved dramatically and his exhibitionistic tendencies had disappeared. These improvements had been maintained six months after the termination of therapy, thus supporting the hypothesis that the exposing behaviour constituted a simple escape strategy.

There are many such cases where the individual engages in undesirable behaviour, not because it is intrinsically rewarding in itself, but because it serves to reduce feelings of failure, or loneliness. Logic would dictate that a direct attack on the symptomatology of such people would be a fairly futile exercise. The skill here is in isolating precisely why the behaviour is carried out (and this is often the most difficult part) and deciding on the best course of action to take. This is the essence of the behavioural psychotherapy approach. In fact, only if behaviour modifiers are prepared, and are properly trained, to carry out this difficult time-consuming procedure, can they really be considered to be psychotherapists in any meaningful sense of the word.

An Ethical Note

As stated at the beginning of this section, behaviour therapists do not (or at least should not), set themselves up as custodians of traditional moral standards. Rather they see themselves as helping individual clients to overcome problems which are causing them distress, or to help them extend their behavioural repertoires. Thus they would never, for instance, consider attempting to reorient a homosexual against his will. However, despite the constantly voiced assertion that behaviour therapy is not tied up with a particular value system, it has to be conceded that the great bulk of the literature has been concerned with ways of converting sexual deviants to heterosexuality. In fact a study described by Fensterheim (1972) in which six male homosexuals were treated successfully for impotence (in homosexual situations) is the only one which I have come across where heterosexuality has not constituted the ultimate goal. Nevertheless, despite the dearth of such pro-liberal investigations, few clinicians would dispute the assertion of Wilson and Davison (1974) that:

> "behaviour therapy has much to contribute to helping homosexuals to participate fully and meaningfully in everyday life *as homosexuals*" (p. 25).

The ethical issues are clearly much more complex where voyeurism, exhibitionism, and paedophilia in particular are concerned.

Summary

In this chapter an attempt has been made to give some idea of the wide range of techniques which have been devised by behaviourists, and by clinicians unknowingly operating within a learning theory framework, to enable individuals to derive more satisfaction from their sex lives. Throughout, it has been emphasized that there should be a sound theoretical rationale underlying every treatment programme based on a full analysis of the behaviour. This is in sharp contrast to the commonly practised "technique-tinkering" approach, which is very often not only a futile exercise but also a potentially destructive one, leading as it sometimes does to general therapeutic disillulutionment on the part of the client. It has also been stressed in this chapter that behaviour therapy is just a set of principles and techniques, which is independent of any value system. With the exception of certain sexual activities universally accepted as criminal, it is felt to be the client's responsibility to decide both whether he needs help, and the kind of help he should receive. Thus where behaviour therapy is practised as a complete psychotherapeutic approach, with the client's best interests clearly in mind, it can contribute considerably to alleviating much of the distress which is brought about by sexual problems.

References

Bancroft, J. (1970). A comparative study of aversion and desensitization in the treatment of homosexuality. *In* "Behaviour Therapy in the 1970s." (Burns, L. E. and Worsley, J. L., Eds), pp. 1—22. John Wright and Sons: Bristol.

Bancroft, J., Jones, G. J. and Pullan, B. R. (1966). A simple transducer for measuring penile erection, with comments on its use in the treatment of sexual disorders. *Behaviour Research and Therapy*, 4, 239—241.

Bandura, A. (1969). "Principles of Behavior Modification." Holt, Reinhart and Winston, Inc: New York.

Barber, T. X. and Hahn, K. W., Jr. (1964). Experimental studies in "hypnotic" behaviour: Physiological and subjective effects of imagined pain. *Journal of Nervous and Mental Disease*, 139, 416—425.

Beech, H. R., Watts, F. and Poole, A. D. (1971). Classical conditioning of sexual deviation: A preliminary note. *Behaviour Therapy*, 2, 400—402.

Belliveau, F., and Richter, L. (1970). "Understanding Human Sexual Inadequacy." Bantam: New York.

Bond, I. K. and Hutchison, H. C. (1964). Application of reciprocal inhibition therapy to exhibitionism. *In* "Experiments in Behaviour Therapy." (Eysenck, H. J. Ed.), pp. 80—86. Pergamon Press: Oxford.

Brady, J. P. (1966). Brevital-relaxation treatment of frigidity. *Behaviour Research and Therapy*, 4, 71—77.

Breger, L. and McGaugh, J. (1965). Critique and reformulation of "learning theory" approaches to psychotherapy and neurosis. *Psychological Bulletin*, 63, 338—358.

Cautela, J. R. (1967). Covert sensitization. *Psychological Reports*, 29, 459—468.

Cautela, J. R. and Wisocki, P. A. (1968). The use of male and female therapists in the treatment of homosexual behavior. *In* "Advances in Behavior Therapy." (Rubin, I. R. and Franks, C. M., Eds), pp. 165—174. Academic Press: New York.

Cautela, J. R. and Wisocki, P. A. (1971). Covert sensitization for the treatment of sexual deviations. *Psychological Record*, 21, 37—48.

Clarke, D. F. (1963). Fetishism treated by negative conditioning. *British Journal of Psychology*, 109, 404—408.

Cooper, A. J. (1969). Disorders of sexual potency in the male: A clinical and statistical study of some factors related to short-term prognosis. *British*

Journal of Psychiatry, 115, 709—719.

Davison, G. G. (1968). Elimination of a sadistic fantasy by a client-controlled counterconditioning technique: a case study. *Journal of Abnormal and Social Psychology*, 73, 84—90.

Dengrove, E. (1971). The mechanotherapy of sexual disorders. *Journal of Sex Research*, 7, 1—12.

Evans, D. R. (1968). Masturbatory fantasy and sexual deviation. *Behaviour Research and Therapy*, 6, 17—19.

Eysenck, H. J. (1960). "Behaviour Therapy and the Neuroses." Pergamon Press: Oxford.

Eysenck, H. J. (1964). (Ed.) "Experiments in Behavior Therapy." Pergamon Press: Oxford.

Eysenck, H. J. (1968a). A theory of the incubation of anxiety fear responses. *Behaviour Research and Therapy*, 6, 309—321.

Eysenck, H. J. (1968b). "The Biological Basis of Behaviour." Thomas and Co: Northants.

Feldman, M. P. and MacCulloch, M. J. (1965). The application of anticipatory avoidance learning to the treatment of homosexuality. I. Theory, technique and preliminary results. *Behaviour Research and Therapy*, 3, 165—183.

Feldman, M. P. and MacCulloch, M. J. (1971). "Homosexual Behaviour — Therapy and Assessment." Pergamon Press: Oxford.

Fensterheim, H. (1972). The initial interview. *In* "Clinical Behavior Therapy". (Lazarus, A. A. Ed.), pp. 22—40. Brunner/Mazel: New York.

Frankl, V. E. (1960), Paradoxical intention: A logotherapeutic technique. *Journal of Psychotherapy*, 14, 520—535.

Friedman, D. (1966). A new technique for the systematic desensitization of phobic symptoms. *Behaviour Research and Therapy*, 4, 139—140.

Gebhard, P. H. (1966). Factors in marital orgasm. *Journal of Social Issues*, 22, 88—95.

Herman, S. H., Barlow, D. H. and Agras, W. S. (1974). An experimental analysis of classical conditioning as a method of increasing heterosexual arousal in homosexuals. *Behaviour Therapy*, 5, 33—47.

Jackson, B. T. (1969). A case of voyeurism treated by counterconditioning. *Behaviour Research and Therapy*, 7, 133—134.

Jones, M. C. (1924). A laboratory study of fear: the case of Peter. *Journal of Genetic Psychology*, 31, 308—315.

Kanfer, F. H. and Phillips, J. S. (1970). "Learning Foundations of Behavior Therapy." John Wiley and Sons: New York.

Kanfer, F. H. and Saslow, G. (1969). Behavior diagnosis. *In* "Behavior Therapy: Appraisal and Status." (Franks, C. M. Ed.), pp. 417—444. McGraw-Hill Book Co: New York.

Kelly, G. L. (1961). Impotence. *In* A. Ellis and A. Abarbanel, "The Encyclopedia of Sexual Behaviour." Vol. 1. pp. 72—96. Hawthorn Books Inc: New York.

Kinsey, A. C. and Gebhard, P. H. (1953). "Sexual Behavior in the Human Female." W. B. Saunders Co: Philadelphia.

Kinsey, A. C., Pomeroy, W. B. and Martin, C. E. (1948). "Sexual Behavior in the Human Male." W. B. Saunders Co: Philadelphia.

Lang, P. J. (1968). Fear reduction and fear behavior: problems in treating a construct. *In* "Research in Psychotherapy." (Shlien, J. M. Ed.), pp. 90—102. American Psychological Association, Washington DC.

Lang, P. J. (1969). The mechanics of desensitization and the laboratory study of human fear. *In* "Behaviour Therapy: Appraisal and Status." (Franks, C. M. Ed.). pp. 160–191. McGraw-Hill: New York.

Lazarus, A. A. (1961). Group therapy of phobic disorders of systematic desensitization. *Journal of Abnormal and Social Psychology*, 63, 504–510.

Lazarus, A. A. (1963). The treatment of chronic frigidity by systematic desensitization. *Journal of Nervous and Mental Disease*, 136, 272–278.

Lazarus, A. A. (1966). Behaviour rehearsal vs. non-directive therapy vs. advice in effecting behaviour change. *Behaviour Research and Therapy*, 4, 209–212.

Lazarus, A. A. (1968). Behaviour therapy in groups. *In* "Basic Approaches to Group Psychotherapy and Counselling." (Gazda, M. Ed.), pp. 149–175. Charles C. Thomas: Springfield, Ill.

Lazarus, A. A. (1969). Group treatment for impotence and frigidity. *Sexology*, 36, 22–25.

Lazarus, A. A. (1971). "Behavior Therapy and Beyond." McGraw-Hill Book Co: New: York.

Lobitz, W. C. and LoPiccolo, J. (1972). New methods in behavioral treatment of sexual dysfunction. *Journal of Behavior Therapy and Experimental Psychiatry*, 3, 265–271.

LoPiccolo, J., Stewart, R. and Watkins, B. (1972). Treatment of erectile failure and ejaculatory incompetence of homosexual etiology. *Journal of Behavior Therapy and Experimental Psychiatry*, 3, 233–236.

McCary, J. L. (1973). "Human Sexuality." (2nd edition). Van Nostrand Reinhold Co: New York.

McGuire, R. J., Carlisle, J. M. and Young, B. G. (1965). Sexual deviations as conditioned behaviour: A hypothesis. *Behaviour Research and Therapy*, 2, 185–190.

Marmor, J. (1971). "Normal" and "deviant" sexual behavior. *Journal of the American Medical Association*, 217, 165–170.

Marquis, J. N. (1970). Orgasmic reconditioning: changing sexual object choice through controlling masturbation fantasies. *Journal of Behavior Therapy and Experimental Psychiatry*, 1, 263–271.

Masters, W. H. and Johnson, V. E. (1966). "Human Sexual Response." Little, Brown and Co: Boston, Mass., USA.

Masters, W. H. and Johnson, V. E. (1970). "Human Sexual Inadequacy." Little, Brown and Co: Boston, Mass., USA.

Meichenbaum, D. H. (1973). Cognitive factors in behavior modification: Modifying what clients say to themselves. *In* "Advances in Behavior Therapy." (Rubin, R. D., Brady, J. P. and Henderson, J. D. Eds), Vol. 4. pp. 21–36. Academic Press: New York.

Meyer, V. (1973). The impact of research on the clinical applications of behavior therapy. *In* T. Thompson and W. D. Dockens III (Eds), "Proceedings of the International Symposium on Behavior Modification." pp. 165–193: Appleton-Century Crofts: New York.

Meyer, V. and Liddell, A. (1975). Behaviour Therapy. *In* "Issues and Approaches in the Psychological Therapies." (Bannister, D. Ed.), pp. 223–240. John Wiley and Sons: Chichester.

Migler, B. and Wolpe, J. (1967). Automated self-desensitization: a case report. *Behaviour Research and Therapy*, 2, 191–200.

Morgenstern, F. S., Pearce, J. F. and Rees, L. W. (1965). Predicting the outcome of behaviour therapy by psychological tests. *Behaviour Research and Therapy*, 2, 191–200.

Mowrer, O. H. (1947). On the dual nature of learning — a reinterpretation of "conditioning" and "problem solving". *Harvard Educational Review*, 17, 102–148.

Murphy, C. V. and Mikulas, W. L. (1974). Behavioral features and deficiencies of the Masters and Johnson program. *Psychological Record*, 24, 221–227.

Neumann, F. and Elgar, W. (1966). Permanent changes in gonadal function and sexual behaviour as a result of early feminization of male rats by treatment with an anti-androgenic steriod. *Endokrinologie*, 50, 209–224.

Obler, M. (1973). Systematic desensitization in sexual disorders. *Journal of Behavior Therapy and Experimental Psychiatry*, 4, 93–101.

Palmer, R. D. (1973). Desensitization of the fear of expressing one's own inhibited aggression: bioenergetic assertive techniques for behaviour therapists. *In* "Advances in Behaviour Therapy." (Rubin, R. D., Brady, J. P. and Henderson, J. D. Eds.), Vol. 4. pp. 241–254. Academic Press: New York.

Patterson, G. R. and Hops, H. (1972). Coercion, a game for two: Intervention techniques for marital conflict. *In* "The Experimental Analysis of Social Behavior." (Ulrich, R. E. and Mountjoy, P. Eds), pp. 424–440. Appleton-Century-Crofts: New York.

Pavlov, I. P. (1927). "Conditioned Reflexes." Oxford University Press: London.

Quinn, J. T., Harbison, J. and McAllister, H. (1970). An attempt to shape human penile responses. *Behaviour Research and Therapy*, 8, 213–216.

Rachlin, H. (1970). "Introduction to Modern Behaviorism." Freeman and Co: San Fransisco.

Rachman, S. (1966). Sexual fetishism: an experimental analogue. *Psychological Record*, 16, 293–296.

Rachman, S. and Hodgson, R. J. (1968). Experimentally induced "sexual fetishism": replication and development. *Psychological Record*, 18, 25–27.

Rachman, S. and Teasdale, J. (1969). "Aversion Therapy and Behaviour Disorders." Routledge and Kegan Paul: London.

Salter, A. (1949). "Conditioned Reflex Therapy". Creative Age Press: New York.

Semans, J. H. (1956). Premature ejaculation: A new approach. *Southern Medical Journal*, 49, 353–361.

Shaw, W. (1954). "Operative Gynaecology." Williams and Wilkins: Baltimore.

Skinner, B. F. (1953). "Science and Human Behavior." Macmillan and Co: New York.

Stevenson, I. and Wolpe, J. (1960). Recovery from sexual deviations through overcoming of non-sexual neurotic responses. *American Journal of Psychiatry*, 116, 737–742.

Stuart, R. B. (1969). Operant interpersonal treatment for marital discord. *Journal of Consulting and Clinical Psychology*, 33, 675–682.

Thorpe, J., Schmidt, E., Brown, P. T. and Castell, D. (1964). Aversion relief therapy: A new method for general application. *Behaviour Research and Therapy*, 2, 71–82.

Watson, J. B. and Rayner, R. (1920). Conditioned emotional reactions. *Journal of Experimental Psychology*, 3, 1–14.

Wilson, G. T. and Davison, G. C., (1974). Behavior therapy and homosexuality: A critical perspective. *Behavior Therapy*, 5, 16–28.

Wolpe, J. (1958). "Psychotherapy by Reciprocal Inhibition." Stanford University Press: Stanford, USA.

Wolpe, J. and Lazarus, A. (1966). "Behavior Therapy Techniques." Pergamon Press: New York.

II

Psychosexual Problems and the Life Cycle

5 | *Adolescent Sexuality and Chronic Handicap*

H. C. CAMERON

Physically Normal Adolescent

General

Developing sexuality is the key to adolescence. Yet the manifest sexual behaviour of the teenage years is just one aspect of the inner world of changing feelings and attitudes. Normal adolescent sexuality can be understood as a display with a sexual flavour of early childhood conflicts. The sexual problems of adolescence have the same roots but carry a more urgent seeking for expression.

Adolescence is a recognized age of an individual's life — the teenage — when particularly momentous developments occur. Adolescence begins when new hormones circulate and cause the changes of puberty in the child roughly at thirteen. The chronological age of puberty varies markedly between the sexes and between individuals. Girls' puberty at twelve is on average two years ahead of boys' at fourteen.

During the adolescent years the gradual physical and hormonal changes are accompanied by psychological developments which often occur in a stepwise manner. The normal erratic progress shows itself as very adult behaviour at one stage being followed by regressed childlike behaviour shortly after. There are marked individual differences in the intensity of these swings. The end of adolescence is as difficult to pinpoint as the beginning; it is often marked by the individual leaving home to set up an independent life as an adult.

Environment

The sexual development of the individual growing into adolescence
cannot be thought of in isolation. The experience of the early childhood years, the stability and happiness of the home, and present
relationships with mother, father, brothers and sisters all have a great
effect on the individual teenager's sexual attitudes and behaviour.

Often the pre-adolescent child seems particularly content and
settled. The person he wishes to be (his ego ideal) and how he finds
himself coincide. He is calm and can channel his attention on tasks
in the outside world. With the onset of adolescence this calm gets
interrupted both by changes in the external world, and by even more
insistent internal psychological changes.

Adolescence is a time of environmental changes which stretch
the individual. There are school changes at eleven or thirteen from a
protected children's environment to a threatening near adult one.
In school there is forced close contact in a single sex or mixed sex
community. At sixteen or eighteen there is the move from school
either to work or to higher education. At eighteen, the teenager
acquires the right to vote. The process of maturation of the adolescent may keep pace with the chronological age, but often it does
not. Then it is the teenager's different levels of functional maturity
that are the key factors in understanding, rather than the chronological age.

Central Change in Relationships

There are two central mental changes in adolescence. A new form of
relationship is developed, a sexual one. The other key change is that
intense emotional relationships move from within to outside the
family and involve a new set of people. The old secure signposts
guiding relationships within the family are preserved on one side and
new guidelines have to be found by the adolescent as he explores a
wider society. Sex is the cause of this change.

Physical Changes and Problems

Awareness of changes in body size and shape can be acute in early
adolescence. The young adolescent may worry greatly about devia-

tion from what is perceived as normal within the peer group. This
is often so around the onset of puberty. Many of the problems are
simple and arise from inadequate sex education and poor understanding by the pupil (see Chapter 19). Girls may worry about the onset
of menstruation or be concerned about unequal breast development.
(This almost always evens up by adulthood.) Girls may mourn the
passing of their childhood and the passing of the fantasy that one
'day they would be a boy. They may be concerned about the effect
of tampons on their virginity. Boys may be concerned about
masturbation, the size and shape of the penis, early morning
erections and nocturnal emissions.

Both early and late developers feel the odd one out and different
from their peers. Their sensitivity may provoke other teenagers to
tease them. This can be so pronounced as to lead to an avoidance
of potentially embarrassing situations like games or gymnastics,
where clothes have to be changed in public. However peer group
pressure may overcome inner feelings. One teenager, who always
previously kept herself covered up, agreed to take cold showers with
other girls once she was placed at a boarding school where the
community of girls had approved inflexible rules about showers.
Even so, fortunate is the teenager who is inconspicuously average
amongst the group in terms of physical sexual development.

Self-consciousness and worry about an unusual bodily feature
may get out of proportion if other anxieties are channelled along a
single symptom path. Understanding acceptance of the presenting
symptom is essential if the teenager is to be helped to acknowledge
the underlying worries.

Phases of adolescence

Adolescence is a continuous process of physical, sexual and psychological development. But within this continuity distinct phases are
recognizable. From an environmental viewpoint there is a distinction
between the teenager at school at fifteen and the young worker at
sixteen. Though leaving school provokes an inner change in the
individual's self-awareness, this is not nearly as marked as the distinction made by society between the school child and young worker.

Adolescence can be thought of in three phases, early, middle and
late which merge into one another. In early adolescence girls and
boys keep within their own sex groups. Boys do not contact girls;

they think of them as weak and soft. Boys are troubled by an awareness of sex and aggression and a fear of loss of control (based on
spontaneous erections and emissions). Girls at this stage may develop
a "crush" on another girl and their interest in boys is only just
awakening.

In middle adolescence the girl begins to look for a boy to love.
The girl matures faster and chooses a boy about two years her
senior who will be emotionally at her stage of development. Boys in
middle adolescence remain more aware of their peers. They engage
in competitive activities with other boys and if they do take an
interest in girls, it is only to flaunt their success in front of their
mates.

Late adolescence, around the age of eighteen, is the time when
the adolescent, beginning to be self-aware, seeks solutions to personal
problems on his own. There is by now a greater separation from the
family and a willingness to try out new relationships — practice for
the eventual aim of creating a new family unit (Laufer 1974).

Psychodynamic Themes

Throughout adolescence there are psychodynamic themes forced
into the teenager's mind by the upsurge of sexual interest. This
normally leads to a psychological move away from individual
members of the family towards outsiders. The variability of the
adolescent is so great that sometimes one and sometimes another
theme predominates, but the themes are present in all adolescents.
If a manifest sexual problem exists, one theme will usually occupy
the centre of the adolescent's mental life.

Ego ideal, Regression, Narcissism and Leaps Forward

The individual becomes established as a certain sort of person in
childhood. The average child aged nine or ten feels a correspondence
between how he would like to be (ego ideal) and how he is. Then
puberty brings sexual changes. The force of sexuality creates a gap
between the self and the ego ideal. The individual (ego) regresses
to a more childlike state for protection. There is an upsurge of preoccupation with the self (a state of narcissism) to enable the teenager
to retain his past achievements. But his old childhood ego ideal,

derived from past identifications with the parents, will have to change. During regression of the ego there is self denigration and partial withdrawal from social contact while a solution is found. The impact of the change in aim, which has become sexual, and object (i.e. the individual to whom he is attracted), which has moved from within to outside the family, necessarily causes a change in self concept. Gradually the new adolescent sexual self is accepted and a new ego ideal created. Identifications with people outside the family are added to the original parental identifications. Psychologically less stable solutions where there is a leap into precocious adulthood, or where the teenager turns totally outside to a mystical God for a resolution of the problem are seen from time to time. Occasionally though physical development proceeds the individual gets stuck (fixated) psychologically at a pre-pubertal stage. Such an arrest in development may lead later to adult sexual problems such as non-consummation of marriage.

Super-ego, Splitting

The disciplining and at times disapproving super-ego has been fairly quiet during the years from five to eleven. As the force of developing genital sexuality makes itself felt there is a response from the super-ego which becomes harsher to resist the new movement. The conflict whether or not to respond to genital feelings enhances super-ego activity. Guilt about sexual urges can be extreme.

The force of the super-ego can lead the adolescent to "split" his feelings about people so that one individual may be seen idealistically as totally good, whereas another is recognized as totally bad. The adolescent in the latter case sees all his own bad attributes in the other person and then defiles them.

Oedipus Complex: Idealization

Adolescence is accompanied by revival of the Oedipus complex and a further loosening of pre-Oedipal attachments.

At the age of five or thereabouts, the boy will have had an intense jealous love for the mother. This will have produced a conflict in him, because he is also fond of the father as well as fearing his strength, strength which he feels might be used against him (e.g.

castration). The hostility he feels against the father he imagines
coming back against himself. So the Oedipus complex develops. Its
resolution, necessarily unsatisfactory, involves the decision to give up
the idea of marrying his mother, and instead to grow up to be like his
father and choose to marry someone like his mother. Direct rivalry with
the father is avoided and mourning for the loss of his mother/wife
accepted. In this way is built the taboo against sexual links with
the mother and hence within the family. During the latency period
(seven to eleven) thoughts of a sexual nature though present are
fairly quiet. However with the onset of puberty there is a revival of
all the Oedipal feelings. In some cases the father in adolescence is
once again seen as the threatening figure but the mother too may
assume this guise. She may be seen as seducing and castrating —
certainly dangerous and to be avoided possibly with homosexual
defences, until the ego is stronger.

The Oedipal situation in the girl involves retaining a dependent
link with the mother while elaborating in her mind a sexual link with
the father. The move to the father is brought about in part by the
little girl's discovery that the boy has a penis and she has not. She
envies the boy, blames the mother for the situation and turns to
her father for consolation. At the age of five the little girl has a
romantic image of being in love with and flying away with her
father, balanced by a sense of guilt directed against her mother that
if she were to do this then some awful punishments (possibly painful
and sexual) could happen to her. The resolution of the girl's Oedipal
situation involves an acceptance of and identification with the
mother and a willingness to choose a partner like the father instead
of father himself.

Oedipal fantasies are re-awoken at puberty and the burglar breaking in dream or the man following her in the street are outward signs
of her inner wish and fear. The erotic sensations of puberty often
make it difficult for the girl to accept the normal non-sexual atten-
tions of father. These same feelings re-ignite the hostile feelings
against mother. Should the father on the other hand be seductive
in his manner, the strength of the adolescent girl's feelings may force
her into boy-crazy behaviour to prevent the development of an
incestuous relationship.

Idealization is one aspect of the resolution of the Oedipus
complex. The child in giving up the parent retains an idealized
image. This comes under scrutiny at adolescence. Both girl and boy
have the fantasy of the chaste mother and to some extent make

a distinction between the good (sexually aloof) girl and the bad
(sexually approachable) girl. This attitude results in devaluation of
the partner following sexual activity; all the badness is seen in the
partner and the girl often shuns any form of contact with him
again. An identical process is seen in the young man who seeks
intercourse with a prostitute rather than debase the idealized girl
friend (who stands for the chaste mother, Chapter 19).

Bisexuality

Both boy and girl as they enter adolescence are troubled by bisexual
anxiety. This is caused partly by the inner psychological move from
mother to father and the vacillation between them in the resolution
of the Oedipus complex. The choice of clothes and dress of some
adolescents seems to express a hidden anxiety about sexual role.
At times the uniform of long hair (feminine) tight tattered old Levis
(masculine) makes it difficult to distinguish male from female.

Homosexuality in adolescence may be an expression of bisexual
conflict. More often it is the outcome of narcissistic regression
where ideal love is showered by the teenager onto a younger person
who represents one's own former (pre-pubertal, but now weakened)
ego ideal. Such a relationship can often be the forerunner of a tender
ideal heterosexual love where the chosen person again has some
qualities of the pre-pubertal ego ideal.

Precocious Sexuality

In our culture this is particularly a problem for the teenage girl
because of the undesirable side effect of pregnancy

The theme of adolescent sexual freedom may not be genuine, for
many adolescents feel themselves forced by group pressures into
premature sexual activity. The teenage girl who admits to no sexual
experience is ridiculed by her peers as being odd and in need of
treatment. The need to conform to group pressures is very strong,
but such girls may in later life regret that they were so influenced.
They have a deep sense of guilt based on a sense of distance from
the idealized mother.

Some unhappy adolescent girls regress to a pre-Oedipal state where
they seek the mother's warm embrace. Too easily the boy's embrace

comforts like the mother's and the price of the comfort is sexual intercourse. Sometimes the teenager feels she is angrily shaking off the regressive tie to her mother, but her sexual activity is so obviously comfort seeking rather than genuinely loving another adult being, that the term "pseudo-heterosexuality" can be applied.

Sometimes the girl seeking a sexual relationship is not looking either for sexual gratification or for comfort at a pre-Oedipal level. She wants a baby. She wants someone exclusively of her own both to love and be loved by. Sadly these girls are disappointed for when it comes the baby seems to have the same insatiable demandingness as she experiences within herself.

The girl's developing heterosexual interest may meet an accomplice in the mother. Sometimes parental uncertainty and a wish not to thwart real progress will lead the mother to condone when the teenager wants a halt to be called. Occasionally a mother encourages her daughter so that she can have vicarious pleasure out of escapades which she herself had avoided as a teenager. Parents may seem over anxious about homosexuality and thus encourage precocious heterosexuality to reassure themselves about the sexual "normality" of their children.

Sublimation

The force of the new genital sexual energy in some teenagers demands expression. In others, the energy is an opportunity for sublimation into academic work, music or other notable achievements of adolescence. Postponement of gratification is a key element in the process of sublimation and essential for the individual's development to maturity. It seems that too little sublimation and too early sexual activity in adolescence can result in a failure to realise early promise.

Masturbation

In adolescence nearly all boys and over half the girls masturbate. While doing so there is normally a relationship to other people or situations in a daydream. With the change in attitudes in our society there is now less guilt associated with the physical act of masturbation. The associated fantasies however can worry the teenager. The teenager while masturbating may alternate in imagination between the active male or passive female. At the same time sadomasochistic, exhibitonistic and voyeuristic ideas may occur. Sometimes infantile fantasies occur of defaecating or urinating while masturbating. Incestuous fantasies may also arise. Though there will be guilt in an adolescent having such fantasies, the bizarre nature of the ideas does not at all imply that sexual difficulties will be met in the future.

Sexual Problems of Adolescence

The number and variety of sexual problems of adolescence is as numerous as the different phases and stages of development through which the individual has passed. All adolescents have sexual worries but the majority overcome them without professional help. The teenager finds comfort and support within peer group and family, and manages to work out most problems with their help on his own. It is a minority of teenagers that seeks help with manifest sexual problems.

Only a small part of sex relates to physical factors and intercourse. The adolescent is equally concerned to know how well he or she fulfils the appropriate sexual role in society, as he is about specific genital sexual problems.

The older adolescent is concerned with relationships and how to use sexuality alone or with others. There may be problems around masturbation and heterosexuality. Worries about the possibility of homosexuality are common. Questions about contraception and venereal disease occur.

Talking with Teenagers

Whenever a teenager comes for help the relationship will succeed if it is based on communication and understanding. Berne (1966) pointed out that when relating to another we can do so as a parent, an adult or a child. In work with adolescents it is essential to speak at an accepting adult level, so that the teenager will give his trust. There has to be emphasis on integrity and respect for the other.

Questions are often felt by the adolescent to be intrusive and persecutory and it is better to avoid asking specific sexual questions.

A general review of work, social and family relations will usually
give an understanding of the individual teenager's dilemma. During
the interview it is helpful to listen to what the teenager is saying and
at the same time judge by his manner and attitude the nature of the
unspoken question. The non-verbal cues may enable the counsellor
to find out what the teenager is really thinking.

Advice, even if it is right, is rarely helpful. It is so easily felt by
the teenager as if it comes from the disapproving parent. Even if the
teenager asks a bald question, it is more helpful to ask oneself why
the question is being asked, and then ask him to discuss the question
a little more to help you understand the point better before you
answer. Sometimes in such a way the teenager can find the answer
for himself.

Meeting teenagers with sexual problems often leads to contact
with parents. Most parents would agree that they want their teenage
offspring to grow up and have physical sexual satisfaction within
their ultimate marriage. But a curtain is drawn across adolescence.
The impression is often given that so far as sex is concerned parents
would prefer their children to rush through adolescence and get
safely married before the question of sex is raised at all. The denial
of the existence of adolescent sexuality can be dangerous. Too little
interest in adolescent sexuality leads to unwanted pregnancies.
Certainly early dating associated with lack of adequate sex education
and lack of proper supervision is the recipe for trouble.

Adolescents respect simple rules and guidance even though they
may protest. The teenager whose parents don't care what hours are
kept feels uncared for. Parents should know with whom their teenager is going out, where they are going and when they will be back.
Often the very strict parent having trouble with a sexually active
daughter is severely split in his attitudes. On the one hand there are
unreasonable rules for time-keeping and on the other hand gross
indulgence (e.g. excessive pocket money). It is hard for such a
family to change but an attempt has to be made to establish reasonable adult agreements guided by commonsense between the teenager
and the parents.

Summary

The coming of sexuality in adolescence changes relationships to a
sexual one and gradually leads the teenager to relate more intimately

to people outside the family. At the same time early childhood conflicts and identifications become active again. It is these personal historical feelings and experiences which both determine the nature, and lead to an understanding of, the sexual problems of the adolescent.

Handicapped Adolescent

General

Handicapped adults have sex lives (Chapter 13); so too do handicapped adolescents. The amount of sexual expression shown by the handicapped depends not only on the limitations imposed by the handicap itself, but also on whether those who care for them are able to encourage the development of sexuality.

As the fact of handicapped people having sex lives becomes accepted, questions and doubts are put forward. How can the handicapped be helped with their sex lives? Who should help them? What about the attitudes and beliefs of those who care for the handicapped when questions about sex are raised?

The handicapped are a group of people with many different sorts of physical disabilities which prevent their leading a full normal life. They have a range of disability which extends from minor disfigurement to a total inability to survive without help. The problems of those handicapped people who are necessarily dependent on others because of their disability are being considered here.

The blind are a large group. They come to rely on touch to help them understand the world. The deaf can learn from vision but should there be a dual handicap — affecting both vision and hearing — then the person is severely hindered in learning ability.

The physically handicapped form a large mixed group. Some are congenitally physically handicapped and are born with disabilities, (e.g. Spina bifida, limb deficiencies). The thalidomide children born with varying degrees of limb deficiency (and often other handicaps as well) form a special group. The most severely affected have no arms or legs, just a rudimentary finger at the shoulder or toe at the hip, and are usually intellectually normal. Some less severely affected have legs but no arms. Some physical handicaps are acquired, for instance following accidents (e.g. road traffic accidents) or infections such as poliomyelitis which leaves the individual with varying degrees of disability. A large group of people with a mixed physical and intellectual handicap are the spastics. Their locomotor and co-ordination disabilities dominate the clinical picture and tend to make the intellectual retardation seem more severe than it is. Though very dependent on outsiders for help their residual abilities can be used to encourage independence in many areas of their lives.

The list of causes of disability is large but when it comes to helping the handicapped person what matters is the amount and distribution of normal motor and sensory function still intact. It is on these remaining positive assets that any rehabilitation programme is built whether it is concerned with a work task or with developing the individual's sexual activity.

Right to Full Life

A moment's reflection makes it clear that the physical and psychological changes of puberty described in the first part of this chapter occur with undiminished force in the handicapped adolescent. However there has only recently come about a more open acceptance of the sexuality of adults and teenagers who have major physical or mental handicaps. People are beginning to accept that the great majority of handicapped individuals have as full sexual fantasies, urges, wishes and bodily responses as their able bodied peers.

In looking after a handicapped person, the professionals may unwittingly encourage regression to an infantile state. In our society the non-handicapped adult plays his part in a comparable way by giving up his clothes when he goes into hospital and then stays in bed, thus becoming an asexual non-aggressive being. It helps the nurses to care for people if they remain in such an asexual dependent role. Signs that the individual is about to leave hospital are the return of ordinary day clothes. Possibly at the same time more adult exchanges occur with the nursing staff. The same tendency to infantilize the handicapped individual is often difficult to resist. But he is not ill or a patient at all. Physical or mental handicaps are certainly disadvantages but they are not "illness". Recognizing this means that the handicapped should not be nursed, but rather educated and led out into as full and enriching a life as possible. In the area of sexual behaviour and practice handicapped individuals are capable of much more than we have been prepared to recognize in the past. But if they are going to realize this potential, education, advice and practical physical help are necessary. Such help will succeed only if it is given with a sensitive understanding of underlying psychological difficulties.

Overprotection

The acceptance of the infantile role by the handicapped dovetails with the overprotection shown by the caring staff, whether they are professionals in an institution, or relations of the handicapped person looking after him in his own home. Being overprotective to a handicapped person is never kind. They need enough help to support them through a current obstacle and then must be allowed to make their own way. The thalidomide child lacking legs is well able to move about a room and if he wants or needs to be lifted onto a chair, he will ask. Some who care for the handicapped feel so guilty in themselves that they do too much for the very people they are trying to help. In a private home this quickly leads to a "hot-house" atmosphere and in an institution to a "warehouse" atmosphere (Greengross, 1975) where even tasks the handicapped can perform are denied him. It is striking how often the more overprotective the method of care, the greater resistance there is on the part of those who look after them, to encouraging handicapped teenagers to find out about sex.

Positive Help

The end is not merely survival, the end is to live and survival is merely the means to it (Fleming, 1973). It is now accepted that we should promote as full a life as possible for the handicapped person up to the limit that his handicaps will allow. This puts a different emphasis on caring as it implies a searching out of new ways to overcome obstacles. The disabled do not want sympathy and consolation (Rosenheim, 1973) from professional staff. They want positive help in the shape of knowledge and hard facts. They need to feel the caring professionals are fighting for them in an imaginative way to develop new methods of overcoming their problems.

Sexual Feelings

The handicapped have the same hopes and feelings, fantasies and fears, doubts and anxieties about sexual matters as the rest of the

population. They too live in a society where sexual titillation is
normal and accepted. Feelings are aroused in the handicapped and
ways have to be sought to allow gratification, release and understanding.

All human beings whether or not they are handicapped have a
sexual drive. This sex drive exists in children and continues into old
age. It is individual, varying from very weak in some people to very
strong in others. All people have a sex life in whatever way it may be
constituted — heterosexual relationships, homosexual relationships,
masturbation or sublimation (Rea, 1973). And this is equally true
for the handicapped. As other people learn to come to terms with
their sexuality so too do the handicapped.

Previous Attitudes to Sexuality of the Handicapped

It used to be felt that it was unfair to burden the handicapped
individual with knowledge of things he could never fully experience
himself. Sometimes those caring for the handicapped found the
thought of those distorted bodies or backward minds involved in
sexual union deeply disturbing. Thus the topic would be swept
under the carpet because of embarrassment in the caring staff. But it
is the handicapped who suffer when an area of life has to remain
closed because of resistance in those who care for them.

Some have argued against discussing sex with the handicapped.
(1) As marriage is not for the disabled then there is no need to talk
about sex. (2) Discussion of sex might cause promiscuity in the handicapped. (3) Knowledge about sexual matters should not be given
because it would be of no practical use. (4) Physical sex is an important expression of an independent person, and as the handicapped
will always be dependent for physical help, there can be no sexual
life for them.

The handicapped person's life is expanded or restricted by those
who care for him. However much the handicapped individual may
wish to be involved in sexual activity, if such activity calls for outside
assistance then whether and how well the activity succeeds depends
to a large extent on the attitude of the caring staff. These points
emphasize how much of the resistance to a sexual life for the handicapped lies in the attitude and beliefs of those who look after them.
Any attempt to help the handicapped with sexual problems needs
to have a twin aim of simultaneously helping both the disabled

person and the person who looks after him. In this way a fuller age appropriate normal sexual life may be developed and encouraged.

Education/Psychotherapy

Psychotherapy always has an element of relearning within it and in this sense is educational. But a strong educational bias is needed when it comes to working with the sexual problems of the handicapped adolescent. Often in the past, indications that help was needed for a psychosexual problem in the handicapped was dealt with by straight denial of the fact that disabled people have sex lives at all, and so there could not be any problem. Workers with the handicapped today need to be good listeners and also authoritative suppliers of correct information about sex.

Sources of Information

All developing children and adolescents, whether or not they are handicapped, are picking up information about sex all the time. Some information comes from the classroom, some from home and peers. A major source of information is the growth, changes and feelings experienced in the developing body and the ideas and fantasies thereby awakened. There can be no question of choice whether handicapped people should be taught about sex, or not. It is happening already. This being the case, there can be no effective argument against handicapped people receiving honest, full information on all subjects including sex, to the limit of their ability. If that is not done they will continue to be ignorant or hear half-truths, myths and distortions that cause great human suffering (Wagner, 1974). The important questions are who should do the teaching and what and how much to teach?

Who Should Teach?

Those professionals in contact with handicapped adolescents have a responsibility to guide and inform them about sex. It is unlikely that parents will do this; as a survey of non-handicapped adolescents showed that nearly 70% of the boys and 30% of the girls had no advice on sex whatsoever from their parents (Schofield, 1968).

Furthermore, the same survey showed that if the parents have not given any instruction by twelve or thirteen years then it is highly unlikely they will ever do so. Knowing the psychological difficulties faced by parents of handicapped children in the area of sex education it is essential that the professionals should broach the subject and give a firm lead.

The experienced teacher presents new material in a form and at a rate appropriate to the age and knowledge of the pupil. The same principle holds good for helping the handicapped teenager learn about sex. But questions about sex are not necessarily directed at a teacher — the topic tends to come up almost anywhere. So it is that parents, nurses, ward cleaners or other staff, may suddenly find themselves being asked questions which they find outside their competence to answer. They need to have a back up of formal discussions with a skilled leader to enable them to respond to questions in a positive manner. The atmosphere of a unit for the handicapped can in this way be helped towards being more open and frank about sex.

What to Teach?

The content of what is taught reflects the objectives of the teacher. Psychosexually mature people show evidence of responsible, mature sexual attitudes and behaviour appropriate to the culture in which they live. There can be no reason for aiming at less for the handicapped adolescent.

Teachers and others may be comfortable talking about anatomy, physiology and reproduction. Undeniably this is a necessary starting point. But all adolescents, and the handicapped are no exception, want to know about other things. The question of how much to teach about masturbation, hetero- and homosexuality has to be faced. The living part of sex (not reproduction) is what fascinates the teenager and this is what he wants to learn about. It can help the teacher decide what to teach if he accepts that the handicapped adolescent already knows quite a lot about sexual practices, some of the information being wrong. To leave him with faulty information may lead to educational and sexual problems in addition to his other handicaps. Surely it is wise to make certain that a handicapped adolescent has as full an account of correct information about himself and his body as possible.

There can never be a simple rule of thumb to cover what to teach

for all handicapped adolescents. Different teenagers require different
information at different stages of development. The right balance has
to be found for each teenager somewhere along a continuum between denying their sexuality utterly and going overboard in an
excess of instruction. The person who is comfortable with his or her
own sexuality can be sensitively aware of each teenager's development and be ready to raise and discuss certain topics when the
moment seems right.

Adjust Teaching to the Individual

Whoever is working with a handicapped adolescent will be effective
if one major difference is born in mind. The handicapped child
and teenager has very little if any opportunity for exploring and
discovering about sex on his own. His non-handicapped peer in
contrast has almost limitless opportunity for finding out things
about sex away from adults, alone, or with a companion. It is a duty
of the professionals concerned to make sure that extra instruction
is given to compensate for this lack of independence. The handicapped individual gets our support to surmount his physical handicaps and explore the world about him. The same support should be
given in the exploration and finding out about sex.

   Close to every handicapped teenager is a parent, anxious about his
or her child. All advice, education or therapy must have parental
agreement otherwise it may fail. Parents need to feel they are included in and know about any programme of instruction. Showing
them the material and discussing progress not only gets their agreement but also ensures knowledgeable co-operation when the teenager asks them questions which they might otherwise find difficult.

   The helping person, knowing the normal states of adolescent
sexual development, will have the aim of enabling the handicapped
person to approximate towards the normal. When thinking of the
disabled we need to think positively about what they can do — and
then ask what they may do given a little more help.

Particular Instances

Each handicap has its own special problems to be met and overcome.
There are very many different kinds and degrees of handicap and
the worker needs not only to know the individual well but also the

limitations imposed by the handicapping condition before informed help can be given.

The severely physically handicapped person who is chair-bound due to poliomyelitis or spina bifida might well find the task of bringing up children too much. Yet this same person can be sexually active given appropriate help. The same applies to individuals with a traumatic paralysis, and to the fortunately rare individual with a congenital absence of limbs. Adolescents with such handicaps need discussion of their sexuality appropriate to their age and disability. They may need help over the practice of masturbation. When as older adolescents they start petting, if they pair with another handicapped teenager, they may need practical help positioning themselves and especially they need privacy.

Even if a handicapped teenager is physically incapable of achieving an erection this does not necessarily mean that he is incapable of becoming a sexual human being (Jackson, 1972). However he could not have the normal goal of heterosexual intercourse. Clearly heavy petting is less satisfactory than full intercourse, but if from physical causes no more is possible, who is to deny the individual that pleasure?

Mental retardation (IQ 40—70 range) presents the same question of non reproductive sex, and raises the question whether these people can handle information about human sexuality responsibly. If they are denied full information about this important area of their lives we hinder their opportunity to be more complete human beings. Without full information and understanding they are more likely to be influenced by impulse. Knowledge is more likely to protect them than to lead them astray.

The blind present a difficult problem. The blind develop heightened powers of hearing and touch in the mastery of their world. The blind learn to have some sense of "seeing" the other person by running a hand over the face. How is the blind adolescent to learn about differences between males and females? Their opportunity to play "doctor" games is limited as they cannot know when they are being watched or if they are alone.

Advantages of Full Information

Adolescents with handicaps need more active teachers than the non handicapped to compensate for their disability and their lack of freedom to explore and experiment. With such help the handicapped learn to cope adequately with their own sexuality. Full information about sex given honestly and frankly to the handicapped teenager has two main benefits:

(a) it allows understanding and hopefully mastery of otherwise incomprehensible bodily urges and psychological feelings and attitudes;
(b) it builds self esteem so that they feel better accepted by their peers and with fuller knowledge they are less vulnerable to sexual exploitation.

Groups of Handicapped Adolescents

Attitudes of Staff

The attitude of the staff plays a central part in deciding how the handicapped adolescents will come to regard sexuality. Once staff acknowledge that sexual education of a sort is occurring all the time they will be able to make a choice about giving deliberate instruction. Knowledge in itself can never be harmful. It is faulty application of knowledge which harms. If the information is too advanced it will go over the pupil's head.

Most staff in adolescent units have some qualms about dealing with sexuality in their charges. The recollection of their own or their parents' embarrassment about these things can be worked through. More fixed ideas against sexuality generally might well call for a transfer to a different work place.

The staff need to think positively about what the handicapped teenagers can do and what they may be able to do with a little more imaginative help. They need to help the adolescents conform to sexual and other behaviour appropriate to the developmental stage reached.

Fostering Sexuality

When they begin to show an interest in each other, boys and girls should be allowed to hold hands, kiss and share much of their life together. But sensible limits as in any family should be imposed. Thus the young adolescents should know that a line is drawn both between public and private behaviour and the difference between teenage and adult behaviour. Although the teenagers may sit beside each other on a coach ride they are not allowed too long cuddling on a sofa together.

Occasionally the problem of excessive masturbation is raised, but an individual doing too much of any normal human activity is in trouble, be it smoking, drinking, eating or working. The problem usually lies in the factors which allow him too much time on his own.

The theme is that the handicapped are entitled to as much freedom in their emotional and sexual life as the non-handicapped enjoy.

There needs to be a steady increase in freedom given to the older handicapped adolescent both in general and in sexual terms. More and better boarding accommodation is needed and the rooms should be large enough and private. The young adult handicapped person is clearly going to wish for some form of sexual activity and this applies too to the older adolescent. The attitudes of the caring staff will decide at what age such a freedom can be allowed.

Unresolved Problems — Physical Help

Kinsey emphasized that masturbation occurs in nearly all men and over 60% of women. A problem arises when a handicaped adolescent wishes to masturbate but is unable to do so because of physical handicap. Some have taken the view that in such cases it is the duty of professional staff to carry out the teenager's wishes. There can be no general answer to this question. Each individual and the people who look after him have to make their own decision after considering all the facts.

The older handicapped adolescent may wish to have a physical heterosexual or homosexual contact but is unable to arrange this privately without help because of the severity of the disability. The non-handicapped older teenager is well able to choose when, where, and with whom, to engage in sexual activity. The handicapped adolescent can rely on the vigorous support of those caring for him if there is a wish expressed to go to a theatre, or visit a library. But what happens when the wish is to go to bed with someone else — and this cannot be achieved without help from an able bodied person? There is no simple answer to this or other difficult questions. But by being involved in a dialogue about such problems, some difficulties grappled with may disappear. Some may remain.

Summary

The handicapped adolescent has the same sexual development and feelings as the non-handicapped. It is a right of the handicapped to be educated and led into as full a sexual life as possible. Being aware of the lack of freedom to explore sexually on their own, the handicapped deserve full instruction. The sexual problems of the handicapped are often inextricably entwined with the confused sexual attitudes of those who care for them. Being sexual means more than just heterosexual coitus. Sexual problems of the handicapped can be resolved by the enlightened application of skills derived from education, psychotherapy and nursing.

References

Berne, E. (1966) "Games People Play." Andre Deutsch: London.

Blos, P. (1962). "On Adolescence. A Psychoanalytic Interpretation." The Free Press: New York; Collier-Macmillan Ltd: London.

Brown, F. (1972). Sexual problems of the adolescent girl, *Pediatric Clinics North America* 19, 3, 759—764.

Casson, F. R. C. (1964). "Sex and Adolescence." W. & G. Foyle Ltd: London.

Connell, E. B. *et al.* (1971). Pregnancy, the teenager and sex education, *American Journal of Public Health* 61, 9, 1840—1845.

Deutsch, H. (1968). "Selected Problems of Adolescence." The Hogarth Press and The Institute of Psychoanalysis: London.

Fleming, W. L. S. (1973). Physical disability — the challenge and the response. *Proceedings Royal Society of Medicine*, 66, 132—133.

Fox, J. (1971). Sex education — But for what?, *Special Education* 60,2, 15—17.

Garrett, J. (1971). Sex education: a second opinion, *Special education*, 60, 3, 16—17.

Greengross, W. (1975). Sex problems of the disabled, *Rehabilitation* 93, 9—13.

Howells, J. G. (1971). Modern Perspective in Adolescent Psychiatry." Oliver and Boyd: Edinburgh.

Jackson, R. W. (1972). Sexual rehabilitation after cord injury, *Paraplegia* 10, 50—55.

Knight, L. (1975). A kind of loving, *Community Care* 70, 16—19.

Laufer, M. (1974). "Becoming a Separate Person in Adolescence." Monograph 5, Brent Consultation Centre: London.

Masham of Ilton (1973). Physical disability — the challenge and the response. The psychological and practical aspects of sex and marriage for the paraplegic, *Proceedings Royal Society Medicine*, 66, 133—136.

Miller, D. (1974). "Adolescence. Psychology, Psychopathology and Psychotherapy." Jason Arouson Inc: New York.

Nash, D. (1975). Expectations for the handicapped adolescent. Spina bifida: training for adult life, *Proceedings Royal Society Medicine.* 68, 317—319.

Rosenheim, Lord (1973). Physical disability — the challenge and the response. *Proceedings Royal Society of Medicine,* 66, 131—132.

Schofield, M. (1968). "The Sexual Behaviour of Young People." Penguin Books: Harmondsworth.

Secker, L. (1973). Sex education and mental handicap. *Special Education* 62, 1, 27—28.

Semmens, J. *et al.* (1972). Sex education of the adolescent female. *Paediatric Clinics North America* 19, 3, 765—778.

Wagner, N. (1974). "Sex education for handicapped people." Inform 5, FPA National Information Resource Centre: London.

Wolfish, M. (1973). Adolescent sexuality, *Practitioner* 210, 1256, 226—231.

6 Sexual Problems of Young Adults

PHILIP CAUTHERY

Post-Adolescence

The years of young adulthood correspond to the stage of personal development known as post-adolescence. What has to be achieved in these years is the integration and synthesis of all the strands of earlier development and the implementation of life-tasks in the external world. Instinctual needs and personal interests come to be organized in a relatively harmonious manner within the self and within the context of the environment (Blos, 1962). The psychic structure becomes stabilized and the individual begins to settle down.

The stage is thus the final step towards maturity and the individual, with all his increasingly evident uniqueness, accommodates to society and finds his own place within it. Dependence on the parental generation and other external resources lessens and sustainment from within increases (Parens, 1970). The right of the emergent adult to assume responsibility for himself is recognized. Self-reliance, self-esteem and personal dignity increase and in many instances genuine friendship with the parents is established as between other adults. Re-evaluations of attitudes on both sides often lead to the discovery of a surprising degree of mutual admiration between parents and children and this state, combined with its underlying goodwill, is undoubtedly the best and healthiest termination to the child/parent relationship.

Detachment from Parents

Some parents and some children cannot achieve the degree of detachment necessary to establish the young adult on his own feet. In the case of "parental adhesion", which is maintained with bribes and threats, the child must either break the relationship himself or be committed to a prolonged adolescence in which he either remains with the parents or, even if he partly escapes into marriage, is subject to parental direction, criticism and control. The condition of "child adhesion" is usually associated with serious disturbances in the earlier child/parent relationship, in which the parents, due to partial rejection, have undermined the child's confidence by their criticisms and hostility. As Schonfeld (1966) discovered, this may manifest itself in profound disturbances of the body-image, which must frequently result in a diminution of the capacity to form relationships outside the home. This is true of both sexes although exceptions may be those women who remain single and who Knupfer *et al.* (1966) found more likely than married women or men to have had a happy childhood; they differ from other women in their degree of "moral strictness".

The disorders which underlie failures of the parent/child separation process carry with them high risks of diminished or deviant sexuality in the child.

Sexual and Emotional Changes

Adolescents have to contend with their body changes and enhanced sexuality; they do so with varying degrees of success. For most, the period involves the acceptance of themselves and their sexuality, in the form of masturbation at first, but eventually members of the opposite sex are involved in most cases. Contrary to popular prejudice the stage is usually one of slow heterosexual progress and experimentation.

Sexual experimentation may well continue into young adulthood and relationships with potential love objects represent all possible combinations of degraded, idealized, sexual and tender love (Blos, 1962). For most young adults, however, the aim to obtain relief from sexual tension with the assistance of the opposite sex is increasingly subordinated to the increasing desire to establish a significant emotional relationship.

Forerunners of this desire are often seen in adolescence but the necessary emotional capacity to establish and sustain a relationship does not appear to be available until the end of adolescence. The reason is almost undoubtedly the lack of final integration in the adolescent and the relationship with the parents which still occupies a part of his capacity. This is not to say, of course, that adolescents are incapable of loving a member of the opposite sex, indeed they may do so to the limit of their emerging capacities, but elements of fantasy limit the perception of reality and the situation is further confused by factors such as girls exaggerating their loving feelings in order to reduce sexual guilt, and the tendency for adolescent love affairs to reflect the total life situation (Duvall, 1964). A fair summary might be to say that whereas adolescents are learning both in fact and fantasy how to express their sexuality and their loving feelings, the young adult must begin to integrate them, not only together but with his personality and his environment.

Various factors assist in bringing about the change. For one thing, masturbation and emotionally insignificant heterosexual activity become less satisfying. Earlier romantic fantasies give way to more practical considerations concerning the establishment of a significant relationship. Interest in such a relationship and the conscious desire for it increases, first in girls and later in boys. The period spanning the last portion of late adolescence and the early part of young adulthood can be a very trying time for girls in which they are prone to fears that they will not be wanted and will not be loved by anyone. Minor reverses in their relationships can precipitate disproportionate depression and this measures their real preoccupation with this need. More superficially they may deny any such intent and indeed many do manage to retain a sense of balance about it and can be increasingly relied upon not to enter ill-considered relationships in the hope of filling the need. However, in love as in sex, it is the increasing consciousness of desire and need which overcomes fears and furnishes the motivation to face up to the problem and solve it.

Another factor, and a very surprising one at first sight, is the manner in which the high-water mark of the sex drive is reached and passed around this time, at least in males (Kinsey, 1948). Currently available statistics do not show the same phenomenon in the female; she seems to be still building up to her sex peak. However, clinical psychosexual practice would support the supposition made by Sturgis (1907) long ago that our conventions make it less possible for females to provide easily the necessary information about their sexual practices on which an accurate statistical picture could be constructed. In fact, clinical evidence, admittedly somewhat limited, suggests, as would be predicted on developmental grounds, that the female reaches her peak during, or soon after, mid-adolescence. It is as if the rising tide of sexuality in the earlier portion of adolescence pushes the individual into what might be termed "practical sex" i.e. physical contact, perhaps not amounting to intercourse, with the opposite sex. As the tide begins to ebb, emotional considerations begin to acquire importance over purely physical drives.

The freedom so gained permits a concomitant reduction in dependence on the super-ego for exercising moral control. Combined with increasing self-confidence this makes it possible for the young adult to proceed in the task of creating an effective relationship. Physical attractiveness and availability alone are insufficient to necessarily establish a relationship — and discrimination between potential partners is increasingly based on considerations of personality. Ideally, a relationship so established should have a chance of yielding continuing and ever increasing satisfaction to the partners over the years, with all its benefits to social stability and child rearing, but the proportion of successful marriages is variously estimated to range from 75% to 10%. The causes of failure often have distant origins in childhood, and may be related to the parents' own marriage (Woodruff et al., 1972), but better management of post-adolescent relationships by the individual could, perhaps, have prevented the failure. Lederer (1973), gives the causes as the wrong (i.e. incompatible) people marrying for the wrong reasons (i.e. romance and sex only) under a system which is poorly adapted to modern life.

For most people young adulthood is, biographically, the stage of serious courtship and the early days of marriage. Since this chapter is not directly concerned with marriage it receives no further consideration as such but the pre-marital stage clearly has implications for what follows.

Maturity

Chronologically, young adulthood commences around 19 to 21 years in women and 20 to 23 years in men. Although not everyone would agree it is probably best to regard it as ending with first childbirth in women or at about 25 years. In men its termination is vague and with some it seems to extend even into old-age. For most, perhaps, it ends between 25 and 30 years. The mean age at first marriage is 22.72 years in women and 24.86 years in men.

The young adult is not fully mature. The stage ends when maturity is achieved. Maturity has been described by Saul (1971) and my views have been expressed elsewhere (Cauthery, 1973). Although the component structures of the psyche are mainly in fixed form, the young adult's adaptability is derived from the relationships between the structures and the ego not yet being organized in permanent fashion.

This permits further learning and adjustment. It is of especial value to the early man-women relationship; for example, the attitudes and interests of couples become more similar as a relationship progresses than they were before it was established (Snyder, 1966).

Some of this necessary flexibility probably derives from the re-evaluation of parents. For example, in most families the late-adolescent daughter is not able to perceive the mother as a sexual being like herself. She tends to regard herself as "bad" and her mother as "good". The inhibitory effect of this childish view is lost when the mother is more accurately perceived. Similarly, as Blos (1962) observes, a girl who earlier rejected domesticity might suddenly discover she is a good housekeeper and say she learned it from her mother.

In these ways new patterns of interaction with a member of the opposite sex become possible and these are extensions, rather than repetitions, of, especially, the earlier relationship with the opposite sex parent. Many fail to acquire this capacity, for one reason or another. For example, a man may expect a women who claims she loves him to continuously mother him and take responsibility for him, being resentful or spiteful at any sign of refusal or rebellion.

With the possible exception of intercourse apart, the larger adaptive change is probably required from the young adult male. From clinical experience it seems that one very important adaptation is the shedding of his fear of the female which is primarily, but not solely, founded partly on reality-based fears of his experience of his mother as a child and partly on oedipal apprehensions. It is a vital step in the achievement of male maturity. Once it is attained his male ego is strenghtened and women are no longer seen either as a challenge or as prey. He can then respond flexibly, constructively and maturely to his partner's needs, distresses, moods and criticisms. The way is open to realistic understanding and real care, which is friendship. Severe failure paves the way for subsequent neglect, sulking, hostility and even partner-battering, all of which are immature modes of response to difficulty and conflict. Some men never attain a state where they can withstand any threat, challenge, apparent rejection or criticism from a woman but respond with depression or massive anger. The woman is thus deprived of the right of free self-expression and loses love into the bargain. The root cause is the man's inability to perceive, emotionally, women as anything but mothers. The equivalent failure in women is less disastrous since it simply leaves the woman somewhat over-dependent and perhaps a little fearful. In fact, it is generally true that the woman's personality is of less importance than the man's in marital success.

The chief aspect of the maturational process for the young adult, then, is the establishment of a capacity to relate to a member of the opposite sex as a whole person and on a fairly realistic basis which is not over-influenced by physical needs or by the negative aspects of the earlier relationship with the opposite sex parent.

Premature and Immature Relationships

Because industrialization is making our society increasingly complex it follows that adjustment towards it is becoming more prolonged and difficult. The attainment of social maturity, particularly educationally and economically, is being delayed whilst biological maturity and marriage are occurring earlier.

However, just as clinical experience shows that is is good advice to the adolescent not to rush into intercourse, so it is good advice to the young adult to avoid too early commitment to marriage. The intervening period should be used to learn more about the self and the opposite sex through relationships. This is an important contribution to the attainment of ultimate happy marriage (Burgess and Cottrell, 1939). One danger is that the termination of a relationship which one partner wished to continue can damage the self-esteem, sometimes irreparably. Nevertheless, premature marriage is associated with a high risk of divorce.

It could be argued that provided there are no children divorce is little different to a broken engagement or terminated affair. Often there are children and even if the dangers of divorce to children have been over-emphasized, the findings of Chester (1971) indicate that divorce hurts the individuals involved to a greater extent than is usually accepted and leads to high psychiatric referral rates in both sexes (Robertson, 1974). Fletcher (1973, p. 156), shows that although the pattern of divorce following early marriage is the same as for other groups it is much higher and the risk even after 25 years of marriage is still higher than for all other groups. The factors which contribute to premature marriage evidently contribute to its failure.

Clinically the most glaring common features leading to early marriage are ego-weakness and seriously unresolved conflicts concerning the parents. Girls, as is well known, may marry early to escape from home or because they feel no-one else will want them unless they take the present opportunity. Some, contrary to their conscious attitudes and actual behaviour, are found to feel so guilty that they wish to obtain religious and legal sanction for their sexual activities. Boys involved in early marriage are usually found to be over-fearful of competition with other males, for which they may over-compensate in some way, and to be more than averagely ambivalent towards their parents or sometimes a sister. The sexual impulse is usually fairly weak. In most cases the male still feels inferior to women and ashamed of his sexual needs for them. Only the prior offer of marriage permits him to make advances and is aimed at disarming the woman so that she will accept and not injure him.

To him women are powerful and fear inspiring although his underlying attitudes may be of hostility to them. In lesser form the same motivation is found behind the behaviour of those boys, and men, who profess love to a woman on short acquaintance.

In early marriages the woman is usually, sooner rather than later, over-burdened with a child for whom she tries to do her immature best. Pregnancy is often the precipitating cause of the marriage and the conception may not have been as accidental as it appears at first sight. It is sometimes wilfully induced by the boy in order to secure the relationship and obligate the girl to him for marrying her. Girls who are disadvantaged in ways other than pregnancy are also attractive to such males for the same reason. It is becoming much less common for girls to risk pregnancy, or even pretend they are pregnant, to force marriage.

Coombs *et al.* (1970) found that in the US, at least, the presence of a pre-marital pregnancy, which is common in young marriage, imposes a disadvantage on the marriage at whatever age it occurs. This is partly explained on economic grounds due to the loss of the wife's earnings. Young marriage is associated with meagre education and this also has economic implications.

Thus escape, guilt and fear of being unwanted by the opposite sex are motivations towards early marriage as is the desire to increase the sense of personal identity and self-worth to compensate for feelings of inferiority. After the marriage the male is usually excessively jealous and restrictive, often being worse than the girl's father. Even so, both partners are likely to become involved with others and the marriage drags to an end, more or less in poverty and perhaps with the wife being battered (Scott, 1974). The highest rates of divorce are found where marriage has been postponed until the woman is at term (Christensen and Meissner, 1953).

The immaturity of those who marry too early is usually obvious. Frequently less obvious is the immaturity which is present in some individuals chronologically well past adolescence. In general their relationships follow the pattern of the premature marriage by reason of their instability, ambivalence, weak sense of personal or sexual identity, excessive dependence, narcissism, egocentricity and unresolved personal conflicts.

Where the opportunity arises, perhaps because an abortion is considered, doctors and counsellors placed in contact with couples intending this form of marriage can endeavour to influence the situation by discovering and treating the underlying causes and discussing the facts. Usually a great deal of resistance is encountered.

Romantic Love

Early and/or inappropriate marriage — as well as some extra-marital liaisons — may be the product of an excess of romantic love or the emphasis on the love aspect of the relationship may disguise guilt about sexual needs. Our culture has received the blame due to its pre-occupation with "love-at first sight" in everything from fairy stories to films.

A distinction is to be drawn between real love and the condition of being in love with love. The first is the product of interaction with a more or less realistically perceived object whereas the latter is more concerned with a largely object-independent fantasy.

The young will usually respond to counselling in this state.

Partner Selection

If sex is regarded as the manifold differences between the sexes,
then the most momentous sexual problem of the young adult is
partner choice. Counsellors and others frequently become involved
in the problem one way or another. For example, a young person
making a suicidal gesture because of insecurity in his or her relationship may need assistance in evaluating that relationship.

A certain amount of (although still too little) research has been
undertaken in this area and the main conclusions to emerge are that
the more nearly homogamous, or similar, the individuals are in
origin, rearing, attitudes, abilities, ambition and so on, the better
the chance of the association affording stable satisfaction. May and
Childs (1972) furnish a neat example of the consequence of a lack
of homogamy in IQ where the wife on the WAIS was found to be 73
and the husband 134. He interpreted her incompetence as failure
to make the necessary effort to improve and she attempted suicide
in a state of depression arising from his criticisms.

Although some investigators dispute the importance of homogamy
it is probable that similar people from similar backgrounds are more
likely to meet through similar social, occupational and recreational
interests. It is also probable that friendships are more likely between
such individuals and that it is easier for them to assess each other
fairly realistically. Mutual adaptation should also be easier. What is
less obvious, although striking clinically, is the unconscious estimates
which are made, especially in respect of sexuality. Contrary to any
superficial appearances which may be present, it recurrently emerges
in psychosexual work that men and women tend to become involved
with individuals of similar sexual tastes and drives to their own. This
emerges even if their sexual compatability has not been put to the
test. In spite of this advantage Landis (1946) found that sexual
adjustment takes longer than any other adjustment.

The initial attraction is undoubtedly physical but it is extraordinarily difficult to discover what the real basis of this may be in
any particular individual. For example, a man who claims to be
fascinated by large breasts and who, perhaps, functions with maximal
arousal and pleasure with such a partner may nevertheless fall in love
and enjoy even better sexual experiences with a woman with small
breasts. Although men emphasize physical factors it seems that the
overall impression counts most after adolescence. In biological terms
it would seem reasonable to suppose that the female is the decorated

and therefore the exhibitionist sex. She, in this sense, is the seducer
and the various lures she uses are, according to the artists, most
pleasing in the years of young adulthood. The signals she transmits
have been classified by Crook (1972) as distant e.g. body form, gait,
breast deportment, middle-distant e.g. voice, complexion and close
e.g. eye glitter, body flush, scent, areolar tumescence, etc.

Whereas adolescent girls are almost invariably critical of their
bodies and general appearance, the young adult woman is more
realistic and less prone to neurotic over-concern. The reason could
be that most have proved their ability to attract males before adolescence ends combined with the relative de-emphasis on sex as other
characteristics become of increasing importance.

The female, thus, attracts attention to herself and arouses sexual
interest. She is then in the position to accept or reject the advances
that are made. In this sense she exercises sexual selection. Her fear
is that no advances will be made — while for the man the main fear is
of rejection.

These fears are a real problem for adolescents but by young adulthood some skill should have been acquired in dealing with them. Ill-
favoured, isolated, under-confident, depressive and socially-graceless
individuals have special difficulties and some can be helped by
therapy of various forms or even by the better "friendship and
marriage" bureaux. It is a pity that these are not more highly developed,
more scientifically managed and more widely accepted than they are,
as is the case, for example, in Germany and Egypt.

Clinical experience indicates that once an association has been
established it is better if sexual progress is fairly slow and that more
attention is paid to the personalities and interests involved. Quite a
lot of work has been carried out on the prediction of successful
relationships but, in practice, it can probably be reduced to five
questions; if the answers to these are mutually and strongly affirma-
tive, it can be predicted that the relationship is likely to be good.

1. Sex apart, could a strong and enduring friendship be established?
2. Is the partner fully acceptable to friends and parents?
3. Is there evidence of mutual contentment and happiness based
on non-physical aspects of the relationship?
4. Is there an equally strong physical attraction on both sides and
is this of a fairly similar character?
5. Are the discrepancies between the partner and the individual's
concept of the ideal partner maturely and realistically perceived

and are they within the adaptive capacities of the individual to
overcome.

Various estimates have been made of the proportion of the opposite sex with whom a successful relationship could be created. These
vary from the "one in a million" of the women's magazine romance
to the statement by Blacker (1958) that 65—75% of individuals
would make good general-purpose husbands or wives no matter who
they married. A further 25—35% need a rather special kind of
spouse and 1—3% are virtually unmarriagable. He studied 8,000
case notes at the Maudsley Hospital and estimated the percentage
of broken marriages by diagnostic category. The average for the
whole group was just over 10% but psychotics constituted 7.5%,
psychoneurotics 10.1% and the personality disorders 22.5%. The
sexually deviant men were only just above the average at 12%. It
could be concluded from this that good relationships will tolerate
sexual disorders (and serious psychiatric illness) whilst disturbed
interpersonal relationships are highly destructive. Blood and Wolfe
(1960), in their survey of over 900 US marriages similarly found
that few relationships can withstand attacks on the partner's personal
behaviour. All this again stresses that relationships are primarily
between people rather than genitals and so the question of the proportion of the opposite sex with whom a successful relationship
is possible revolves round personality and not sexual factors. The
true answer is probably that it is most related to his or her capacity
to form friendly relations with others, especially of his or her own
type, and freedom from negative attitudes towards the opposite
sex. In fact, the more the opposite sex is valued the better. Occasionally isolates or inadequates create excellent relationships with each
other, the sum being infinitely greater than the parts.

Young Adult Sexuality

However, physical sex is of importance in young adult relationships
and its role therefore needs further definition. On questioning, a
surprisingly large proportion — over a third — report that they do
not find sexual activity particularly satisfying. Schofield (1973), in
re-questioning 376 young adults (age 24—26 years) of the 790
sample interviewed seven years earlier as adolescents (17.6—19.6

years), found that 88% (95% of those with experience) enjoyed sex but that 41% had reservations; 5% did not enjoy it at all.

In clinical practice, young women who do not enjoy sex are largely the inhibited and the guilty, often unconsciously so, but in a proportion, fears of pregnancy or of the contraceptive being used are scapegoated (Orchard, 1969). Psychosexual assessment nearly always reveals finally a strong and sometimes a very strong, libido overlaid with conventional moral attitudes and even marked reaction-formation against the libido. Often there is a wide discrepancy between what the woman says and what she does, the gap being filled with a rationalization. Surveys, and superficial clinical questioning, always underestimate the strength of the feminine libido due to failure to penetrate these defences.

This is understandable in a culture which has been biased against female sexuality for two millenia — Eve, after all, unleashed all manner of disasters on the world due to her concupiscence — but more problematical are the unenthusiastic young men. Closer scrutiny reveals some to be heterophobic, some surprisingly to be promiscuous, some to possess undue performance fears, some are inhibited, some feel inferior, and others seem to have a largely un-conscious notion that they are dirty for being interested in women and wanting them. This belief goes in parallel with the attitude that women have intercourse only to please men and not themselves. Some men never make use of photographic aids to fantasy in mastur-bation for this reason. However, the inhibition operates mainly in an unconscious way and usually co-exists with a good deal of intel-lectual knowledge about, for example, female masturbation and the physiology of female response. This knowledge is sometimes encyclopaedic and this should always raise clinical suspicion when dealing with a male sex or relationship problem.

As a group, young adults do not give the impression clinically of mad enslavement to sex but rather of nervous learning to adjust to their partner sexually. That it needs time to master the art of intercourse (as opposed to copulation) should be stressed or discouragement can, for some, become a serious problem later. In terms of psychosexual development young adulthood conforms to the general description given above, in that the instincts and earlier experiences are synthesized in order that intercourse, that is, significant sexual communication, with the opposite sex is learned.

Adolescence is the stage of physical sexual development where the individual learns to cope with masturbation. This is commonly extended to the opposite sex by the use of their genitals for copulatory purposes, which, in essence, is really making use of them as masturbation aids. Young adulthood is the stage at which it becomes possible to learn to have intercourse. It is the outgoing nature of personality and emotional development at this stage combined with its immature flexibility which makes it possible. Good adjustment and good-will between the participant personalities added to warm emotional feelings engendering trust and the wish to please and be pleased, combined with mutual desire, freedom of communication and some degree of uninhibited genital proficiency are the ingredients of good intercourse. This combination of capacities does not arise in the individual before young adulthood and neither does the ability to find an appropriate partner and establish a relationship of the necessary type. Conversely, personality and emotional disorders in the individual or interpersonal or interemotional disorders in a relationship may prevent intercourse being established or maintained.

Provided the drive and drive characteristics are fairly well matched then sex is not likely to be a problem. Due to inhibitions the drive finally available can be so low that intercourse is a rare activity and yet both partners may remain satisfied if they are well matched.

Although most learning is associated with some tension, the learning of intercourse probably has a higher anxiety component than the learning of other tasks due to the very significance attached to sex in our culture. High anxiety interferes with learning so mislearning becomes more frequent. If learning to masturbate be regarded as analogous to learning to talk then learning to have intercourse is learning the art of conversation. Due to the presence of a social phobia or just general inhibition a good talker may be a poor conversationalist. Something similar happens in heterosexual learning due to the presence of special and disabling attitudes towards the opposite sex or just their genitals. For example, men with special fears of women or even, as some have, actual distaste for the appearance, feel and odour of the vulva, will be poor learners. A comparable fear in women is the dislike of semen (Shengold, 1968). Some individuals always experience sexual activity, or even just sexual arousal, as a source of intense anxiety.

As learning proceeds with a partner in a significant relationship anxiety usually lessens. Anxiety reduces sexual pleasure so pleasure increases as anxiety slackens. It is probably this factor which tends

to make sexual pleasure increase with experience for the young
adult. Changes in conventional attitudes tending to reduce female
sex guilt probably account for the increase from a half to two-thirds,
over the two decades to 1967, of US women students who report
pleasure on first coital experience (Packard, 1968). So time,
experience and social changes increase pleasure. The intimate nature
of learning to adjust to, and have good intercourse with, a loved
member of the opposite sex obviously contains within it the potential not only of cementing the bond but of extending communication
and understanding since intercourse is, or should involve, a total
transaction rather than just a genital one. In addition to satisfaction
good intercourse also carries a sense of obligation on which sexual
loyalty is based and furthermore a willingness not to provoke conflict over small issues. Conversely, almost any aspect of the appearance
or behaviour of the partner may be used to inflict punishment for
bad sex. Withdrawal from intercourse is also used, particularly by
women, for retribution.

The role of the sexual factor is clearly complex and it cannot be
usefully discussed in the simplistic manner of the Church, the "sex-
cures-everything" school or even the sex-therapists of current vogue.
Sex is probably maximally complex for the young adult since it is
the time in which personal sexuality is revealed and integrated with
that of a member of the opposite sex with whom an important
relationship exists.

Pre-Marital Sex and Early Problems

Much tedious research effort has been expended on discovering the
extent and consequences of pre-marital intercourse. Nearly all of it
is preoccupied with the female.

Clinically, one would estimate eight to nine out of ten couples so
indulge and that in the remainder the failure to do so is frequently
a sign of an underlying difficulty — more often than not in the man —
which will manifest itself later to the detriment of the relationship.
If, however, attention be paid to statistics obtained by survey then,
in England, one quarter of men and two-thirds of women claim to
be virgins on marriage (Gorer, 1971). Schofield (1973) found that
one fifth of men and 39% of women made such claims. Obviously,
to some extent, conventional attitudes rather than the apparent

biological facts under discussion were being measured, especially perhaps when, as seems to be common in such surveys, women interviewed women.

Interestingly, the double standard implied by these results are maintained predominantly by the women who invoke generalizations about the male's sexual nature to justify his behaviour. This is consistent with the typical psychosexual findings that in fantasy women attribute irresistible passion and ardour to the male, presumably to minimize objections from the super-ego. Perceiving herself, both in fantasy and practice, as being "taken" by the male (whether as the result of her desirability, her seductive behaviour or the romantic atmosphere) permits most women to function more efficiently than would otherwise be the case in both masturbation and intercourse. One of the subsidiary difficulties which arise is that for some any failure of her partner to function in this way in real life undermines her confidence regarding attractiveness. Until she has obtained some experience and understands male sexuality more realistically this can be a problem, especially for the relatively inexperienced young adult. If she comes, over the years, to believe that any lack of passion is an attribute of her particular partner which is not shared by other men then this is a potent motive for seeking extra-marital relations.

Common sense would indicate that once it has been ascertained that a relationship is good then the sooner that the long process of sexual adjustment commences the better. The findings of Karim and Howard (1958) appear to support this conclusion. A criticism of this view is that it overlooks the point that sexual behaviour is not, especially for the young, a pure expression of the id but is, in practice, the product of an unstable balance between the instinctual and anti-instinctual forces which is further complicated by attitudes towards the opposite sex and towards love objects. Generalized advice is probably dangerous in such a complex area, in the absence of yet further research (Hamblin and Blood, 1956).

Pre-marital sexual behaviour goes no further than kissing for some couples whereas for others everything or anything short of actual intercourse is acceptable. The most important point clinically is not what is the actual sexual behaviour, or lack of it, but are the desires and fantasies strong and appropriate. If they are, later problems are unlikely. Very often, however, they are not.

Marriage, in itself, is never a cure for a sexual problem and difficulties or deviation which exist before it will continue to exist afterwards. Thus, couples who do not have intercourse before marriage contribute an undue proportion of all sexual problems which come for treatment. Occasionally, the late start and early discouragement mentioned above are the simple cause but more commonly unresolved oedipal conflicts are found in the male. These may be manifest as sheer disinclination, apparent homosexual interests, arrests in fore-play in which case the breasts or oral sex tend to figure prominently, or in desires to observe the partner having intercourse with others. Sometimes the difficulty is presented in the guise of an avoidance manoeuvre such as failure to erect. Several cases have been en-countered where in spite of hundreds of attempts with a willing and even experienced partner who has given every assistance, the man has been "unable to find" the introitus but has finally ejaculated extra-vaginally in the attempt.

The cases with the best prognosis are those in which fantasies of intercourse do occur and may even lead to erection or masturbation whilst at work but all desire for intercourse seems to evaporate when actually confronted with the partner. Of greater difficulty are those cases where direct masturbation has been absent or inadequate in adolescence and where fantasy has been absent or has never reached the stage of penetration or has invariably involved unattainable, homosexual or incestuous partners.

When confronted with a failure to establish intercourse in the presence of a desire to do so in a young couple, whether married or not, the questions — which also have some applicability to any sex problem — the clinician must seek to answer are:

1. is the problem real or imagined?
2. is it a learning difficulty or a misunderstanding?
3. is it the product of a deficiency, defect of deviation in one partner?
4. is it an adaptive difficulty i.e. both partners are normal but the problem lies with that particular union;
5. is the problem a superficial manifestation of a deep, and non-sexual, disharmony?

An accurate diagnosis should preceed the prescription of treatment in psychosexual medicine just as much as in any other branch. The present pre-occupation with therapeutic techniques to the neglect of diagnosis is poor practice but this does not imply that any underlying psychological cause necessarily requires specific psychotherapeutic attention. Therapy has to take its existence into account but may not be required to deal with it directly.

A note of warning regarding pre-marital intercourse is sounded by Kinsey (1953) who finds that in US women, at least, those who have intercourse before marriage are more likely to indulge in extra-marital relations later.

Formal and Informal Engagements

Formal engagements seem to be declining but whether formal, semi-formal or totally informal the procedure has uses. The chances of subsequent marital happiness are definitely lowered without it (Cole and Hall, 1970).

The statistics, gained by survey, for engagement are, according to Gorer (1971), 4% no engagement, 8% married within six months of engagement, 29% married between 6 months and a year and 28% between one and two years: 18% of men and 30% of women had seriously considered marrying someone else. Schofield (1973) found that 16% of those married had no prior engagement, 16% married in less than six months, and 58% were engaged for between six months and two years prior to marriage: 18% of those married had had no other boy or girl-friend and 9% had been engaged to someone they did not marry. Parents approved in 82% of cases. In a survey of 1,000 engaged US couples Burgess and Wallin (1953) found that about a third of the men and half the women had been previously engaged to someone else.

Unless the feeling is mutual and accepted it is clearly wrong for a young adult, particularly a woman, who wishes to marry to be held in a relationship where the other does not intend marriage. An engagement is a statement of intent in principle. The use of the engagement is to test the basic quality of the relationship, assess compatability and commence adaptation. Clearly it is better that the commitment to marry be abandoned if or when the relationship begins to appear to be unsatisfactory. Special difficulties arise in those who remain engaged for long periods but cannot bring themselves actually to marry — due, usually, to immaturity with or without attachment to parents. A second problem is those suffering from engyesis. In this condition, which in lesser forms is probably more widespread than appreciated, health deteriorates during the engage-

ment. Anxiety, depression, insomnia, weight loss, headaches, loss
of concentration and indecision regarding the marriage occur,
Davies (1956). Of the 50 patients on whom Davies reported, 21 (out
of 33) were "especially obsessional" but in only two cases did
marked sexual tension appear to be present. Of the much smaller
number of cases known to me all were markedly obsessional and
the psychosexual history of all displayed intense sexual conflicts,
first seriously manifest in adolescence. The engagement, or even the
realization that the individual had become involved in a significant
affair involving severe sexual desire, precipitates the initial attack.
Engyetics often have a history of broken engagements.

A problem of another type arising from engagements pertains to
those that are informal. The number of girls believing they are in
such a relationship greatly exceeds the number of men who hold
the same belief. This probably comes about for reasons already
mentioned, namely, girls exaggerating their loving commitment
and boys declaring love in order, not so much to gain favours but,
to reduce their fears. Thus, it comes about, as Burgess and Wallin
(1953) put it:

> "The men do not think of themselves as having seriously discussed getting
> married whereas the women do."

Obviously, the potential for women being harmed from this situation
is high and is a common cause of attempts at suicide. In general
terms the problem is most intense in young couples of about the
same chronological age since women mature earlier than men and are
therefore ready at a younger age for full emotional commitment.
They probably take the topic of marriage seriously whilst the man is
speaking superficially or defensively. The matter often comes to light
when it is discovered that the man is meeting other women.

Distress from broken engagements is often sufficiently serious to
require medical support. In addition to symptomatic therapy the
point to stress is the one made above that it is better now than
later. It is also worth stressing that what is involved is mutual suita-
bility and not some absolute judgement of the individual as a man
or a woman. In point of fact individuals should learn more about
themselves and about the probable characteristics of a member of
the opposite sex likely to afford mutual satisfaction, from every
failed relationship.

The opinion of counsellors, for example, that of Lantz and Snyder
(1969), is that where it is desired to break an engagement it should

be done straightforwardly and the one breaking it should be resolute in resisting special pleas of "blackmail" such as threats of suicide. The writer would feel that whilst this is sound advice in general it requires modification depending on the circumstances and the other individual involved. Some couples occasionally break the engagement temporarily in order that they shall be free to meet others and then arrive at a decision regarding the future of their relationship. This can be an excellent tactic where both partners have little experience of others. It permits them to discover the real value of the relationship. If this is not assessed before marriage, extra-marital affairs are likely subsequently. It seems that probably most members of both sexes are better for sowing a few wild oats.

Living Together

It is becoming increasingly common for young adults to live together on the understanding that no commitment to subsequent marriage is involved. In a sense it may amount to a "trial marriage" and more often than not the couple do eventually marry. In these cases it is probably an informal engagement but for reasons of immaturity or doubt it is not so perceived. Many such young adults say that they are still unsure about what love is or whether they do in fact love. This seems to be some form of emotional counterpart to the tentativeness they display about sex and frequently their behaviour is very loving. In other cases the individuals are expressing doubt about their own ability to discriminate between someone they can get on with as opposed to someone they love.

Provided no deception is involved, living together seems to be more helpful than harmful. It is a breathing space during which the individual is free to come to more certain conclusions not only about that particular relationship but about himself or herself and the opposite sex. It seems to be more born of caution than sin.

Promiscuity

Our culture has been concerned with the problem of promiscuity for the better part of 2,000 years. It has been confused with prostitution

and those who troubled their minds with these issues in the past
have argued as to the number of partners which should earn a woman
the appellation of harlot. Estimates, in the early years of the debate,
varied from thousands to three. By the third century, however, any
woman who had intercourse for any purpose except procreation was
held to be a prostitute, whether paid, married or not. These attitudes,
which exist in the form of unconscious prejudices, still influence all
discussion about promiscuity, and much else as well.

Clinical observation, as opposed to more theoretical discussion,
suggests three conclusions. The first is that as judged from fantasies
and dreams, as well, perhaps, as their behaviour, everyone is potentially promiscious and it is presumably this tendency which keeps the
topic alive. The second is that the potential for promiscuity is a very
powerful socializing force. This is not only true in the narrow physical sense but in a wider sense of outgoing attitudes and behaviour,
friendliness, appreciation of and consideration for the opposite sex,
tolerance of others, lack of censoriousness, and emotional promiscuity i.e. flirting. Although flirting is a sexual activity, for most people
it amounts to an expression of liking for the other member of the
opposite sex rather than a substantial attempt at seduction. Of
course, in some instances it does lead to intercourse but all heterosexual relationships, whether permanent or temporary, start at this
point, hence the importance of the acquisition of the social skills
necessary to support flirting. No matter how obvious it is true that
the initial attraction between the sexes is sexual.The general interaction between the sexes, which underpins society, has an almost
exclusively good social effect on the behaviour of the individuals
involved.

Regarded from the point of view of the individual, rather than
society, it seems to be reasonable to say that all "normal" people,
or perhaps everyone basically, wants to love and to make love and
be loved. Since copulation is possible with almost every member of
the opposite sex, the real issue is one of love. The potential for
promiscuity, in a sense, makes every member of the opposite sex a
possible partner but, some attract a great deal more than others.
Fortunately, these "best choices" are based on catholic taste combined with some sense of personal realism. Thus, beyond mid-
adolescence particularly, individuals develop their own tastes and
so no one member of either sex is attractive to more than a proportion of the opposite one. Individuals with a poor self-image may
not attempt to form a relationship with someone they really want

but rather with someone they think they can obtain. This must be one cause of bad marriage. Amongst the young, due to their inexperience, and lack of emotional maturity, bad relationships are formed, and then with luck, abandoned and fresh ones take their place. In this way, hopefully, they learn lessons helpful in attaining good adjustments in their final relationship. If the final relationship is good, and based on a mutually ego-enhancing one-to-one love bond, then the potential for promiscuity is held in check. If the relationship is unsatisfying the participants are likely to return to the "promiscuous pool" i.e. to search for a fresh partner and a new relationship. It is this need for a relationship, rather than just genital activity, that makes remarriage "a triumph of hope over experience". Although much of this is labelled "promiscuity" by moralists it is really to be viewed as an expression of the need of individuals to form a love relationship and it is not primarily based on genital drives.

The third observation regarding promiscuity is that there are individuals, of both sexes, who are routinely prepared to undertake prompt copulation on scant acquaintance and with little or no real intention of being involved in a relationship. This is real sexual promiscuity and, since, money does not change hands, it seems to the superficial observer as if the 5–10% of the population so involved are "sex-mad" and have intercourse solely for gratifying lust. On this basis the promiscuous person is worse than the prostitute who, at least, has the justification of receiving cash and giving specialized attention in return. In fact on closer investigation it is usually, if not invariably, discovered that the promiscuous have weak libidinal drives; the women often experience failure of lubrication and most have no conscious acknowledgement of orgasm. Their personal psychosexual histories tend to be impoverished and masturbation has often not been properly established. The prime feature of their histories is of sexualized relations with others although, as a rule, the women is more sinned against than sinning. They are usually depressive, in the sense that they feel inferior, useless, unloveable and lacking in merit. They are convinced no man would ever want them if he really knew what they were like — and so they remotivate the male to genital activity in order to escape the scrutiny they would otherwise receive. It is often said that such women are seeking for love, and in a sense they are, but they entertain no hope of attaining it. The usual romantic fantasies found in women are minimal in them: they are very unhappy and stand in need of psychotherapy aimed, not at stopping the sexual behaviour, but at strengthening the ego.

Promiscuous men usually have messy sexual fantasies about women and tend to be fundamentally afraid of them. The borderline between them and the heterophobically homosexual man is blurred; many indeed have a history of bisexual activity. Out of fear, they wish to dominate and humiliate the woman i.e. they are in various degrees sadistic. Intercourse, or rather copulation, amounts to humiliating the woman but it is the woman's willingness to submit and not the actual intercourse which is the attraction. Promiscuous men have all the boldness of those who do not have genuine sexual desire and this accounts for their success. The veneer of skill they acquire in their social dealings with women along with their bold directness makes them attractive to many women. Promiscuous men estimate that at least half of all the women they approach will fairly promptly agree to their overtures. When, and if, promiscuous men fall in love they are not infrequently impotent. They then illustrate the so-called princess—prostitute syndrome. The princess stands for the pure mother and vaginal access is prohibited. Promiscuous men are difficult to treat and, because of our double standards, they may even meet a certain degree of approval from society. The fact that they are psychosexually ill is not readily apparent to themselves or others.

When dealing with apparently promiscuous young adults it is necessary to sharply distinguish between what may be labelled "biological" promiscuity, which is basically a search for a suitable partner, and real promiscuity. Care should be taken to label individuals, and not particular pieces of behaviour, promiscuous. Even then it should be recognized that it is a symptom and not a diagnosis.

Bouts of periodic promiscuity can occur in otherwise non-promiscuous young adults. Women moving into depression may behave promiscuously as may women who wish to hit back at society, for example, following a police charge which they feel is unjust. Psychiatric states can be heralded in by promiscuity — and drugs, including alcohol, can lead to temporary disinhibition. Almost anyone is capable of occasional lapses of behaviour, especially when away from home or abroad, and may then indulge in sex for the sake of sex itself but this is more opportunistic and lacks the routine quality of the truly promiscuous. Similarly, what may be termed "friendly intercourse" can occur between young men and women who are friends but who are not boyfriends or girlfriends in the relationship sense. It is an expression of mutual esteem and should be so evaluated. Sometimes women undertake this type of intercourse primarily to help a man they like who has a sex difficulty and because he feels less tense with her he can often succeed. Young adults not infrequently have a friend of the opposite sex with whom they discuss their relationship and this is the type of context in which intercourse may arise.

Infatuations

Young adults, and late adolescents, may become involved in infatuations with inappropriate partners. Men who are afraid of women of their own age may concentrate on 14-year-old schoolgirls or on much older women who they trust to love them, and not hurt them, as their mother did. They are less afraid of criticism and rejection from much older women and as Vincent (1968) points out, their acceptability to the woman proves to them that they can compete with older men.

Similarly, older women may concentrate, particularly, on young men who are unsure of themselves and young women, as is well known, frequently conceive passions for older men. To some extent all this is normal and represents a weaning stage from oedipal objects. There is truly no generation gap as far as sex is concerned. It is only when the young person becomes stuck in such a relationship and fails to make progress beyond it that harm may perhaps arise. Where there is apparently intense love in this sort of situation an infatuation exists. On the part of the older person the motive may be of a reverse oedipal nature. For example, the older woman who was intensely preoccupied with her only son as he grew up may establish a passionate emotional and sexual relationship with a young adult male who never quite succeeded in successfully resolving his own oedipal conflicts. Because the basis of these relationships is distorted and neurotic they tend not to last.

Homosexuality

In so far as homosexuality in young adults is concerned two problems arise in practice. The first is diagnostic. Sometimes the problem

presents in the form of psychological symptoms unrelated to homosexuality or, occasionally as a symptom such as rectal gonorrhoea. In
other cases the patient, usually a man, directly reports homosexual
practices, fantasies, dreams or fears (the last being sometimes induced
by an approach from a homosexual) and asks for assessment or treatment. However, the fears concerning sexual identity found commonly
in adolescents are relatively uncommon in young adults.

The history is of crucial importance but is often distorted along
the line that the individual has no responsibility for the state in
which he finds himself. Thus the image which is projected is of being
involved in tendencies towards homosexuality from "as far back as
I can remember" or of seduction during childhood by others. The
paranoid tendencies found in many total homosexuals and their
literature shows how defensive they still feel about their plight. In
many of the marginal cases found in adolescents and young adults
the real diagnosis is often one of heterophobia and not homosexuality;
they only prefer their own sex due to fear of the opposite one. The
underlying causes of the heterophobia are often susceptible to psychotherapy in young adults. Clinically, the prevalence of homosexuality is a good deal less than many surveys indicate.

The other problem is of the bisexual and this not so much in
respect of themselves but of their heterosexual partner. On the whole
men appear to be more tolerant of occasional lesbian behaviour
than women are of homosexual activity. Advice, if requested,
can only be based on joint discussion and assessment.

Sexual Difficulties and Young Adults

Whether the incidence of sexual difficulties is increasing or whether
the incidence with which they are being reported is increasing is
impossible to decide. The clinical impression is that they are indeed
waxing. A part of the contributory background could be the
technical nature of the contemporary sexual discussion. All knowledge is good, particularly about sex, but clinical practice confirms
that it is frequently misunderstood and usually ill-digested. For
many young men — and they are the generation most affected —
intercourse has become an almost laboratory exercise in which the
women's reactions are observed and discussed, even during the
act, in a way which makes it difficult for her to lose ego control.

Young men are increasingly self-conscious about their ability to
"satisfy" their partner, by which they mean their capacity to induce
orgasm in her but which to a woman may mean something different,
and their anxieties are thereby increased. One anxiety coming into
prominence is their fear that their partner will seek satisfaction elsewhere (Gorer, 1971), unless he is a competent performer. Kinsey's
(1948) discovery that the rates of intercourse are falling in each
generation compared with the previous one is probably still operating.

Young adults who are sexually inexperienced may seek to avoid
the experience although they are in an otherwise good relationship.
Usually moral, religious or parental grounds are put forward to
account for the lack of any sexual activity or a man may speak of
the respect he feels for his partner. Experienced young adults in a
relationship which involves intercourse may, like other age groups,
seek to reduce or abolish intercourse by diversion to work or leisure
pursuits and then claim to be too tired or too short of time. The
same end may be obtained by secondary gain from symptoms such
as intercourse-related pains in the head, groins, testes or introitus, or
by functional symptoms such as anomalous bleeding or discharges
for which no cause is found. Others reduce intercourse by the
rejection of advances from the partner or by apparently not enjoying
the act in order to discourage future advances. Although either partner may accuse the other of being over-sexed, due to their demands,
such an assertion generally disturbs a young woman more than a man.

More directly, intercourse can be avoided by men through performance failures including failure to erect, failure to erect properly,
loss of erection before or after penetration, ejaculation whilst flaccid
or semi-erect, ejaculation before penetration or soon after penetration,
or failure to ejaculate intra-vaginally. A woman can obtain a deterrent effect through sensation failures of which she makes the man
aware, perhaps bitterly. Many women, of course, are satisfied
although they do not consciously experience an orgasm and so do
not complain; a woman may act an orgasm in order to please the
man or because she feels that she, and not the man, is really to
blame. Occasionally men complain of sensation failures, in that the
penis, or just the glans, is anaesthetic. This symptom is usually
variable and in some cases reflects the current emotional stresses
in the relationship. Performance failures can also occur in women
and the commonest is a failure to lubricate ("female impotence").
Vaginismus is a fairly rare cause, even in young adults, and where
it occurs, in the absence of physical cause, the characteristic feature

is a disturbed body image in relation to the vagina which usually takes the form of, in effect, denying its existence. However, in general, sexual difficulties in men relate to performance and in women to sensation.

Symptoms of impotence or frigidity, where the cause is not physical, are often underlaid by excessive anxiety, although it may not be consciously or fully acknowledged, and many such cases display typical approach/avoidance conflicts. Examples are the man who erects and the woman who lubricates in foreplay but the excitatory state is not maintained as penetration approaches. Many such individuals often have overwhelming desires for intercourse with their partner when, for a variety of reasons such as non-availability, menstruation, or inappropriate location, it is impossible but all desire evaporates when the partner is available. When the psychic apparatus is adjusted to avoidance, the anxiety level falls although, in men, the presence of impotence in many, but not all, is associated with secondary anxiety. In cases of extreme avoidance, impotence may be present in masturbation, as well as intercourse and functionally the individual is a castrate. Although such men may complain they are often not very distressed and attend more at their partner's insistence or because she is threatening to leave. Such men are usually very jealous sexually.

Theoretically the cause of a sexual difficulty lies in the individual or in the relationship. Within the relationship indifference, resentment, distaste, aversion, hatred, the desire to punish, identification of the partner with the opposite sex parent, frequent rejection, recurrent failure to satisfy self or partner, the lack of real communication, habitually inadequate foreplay, fear of injuring the partner or self, fear of disease, fear of detection, fear of ridicule, fear of pregnancy by that particular partner and so on, are all common causes of difficulty.

Within the individual the causes may lie with the personality or in an emotional disorder, but when the sexuality is at fault the causes appear to be unresolved sexual conflicts from childhood or negative learning inspired mainly in childhood. Retrospectively, as seen clinically in treating young adults, the difficulties arising in childhood from negative learning include the association of sex with excretion i.e. *dirty sex,* failure to name or acknowledge the existence of the sexual parts i.e. *castrated sex,* expectation of divine hostility and punishment, which is widespread if largely unconscious i.e. *sinful sex,* and fears induced through rebuke which associate anxiety with sexual interest, display, arousal, desire or fulfilment involving self and/or activity (or the guilty wish for it) with others i.e. *fearful sex.*

These upsets are manifest as specific delays in psychosexual development i.e. the correct stage is not attained at around the correct age, total or partial inhibition of the libido or the distortion and deviation of psychosexual development. Although the consequences may affect both the personality and the emotions (as, for example, in a general hostility to the opposite sex with desires to harm or humiliate them and obtain revenge against them) as far as sex itself is concerned a variety of outcomes are possible depending on circumstances. These are the total suppression of sexuality, the partial suppression of sexuality with or without the normal patterns of development having been followed, or choice of inappropriate objects e.g. animals, much younger or older people, own sex or even the self.

In clinical form a patient so afflicted may present in one of a variety of ways. Depending on individual circumstances, past and present, and the best compromises of which the individual is capable between drive and inhibition, he or she may:

1. appear totally sexless or nearly so;
2. be capable only of sexual activity mainly involving himself or herself e.g. fantasy, masturbation, voyeurism, exhibitionism, transvestism;
3. sexual expression with others may be possible but does not attain the level of mutual genitality e.g. mutual masturbation only, oral sex only, frotteurism, sado-masochistic practices which are an end in themselves such as men who ejaculate when whipped by a woman or when she urinates on him, and all other cases where arrest occurs at the level of foreplay;
4. genital interaction is desired and even attained occasionally but usually avoidance manoeuvres are put in its place;
5. conditions are imposed on intercourse which make success unlikely, such as women who will not tolerate the "dirtiness" of foreplay or who are totally passive because of a belief that sex is something men do to women;
6. genital union is achievable but special circumstances must be present for real satisfaction e.g. fetishism, coprolalia, wife-swapping, orgies, mock-rape, partner must be of some particular type such as dominant, coloured or a prostitute;
7. some special position must be used such as standing or female superior;

  8. normal intercourse can be attained but is experienced as
unpleasurable or unsatisfying in some way;

  9. total release cannot be obtained and orgasm is not reached with
the penis contained in the vagina;

10. normal intercourse is possible with other individuals but not
with the loved partner because of an unconscious fear that sex may
lead to the loss of love;

11. sexual release is preferred, or is only possible with, an inappropriate human, non-human or inanimate object.

Some of these items verge towards normal experience and this is
the particular area in which women, especially young ones, encounter
difficulty. Because of her passive role she can always copulate, and
her body may well show the signs of sexual arousal and response,
but it is at the levels of satisfaction and of the psychic interpretation
of sexual stimuli that matters go awry. Nice girls do not seek, provoke, or enjoy intercourse. The attitude lies in the unconscious and
her conscious mind, superficial approach and behaviour may appear
to be in total contradiction. However, in both sexes it is the unconscious which determines sexual response and pleasure. Men
cannot will themselves to erect and women cannot force themselves
to lubricate. Thus, women will embark on behaviour motivated
towards making intercourse occur but they may be totally, or nearly,
unconscious of the real motivation and so fail to protect themselves
against the consequences. Some young and guilt-ridden women discover
they can attain orgasm with "nasty" men because they tap the "nasty"
i.e. sexual, portion of herself and others find that they are disinhibited
with a stranger they will never see again and whose regard, therefore,
they do not value. It is this type of situation that sometimes lies
behind those cases of unwanted pregnancy where the woman claims
she did not know what was happening or that she was carried away
or that the man, whilst not exactly raping her, forced her to do it.
Such women will often explicitly state that they had no intention
of behaving in this way when they went out. Many women function
in a split fashion sexually in that they deny the desire or intent,
undertake the act, then deny the pleasure and thereby, partly or
totally, deny the act.

Similar, and infinitely more subtle, expressions of this formula
are found in the sexual behaviour of women, both married and
unmarried, of all ages but particularly in the young. It is a common
cause of apparent or pseudo-frigidity. It is often said that a woman
who asks what an orgasm is has never had one but this is a good deal

less than true. Physically most, if not all women, do experience orgasm, although not perhaps in heterosexual intercourse, but whether they can psychically accept the experience is quite another matter. In one case referred for "absolute frigidity" the patient was discovered to regularly attain status orgasmus and in many others it is found, if suitable investigation be made, that the patient does experience sensations, which may be perceived as being of a minor nature or they may not be experienced as being connected with the genital area or even the genital act, but nevertheless they are physically orgasms and can be "expanded" to normal levels of intensity by psychotherapy. Due to these considerations frigidity is best described, rather than defined, as the inability to acknowledge orgasm from any source. It is noteworthy that many women who claim to be frigid in masturbation and/or intercourse describe the typical post-orgasmic sensations on completing the act.

The difficulty is psychological and the best therapy is psychologically based but all therapy does have psychological implications. It may be this unacknowledged psychological component of the therapy which brings success to the apparently physical methods of treatment but the so-called new therapy of Kaplan (1974) explicitly combines the two. If a doctor instructs a "frigid" woman who may well, through the operation of the aforementioned processes of self deception, deny auto-sexual practices, to purchase a vibrator and use it to stimulate her vulva, the fact that she has been given the direction to masturbate herself by an older man whom she trusts and vest with authority is probably of much more importance than the vibrator. In certain cases, due to considerations of aetiology, the instruction may be more effective if delivered by a woman.

With the possible exception of deviation in object choice, the key to comprehending and treating primary psychosexual difficulties (i.e. those that are not secondary to physical or psychiatric illness or marital disharmony) lies with the super-ego. In general form it could be said that the possession of the super-ego permits the individual to be "civilized" so that he or she eventually fits into the culture and background to which he is born. In the vast majority of psychosexual problems the super-ego has been "trained" to raise very strong objections to the libido so that normal, enjoyable, sexual self-expression became impossible. The resultant conflicts lead to anxiety if the super-ego is challenged. The libido will commonly find ways of "cheating" the super ego, especially in women, but the price is usually some form of malsensation. In men "cheating" is less possible, due to their active role, so the problem is evidenced as malfunction and their anxiety Cooper (1969), is perhaps more obvious for this reason. Of course, concentration on the super-ego in therapy does not mean that the id is ignored and one aim should be to promote the welfare and strength of the id relative to the super-ego. More peripherally, matters of concern to the ego such as body-image, self-esteem, an inadequate, selfish, or over-rigid personality, social skills, interpersonal relationships and emotional expression may all require attention in addition to the central sexual issue. In a proportion of cases it is found that the fulcrum of the problem lies more in an area apparently peripheral to sex than in the sexuality itself. The clue is the presence of "normal" autosexuality.

Sex Problems in Relation to Marriage

On the insistence usually of the woman, many couples cease intercourse as marriage approaches. It is probably an unconscious attempt at guilt reduction rationalized as "saving it up" for the honeymoon. Oral contraception may be stopped to reinforce the embargo and pregnancy can result.

It is becoming increasingly common for a woman who experienced orgasms in intercourse beforehand to lose the capacity immediately after marriage. Sometimes the loss of the element of "naughtiness" is to blame but in others it appears to be a guilty reparation for earlier misdeeds. In other cases the ready and easy availability of intercourse after marriage makes it less attractive. The loss of freedom troubles others and they become intensely preoccupied with thoughts of extra-marital intercourse. Early doubts about the relationship are common. Disappointment because of the prior expectation that sex would become suddenly even better after marriage can adversely influence both men and women against it.

Some men lose interest after marriage sometimes for reasons similar to those given above but more commonly out of discontent with the woman or even fears of her emerging sexuality.

Importance of Masturbation in Relation to Problems

Attention to masturbation is of importance in therapy, especially in women since they are more commonly inefficient than is the male, especially when young. Due to their different psychosexual organization, their innately higher responsiveness, their greater sexual capacity and the unobvious nature of arousal and orgasm compared with men, self-deception is endless. It can involve stimulation of areas other than the genital one, the use of a routine activity which is not obviously masturbatory in character, such as washing the vulva, riding bicycles and so on (endlessly), the use of muscular or simply psychic activity as well as the denial or displacement of orgasm. Many of these women are, at a conscious level, genuinely unaware of their practices. Others will suppress sexual fantasy during manipulation and so fail to acknowledge the act. During intercourse they will concentrate intensely on a non-sexual theme. More often, women deny masturbation in a verbal fashion. For example, a Catholic girl may confess to disobedience without adding that she is referring to a parental prohibition against masturbation. A woman may define masturbation to herself as vaginal insertion and then deny the act because her behaviour lacks the essential ingredient she attributes to it. This is a common motive for denying orgasm. All such denials and self-deceptions are harmful to the patient's psychosexuality.

Another area of trouble which is commonly first manifest in young adulthood is where, due to fears of punishment or rebuke, the woman adopted a concealing method of masturbation in childhood. Thus, she may have learned then to masturbate prone, or erect, or with her legs extended and adducted, or through her underclothes, all in order to disarm parental suspicions. In later life she is found to be able to attain orgasm only under the same sort of circumstances and in many cases these are incompatible with intercourse. Re-training is often inordinately difficult. In a similar way masturbation is relegated to sleep, or a sleep like state, usually by women but occasionally also by men. Cases have been encountered where women can only enjoy intercourse if it occurs, like a dream, in the middle of sleep or where the initiation of intercourse induces a prompt narcoleptic response (but the physiological response continues).

In both sexes non-manual and bizarre methods of masturbation clinically appear to be associated with later inefficiency at intercourse. Other signs of difficulty are sudden changes in fantasy, position or method just prior to orgasm. In the absence of deliberate delay in the attainment of orgasm, which is common, prolonged efforts to achieve orgasm in masturbation are a further sign of diffi-

culty in either sex. Absent or substantially deviant fantasies can
indicate trouble as can the non-involvement of self in fantasy.
Women, who involve the vagina in their masturbatory techniques
and fantasies, which usually first occurs in mid-adolescence, rarely
seem, clinically, to have much difficulty in obtaining an orgasm with
the penis in the vagina. Their fantasies express their high vaginal
drives, which seem to be present in some degree in all women, but
they may be partially or even totally inhibited thus preventing
orgasm being induced via the vagina or, in some cases, from any
part of the genital region. Such women, however, usually respond
well physiologically to stimulation. It is as if special prohibitions
against acknowledging vaginal pleasure have been induced in them.
A good proportion of women report that occasionally if they are
feeling aroused, orgasm is obtained at the outset of masturbation
and these women, again, appear to experience few difficulties.
The implications for therapy are obvious. It is because young adulthood is so concerned with the establishment of effective close relationships that any earlier failures in development, including psychosexual
ones, must be made good.

Treatment of Sexual Difficulties

Once a diagnosis has been made, the early and effective treatment
of sexual disorders in the young is vital. It should be properly
planned and an appropriate selection from the available therapies
can be used to supplement psychotherapy and re-education. General
measures should include optimism, positive suggestion, encouragement and the de-emphasis of the technical symptom. The promotion
of touch and body contact bear special significance since it is the
primary (i.e. infant) way in which trust and love are expressed. The
emphasis should be on the mutual physical pleasures and joint desires
rather than intercourse which should be regarded as arising spontaneously from contact. Techniques of foreplay and intercourse may
require adjustment or intercourse may be temporarily banned. Total
honesty between the couple should be encouraged in relation to
fantasies, desired stimulations and sexual expression generally but it
does have a risk of shocking, or even averting, the young male. The
taking of a good psychosexual and general history in a relaxed
fashion is therapeutic in itself for many individuals, especially young

ones. In fact re-education commences as the history is taken. Pills,
aids, and devices can help but their contribution is probably more
psychological than physical. In practice hypnosis appears to be relatively valueless in the majority of cases of sexual difficulty but
hypnotics, in sub-hypnotic doses, taken before sexual contact can
very greatly assist the early stages of therapy due to their effect on
the super-ego. Their use should not be routinely continued.

In spite of what was said earlier (p. 179) the use of surrogates, or
any form of extra-marital partner, for "instruction", whether self
or medically prescribed, is found in practice to be much more
frequently harmful than helpful in young adults. Since it is hazardous it should not be used except, possibly, as a very last resort.
Suggestions from the patient that this course be followed should be
opposed and the reasons supplied. Occasionally, the successful
completion of intercourse with another partner boosts the ego
to such an extent that difficulties are overcome in the prime relationship but amongst the young, the inexperienced, the poorly adjusted,
the insecure and those in relationships with any difficulties, the
final outcome is nearly always to disrupt the bond. If the relationship was otherwise good, and really it was only having difficulties
in adjustment and learning, then to risk its disruption is bad practice.

An element of importance in therapy is that the therapist is
granting the patient permission to "let go" which capacity was
inhibited, at some stage, by the parents. There is a fear, especially
in women, of totally submitting to sexual urges with abandon. Where
the inhibition is high it may be impossible to obtain an orgasm in the
presence of another individual or, in some cases, only in the presence
of the opposite sex. In lesser forms some people cannot permit
themselves to have an orgasm if they are being watched. The presence
of such inhibitions is less obvious in men than in women but it
can affect their orgasmic enjoyment and ejaculatory force.

The Unwanted Pregnancy

Statistically, unwanted pregnancy and abortion is a problem of the
young adult age-group in that 20 to 24-year-olds furnish, at around
27% of all abortions, the largest group and their rate of abortion,
at something over 13 per thousand, is also the highest of all age groups
(Lane Committee, 1974).

The one aspect of the unwanted pregnancy which receives little or no attention is the question of aetiology. To the uncharitable, the patient has been simple, sinful or silly and to those who seek to assist her she has been unfortunate, imposed on, or impetuous. And yet the question remains as to why, in an age of totally efficient and reversible contraception, namely the pill, should a woman undertake unprotected intercourse and a few weeks later be demanding a termination of the pregnancy. When regarded in this way it is easy to see that those who are opposed to abortion can come to believe that really the woman wishes to have a baby and that to assist her to abort is tantamount to something close to murder.

The two facts to keep in sight when considering the problem are that a good proportion of sexual motivations are unconscious, especially in young women, and secondly, that sexual desire is not directly geared to reproductive intent. It is sexual tension or desire which leads to intercourse and not the wish to reproduce. Throughout the animal kingdom man must be the only living creature who realizes that sexual practice has procreative consequences but, in general as with all other living things, his level of sexual, and reproductive, activity is much higher than is required to ensure numerical replacement of the species. Over-reproduction and the survival of the fittest (from conception onwards) is the rule. Since a woman is more or less capable of sexual activity all the time but is only able to conceive for about 10% of it, the biological presumption must be that in man, as in the other higher animals, sex serves manifold purposes.

Although no evidence on the point is known to the writer, it would seem reasonable to assume that young adults who have abortions later do have babies, probably at more or less the same rate as other women. Viewed in this way it could be argued that they are postponing pregnancy until they are better adapted to parenthood. Thus abortion in this age group is probably a highly responsible social act.

An attempt at a brief summary of the aetiology of the unwanted pregnancy is given below and identifies four main groups of causes. They are based on clinical experience with young adults seeking contraception or abortion.

Male Factors

1. Due to earlier orchitis, genital disease or abnormality the man fears or believes he is sterile and tests his potency on his female partners, they being unaware of the risks being run.

2. Men with weak male egos will undertake intercourse more or less forcefully, whether it is safe or not, since to accept a refusal would be to submit to female domination.

3. Some men, especially certain immigrants, will seek to make as many women pregnant as possible since in their sub-culture it proves their masculinity.

4. Some men, usually with sadistic fantasies about women, will deliberately expose the woman to pregnancy in order to enhance their pleasure and sense of power over her.

5. Men may make holes in sheaths in order to induce pregnancy' in the hope of securing a relationship.

6. Some men are opposed to the use of oral contraception by their partner, sometimes out of fear of infidelity and sometimes out of a fear of increased sexual demands. This is usually rationalized on religious or medical grounds and the woman is compelled to use less safe methods.

7. In casual encounters, if nothing is said, a man may assume a woman is taking the pill and she may assume he will withdraw.

Conception and pregnancy are neither sought nor welcomed by this group of women.

Bad Luck and Bad Advice — Apparent or Otherwise

1. Method failures — which, actually, may not be as random as they seem.

2. Bad advice e.g. to stop oral contraception on unnecessary grounds. Sometimes the woman, due to underlying guilt, produces symptoms which alarm the doctor and are designed to persuade him to take the responsibility for stopping contraception.

3. Occasional risk taking — which probably afflicts nearly every couple from time to time.

4. Change of circumstances following conception e.g. relationship collapses.

Conception may be unconsciously desired in this group and investigation of the underlying motives is required.

Falsely Motivated Conceptions

In these cases the chance of conception is partially welcome at the time mainly with the intent of filling some other motive which often becomes less desirable when conception is actually achieved. There are many causes and the following are only an illustration.

1. The woman wished to secure or strenghthen a relationship.
2. The unmarried woman may wish to punish parents.
3. A student may wish to escape a course of study or a woman from her employment.
4. Depressive women may feel that conception would not matter since it would provide a dependent love object for them.
5. A "neurotic" woman may feel, or even be advised, that having a baby will cure her.
6. Out of jealousy of a sister or friend who is pregnant a woman may risk conception although pregnancy is not really desired.
7. A woman who was illegitimate herself may seek to repeat the process in order to "prove" that it is not the awful business she really believes it to be.
8. Women who feel they wish to seek revenge against an unpleasant or unfaithful partner may run the risk of conception outside the relationship.
9. Women who feel hard done by to society often hit back with sexual incontinence. It is the equivalent of delinquency in men.
10. Women who fear they are sterile have desires to test themselves. Common causes are:
    a. unguarded comments by gynaecologists;
    b.   reading articles to the effect that oral contraception or a previous abortion can cause sterility.
    c. attention to anti-VD propaganda which nearly always stresses that gonorrhoea can cause sterility and that women often do not know they have it. Thus unnecessary fears about both VD and sterility are inspired;
    d. frequent unprotected intercourse in the past which has not led to conception (due to juvenile sterility);
    e. fears based on small breasts, hirsutism or scanty periods are commoner in adolescents than young adults.
11. Some women with sadistic or resentful attitudes towards men may run the risk of conception unknown to the man, for example by missing pills, in order to give him something to worry about.

The Psychosexually Disturbed

Although the sexuality in general is an expression of the personality,

psychosexual illness or inadequacy is not necessarily evident in any
other aspect of behaviour, emotions, intellect or personality. The
guilt, self-deception, denial and inhibition which underlie the
disturbance often show up only in the psychosexual history and
the associated lack of adequate sexual sensation. Unwanted conception is always a possibility. Examples include:

1. "Promiscuous" women who often fail to contracept sometimes in an endeavour to control themselves and sometimes because
their aims, not being sexual, pay little or no attention to contraception.
2. "Over-fertile" women, who often start having babies early in
life, may feel that reproduction is the only justification for sex.
3. Women who strongly equate sex with sin may secondarily
associate pregnancy with punishment and the risk therefore has
to be present if they are to feel any pleasure.
4. Young women at the outset of their heterosexual careers
frequently fail to obtain contraception because, in effect, they
are persuading themselves that they are going to stop until they
are married. Requests for contraceptive advice from virgins are
rare.
5. Some women fear that all restraint will be lost on oral contraception and therefore avoid it.
6. Some young women are too embarrassed about their sexuality
to seek any advice.
7. Women who are intolerant of all contraception because of its
implications for their sexuality i.e. they cannot acknowledge their
needs.
8. Women who cannot admit their intentions to themselves and
so fail to take precautions. They are therefore "carried-away",
often after the consumption of a trivial amount of alcohol.
9. Women who produce adverse physical, psychosomatic and
psychological reactions to oral contraception and so cease using it.
10. Immature women, for example:
    a. those who strongly wish to be mothered rather than be
    a mother;
    b. women with strong erotic attachments to the father;
    c. women with large overt or unconscious hostility to
    the mother, who they may wish was dead and therefore
    fear death if they become a mother;
    d. women who have not fully accepted their female role.

If such women do become pregnant they frequently demand an abortion.

The treatment of this group is the treatment of the root cause and is not a mere exercise in contraception. Most repeat abortions come from this group and the majority of individuals who have a very adequate knowledge about contraception, such as doctors and nurses, but who nevertheless become unwantedly pregnant are usually found to belong to it.

Difficulty in Oral Contraception in Young Adults

Young women may react badly to oral contraception and the drop-out rate amongst them as a group is high.

The symptoms of which they most commonly complain are headaches, irritability, nausea, depression, weight-gain and loss of libido. Clinical experience, the results of cross-over trials such as that of Goldzieher *et al.* (1971), placebo investigations such as that of Ramos *et al.* (1969) and the dose and preparation independence evident in most cases as well as most well conducted investigations such as those of Kutner and Brown (1972) and the Royal College of General Practitioners (1974), suggest that the majority of symptoms are psychogenic rather than pharmacological in origin, although there is conflicting evidence such as that of Grounds *et al.* (1970). Some symptoms, such as thrombosis or breast tenderness, are assumed to be pharmacogenic but even here the evidence is not absolutely certain.

A common chain of events on commencing oral contraception is initiated by unconscious conflicts manifest in headaches, bad dreams, tiredness and resentment at environmental distractions i.e. irritability. The associated self-criticism and withdrawal of approval by the super-ego leads to depression. Orality is increased in many women when depressed and so over-eating and weight gain occur. This may be reinforced by a shift in the libido from the genitals to the mouth. The decathexis of the genitals affirms to the super-ego that the primary intention of pill-taking was not sexual gratification and thereby sexual drive, and often orgasmic capacity, is lost. The unconscious fear of punishment leads to symptom exaggeration and even panic attacks.

Treatment rests not in changing the preparation, provided it is otherwise suitable, and even less in changing the contraceptive method, but in recognizing and dealing with the underlying guilt.

Summary

Young adulthood is the time in which personality development enters its final phase. The individual becomes self-reliant and accommodates to society. Emotional development makes it possible to form a significant and potentially enduring relationship and sexuality is extended beyond its earlier physical boundaries to become a form of pervasive intercommunication with a special member of the opposite sex.

The complexity of the processes involved affords plenty of scope for error but the flexible immaturity of the young adult permits correction. The same feature can also allow for unresolved conflicts from the past to find a solution. Although the phase is essentially one of integration it is also one of expansion and development. It prepares the way for parenthood and its sound management has implications for marriage, child-rearing and society.

Sexual problems may arise directly from difficulties in adaptation but more commonly they are the expression of sexual and emotional hindrances acquired in childhood. Earlier clues to their presence may have only been slight but even so they can still be severely disabling when they finally manifest themselves. Treatment, it is argued, should be preceeded, as far as possible, by an exact diagnosis or formulation of the real causes of the symptoms. Causes must be distinguished from their effects or symptoms. Different patients may exhibit the same symptoms but aetiologically they are all different. Although the underlying causes may not receive specific attention, or even be imparted to the patient, they exert an effect on the choice of therapy and prevent both mistakes and a waste of effort. As in the rest of medicine, but even more so in psychosexual practice, treatment is primarily of the patient rather than just the disease.

The special problems of young adults do not demand special treatment as such, but the best selection of available standard therapies is influenced by their special needs which, in practice, are largely related to their inexperience, fears and inhibitions. It is usually found that in all but the simplest cases treatment follows multiple lines but the central effort is always psychotherapeutic.

Unwanted pregnancy and difficulties in contraception particularly afflict this age group and sound treatment is based on comprehending the aetiology.

References

Blacker, C. P. (1958). Disruption of marriage, *Lancet*, 1, 578–581.

Blos, P. (1962). "On Adolescence." pp. 148–158. Free Press: New York.

Blood, R. O. and Wolfe, D. M. (1960). "Husbands and Wives." p. 250 Free Press: New York.

Burgess, E. W. and Cottrell, L. S. (1939). "Predicting Success or Failure in Marriage." pp. 128–132. Prentice-Hall: New York.

Burgess, E. W. and Wallin, P. (1953). "Engagement and Marriage." Ch. 9. Lippincott: Philadelphia.

Cauthery, P. (1973). "Student Health." Priory Press: London.

Chester, R. (1971). Health and marriage breakdown, *British Journal of Social and Preventive Medicine*, 25, 231–235.

Christensen, H. T. and Meissner, H. H. (1953). Studies in child spacing: III – Premarital pregnancy as a factor in divorce. *American Sociological Review*, 18, 641–644.

Cole, L. and Hall, I. N. (1970). "Psychology of Adolescnece." Holt, Rinehart and Winston: New York.

Coombs, L. C., Freedman, R., Friedman, J. and Pratt, W. F. (1970). Premarital pregnancy and status before and after marriage, *American Journal of Sociology*, 75, 800–820.

Cooper, A. J. (1969). A clinical study of "coital anxiety" in male potency disorders, *Journal of Psychosomatic Research*, 13, 143–147.

Crook, J. N. (1972). Sexual selection, dimorphism and social organisation in the primates. *In* "Sexual Selection and the Descent of Man." (Campbell, B. Ed), Heinemann: London.

Davies, D. L. (1956). Psychiatric illness in those engaged to be married, *British Journal of Social and Preventive Medicine*, 10, 123–127.

Duvall, E. M. (1964). Adolescent love as a reflection of teenagers' search for identity, *Journal of Marriage and the Family*, 26, 226–229.

Fletcher, R. (1973). "The Family and Marriage in Britain." p. 156. Penguin: Harmondsworth.

Goldzieher, J. W., Moses, L. E., Averkin, E., Scheel, C. and Taber, B. Z. (1971). Nervousness and depression attributed to oral contraceptives, *American Journal of Obstetrics and Gynaecology*, 111, 1013–1020.

Gorer, G. (1971). "Sex and Marriage in England Today." pp. 22, 30, 84. Nelson: London.

Grounds, D., Davies, B. and Mowbray, R. (1970). The contraceptive pill, side effects and personality, *British Journal of Psychiatry*, 116, 169–172.

Hamblin, R. L. and Blood, O. R. (1956). Pre-marital experience and the wife's sexual adjustment, *Social Problems*, 4, 122–129.

Karim, E. J. and Howard, D. H. (1958). Post-marital Consequences of pre-marital sex adjustments, *American Sociological Review*, 23, 556–562.

Kaplan, H. S. (1974). "The New Sex Therapy.' ' p. 193. Balliere Tindall: London.

Kinsey, A. *et al.* (1948). "Sexual Behaviour in the Human Male." pp. 219, 148–158. Saunders: Philadelphia.

Kinsey, A. *et al.* (1953). "Sexual Behaviour in the Human Female." pp. 358, 427. Saunders: Philadelphia.

Knupfer, G., Clarke, W. and Room, R. (1966). The mental health of the unmarried, *The American Journal of Psychiatry*, February, 841–851.

Kutner, S. J. and Brown, W. L. (1972). History of depression as a risk factor for depression with oral contraceptives and discontinuance, *Journal of Nervous and Mental Disease*, 155, 163–169.

Landis, J. T. (1946). Length of time required to achieve adjustment in marriage *American Sociological Review*, 11, 666–677.

Lane Committee (1974). Report of the Committee on the working of the Abortion Act, HMSO, Vol. II, pp. 38 39.

Lantz, H. R. and Snyder, E. C. (1969). "Marriage." pp. 198–203. Wiley: Chichester.

Lederer, W. J. (1973). "Marriage: For and Against". Dent: London.

May, A. E. and Childs, D. (1972). Homogamy in intellectual abilities, *British Journal of Psychiatry*, 120, 623–624.

Orchard, W. H. (1969). Psychiatric aspects of oral contraceptives, *The Medical Journal of Australia*, 56, 872–876.

Packard, V. (1968). "The Sexual Wilderness." Longmans, p. 398: London.

Parens, H. (1970). Inner sustainment, *Psychoanalytic Quarterly*, 9, 223–239.

Ramos, A. R., Velazquez, G. J., Ricalde, L. R. and Manautou, M. J. (1969). Incidence of side effects with contraceptive placebo, *American Journal of Obstetrics and Gynaecology*, 105, 1144–1149.

Robertson, N. C. (1974). The relationship between marital status and the risk of psychiatric referral, *British Journal of Psychiatry*, 125, 433–441

Royal College of General Practitioners, (1974). "Oral Contraceptives and Health." pp. 32–33. Pitman Medical: London.

Saul, L. J. (1971). "Emotional Maturity." Lippincott: Philadelphia.

Schofield, M. (1973). "The Sexual Behaviour of Young Adults." pp. 136, 166, 186. Lane (The Bodley Head): London.

Schonfeld, W. A. (1966). Body-image disturbances in adolescents, *Archives of General Psychiatry*, XV, 16–21.

Scott, P. D. (1974). Battered wives, *British Journal of Psychiatry*, 125, 433–441.

Shengold, L. (1968). The smell of semen, *Journal of the Hillside Hospital*, XVII, 317–325.

Snyder, E. C. (1966). Marital selectivity in self-adjustment, social adjustment and IQ, *Journal of Marriage and the Family*, 28, 2, 188–189.

Sturgis, F. R. (1907). Comparative prevalence of masturbation in males and females, *American Journal of Dermatology*, September, 396–400.

Vincent, E. C. (1968). Sexual interest in someone older or younger, *Medical Aspects of Human Sexuality*, 2, 6, 6–11.

Woodruff, R. A., Guze, S. B. and Clayton, P. J. (1972). Divorce among psychiatric out-patients, *British Journal of Psychiatry*, 121, 289–92.

7 | *Sexual Minorities*

PREBEN HERTOFT

Normal Sexuality – Deviant Sexuality

The diversity and great individual variation in sexual functioning
make it difficult to draw the border between what is considered
normal and what is considered deviant. There are textbooks of
sexology, which completely avoid the concept of sexual deviance
and which only refer to minority groups or use the term "sexual
variations". The advantage of this approach is that it calls into
question a categorization of sexual behaviour, which is often based
on emotional and culture-bound factors. The risk of this approach
is that it will result in the watering down of the concepts and a loss
of distinction among them.

What should one do, if a patient comes and asks: "Is this or that
abnormal?" Will the patient be satisfied, if the doctor answers "That
is just a little variation?" Will he not interpret such a glib remark
as a rejection, an indication that his problem is not being taken
seriously? It is easy to be pseudo-liberal. Such an attitude has nothing
to do with real insight. In describing sexual behaviour one or more
frames of reference are necessary. Frames of reference which have a
philosophical or religious basis can be used, but these are outside of
the scope of this discussion. On the other hand it is possible to take
as a point of departure a number of concrete observations. For
example, it is possible to attempt to draw conclusions from the
behaviour of animals. However, it will rapidly be discovered that
such observations can be used to provide support for almost any
concept. The same holds true to a certain degree for studies which

are based on a comparison among different cultures. Whether these comparisons are historical or concurrent, they can be used to confirm or refute almost anything depending on the intentions of the author. Statistical data can be used as a starting point. One can consider how frequently this or that occurs, which is the approach taken by Kinsey's group and others. This approach has its advantages but also has its pitfalls.

From a purely medical standpoint, there are two frames of reference, complementary to a certain degree, which are perhaps particularly productive and which yield insight. One of these can be called the psychobiological frame of reference and is based upon our knowledge of those biological and psychosocial factors that influence the development of sex and gender (Money and Ehrhardt, 1972). The other frame of reference is based on the work of Freud and his followers and can be called the psychodynamic model. This will be briefly described in a subsequent section.

Instead of setting up the dichotomy normal – deviant, one can ask: with which form of sexual behaviour, normal or deviant, does the individual feel comfortable, and which form causes problems for him? The reason that a form of sexual behaviour causes problems can be sought in *the individual* himself (psychological strength, independence with regard to setting own norms, feelings of shame, disgust, anxiety, etc.), or in the *environment* (the partner, risk of social degradation, societal sanctions, etc.). Certain forms of sexual behaviour are not deviant in themselves, but can easily elicit sanctions from the environment – for example an adult man's relationship with a girl, who is a minor but who is sexually mature, certain forms of rape, etc. Not all sexual criminality is identical with deviant behaviour. Conversely many forms of sexual behaviour traditionally considered to be deviant are not criminal matters in many countries (for example, homosexual relationships between consenting partners over a certain age, transvestism, sexual relations with animals, and so on). However, these forms of behaviour often elicit unpleasant reactions, if they become known to people in the surroundings. Finally, it should not be forgotten that so-called deviant relationships are not necessarily expressions of a deviant attitude, but may be substitute relationships in situations in which there is a lack of possibilities for establishing so-called normal relationships (the cowman and the cow, homosexual relationships in unisexual institutions or in certain periods of life, etc.). Furthermore, some mentally retarded or elderly debiliated individuals engage in relationships, which are not the result of a sexually deviant attitude, but which may be considered to be a kind of substitute relation or an indication of lack of judgment and weakened inhibitions of normal sexual impulses.

People, who have problems with their sexual lives, will — sometimes of their own accord, other times forced by others (spouse, parents, social agencies, legal authorities) — seek the help of a doctor. What can the doctor do? It is rare that he can effect a basic change. He must often recognize that he can only help the patient to live with his characteristics in the best way possible, both internally and externally. In some cases extreme measures have been resorted to, as for example castration and stereotactic procedures involving the hypothalamic nuclei, although such interventions are rare. In other cases treatment with so-called anti-hormones and different forms of psychotherapy have been tried. These treatment modalities will be discussed in more detail below. It is, however, necessary when speaking of sexual deviations to be aware that it is often the deviation itself that gives the individual his real instinctual satisfaction (the exhibitionist prefers to exhibit himself rather than have intercourse with his attractive wife) and that rational or ethical arguments rarely have any decisive effect. Furthermore, it should be remembered that the sexual deviation is often just as incomprehensible, although irresistible, for the individual himself as for those around him. He has no choice. His choice has been made for him.

The Psychodynamic Model

In "Three Essays on the Theory of Sexuality" (1905, 1949) Freud states that:

> "The normal sexual aim is regarded as being the union of the genitals in the act known as copulation, which leads to a release of the sexual tension and a temporary extinction of the sexual instinct."

But Freud maintains that:

> "no healthy person, it appears, can fail to make some addition that might be called perverse to the normal sexual aim; and the universality of this finding is in itself enough to show how inappropriate it is to use the word perversion as a term of reproach. In the sphere of sexual life we are brought up against peculiar and, indeed, insoluble difficulties as soon as we try to draw a sharp line to distinguish mere variations within the range of what is physiological from pathological symptoms."

As early as 1905 the word "perversion" had already developed a negative connotation. It appears that then as now one "is brought insoluble difficulties", if one draws a sharp border between "normal" and "abnormal".

In addition to the final sexual aim Freud talks about preliminary sexual aims — for example everything that goes into foreplay and which can be sexually exciting but which leads to the definitive sexual aim: sexual intercourse. Accordingly the perversions are defined as:

> "sexual activities, which either
>
> a. extend in an anatomical sense, beyond the regions of the body that are designed for sexual union
>   or
> b. linger over the immediate relations to the sexual object which should normally be traversed rapidly on the path toward the final sexual aim".

However, what particularly differentiates between normality and abnormality is:

> "if a perversion instead of appearing merely *alongside* the normal sexual aim and object . . . takes the place in *all* circumstances — if, in short a perversion has the characteristics of exclusiveness and fixation — then we shall usually be justified in regarding it as a pathological symptom."

In Freud's view — which is shared by many others, often on the basis of completely different frames of reference — the foundation of sexual disturbances are laid down very early in life, during the first years of life, even though they usually are first clearly manifested after puberty.

If psychosexual development is seriously disturbed the result — depending in the nature and degree of the trauma as well as on the individual's power of resistance and mode of reaction — is either

a. a decreased ability to act out sexual impulses, but with the maintenance of "normal" instinctual direction and object choice. The disturbances in these cases may manifest themselves as a "sexual dysfunction" (e.g. frigidity, impotence).
or
b. a change in the "normal" impulses and forms of behaviour toward those conditions which are considered to be deviant.

Sexual dysfunctions (frigidity and impotence) and sexual deviations can be considered to represent different attempts to solve unconscious conflicts.

Ismond Rosen has formulated his view of sexual deviations in the following way:

> "Sexual perversions are the living out of pieces of infantile behaviour which have been retained in the personality in order to hold in check other more undesirable elements, or to defend the individual against the threat of castration or the effects of object loss .... The perversion allows the free expression of selected elements such as the exhibitionism or voyeurism while the deeper incestuous wishes, castration fears and primitive sadistic wishes of particularly oral type are kept in check."

If this view is accepted, it can be understood, why experience has shown that it is so difficult, often impossible, to get a patient to give up his perversion in favour of so-called "normal" behaviour. The road to this apparently uncomplicated behaviour is blocked, because he (unconsciously, of course) fears — on the basis of all his painful experiences — the accompanying confrontation with distressing, frightening intrapsychic material. The perversion is, despite the psychological and sometimes also social problems that accompany it, a lesser evil which insures to a certain degree his continued psychological integrity.

Classification of the Sexual Deviations

The following schematic list of sexual deviations has its weak points, but it is for the most part useful.

Deviations, which are manifested by a change of *sexual aim:*

Exhibitionism — impulse to exhibit oneself.
Voyeurism (scopophilia) — sexual pleasure in secretly watching others.
Sadomasochism (algolagnia) — sexual pleasure in humiliating others and in being humiliated.
Saliromania, Coprophagia, Coprolalia — sexual pleasure associated with excreta.
Fetishism — sexual pleasure at the sight of or contact with particular objects, materials, parts of the body, etc.
Kleptomania — sexually motivated impulse to steal.
Pyromania — sexually motivated impulse to set fires.

Deviations, which are manifested by a change of *sexual object:**

---

* Pedophilia, sexual relations with children (heterosexual or homosexual pedophilia) will not be described separately, but only in relation to the other deviations.

Zoophilia (*crimen bestialis*) — sexual relations with animals.
Necrophilia — sexual relations with a corpse.
Homosexuality — sexual relations between persons of the same sex.

Deviations, which are manifested by *altered sexual role or sexual identity*:

Transvestism (eonism) — impulse to dress in the clothing of the opposite sex.
Transsexuality (gender dysphoria) — desire to "change sex".

It should be stressed that several of these terms — most of which originated around the turn of the twentieth century — are used imprecisely. This will be commented on further below. It should also be remembered that these are not sharply delimited conditions. Some of the deviations mentioned occur rarely, others frequently. Some are clearly of societal interest, while others are only of limited relevance. Some of the deviations occur much more frequently or exclusively in men. This is true for example of exhibitionism, voyeurism, and heterosexual transvestism.

Exhibitionism and Voyeurism (Scopophilia)

Sexual deviations are often best understood, when they are considered together. This is particularly true of exhibitionism and voyeurism.

The term *exhibitionism* is often used imprecisely, almost as a synonym for the transmission of very direct sexual signs. Thus it is not uncommon in everyday speech to hear women in low cut dresses, very short skirts, or otherwise "provocative dress" referred to as exhibitionists. Similarly, men who like to wear very tight pants or who in other ways try to emphasize their sexual characteristics are called exhibitionists. However, from a sexological point of view these are not examples of exhibitionism. On the other hand, some of this behaviour may be an expression of aggression, in which there is pleasure in exciting and then, when the effect is achieved, in refusing sexual advances.

An exhibitionist is a person, who has an irresistible, repetitive impulse to show his sexual organs, usually to strangers, in order to achieve a psychic discharge that other sexual practices do not give him. Defined in this way exhibitionism occurs only in men. While exhibiting himself, the man in some cases has an erection, while in other cases he does not. Sometimes he ejaculates, at other times he does not.

Usually, this impulse becomes manifest after puberty and remains throughout life. Many exhibitionists hope that by entering into a stable relationship, they can weaken their inclination to exhibit themselves, but they discover that it is the exhibitionism, which gives them their real impulse gratification and that coitus is only a surrogate for the exhibitionism.

Most cases of exhibitionism do not come to the attention of the police. Even so exhibitionism is one of the most frequently prosecuted forms óf sexual criminality. In recent years the number of reported cases of exhibitionism in Denmark has decreased considerably. This is not·the result of fewer cases, but rather of the fact that people today less often report exhibitionists than they did previously because of a change in attitude (see for example Kutchinsky, 1973). Exhibitionists are usually rather harmless and flee as soon as they have achieved their goal. Often the entire episode lasts only a few minutes. It is their own welfare, rather than that of others, that is threatened by their irresistible urge to exhibit themselves.

To punish these individuals, for example by imprisonment as provided for by the legal code of most countries, of course does no good. Perhaps all parties would best be served, if this deviation did not come directly under the jurisdiction of the criminal code and instead came under the jurisdiction of local police regulations and only under certain circumstances was punishable by a fine. In this way considerable social damage to the individual exhibitionist could be avoided.

Usually the exhibitionist has a particular "stimulus type", which arouses the impulse in him — it can be a particular age group (children or adults), a particular hair colour, hairdo, or clothing, particular population groups, etc. Some exhibit in stairways, others prefer parks or exhibit themselves from their car, while they wait for passers-by. The exhibitionistic behaviour is often very stereotyped. Some exhibitionists plan their exhibitionistic excursions carefully. Others are more impulsive and exhibit themselves only if they are in a particular psychological mood or if their interest is suddenly awakened by a passer-by. Exhibitionism occurs in all social groups and is not an indication of particular "primitivity", "crudity" or lack of responsibility. On the contrary, many exhibitionists are deeply unhappy partly because of the social risk to which this impulse exposes them and their families. However, many exhibitionists are unhappy, particularly because they recognize that this form of sexual release is a very isolated, impoverished form of sexuality, which does not include any possibility for mutuality or for the affectual aspects, which more normal forms of sexuality can provide. Therefore, the exhibitionist himself feels that there is "something wrong with him", that he is abnormal — and he feels this particularly, when he realizes that his partner, to whom he otherwise feels closely attached and of whom he is fond, cannot provide him with sexual gratification, which only the particular circumstances connected with the act of exhibitionism gives him.

The term voyeurism (Fr. voir) or scopophilia (Gk. skopein: see, examine) indicates the impulse to spy upon others — usually strangers — as they undress, have sexual intercourse or in some cases while they defaecate or urinate. However, the term voyeurism applies only if the impulse entirely overshadows the desire to have sexual relations. Ordinary sexual curiosity, which today there is ample opportunity to gratify, is a common personality feature and of course is not an expression of voyeurism.

Voyeurism also occurs only in men. There are no reports of women seeking gratification of their sexual impulses by, for example, roaming around military bases and spying on soldiers. The voyeur is also subject to an irresistible, repetitive urge, which he seeks to satisfy by spying on others through windows, doors, public toilets, in parks, woods, on the beach, and so on. This is the way he obtains his impulse gratification. Just like the exhibitionist, the voyeur is usually harmless and flees frightened, if he is discovered. Sometimes the object of his spying is not entirely innocent in the incident, but has, for example, undressed in a lighted room without drawing the curtains. Some voyeurs also complain, probably not without some justification, that they are repeatedly provoked. In some cases the voyeur, usually after feeling intensely stimulated or provoked, will let his presence be known, will exhibit himself or ask the girl to touch him or even to masturbate him. Cases have been described, in which the voyeur has tried to force the victim to have sexual intercourse with him. However, such cases are exceptional.

In situations, where there is a possibility for close physical contact, for example in trains, buses, in front of movie theatres, etc., some men find satisfaction in rubbing themselves up against women, while they masturbate to orgasm, but without seeking verbal contact. Such cases can be called examples of "frotteurism".

Many exhibitionists and voyeurs indicate that they have missed emotional warmth and security during childhood and that they themselves feel a lack of ability to give themselves to another person and feel secure in doing so. Similarly, they frequently complain that they do not feel sufficiently masculine, which they believe must also be evident to others. By exhibiting themselves and spying on others, and by being content with this, they avoid becoming dependent on others and avoid the risk of rejection and thus of further frustration. The element of aggression, which is hidden behind both exhibitionism and voyeurism, undoubtedly serves to strengthen the feeling of masculinity. The illegality itself is part of the sexual stimulus both for exhibitionists and for voyeurs. The stimulus includes the risk, the fear of degradation, the moment of surprise, and the urge to shock. All in all it is of course true that attempts to find rational solutions to this type of problem rarely succeed. If it were so simple, human sexuality would not so often in fact be accompanied by difficulties and even actual tragedies for those involved.

Sadism and Masochism (Algolagnia)

Electrical stimulation of a number of large and small regions of the hypothalamus, which are interconnected with one another, results in either sexual or aggressive impulses.

This is entirely or partially the neurophysiological substrate for the general experience that sexuality and aggressiveness are closely connected. Frustrated sexuality can be converted to aggressiveness. Conversely aggressive fantasies and forms of behaviour often contain a sexual element. In order for a sexual relationship to be successful, it is necessary that both partners have the ability both to be able to subordinate themselves, to give themselves, to take pleasure in being the recipient, and to demand, to be active, to take initiative. When this necessary balance is not present for various reasons, the result can be a sexuality characterized by sadomasochism.

The Austrian author Leopold v. Sacher-Masoch wrote the novel "Venus in Fur", in which the hero passively, both psychologically and physically, accepts subjugation by a cruel and tyrannical woman and clearly finds pleasure in this. The French nobleman Donatien Alphonse de Sade described in a number of novels, including the famous Justine (1791, 1797) the sexually pleasurable feelings derived from degrading others and causing them pain, even from mutilating them to the point of death.

Thus in the case of both of these deviations there is an aspect of untamed aggressiveness, which can either be directed outwards (sadism) or inwards (masochism). Sadism and masochism are two sides of the same coin and usually one talks about sadomasochism.

In accordance with what was said above about perversions, sadomasochistic forms of behaviour are considered to reflect a perversion only when they become the actual sexual goal. Many people have moderate sadomasochistic features in their sexual lives without being considered deviant. Rape often contains sadistic elements, and murder for sexual pleasure is the extreme of sadism. How close sadism lies to the surface is demonstrated during war, during which sadistic excesses almost always occur. Books and films which contain descriptions of sadism enjoy a large audience, and the same is true of pornographic descriptions of bondage and spanking. Some people seek prostitutes or certain clubs as outlets for their sadomasochistic impulses. Masturbation is sometimes carried out in connection with sadomasochistic arrangements, in which the individual brings himself into a dangerous situation in order to increase his sexual pleasure. Sometimes the result is death. The reader is referred to descriptions of of such cases in textbooks of forensic medicine.

Saliromania, Coprophagia and Coprolalia

In periods children are very preoccupied with examining, playing with and tasting their urine and faeces as part of their discovery of themselves and their surroundings. Later on "naughty words" are the object of their attention. Some adults remain sexually preoccupied by urine, faeces, and dirt. If this becomes a dominant characteristic it is referred to as saliromania (Fr. salir: dirt). Such an interest may be expressed in various ways. For example there is the previously mentioned interest in seeing others urinate and defecate. The anonymous author of the probably authentic Victorian autobiography "My Secret Life" describes repeatedly in great detail how he gratified such a desire by hiding himself in public lavatories or by having prostitutes urinate while he watched. Some go further and themselves wish to urinate or defecate on others or to be the object of this. Similarly some find it pleasurable to ingest the excreta of others. Such cases are referred to as coprophagia (Gr. kopros: manure — phago: to eat).

In the so-called personal advertisements in newspapers such desires
are often expressed. These deviations are closely related both to sadomasochism and to exhibitionism and voyeurism, and their regressive
features are obvious. Some people feel clear sexual pleasure in using
vulgar expressions, for example during telephone calls to strangers,
in letters with very crude sexual contents or in attacking passers-by
with obscene remarks. Such cases are referred to as coprolalia (Gk.
lalein: to talk).

Fetishism

A fetish is an object endowed with particular, often supernatural
characteristics and which is venerated (Portuguese feitio: amulet).
The child's teddy bear, security blanket, etc. can be regarded as
security-providing fetishes.

Fetishists, usually men, are sexually aroused by non-genital parts
of the sexual partner (often the hair or the feet) or by particular
pieces of clothing or material (underwear, corsets, shoes, boots —
rubber, plastic, leather, shiny or particularly soft material, etc.).
Sadomasochistic practices are often associated with the fetishistic
use of boots, shoes, leather or rubber pieces of clothing, and so on.
An essential part of transvestism (see the description of this) is a
fetishistic preoccupation partly with the female wardrobe and partly
with the woman as such. Certain people feel sexually attracted by
handicapped individuals in a fetishistic way.

Kleptomania and Pyromania

These two terms are often applied imprecisely as designations for
poorly understood, apparently purposeless thefts or fire-setting (Gr.
kleptein: to steal — Gr. pyros: fire).

Sexologically kleptomania refers to an obsessive inclination to
steal and thereby achieve sexual pleasure. As far as is known it is
particularly women, who demonstrate this inclination, which may
be especially evident during certain days of the menstrual cycle or
during the menopause.

Those cases in which fire-setting is accompanied by sexual arousal
may be expressions of a perversion. Most so-called acts of pyromania
probably have another origin — for example the motive of revenge.

Zoophilia

Sexual relations with animals, also called *crimen bestialis* (Lat. crimen: crime — bestia: animal) or, less accurately, sodomy (after the biblical town of Sodoma — sodomy is most frequently used as a synonym for anal coitus), may be an expression of a sexual deviation. However, in some cases it is more likely to be a substitute gratification resulting from the absence of a human sexual partner or to reflect a desire for variation. In earlier times zoophilia was considered to be such a serious crime that it was punishable by death and the animal was also killed. Today it is only prosecuted in cases of cruelty to animals.

Necrophilia

Sexual interest in corpses (Gr. nekros: corpse), including sexual relations with dead persons, and even ingestion of the flesh of the dead, is called necrophilia. It is the opposite to the fantasy of vampires, dead individuals who find and exsanguinate the living.

Homosexuality

From the description of exhibitionism and also of several of the other deviations mentioned earlier, it appears clearly that these deviations are very isolated forms of sexuality. Consideration of the partner plays no role. No real relationship exists, let alone a love relationship. Even the sexual act differs essentially from that in a usual relationship. Exhibitionists, voyeurs, etc. often themselves complain that they feel abnormal.

However, it is different in the case of the usual homosexual relationship, which resembles the heterosexual relationship much more closely. With regard to feelings, homosexual relations can be just as genuine as heterosexual relationships, just as the purely sexual aspects do not differ essentially from those of heterosexual relationships. It is therefore not surprising that many homosexuals in no way feel "abnormal" and that they feel insulted in being classified together with bizarre forms of sexuality such as zoophilia, necrophilia, etc. While it may be difficult or impossible to understand exactly how individuals with a number of other sexual deviations feel, and what drives them to act out their sexual impulses, it is possible for most people, if they allow themselves, to understand how homosexuals lead their lives. It is another matter whether people can accept in theory and practice, as advocated by many homosexuals, that homosexuality is a form of life parallel to heterosexuality. However, there are good reasons for emphasizing that of all the sexual minorities homosexuals are the ones that are closest to heterosexuals.

Conceptual Delimitation

A necessary prerequisite for discussing the subject of homosexuality is, that what is being discussed is precisely specified and that homosexual acts and homosexual attitudes are not equated.

A homosexual act is a sexual relationship between two sexually mature individuals of the same sex. There is general agreement about this definition. It becomes more difficult, if an attempt is made to separate people into two well-delimited groups, heterosexual and homosexual (Gr. homos: the same — Gr. heteros: another). Is a person homosexual, if he has either homosexual experiences or only admits to homosexual impulses? It would perhaps be possible to maintain this point of view, if homosexual experiences rarely occurred in predominantly heterosexually oriented individuals. However, today we know that this is not the case. This knowledge stems mainly from two sources, partly from a number of studies of behaviour, of which that of the Kinsey group is the most comprehensive and best known, and partly from a number of psychoanalytic studies. The following sections will briefly consider the degree to which these two frames of reference agree about human homosexuality and on which points they diverge.

The Kinsey Group's Frame of Reference

On the basis of the behaviour of individuals interviewed, but to a certain degree also on the sexual attitude of these people, Kinsey and co-workers (1948, 1953) developed the following heterosexuality—homosexuality continuum:

Table 1

Heterosexual-homosexual rating scale (Kinsey *et al.*, 1948, p. 638).

0: Exclusively heterosexual
1: Predominantly heterosexual, only incidentally homosexual
2: Predominantly heterosexual, but more than incidentally homosexual
3: Equally heterosexual and homosexual
4: Predominantly homosexual, but more than incidentally heterosexual
5: Predominantly homosexual, but incidentally heterosexual
6: Exclusively homosexual.

Grouping individuals in this way, the Kinsey group found the following frequency of homosexual experience in a fairly representative sample of the white American population:

Table 2

Incidence of homosexual experience (after Kinsey *et al.*, 1948 1953).

		1	2
		♂	♀
		%	%
Homosexual feelings, but no experience		13	15
Overt homosexual experience since the onset of adolescence		37	13
Exclusively homosexual		4	2–3

		3	4
		♂	♀
	scale	%	%
At least some homosexual experience	1–6	30	11–20
More than incidental homosexual experience	2–6	25	6–14
Homosexual as much as heterosexual	3–6	18	4–11
Mostly homosexual	4–6	13	3–8
Largely homosexual	5–6	10	2–6
Exclusively homosexual	6	8	1–3

1. Between adolescence and old age
2. Women by age 45
3. In a period of three years or more between the ages of 16 and 55 years
4. Women from 20–35.

It can be seen from the table that it was not possible to obtain exactly comparable figures for the two sexes.

When they were originally presented, the figures attracted a great deal of attention and gave rise to erroneous interpretations.

The Kinsey group itself emphasized that it was not possible on the basis of these figures to conclude that a considerable number of American men and women "actually were homosexual" but that on the other hand the opposite had to be concluded, namely that it was impossible to maintain a sharp distinction between heterosexuals and homosexuals. In principle it should be possible for an individual to move along the entire continuum, but in practice most frequently he or she moves only within a limited portion of it.

This rating scale has its evident advantages. It is relatively easy to use (although apparently not so easy that the Kinsey group itself was able to co-ordinate the data about men and women better than it did), it solves many practical problems, and it does not make value judgments, which may contribute to a desirable de-dramatization of the attitude toward homosexual behaviour. It has also won wide acceptance. However, it is not adequate to cover certain areas, as physicians will readily recognize. To cover such areas other frames of reference must be applied, such as the psychoanalytical model.

The Psychoanalytical Model

The psychoanalytical school agrees with the Kinsey group that homosexual acts in themselves say nothing about an individual's possible homosexual attitude. So many people have homosexual experiences or at least homosexual dreams and fantasies and recognize a certain attraction to their own sex that these must be accepted as entirely normal personality features. However, in addition to these individuals there is a small group of people — those that would score 5—6 on the Kinsey scale — who are distinguishable from the majority. They are distinguishable not so much because of their sexual behaviour as because of a particular development and attitude. The distinguishing characteristic of these people is a lack of heterosexual interest and ability. Although they may be entirely able to carry out sexual intercourse with a person of the opposite sex, their real sexual gratification is obtained only in a relationship with a person of their own sex. These people, the "real" homosexuals, in contrast to most people have no choice between heterosexual and homosexual gratification (physical and psychological) and it is this lack of choice that differentiates them from heterosexuals, who at least in principle are able to decide for themselves, whether they will enter into heterosexual or homosexual relations and can achieve full gratification from both forms.

While the Kinsey group places everyone on the same heterosexuality—homosexuality continuum and in principle it must be agreed that there is a smooth transition and complete mobility between all steps on the continuum, in the psychoanalytic view "real" homosexuals (or as they are sometimes also called, inverse homosexuals) are on a continuum of their own.

There is no reason to set these two points of view in opposition to one another in an attempt to evaluate which of them is better. Each has its advantages and limitations.

In the following sections the word homosexuality is used to indicate those forms of homosexual attitude and behaviour, which would be rated 5—6 on the Kinsey group's rating scale and for the most part correspond to inverse homosexuality.

Bisexuality

Persons who are equally interested, physically and psychically, in relationships to both sexes are called bisexuals. It cannot be denied that some people really may be bisexually oriented, but most often the term bisexual is used imprecisely and covers entirely different phenomena.

In biology and psychology it is often impossible to indicate sharp, well-defined limits, one can only describe a group of persons distinctly different from another group of persons. Borderline cases have to be included in one of the main groups, if they are not so divergent that they ought to be classified in a separate group.

Following a criterion of sexual preference it is possible to divide human beings into heterosexuals and homosexuals. From a logical point of view it might be expected that we need a third classification called bisexuality. In practice it is nearly always possible — provided necessary information is available and useful criteria are at hand — to classify a person as either heterosexual or homosexual; the term bisexual is needless in the majority of cases.

As described earlier, both heterosexual and homosexual persons sometimes engage in sexual relations with both sexes. It is not always possible to equate sexual behaviour and sexual preference. Often there is an agreement between sexual behaviour and preference, but in some cases, more than accepted previously, heterosexual persons engage in homosexual contacts and vice versa. This fact does not necessitate the introduction of a third term: bisexuality;

but instead requires a re-definition of what is understood as hetero-sexuality — if you wish: to extend the concept of normality. And this is what is happening today in Western culture. This new concept of heterosexuality and homosexuality ought not to lead to the mis-conception that there is no difference between heterosexuality and homosexuality, but emphasizes that the differences are shown more in attitudes and feelings than in behaviour.

The word "bisexual" is however, used increasingly. Why is this so? Partly the reason is the growing understanding that many hetero-sexuals are not unaffected by members of their own sex. But nothing is gained if those heterosexuals who, using an expression of Vanggaard (1962), show "normal homosexual inclinations", are separated from other heterosexuals under the special term of bisexuality, because there is no basic difference between this group of heterosexuals and other heterosexuals. On the contrary, it is the heterosexuals with the strongest personality, the greatest flexibility and independence who realize their homosexual potential. As mentioned earlier, the conse-quence must be to extend the concept of normality, not to narrow it down or change it by saying that normality is the same as bi-sexuality.

The second reason for the increasing use of the word bisexual is that many homosexuals prefer themselves and others to be called bisexuals. The explanation is, of course, partly a narrow concept of what is understood as homosexuality, partly the negative attitude towards homosexuality in our culture. The term bisexuality seems more acceptable, lesser discriminating — in short in these cases is used as an euphemism.

The following example will illustrate this.

Two younger men, one married, the other single, sought advice, because the married man's wife threatened to divorce him. The two men had started a homosexual relationship some years ago and still slept together once or twice a week. Originally the wife had accepted this, but felt the situation more and more difficult. The married man said that he was bisexual, because he was very fond of his wife and never had any potency disturbances and often had sexual intercourse with her. He had only had heterosexual relations with his wife and had not known any other woman. His single friend had known several women, but stressed that he felt completely homosexual. He was very much in love with his friend.

The married man had told his wife that if she forced him to leave his friend, it would not be of any benefit, but only make more problems, since it was impossible for him to give up his homosexual satisfaction. Before he met his friend, he had many casual relationships with other men, he met in a park well known as a homosexual meeting-place and this habit he would take up again. Many times during the conversation he stressed that he was bisexual. When asked whether he would meet other women, if his wife really left him, he looked rather astonished and said definitely no. Then he smiled and during the rest of the conversation he did not use the word bisexual. And his friend looked a little triumphant.

If we use the term bisexual, we are in a situation, where this word is used about two quite different groups of people, partly hetero-sexuals, partly homosexuals.

It is hardly possible to eradicate the term bisexuality from daily use. But where precise definitions are needed the word bisexual should be restricted to indicate persons who really are bisexual — if there are any — and not in that imprecise, euphemistical way, in which it is often used today.

Causes of Homosexuality

It has not been possible to explain, why some people become homo-sexuals. It is hardly likely that a single etiological factor will be found, as there is probably an interaction among a number of factors, some of which may be biological and others environmental. The only thing that is certain is that the basis of homosexuality is laid down very early in life, within the first years of life, and is not something which is acquired during puberty or in later years, even if the first manifestations of it occur after puberty.

Our present knowledge about the importance of genetic, hormonal, psychological, and familial factors will now be briefly described, and the question of whether the concept of seduction is of any importance will be considered.

Genetic Factors

It appears that parents of homosexuals, both fathers and mothers, are somewhat older on the average than parents in the general population, and that homosexuals are frequently born late in the line of siblings. Finally, it seems as if there is a concentration of homosexuality in certain families (Bieber, 1962; Slater, 1962; Abe and Moran, 1969). However, it is difficult to decide whether hereditary factors or environmental factors are the most important. Twin research has been used in an attempt to clarify this issue. In the most representative studies there is a 50% concordance rate for homosexuality among MZ twins as opposed to an 8.3% rate among DZ twins (Rosenthal, 1970).

Today it is not possible to specify the importance of hereditary factors any more certainly than Rosenthal does, when he concludes that:

> "it is difficult to evaluate this spotty literature. The twin studies suggest that heredity plays an important role with respect to whether males become homosexuals, but even here, we have only a few small samples that at least suggest that they may not be biased."

Hormonal Factors

It is necessary to distinguish between the influence of hormones during foetal life from their importance later on. If there is a casual association between hormonal factors and homosexuality it will probably be found in foetal life rather than later in life. (Money and Ehrhardt, 1972).

During puberty by far the main importance of hormones seems to be the completion of a development the basis of which has been laid down many years previously.

It has been known for many years that in the case of sexually mature individuals testosterone increases libido in both sexes, but does not influence the direction of the sexual drive. Testosterone given to a feminine, sexually mature man will not make him less feminine. If he is homosexual, it may increase his desire for homosexual relations, but under no circumstances will it increase his interest in women. Similarly, oestrogens given to masculine, homosexual women have just as little effect on their homosexual attitude and will not make them feminine.

It has long been accepted that in sexually mature individuals it is not possible to demonstrate biological differences between heterosexuals and homosexuals. In recent years, however, there have been some reports, which indicate that lower testosterone values have

been found in a group of homosexual men than in a control group
and that higher androgen values have been found in a group of
homosexual women than in a control group. Furthermore, different
androsterone/etiocholanalone ratios have been reported in homosexual men and women compared to heterosexuals (Lorraine *et al.*,
1971; Margolese *et al.*, 1973; Pillard *et al.*, 1974). However, the
results continue to be controversial (Barlow *et al.*, 1974) and so far
no definitive conclusions can be drawn from them. Margolese and
co-workers were only able to go so far as to conclude that:

> "this study lends further support to the hypothesis previously proposed:
> that the metabolic pathway, which results in a relatively high androsterone
> value, is associated with sexual preference for females by either sex,
> whereas a relatively low androsterone value is associated with sexual
> preference for males by either sex."

Changes in hormone concentration may be secondary to a primary
homosexual, psychosocial orientation through cortical influences
on the hypothalamus and hypophysis. John Money indicates that the
authors of these reports have not found anything basically new about
homosexuality, but that they have described a syndrome in which
homosexual behaviour and changes in the levels of sex hormones
occur (Money and Ehrhardt, 1972).

Psychological and Familial Factors

Most researchers agree that the conditions of childhood are of essential importance for the development of homosexuality. Even though
the results of research are not entirely in agreement, attempts have
been focused on certain family constellations, which are felt to be
particularly influential in the development of homosexuality in men
and women. Considerably more effort has been invested in research
on homosexuality in men than in women. "The classical pattern" for
the development of a homosexual man (Bieber, 1962) is a domineering, over-protective mother; a father who is experienced as weak,
hostile, or who — physically or psychologically — is often away from
the home; and a son who as a child prefers quiet games, does not
care for sports or other forms of physical activity, abhors fights and
attaches himself closely to the mother. The relationship to any
siblings is often disturbed, so that there are particularly negative
feelings between the homosexual and his brothers, and in certain
cases also between the homosexual and his sisters.

However, a number of questions remain unanswered: why is it exactly this son and not one of the others in the family that becomes homosexual? Do some children themselves seek out a particularly close relationship with the mother and thus alienate the father and siblings? Studies suggest that it is an *interaction* of unfortunate family factors, which forms the background for a homosexual development. If the mother is a domineering, overprotective type, but the father does not react by rejecting the son, but instead is able to be a good object for identification and to give him the warmth and love he needs, this will counteract the influence of the mother. Similarly, a good sibling relationship seems to a certain degree to hinder a homosexual development.

The family pattern also plays an important role of the development of homosexuality in women. The daughter's relationship to the father is of essential importance (Bene, 1965; Lonely, 1973).

Seduction

For many years it was assumed that seduction played a role in the development of homosexuality. All those with insight into homosexual problems are now in agreement that it is not possible to become homosexual through seduction. The seduction theory held that early homosexual experiences could result in a change from predominantly heterosexual to a predominantly homosexual direction of sexual drive.

The reason for which the seduction theory has been so hard to do away with is that pubescent boys are not difficult to talk into having homosexual relations. However, they do not become homosexuals as a result, if they are not homosexual already. Another reason for the durability of the seduction theory is homosexual prostitution which, like other forms of prostitution, is often accompanied by criminality of different types. Many male prostitutes, when they get into trouble, claim to the police that they entered into this activity, because they previously had been seduced by homosexual men. However, male prostitutes are in themselves the best proof that the seduction theory does not hold in reality. Those male prostitutes, who are heterosexual, when they start as prostitutes, are also heterosexual, when they stop being prostitutes.

The seduction theory has resulted in a higher age limit for homosexual relations than for heterosexual relations in the codes of law in many countries. These laws are intended to protect the young

from homosexual "seduction", and the damage it is believed such
seduction can cause. It has turned out that young people frequently
encounter homosexual advances, but also that they can very well take
care of themselves and do not need special protection from the law
(Hertoft, 1968). On the other hand certain young criminals have
taken advantage of the difference in age limits for homosexual and
heterosexual relations to blackmail homosexuals with whom they
have had relations. As a result of the recognition of the lack of
validity of the seduction theory and because of the possibilities for
abuse provided by different age limits, many countries now have the
same age limit for homosexual and heterosexual relations.

Features of the Homosexual Subculture

Meeting places. In almost all countries, particularly in the big cities,
there are a number of meeting places, which provide possibilities
for making homosexual contact, and which rapidly become known
to those, who need them. They usually include bars, restaurants,
clubs, baths, movie theatres, parks, streets, railroad stations, public
toilets, etc. Of course this is not a fixed system. The places change
depending on fashion, attention from the police or gangsters and
so on. It is characteristic that most of these meeting places remain
inconspicuous to anyone but the interested homosexuals. It is therefore necessary to know a little about the characteristic language and
signal systems, which are used between people, who wish to make
homosexual contact in order to be aware of what goes on in this
subculture. There is nothing mystical about this "language". It consists only of glances (often only a fraction of a second longer than
those normally exchanged between strangers); little remarks which
can be amplified upon, if the other party demonstrates interest;
and characteristic movements, which allow the insider to draw his
own conclusions but which would not be understood by others (see
for example Hoffman, 1968).

Of course this system developed as a result of the generally
negative attitude toward homosexuality and it has both its advantages
and disadvantages. The advantages include the fact that all insiders
know where to go and what to do to make homosexual contact.
Many of the homosexual meeting places make anonymous contacts
possible, which some homosexuals find desirable because of family,
job, and other considerations. Other meeting places make it possible

for the homosexual to relax and be himself without having to pretend as he must do elsewhere. The disadvantages include the resulting "ghetto mentality", and the fact that many homosexuals do not feel very comfortable in the usual meeting places and wish to have other possibilities for making contact. Furthermore, the somewhat older individuals often have difficulty in measuring up in these usual meeting places, which are so clearly part of a youth cult. Aside from a few lesbian restaurants and bars, these meeting places are usually dominated by men. Homosexual women seem to prefer and to be able to contact one another in ways that are different from those usual for men. Furthermore, it is probably easier for homosexual women than for men to establish relationships in which they live together for long periods of time and therefore they do not have such a great need for ways of making contact. Finally it may be that there are fewer homosexual women than men.

Sexual Behaviour

Homosexual relationships develop in much the same way as hetero-sexual relationships. In relations between men the most usual "prac-tices" are mutual masturbation, fellatio (Lat. fellare: to suck) and anal coitus. In relations between women mutual masturbation, cunnilingus (Lat. cunnus: female sexual organs (vulva), lingere: to lick) and coital imitations with or without the use of a dildo (artificial phallus) are most usual. The frequency with which these different types of sexual relations are carried out has been reported by many including, among others, Kinsey. Many authors are particularly pre-occupied with mentioning how frequently anal coitus occurs, as some maintain that it occurs rarely, others that it occurs frequently. What is perhaps most interesting about these different reports is that they once again reflect how taboo-laden is the area of anal coitus.

Many people believe that one partner in a homosexual relationship always or usually imitates the "woman's role" and the other partner the "man's role". In Bieber's terminology for men, one is either "the insertee" or "the insertor". This is undoubtedly true in some cases. However, in many, perhaps most, homosexual relationships the roles change, or the partners have equal roles. Similarly, a person may be the more "active" partner in one relationship and the more "passive" partner in another relationship depending, among other things, on the relative ages of the partners. Many homosexuals claim

that one of the advantages of homosexual relationships compared
to heterosexual relationships is that neither partner is locked into a
definite role.

There are a number of reports, mainly English and American,
about the age of first sexual experience, the number of partners, and
the duration and character of relationships, and the interested reader
is referred to them for further information about these topics (see
for example Kinsey, 1948, 1953). On the average, women seem to
find it easier to establish stable relationships than men. Many homosexual men wish to live in stable relationships, but few are able to
do so. It is not known, how many have established stable, long-
term relationships. A number of studies indicate that some homosexuals live rather "promiscuously" with many one-time relations or
brief relationships.

Homosexual Organizations

Since the time of the second world war, homosexual organizations,
which seek to look after the interests of homosexuals, have developed
in a number of countries. Although they are small in terms of numbers
of members, they have undoubtedly been of great importance as
meeting places and as lobbying organizations. Many of the older
homosexual organizations have characteristically worked within the
existing system and have tried (and succeeded) to better the conditions for homosexuals within that system. However, in recent years
somewhat different, more radical demands have been formulated
by more militant organizations, who have adopted the methods of
action of the American black movement and the feminist movement.
These homosexual groups have separated themselves from the older
organizations and have said that they no longer will accept that
homosexuals are merely tolerated on the terms of heterosexuals,
and that the homosexual way of life has its own value, which should
be recognized. Slogans from the black movement such as "Black
Power" and "Black is Beautiful" have been directly taken over so
that terms such as "Gay Power" and "Gay is Good" are used. Older
homosexuals often have difficulty accepting the methods of these
more radical homosexual groups. On the other hand many younger
homosexuals have difficulty in understanding how massive the suppression of homosexuality was even just a few years ago.

Attitudes Towards Homosexuals

Considerable changes in the attitudes towards homosexuality have occurred in the course of the last century, particularly in the period since the second world war. The publication of the two Kinsey reports in 1948 and 1953 undoubtedly contributed considerably to this by clearly demonstrating how frequent homosexual behaviour is. This change in attitude has, among other things, been reflected in changes in the law in a number of countries, so that homosexual relations between consenting partners has either completely or partially been removed from the list of criminal offences.

However, it can be questioned, whether this legalization of homosexuality means that the animosity towards homosexuals will soon belong to the past. That external sanctions have contributed to the maintenance of this animosity is clear. However, that this animosity will disappear together with most of the sanctions is not so clear. In this connection it is necessary to inquire further: why is it particularly male homosexuality that arouses animosity, while female homosexuality is hardly considered a problem? Furthermore, why is it particularly feminine homosexual men, who are placed furthest down on the hierarchy by both heterosexuals and homosexuals? It is not possible to answer these questions fully here. However, the possible reasons for these attitudes will be briefly mentioned.

The reason that the feminine homosexual man arouses as much animosity as he often does is that he has come to represent something frightening to other men. This in turn is related to the need faced by all people to find a balance between being dominant and submissive (for further information about the dominance-submission problem the reader is referred to Vanggaard, 1972).

Experience shows that men more often than women have difficulty finding a reasonable balance between being submissive and dominant. This is perhaps because they erroneously equate submission with feminity and dominance with masculinity. Many men doubt their own dominant (masculine) abilities and are fearful that others will discover this "weakness" and use their knowledge to dominate (feminize) them. Homosexual men, particularly those of the feminine type, are seen by many insecure men as an example of what could happen to them. Therefore, these men seek to defend themselves against this threat by avoidance, disgust, and possibly aggression. Homosexual women do not have any reason to harbour

the same fear, and they do not. Similarly it is understandable that
women in general do not become so involved in conflict when confronted by homosexuality in either sex.

If it is correct that it is our own conflicts, particularly those concerning dominance and submission, that are reflected in and determine our attitudes toward homosexuality, it is self-evident that
legalization of homosexuality is not sufficient to change the prevalent
attitude toward homosexuality. Similarly a call for "tolerance" is
not of much use. What is it that must be tolerated? It appears in
this connection that what is needed is not so much learning to tolerate
homosexuals as learning to accept oneself. When it comes down to
it, it is not really just a minority problem, a favour to be shown to a
minority, but a more general problem, which in the best interest of
everyone should be solved in the best possible way. A certain understanding of the extent of the problem is probably necessary for the
development of real tolerance. Such a change of mentality requires,
among other things, an upheaval of false ideas about masculinity
and femininity. Furthermore, it would be useful for more people to
learn to use the anxiety that confrontation with homosexuals (and
with their own homosexual feelings) releases to gain more insight
into themselves. Perhaps it would be possible to ask in such situations:
"Why am I afraid?" instead of immediately converting the anxiety
into abhorrence and aggression. Not until this is done will it be
possible for the superficial pseudotolerance, which seems to be the
prevalent attitude towards homosexuals today, to be replaced by
real tolerance, based on insight.

The Doctor and the Homosexual Patient

If the figures from the Kinsey reports can be applied to other cultures, it would be expected that most doctors relatively frequently
are in a position to give advice about problems in which homosexuality plays a role.

It is rare that the doctor is able to "convert" a homosexual to
heterosexuality, even when the patient wishes it. The most optimistic
reports of positive results are based on long-term and special treatment, which cannot be carried out by the practicing physician.

However, it is relatively rare that homosexuals consult a doctor
in order to change their sexual orientation. This is probably partly
because they know that this usually is impossible and partly
because many homosexuals have no desire for such a change. On the

other hand, quite a few people, who are uncertain about themselves and their sexual identity, do consult a doctor. In such cases the doctor can be helpful by pointing out that sexually most people do not function clearly according to an either/or model, as was believed earlier, and that a certain homosexual potential does not mean that an individual is a homosexual and thus cut off from a heterosexual life. Many patients will thereby be helped to gradually discover, where they belong and how to organize their lives. Under the present conditions of society it is easier in many ways to live mainly as a heterosexual, and the doctor should not avoid calling attention to this. On the other hand, he must help those people, who recognize themselves as being completely or predominantly homosexual, to see that although a homosexual way of life makes somewhat different demands and gives somewhat different possibilities than a heterosexual way of life, it is possible to live a satisfying, rich life whether one is heterosexual or homosexual.

If the patient directly asks the doctor's advice about entering into marriage, the doctor must as far as possible determine if the patient should be considered to be a "real" homosexual, as marriage usually is not advisable in such cases. This is particularly true of those patients, who hope that marriage will "cure" their homosexuality. In many cases the doctor will not be able to take a definitive position, but must discuss all aspects of the problem, including those which the patient would probably not take into consideration himself. Then he must make clear to the patient that the patient himself must make the final choice.

It is not possible to give general advice about whether a homosexual should inform his spouse, who is ignorant of his homosexual attitude, about this. In some cases it may be right to do so, while in other cases it would be more harmful than beneficial. Here too an open, comprehensive, unbiased discussion with the patient will often help him to decide for himself. These people often feel very isolated with their problems and have no one but the doctor with whom they dare discuss them. Just being able to talk about these problems will often be of considerable help to them. Sometimes the doctor is asked, if homosexuality is inherited (see section above). What is perhaps inherited is a certain predisposition, beyond which psychological factors in the early years of childhood play the major role. Many people, who fear that a "homosexual predisposition" will be transmitted to their children, feel relieved to hear that a good, affectionate upbringing will outweigh any "homosexual predisposition".

In divorce cases, in which one of the partners is a homosexual, the doctor may be asked for his advice about, who should be given custody of the children. No general rule can be given, except that the doctor should primarily take into consideration the total personalities and life styles of the parents, and only secondarily take their sexual attitudes into consideration.

Homosexual young men sometimes come to the doctor to get a statement indicating that they should be exempted from military service. Before giving such a statement, the doctor should always point out to the young man that a declaration to that effect may later cause him difficulties for example if he would like to enter into an occupation in which homosexuals are not wanted.

Although it sounds banal, it must be mentioned that homosexuals have a number of physical and psychological disorders, which should be handled just as the corresponding disorders would be in heterosexuals.

It is important that therapists, who undertake the treatment of sexual difficulties, have sufficient basic professional training, so that they do not get lost in the sexual problems of the patient and are able to carry out a comprehensive evaluation. Sexual complaints can occur as a part of several medical and surgical disorders, including diabetes, tumours, and organic brain disorders or may occur in connection with the development of a psychosis, which may be a manic-depressive psychosis, schizophrenia, or a senile psychosis. As is known, it is not unusual for complaints related to sexual identity problems to occur during the development of schizophrenia. Such complaints often take the form of a fear of becoming homosexual. The patient may feel that he is changing into a homosexual and that people in his surroundings can see this. He feels this change in himself as something strange, anxiety-provoking, and threatening, and he may have accompanying feelings of changes in his body. For example, young schizophrenic women may complain that their nose and Adam's apple are growing, that they are coming to look more and more like a man, that they are developing a penis. Young schizophrenic men may complain that their face is becoming weak and feminine, that their beard is not growing as much, that they are developing breasts, and that their sexual organs are diminishing in size. Patients of both sexes may have feelings of influence related to the genitals. Complaints such as these should naturally be taken for what they are, namely part of the development of schizophrenia, and should not be considered and treated in isolation.

Disturbances of Gender Identity

Transvestism

Some men experience clear satisfaction in dressing up in women's clothing and in imitating women in various ways. These are referred to as cases of transvestism (Lat. trans: on the other side — vestitus: dressed).

If a transvestite is prevented from acting out his impulse, he has difficulty concentrating and feels depressed and uncomfortable, whereas he calms down as soon as he has the chance to act on his impulse. There are different degrees of transvestism. However, most transvestites undoubtedly yearn to a very great degree to imitate women by dressing in women's clothes from undergarments to outer clothing, using artificial breasts, wigs, makeup, and so on.

This inclination is laid down early in life. In some cases it has been shown that someone close to the patient, undoubtedly someone with less overt sexual identity conflicts of his or her own, has attempted to more or less demasculinize the patient. For example, many transvestites report that early in life they were forced to dress in girls' clothing — as a punishment, in connection with a masquerade, because there were said to be no clean boys' clothes available and so on. They indicate that this experience made a permanent impression on them, and often that their reaction was ambivalent, so that they felt humiliated and frightened on the one hand, but on the other hand they also felt stimulated and excited. The individual experience is not really decisive but is remembered particularly clearly, while more indirect attacks have been forgotten or were never even recognized. In those cases in which the boy on the one hand submits to being dominated, but on the other hand has so much resistance that he doesn't completely buckle under, and is able to preserve the nuclear experience of himself as being a boy/man, the result may be the development of transvestism. If he does buckle under, the basis is laid for a transsexual development (see next section).

Transvestism and transsexuality may already be manifested during childhood as a particular interest in girls' and women's clothing, fashion magazines, makeup and so on. In others it does not become clearly manifested until after puberty. Usually it lasts throughout life. It occurs in biologically entirely normal men. On the other hand transvestism is not seen very frequently in individuals with chromosomal abnormalities, hormonal disturbances, or in intersex conditions in general. At first changing into women's clothes is usually sexually stimulating and is often accompanied by sexual fantasies and masturbation. Thus, transvestism has a fetishistic aspect. As a rule, as the years go by the immediate sexual stimulation associated with dressing up disappears and is replaced by a feeling of security and "inner harmony", which cannot be attained in any other way. Transvestites vehemently deny that they harbour homosexual impulses and they do not wish to be mistaken for homosexuals in any way. Some transvestites have a weak sexual drive, but most maintain that the sexual drive is normal and directed toward woman and that they are normally potent. They often enter into stable heterosexual relationships, many in the hope that they will thus be cured of their transvestism. Therefore, they often hide their inclination from their partner and get rid of their feminine equipment. However, after some time, months or years, the impulse to get dressed up in women's clothes breaks through again so strongly that they can no longer hold it back. Some transvestites then continue to hide their activities from those close to them and may manage to do this throughout life. Others are "discovered" (they often arranged for this themselves) or tell their spouse about their transvestism. The wife's reaction of course varies. Some wives cannot accept the fact at all and demand divorce or make it a condition of remaining in the marriage that the transvestism be given up entirely. Others accept it more or less reluctantly. Still others actively support their husbands in their transvestism, helping them to find a feminine wardrobe, wigs, makeup, etc. and accompanying them to meetings with other transvestites and their spouses. There is almost no information available concerning the effect on children of growing up in a home in which the father is a transvestite.

Transvestites are not psychotic (although transvestism, like other disturbances of sexual identity, can occur as part of a psychosis). They recognize that biologically they are men and they understand that other people may look upon them with surprise and find it difficult to understand them. They usually function well socially, both at home and at work. However, they often find it difficult to understand, how much of a burden their transvestism can be to those close to them and they often have a tendency to minimize the difficulties and idealize the reactions of those around them. Some transvestites are able to imitate women very well, but many exhibit a poor sense of reality with regard to how they appear to others. Sometimes they "overplay" the female role or inadvertently slip

out of it, so that an observer cannot be in doubt that he is in the
presence of a man in disguise.

As the years go by many develop a considerable routine in dressing
up and behaving like the type of women with whom they try to
identify. Many transvestites claim that they have a particular ability
to enter into "the female psyche", a belief that their wives rarely
share. It is probably closer to the truth to say that they try to realize
their ideas about what it is "to be a woman", but make the kinds of
mistakes that men usually do, when they try to imitate women.
Therefore, many transvestites, when they behave like women, resemble
somewhat old-fashioned, conventional, not very up-to-date women.

When a transvestite behaves like a man he is usually unremarkable,
without any particularly feminine features in his way of acting or
dressing.

Some homosexual, feminized men may dress in women's clothing.
Whether they should be called transvestites depends to a certain
degree on how the concept of transvestism is delimited and defined,
and it is self-evident that there will be transitional forms. Such
men often have a very hateful attitude toward the female sex in
general and their dressing up in women's clothes usually has a
very clear aspect of parody to it, which "real" transvestites do not
demonstrate, at least not on purpose. In the entertainment field
there are the so-called female impersonators, men who imitate
women. Some of these are undoubtedly transvestites, others
feminized homosexuals, some are transsexuals, while there are
still others who are none of these but who capitalize on particular
abilities and cultural tendencies.

The term transvestism is generally not used to describe women.
No women are known, who have an irresistible urge to imitate
men and who also consider themselves to be heterosexual. As is
well known it is not unusual that some women try to imitate men,
but these women are either special types of homosexuals or transsexuals.

The phenomenon may rarely occur as part of a psychosis.

There is a cultural and temporal relativism with regard to what are
considered to be feminine and masculine characteristics, what are
looked upon as feminine garb and masculine garb, etc. The fact that
women in Western culture have to a certain degree adopted masculine
articles of clothing such as trousers and shirts has nothing to do
with transvestism, the opposite tendency is also known, but it is not
nearly as marked. The reason that a woman dresses for example in

slacks is not that she harbours "latent" transvestitic tendencies, but rather that she finds such type of clothing practical, becoming, wishes to protest against the accepted female role, etc. Another matter is that there is a tendency today to protest against all overly rigid ideas of sexual roles — a tendency promoted by the fashion industry, etc. — which probably contributes to the fact that a number of sexual minority groups, including transvestites, are not so clearly distinguishable from others, as they were previously and probably also to the fact that they are more readily accepted. However, it is questionable whether this formal acceptance is an advantage.

In any case it is a fact that many transvestites today have difficulty limiting themselves to transvestism, and in increasing degree wish to "completely" become women, that is to "change sex". This would not be so bad, if this solution was the right one, but often this is not the case.

Until recently most countries have prohibited public appearances in the clothes of the opposite sex. In recognition of the fact that transvestism can in no way be considered to threaten law and order and is no longer regarded as an affront to "the public sense of decency", a number of countries have stopped the prohibition of transvestism, so that transvestites are free to walk about dressed up in women's clothing, to publish magazines and books, and to form organizations through which they can exchange experiences, cultivate common interests and meet similarly inclined individuals.

Transsexuality

Some people, women as well as men, indicate that there is a marked disparity between their biological sex and their psychological sexual identity (for example that they "harbour a woman's soul in a man's body"), and that the only solution to this oppressive problem is, through hormonal, surgical, and cosmetic procedures, to bring about as close a correspondence as possible between their psychological sexual identity and their bodily appearance — that they undergo a so-called sex change.

The term transsexuality was introduced by Cauldwell (1949), first came into general use in the 1950s, particularly after a young American, George Jorgensen became Christine Jorgensen through a series of hormonal and surgical treatments in Copenhagen in 1951 – 1952. In the older literature descriptions of transsexuality can be

found under other headings, including of course transvestism. A
certain conceptual confusion continues to exist in this area. This is
not strange, since the term refers to a very heterogeneous group of
people, who have in common only the intense desire to "change sex"
(Meyer and Hoopes, 1974; Person and Ovesey, 1974a, 1974b). In
1973 another term appeared — the gender dysphoria syndrome. This
term places the emphasis on the conflict of sexual identity. Secondary terms can be added, which are intended to indicate something
about the background for the gender dysphoria (for example transvestism, homosexuality, borderline psychosis, psychopathy, etc.).
This is not a question of linguistic hairsplitting, but rather an
attempt to divide up the heterogeneous group of individuals currently
classified under the term transsexuality into smaller groups and
thereby separate out that probably small group for whom a "sex
change" is indicated from the large group of patients with gender
dysphoria, for whom present experience indicates that hormonal
and surgical procedures are not advisable.

There is no doubt that gender dysphoria is a painful condition,
which previously has been underestimated and often ridiculed, and
that patients with this condition need medical help. However, this
does not mean that the solution always consists of a comprehensive
hormonal-surgical-cosmetic "sex change" treatment, no matter how
urgently the patient insists on having such treatment. This is an irreversible, very mutilating procedure, which furthermore involves
many years of hormonal substitution treatment, the side effects
of which are not yet fully known.

In dealing with these patients, one of the most important things
to accomplish is to help them to understand that on the one hand
their complaints are taken seriously and that it is clear how difficult
their situation is, but that on the other hand the help that they seek
is not necessarily only available through a sex change, and that the
therapist will work together with them to try to find the best
treatment. A tug of war between the doctor (or other therapist) and
the patient, in which each tries to show the other who is stronger,
should be avoided. However, some of these patients are so determined
to have a "sex change" that no matter how much one tries, it is
impossible to develop a reasonable contact with them except on
their own terms. They will go from doctor to doctor, until they find
one who "understands" them, that is someone who will give in to
their desire for a "sex change". Or they will try to force the doctor
to submit to their wishes in various ways including making suicidal

threats, suicide attempts, and self-mutilating attacks on their genitals. In some cases the patient's actions are of such a desperate nature that the doctor is forced to give in to him, although in doubt about the correctness of doing so.

It is clear that the easiest course of action is to make absolute rules for decisions in these cases. For example, it is possible to say that all patients, who want to, should be permitted to "change sex". On the other hand one can refuse to participate in "sex change" evaluations altogether.

In those countries, where medical resources are scarce, it may be necessary to give higher priority to more pressing conditions. How ever, if it is possible to take on such problems, there is no doubt that some people experience such a disparity between their biological and psychological gender identity, and that this disparity makes life so unbearable for them that a "sex change" can help them to lead a more harmonious life. However, it is very time-consuming and difficult to decide if it is indicated, and there are no laboratory examinations, psychological tests or other methods of investigation which can with any degree of certainty differentiate the nuclear group of "genuine transsexuals" from the other patients, who want to have a sex change. Some workers only recommend surgical sex change for those men who, from early childhood have exhibited marked feminine features and who continue to appear clearly feminine, who have no regard for or happiness from their genitalia, and who wish to become women, not only to look like women intermittently. Absolute contra-indications include psychotic and border-line psychotic conditions, and sex change is relatively contra-indicated for patients who are or have been married and have been able to have an erection and orgasm during intercourse or in some other way have experienced genital pleasure as an adult. It is also relatively contra-indicated in patients who have an unmistakably masculine appearance or who exhibit fetishistic happiness in the female role.

In the case of female transsexuals, sex change should be agreed to mainly for those individuals in whom decidedly masculine features have been present from early childhood and who after puberty have continued to demonstrate masculinity in life style, way of dressing, choice of job, etc. Absolute contra-indications are the same as those mentioned above for biological men and relative contra-indications are for the most part the same as those for men.

Other workers involved in deciding about indications for sex

change treatment, including many who are very experienced, are
not nearly as rigid in their criteria. However, it should be stressed
that under all circumstances the decision about whether sex change
is indicated should be made by those who, through long-term experience, have developed insight into the problems concerning this
group of patients who are very difficult to evaluate.

Further difficulties arise from the fact that many doctors, on the
basis of very limited or entirely lacking indications, give sex hormones to patients that present complaints of gender dysphoria —
oestrogens to biological men and androgens to biological women.
Although normally these doctors have the right to do this, such
practices must be strongly advised against. When the patient later
comes to a speciality clinic, such a fait accompli will cause considerable difficulties if it is felt that the patient should be advised against
having a sex change. Another problem is that in many countries it
is possible to obtain sex change treatment by fulfilling just one condition — being able to pay for the treatment, which is usually expen-
sive. As transsexuals know very well what they must say in order
to get the doctor to give in to their wishes and also what they can
do to get their wishes carried out if they are refused, it is even more
difficult to make contact with the patient.

These are the reasons which today have resulted in the centraliza-
tion of observation and treatment of such patients to a few departments and for which it is advised that patients should be referred to
such departments early. The observation phase should extend over
at least two years. The follow-up treatment phase may be considerably longer as it may take a long time before the patient is well
established somatically, psychologically, and socially.

The surgical procedure itself will be briefly described. It is preceeded by hormonal treatment of at least one year's duration and
often of several years' duration. In both sexes castration is carried
out. In addition, in biological men demasculinization is carried out
and the left-over soft tissue and skin are used to form labia and an
artificial vagina. It is possible to achieve very satisfactory results
both cosmetically and sexually, so that the patient later can function
as a female partner in a sexual relationship. In some cases the
patient maintains that the ability to achieve orgasm has been preserved. In the case of sex change from a biological woman to a man
the cosmetic results are not nearly as satisfactory. Usually a bilateral
mammectomy is performed, unless the breasts are so small, possibly
due to preceeding androgen treatment, that such a procedure is

superfluous. The internal sexual organs are removed and the vagina is partially or completely closed. In certain cases attempts have been made to create an artificial penis, but the results have been unsatisfactory both from a cosmetic and from a functional point of view. Usually such attempts are advised against, and most transsexual women accept this when they are informed about the practical possibilities. From a purely sexual point of view transsexual women usually function well after a sex change to a man, as the clitoris is preserved and as a result of the androgen treatment often has grown somewhat in size and its sensitivity has become increased.

Often several operations must be performed before a satisfactory result is obtained.

Follow-up evaluations of transsexuals always suffer from the fact that it is difficult to obtain a sufficiently representative material and sufficiently substantiated information. A follow-up evaluation of seventeen men and seven women who underwent a "sex change" at Johns Hopkins Hospital in the United States showed that, judged according to five criteria — occupational ability, stable relationships, need for psychiatric treatment, subjective sense of well-being, and criminality — in most cases the "sex change" resulted in improvement, psychological as well as social (Money and Ehrhardt, 1970. See also Randell, 1969). It must be pointed out that the indications at Johns Hopkins are rather strict and that the patients are offered an adequate follow-up treatment programme. Reports from other places in the United States and from other countries indicate that some patients have regretted the sex change and have sought to go back to their original sex.

The estimated frequency of transsexuality varies considerably. Figures from the USA indicate the prevalence to be 1:100,000 men and 1:400,000 women, but these rates are probably too low. The Johns Hopkins Hospital alone received 1,500 referrals for sex change in a two-year period. A Swedish report published in 1967 (Wålinder) stated the prevalence in Sweden to be 1:37,000 men and 1:103,000 women. In 1971 the same author reported that in Sweden the ratio between men and women was closer to 1:1, which seems surprising. In Sweden the yearly increase in the number of transsexuals over the age of 15 years has been calculated to be 0.2 per 100,000 inhabitants Hoenig and Kenna (1973) estimate that there are 449 male and 127 female transsexuals over the age of 15 years in England and Wales.

Principles of Treatment of Sexual Deviations

It is possible to discuss some of the possibilities for the treatment of sexual deviations only briefly here. However, a short account should be sufficient, since in a number of ways there is no difference between these treatment methods and other psychiatric treatment methods. In this area, as in other areas, it is the object to prevent the development of impairment and to attempt to cure or at least decrease the degree of any impairments that have already developed.

Phrophylaxis

As it becomes understood which factors are of importance in the development of sexual deviations, theoretically, at least, there are greater chances for preventing their occurrence. We know that the foundations for sexual deviations are laid down early in childhood and that they are entirely or partially a product of the interaction between the child and its environment. The reaction of the environment is in turn a product of the conditions under which the key persons in that environment themselves grew up and of their characteristics, as well as of the norms of the times. It can be said that sexual deviations are partially created by society. If for various reasons one is hesitant to formulate the situation in this way, it may be said that sexual deviations are culturally dependent. Preventive work must thus involve changes in those micro- and macro-social structures of society that have been found to be of importance for the development of sexual deviations. This preventive work must partially be aimed at the key persons who apparently are of such importance in the child's development. Preventive work cannot stop here, but must also be extended to those conditions under which we all live. What use is it that the individual may be in possession of both the necessary knowledge and the right intentions and abilities if conditions of society more or less prevent him or her from using this knowledge and from living according to these intentions.

It is not possible in the present context to exemplify the ideas mentioned above, let alone to provide concrete instructions about how such preventive work can be carried out and in what ways doctors may be considered to have particular qualifications and thus particular obligations for undertaking this kind of work. The purpose of these general remarks has only been to emphasize that sexual deviations are not conditions about which nothing can be done but, on the contrary, are conditions the development of which can be either completely or partially prevented. However, it should not be thought that this prophylactic work is simple or easy. The challenge is therefore so much the greater.

Of course, prophylaxis in this area should be aimed only at preventing real sexual deviations and not at making human sexual modes of expression uniform.

Treatment Methods

If the perversion has already developed, the following courses of action may be undertaken:

1. One can try to remove the "necessity" of the perversion through various forms of analytical therapy or other psychological methods of treatment which give the sexually deviant person insight into the reasons for his sexual behaviour and into possibilities for changing this behaviour. As mentioned previously, such analytical work is difficult and requires a great deal of ability and sensitivity.

2. One can decrease the individual's sexual drive, so that the impulses are weakened. This can be done irreversibly or reversibly. Irreversible methods include castration and stereotactic procedures involving the hypothalamic nuclei. Castration has been used to a certain extent in cases of so-called "sexual offences" which are considered so dangerous that they cannot be tolerated. Stereotactic brain procedures are used less often, but have found a number of proponents in recent years, and have been used for the treatment of paedophile homosexuals among others (Roeder *et al.,* 1972). It is sometimes claimed that stereotactic procedures change the direction of drive, but the effect seems to be mainly a reduction of sexual drive. Reversible methods include the use of female sex hormones and anti-hormones. If sufficiently large doses of oestrogens are given to a man, within the course of a few weeks his libido and potency will be markedly reduced or even eliminated. This treatment has a number of side effects, including gynecomastia and changed fat distribution. Similar results without so many side effects have been achieved with the so-called anti-hormones, such as cyproterone acetate. In recent years the use of anti-hormones in the treatment

of conditions such as exhibitionism and voyeurism has increased. The treatment usually extends over the course of a couple of years and while the sexual drive is temporarily reduced, psychotherapeutic and supportive measures are undertaken in the hope that when the drive is no longer weakened, the patient will have gained so much insight and strength that in the future he will be able to channel his sexual impulses into an expression that will be more acceptable both to him and to his surroundings.

After the discontinuation of cyproterone acetate, libido and potency return in the course of 4—6 weeks. Up to the present time there have been no reports of impairment of reproductive function, even after several years of cyproterone acetate administration. However, the anti-hormones have a number of psychological side effects which are very much like those found with castration, and which limit the use of these drugs.

3. One can attempt to modify the deviant behaviour itself in various ways.

a. Through punitive or other sanctions (social, religious, etc.).

In recent years a number of countries have changed their penal codes so that as far as sexual matters are concerned, it is mainly only those involving really harmful acts that are included.

b. Through behaviour therapy, in which a system of rewards and punishments is used to encourage certain acts and to discourage other acts — see the section concerning this form of therapy (Chapter 4).

c. Through intervention so early in the course of the disorder that the deviation has not yet fully developed. In certain cases of homosexuality, transvestism, and transsexuality it is possible to determine at a very early stage that a deviation is developing. In the USA there are a few observation kindergartens which have been particularly interested in markedly feminine boys. Attempts have been made to see if a modification of their behaviour can prevent their rejection by the masculine circle of boys and thereby maintain a number of identification objects and to see if it is possible through psychotherapeutic work with their parents to alter the feminine development which is already underway (Green, 1974). It can not yet be determined if these attempts will have the intended effect, but the attempts are interesting. In these cases the symptom has already developed, but intervention occurs at such an early stage that this form of treatment is very much like prophylaxis.

Finally only this will be said: a prerequisite for any attempt at treatment should be that the individual himself wants treatment, with the exception of those who commit truly harmful acts (markedly sadistic acts, fire setting, etc.). However, the degree to which the patient must be willing is open to discussion. In countries with a restrictive attitude toward sexual deviations, in which the deviant is isolated and rejected, it is rather illusory to talk about voluntary treatment. Those people who undertake the treatment of sexual deviants may find their attention drawn to the conditions under which the sexually deviant person exists and may feel obliged to work towards a change of those conditions.

References

Abe, K. and Moran, P. A. P. (1969). Parental age of homosexuals, *British Journal of Psychiatry* 115, 313–317.

Barlow, D. H., Abel, G. G., Blanchard, E. B. and Mavissakalian, M. (1974). Plasma testosterone levels and male homosexuality: a failure to replicate, *Archives of Sexual Behavior* 3, 571–575.

Bene, E. (1965). On the genesis of female homosexuality, *British Journal of Psychiatry* 111, 815–821.

Bieber, I. (1962). "Homosexuality. A Psychoanalytic Study of Male Homosexuals." Basic Books Inc: New York.

Cauldwell, D. (1949). Psychopathia transsexualis, *Sexology* 16, 274–280.

Freud, S. (1949. – orig. publ. 1905) "Three Essays on the Theory of Sexuality." Imago Publication Company: London.

Green, R. (1974). "Sexual Identity Conflicts in Children and Adults." Basic Books Inc: New York.

Hertoft, P. (1968). "Undersøgelser Over Unge Maends Seksuelle Adfaerd, Viden og Holdning." Akademisk Forlag, Copenhagen. English summary: Investigation into the sexual behaviour of young men (1969), *Danish Medical Bulletin* 16, 1–96.

Hoenig, J. and Kenna, J. (1973). Epidemiological aspects of transsexualism, *Psychiat. Clin.* 6, 65–80.

Hoffman, M. (1968). "The Gay World." Basic Books Inc: New York.

Kinsey, A. C., Pomeroy, W. D. and Martin, C. E. (1948). "Sexual Behavior in the Human Male." Saunders: Philadelphia.

Kinsey, A. C., Pomeroy, W. D., Martin, C. E. and Gebhard, P. (1953). "Sexual Behavior in the Human Female." Saunders: Philadelphia.

Kutchinsky, B. (1973). The effect of easy availability of pornography on the incidence of sex crimes: the Danish experience, *Journal of Social Issues* 29, 163–181.

Loneley, J. (1973). Family dynamics in homosexual women, *Archives of Sexual Behavior* 2, 343–350.

Loraine, J. A., Adamopoulos, D. A., Kirkham, K. E., Ismail, A. A. A. and Dove, G. A. (1971). Patterns of hormone excretion in male and female homosexuals, *Nature* 234, 552–554.

Margolese, M. S. and Janiger, O. (1973). Androsterone/Etiocholanolone ratios in male homosexuals, *British Medical Journal* 3, 5873, 207–210.

Meyer, J. and Hoopes, J. E. (1974). The gender dysphoria syndromes, *Plastic and reconstructive surgery* 54, 444–451.

Money, J. and Ehrhardt, A. A. (1970). Transsexuelle nach Geschlecht Wechsel, *Beiträge zur Sexualforschung* 49, 70–87.

Money, J. and Ehrhardt, A. A. (1972). "Man and Woman, Boy and Girl." The Johns Hopkins Press: Baltimore.

Person, E. and Ovesey, L. (1974a). The transsexual syndrome in males. I. Primary transsexualism, *American Journal of Psychotherapy* 28, 4–20.

Person, E. and Ovesey, L. (1974b). The transsexual syndrome in males. II. Secondary transsexualism, *American Journal of Psychotherapy* 28, 174–

Pillard, R. C., Rose, R. M. and Sherwood, M. (1974). Plasma testosterone levels in homosexual men, *Archives of Sexual Behavior* 3, 453–458.

Randell, J. (1969). *In* "Transsexualism and Sex Reassignment." (R. Green and J. Money, Eds), The Johns Hopkins Press: Baltimore.

Roeder, F., Orthner, H. and Müller, D. (1972). *In* "Psychosurgery." (E. Hitchcock, L. Laitinen and K. Vaernet, Eds), C. C. Thomas, Publisher: Springfield, Illinois.

Rosen, I. (1965). *In* "Sexual Behavior and the Law." (R. Slovenko, Ed.), C. C. Thomas, Publisher: Springfield, Illinois.

Rosenthal, D. (1970). "Genetic Theory and Abnormal Behavior." McGraw-Hill: New York.

Slater, E. (1962). Birth order and maternal age of homosexuals, *Lancet* 134, 69–71.

Vanggaard, T. (1962). Normal homoseksualitet og homoseksuel inversion. *Ugeskrift for Laeger* 124, 1427–1434.

Vanggaard, T. (1972). "Phallos. A Symbol and its History in the Male World." Jonathan Cape: London.

Wålinder, J. (1967). "Transsexualism. A Study of Forty-three Cases." Akademi-förlaget: Göteborg.

Wålinder, J. (1971). Incidence and sex ratio of transsexualism in Sweden, *British Journal of Psychiatry* 119, 195–196.

WHO Report (1975). "Education and Treatment in Human Sexuality: The Training of Health Professionals." Technical Report Series 572, Geneva.

8 | *Psychosexual Problems in Marriage*

SIDNEY CROWN

A significant extension from individual therapy is into the marital field in which the couple, rather than the individual, is treated. In this chapter the social context of marriage and marital therapy will first be considered. This will be followed by a discussion on the technique of assessing a marriage. The major part of the chapter is devoted to the description and understanding of psychosexual problems as these present in marriage. Finally the techniques of marital therapy will be noted.

Social Context of Marriage and Marital Therapy

There has probably never been a time when so many experiments have been made with ways of living with other people. While it would still be true on average that most people aim for a marriage to one person to last a lifetime, many other significant ongoing pairings or groupings are attempted and it is in this context marital therapy must be viewed. Thus the commoner pairings at present are two people living together but not formally married; communal living; and, with less frequency, various bisexual pairings, for example, a woman married to a man and living in the same house as the man's homosexual partner.

Just as the form of marriage is highly significant in relation to marital therapy so too are the major trends in the epidemiology of marriage, separation and divorce. This is discussed fully by Fletcher (1973) and more briefly by the present writer (Crown, 1976). While the prevalence of divorce has steadily risen during this century with high peaks following disturbances especially war, these figures do not necessarily indicate a decrease in the stability of marriage. The figures may, for example, reflect peoples' higher aims for personal happiness so that a marriage which might have been tolerated in previous times even if it was unhappy is less likely to be tolerated now; people feel free to try again. In addition changes in legislation relating to marriage and the family, in particular the Divorce Reform Act (1969), have resulted in persons tending to accept divorce in two or five years, the relationship having irretrievably broken down, rather than contrive grounds for divorce — adultery, cruelty and so on.

As there are several different types of marital therapy available it is important, possibly crucial, to assign a couple to the most appropriate treatment or combination of treatments. The major division is into the psychodynamic versus the behavioural marital therapies. Behavioural marital therapy is discussed by Crowe (1976) and in this book by Mackay (Chapter 4). The writer's main experience is with psychodynamic marital therapy using the joint interview. This has been described in detail elsewhere (Crown, 1976). Group marital therapy techniques are described by Burbank (Chapter 3) and counselling techniques by Newsome (Chapter 2).

When is there a Psychosexual Problem?

It is relatively simple to say in many of the specialized fields dealt with in this book when a psychosexual problem exists. A problem about contraception, for example, may present directly to the gynaecologist (Chapter 16), or a problem of impotency supervene after prostatectomy and present to the urologist (Chapter 15), or a problem of sexual dysfunction to the general practitioner (Chapter 11). In marriage, however, problems are relative to the attitudes, understandings, desires and feelings of the partners; only rarely can they be accorded absolute status as a "problem". Occasionally this is so, of course, and later in this chapter examples (e.g. extreme sadomasochism) will be given. Usually however any absolute and rigid standard of normality, or a view in which normality is equated with the average, or the view that normality is relative to cultural norms is not helpful in evaluating an individual marital problem.

The most useful working definition, although it breaks down with exceptionally deviant behaviour, is that "normal" is what is acceptable to the couple. Abnormality is what is defined as such by one or other of the partners. We are concerned with psychosexual behaviour and it is relevant and necessary to find out, in the course of the marital assessment, what is desired by each of the partners separately and together. Paradoxical situations may be revealed, for example, a man with a sexual appetite which he regards as normal, and Kinsey would rate as average, who finds himself regarded by his wife as being excessively demanding. To take another example: the frequency of anal intercourse in marriage is unknown. It is clear, however, from marital assessments that it is a sexual demand sometimes made by the male partner of the woman who may acquiesce willingly, may acquiesce unwillingly or may find the practice unacceptable, painful or "revolting". Whether or not it is "normal" to have anal intercourse in marriage or whether this suggests that there is a "problem" and with whom the problem lies is something that needs to be worked upon in marital therapy. Similar considerations apply to other areas which may become problematical such as positions in sexual intercourse, or the use of sexual stimulants such as pornographic literature or vibrators to help sexual arousal. (Chapter 4).

Preconceived notions about normality or what constitutes a psychosexual problem have little place in the assessment of a marriage. It is necessary to find out what each partner wants, what each partner finds pleasurable or unpleasurable and, from a therapy point of view, whether there is any room for abandonment of certain modes of behaviour or compromise between what one partner wants and the other is prepared to concede.

Assessing a Marriage

Tripartite Assessment

Although sometimes a marriage problem is referred as such by, say, a general practitioner (Chapter 11), in the majority of cases an individual patient presents to a psychiatrist with anxiety, depression or a sexual problem. A full psychiatric history should be taken. This is followed

by a diagnostic formulation. The assessment of the individual is completed by making a psychodynamic assessment which includes drive
development, ego and defence functioning, super-ego functioning
and functioning in interpersonal relationships (pp. 12–17).

If after this it seems likely that the marriage is implicated then
permission should be sought to interview the spouse. Usually there is
no objection; in fact the spouse may have "asked to come today".
Where this is not so I explain simply that it seems likely that the
marriage is implicated so it seems sensible to involve the marriage
partner in the treatment. I ask both the wife and the husband to come
on the next interview and see the spouse first and then the partners
together. This is the tripartite assessment technique and an idea can
be obtained of the problems and personality of each individual as
well as a direct observation of marital interaction. The last part of the
joint interview is used to discuss with the couple the possible forms of
treatment that are relevant and, of course, which they feel might help
them most. This phase is analogous to the therapeutic alliance in
individual psychotherapy (Chapter 1).

Ethical Considerations

All psychotherapies relate to the personal value systems of the therapist. This is so even afer undergoing specific therapeutic and training
techniques such as psychoanalysis. A therapist's psychosocial background, his parents' marriage, his or her own marriage, his personal
philosophy and view of marriage are important in marital psychotherapy. This is because using the joint interview technique, marital
therapy is a reality-orientated technique with less fantasy on the
patients' part. The therapist is more active which is an important
factor In the establishment of a working therapeutic alliance. Many
couples want to be assured that they are not going to be forced into
some prearranged mould, for example, a "typical suburban marriage"
that they may imagine of their therapist. It is important to convey to
the couple that the aim of therapy is their personal satisfaction and
fulfilment and not to force them into a particular mould. Nor can a
marital therapist be committed to assuring a couple that a relationship will survive. This is where ethical considerations are particularly
relevant.

There are two major ethical considerations: the first concerns
children and the second concerns the future of the relationship. So

far as children are concerned I feel this makes a fundamental difference to the gravity of marital therapy. In this sense psychiatry and
the law have a common interest as, following the Divorce Reform Act
(1969), lawyers and particularly judges are greatly concerned about
arrangements made for children following marital breakdown. Adults
can, or should be able to, take care of themselves but a marital therapist must be aware of the impact of separation or divorce on children
of various ages. A useful rule of thumb here is probably the psychodynamic truism that the earlier the more serious. Adolescent children
can to some extent be involved in the dissolution process directly or
indirectly; young children cannot. Balanced against this, however, is
the equally important, often agonizing, choice as to whether a bad
relationship in which a couple stays together is better or worse for
children than the alternative, usually the absent father or the father
who has "access" to the children.

Whether or not the children are involved, therapy which looks at
the basic structure of a marriage will not necessarily lead to a
strengthening of the bond. A marriage undertaken for strongly neurotic reasons as for example a man or woman whose need for a parent
is more important than their need for a partner; or the homosexual
man who marries in order to protect himself from his sexual deviation, these relationships may well break up once the underlying
psychodynamics are exposed.

The skill is to recognize whether marital therapy is likely to be
relatively straightforward and lead to a closening of the relationship
or whether it is liable to lead to marital breakdown. If the latter then
the couple must be warned of this possibility before embarking on
therapy so that they can go away and think about it and decide
whether for them taking the risk is worthwhile. Intelligent couples,
otherwise insightful, may never have faced up to the imponderable
factors in their relationship and it is an outsider who may see the
dangers. If this is so then prior warning will at least allow the decision
about therapy to rest where it should rest which is with the couple.

Consideration of Therapies

General considerations about choice of therapy follows the same
reasoning as for individual psychotherapy (Chapter 1). If a problem
is a relatively minor one it should respond to a reflective type of
therapy in which problems are thrown back to the couple to discuss

further in the manner of client-centered counselling (Chapter 2). If unconscious motivations seem particularly involved (e.g. in a sado-masochistic relationship) then almost certainly a psychodynamic marital therapy, individual or group, should be used. Where a relationship is basically good and the problems seem to relate to the mechanics of sexuality or to easily identified personality difficulty in one of the partners (e.g. non-assertiveness) then one of the behavioural psychotherapies may be appropriate such as the Masters and Johnson (1970) technique or assertiveness training. As with individual psychotherapy, consideration must be given whether a combination of therapies would be most appropriate for the problem under consideration e.g. a combination of psychodynamic marital therapy and behavioural marital therapy.

Further consideration should be given to the use of a single therapist or more than one therapist. Some authorities, both psychodynamic (Dicks, 1967) and behavioural (Masters and Johnson, 1970) use co-therapists and may specify that the co-therapist should be of a different sex. There seems little evidence to suggest that this is necessary and one thing that is certain is that the chronic shortage of psychotherapists of all types is likely to persist for as long as reasonably can be seen ahead. For these reasons I advocate the development of techniques, both psychodynamic and behavioural, in which one therapist, trained in the principles and practice of several techniques manages the marital problem him- or herself. There are occasions when this is not possible and when more than one therapist needs to be brought in but in my opinion these situations are relatively few and one therapist is the method of choice.

Psychosexual Problems in Marriage

Sexual problems in marriage can be sub-divided into those relating to sexual drive differences, sexual inadequacy and sexual deviance.

Sexual Drive Differences

It seems fully in line with basic biological expectancy and clinical experience that the major drives, sexuality and aggressiveness, vary greatly in different individuals. In the usual clinical situation it is not possible to decide whether an apparent drive difference between spouses is likely to be due to inborn differences or to problems with the expression of the drive, for example, apparently low sexual drive due to sexual inhibition. "Norms" of frequency of sexual intercourse as in the Kinsey reports seem irrelevant to the evaluation of the individual marital problem relating to differences in sexual appetite. Couples can be suited having intercourse every night or more than once per night and they can be suited with intercourse once every three months; what is important is whether or not there is agreement about the expression of sexual need.

It must not be overlooked that a marriage is a relationship extending over a considerable period, sometimes half a life-time or more, so that it is necessary not only to evaluate differences in sexual appetite at the time of presentation for marital therapy but also to try and assess whether there is any evidence of a change in appetite during the marriage. A common example of this is diminished appetite on the wife's part following the birth of a child. A not dissimilar problem may arise with the husband because he feels neglected because of the child's arrival; he may find difficulty in allowing the wife to share her love between the child and him. A change of sexual appetite may occur after major abdominal surgery not because of the direct effect of this surgery but because of the cosmetic effect (Chapter 18). There may be gross age differences between the partners with differences in sexual appetite.

Problems relating to drive differences or change in sexual appetite can be helped in marital therapy whether this is by counselling, psychotherapy or behavioural modification. Thus counselling might allow for couples to compromise on frequency of intercourse, psychotherapy may help a man or woman to unravel the cause of a sexual inhibition and thus release the inhibited sexual appetite; behavioural modification techniques may employ marital contract therapy when change in frequency of intercourse on the part of one partner forms part of the contract in exchange for changes on the part of the other.

Sexual Inadequacy

Male Sexual Inadequacy

The assessment of male sexual inadequacy follows the general lines indicated by Crown and Lucas (Chapter 1). The inadequacy may be erectile or ejaculatory and the sexual process should be considered from the arousal of sexual desire in one or other partner through to the completion of the sex act itself and the relationship between the partners after this. Impotence as a sexual "problem" in marriage may present with the man, his wife or both complaining that his erection is deficient, not maintained or lost after penetration. Ejaculation may be too rapid, or there may be ejaculatory incompetence. The presentation may be more complex, as for example, when erectile or ejaculatory difficulty relates only to the spouse and not either to extra-marital relationships or to pre-marital relationships. Or the man may begin to be impotent when his partner loses interest in her appearance, for example after childbirth or if the woman has the philosophy that generally neglects personal appearance after marriage. The medical causes of impotence as for example diabetes mellitus or hypotensive drugs must always be considered but are rarely seen in the psychiatric clinic; these must, however, be thought of in the general medical or surgical context particularly as a side effect of the use of drugs (Chapter 12).

To some extent the cause of male sexual inadequacy depends on the concepts of the sexual investigator; thus the behavioural psychotherapist may find a sex phobia where a psychodynamic psychotherapist may think in terms of a sexual inhibition. These ways of conceiving the problem may lead to the modality of treatment favoured by the therapist. Another cause of male sexual inadequacy is in the relationship adumbrated particularly by psychoanalysis, between sexuality and aggressiveness. Aggressiveness in excessive amounts in relation to sexuality may lead the man to be apprehensive that his aggression might harm the woman and so lead to malfunction of erection or ejaculation. The joint interview with both spouses is the best way of detecting the more subtle nuances of relationships which might lead to sexual dysfunction. In the majority of cases, at the conclusion of the tripartite assessment an idea will have been obtained about the possible causes of male sexual inadequacy, ideas which can be discussed with the partners to select the most appropriate therapy or combination of therapies.

Female Sexual Inadequacy

Frigidity is an inexact term for lack of sexual pleasure on the part of a woman. This may vary from total inability to be aroused to complaints, stimulated by the popularizations of sex researchers, about lack of ability to have a multiple orgasm. As with male sexuality a systematic assessment will consider the sex act from preliminary arousal through foreplay to orgasm and on to post-coital behaviour. A further factor has to be taken into account in relation to female sexuality: this is that the popularizations of the sex educators and sex researchers, welcome as this is to the serious professional, has brought with it what might be called iatrogenic neurosis in relationship to female sexual satisfaction. It seems likely that a fairly high proportion of women do not consistently achieve sexual orgasm — probably about 60% (Fisher, 1973). This does not mean that they do not enjoy sexuality. Secondly since the physiological studies of Masters and Johnson (1966) have shown the capacity of the female for multiple orgasm, this again has aroused what might be regarded as false aspirations for a number of women who are perfectly well adjusted and achieve orgasm most times but feel that they are missing something. A third point in relationship to contemporary writings is that there has been perhaps too much preoccupation with the capacity to achieve orgasm with the implied suggestion that anything less than this means total lack of sexual satisfaction. This is not so and there are many women who, while not achieving orgasm every time they make love, nevertheless enjoy sexuality in the sense of heightened enjoyment and awareness of a relationship which is important to them. This leads to another point which seems old-fashioned. It seems likely, despite shrill claims for "permissiveness" and playing everything "cool", that sexuality in the sense of the pure mechanics of sex is less often enjoyed for itself alone by women than by men. Thus one presentation of frigidity in the woman and particularly in young people is where both members are striving to achieve a "cool" relationship but whereas the man enjoys his sex, having separated this from tenderness, the woman who would like to achieve this separation at least intellectually fails to do so emotionally. Although the above represents my clinical experience, others deplore the separation of sexing and loving — see the lively discussion by Cole (Chapter 19).

Psychodynamic Considerations

A not inconsiderable proportion of sexual problems relate to the triangular situation called by psychoanalysis the Oedipal situation and by others the princess and the prostitute conflict (see Chapters 6 and 19). Around the ages of three to eight years the child becomes attached to the parent of the opposite sex and rivalrous with the parent of the same sex. In a family where this situation is managed with understanding the child learns to share affection and to tolerate rivalries. The successful resolution of this conflict seems to relate to the later ability to make significant ongoing close relationships including close sexual relationships. From the point of view of marital sexual inadequacy an assessment of the probable Oedipal situation as this applied in childhood is important. This may apply, for example, in problems where sexuality for either the man or woman was satisfying before the relationship was legitimized. Thus there may be no problem when a couple are courting or living together but sexual difficulties start either after marriage or before if there is some symbolic legitimization, for example, an engagement party. An understanding of the Oedipus complex may also be relevant when either spouse is able to achieve an adequate sexual adjustment outside marriage or with a partner of different social, intellectual or ethnic background but not with the spouse. An understanding of this psychodynamic constellation may be relevant to the resolution of marital sexual dysfunction and may be a good reason for suggesting psychodynamic marital therapy rather than behavioural marital therapy.

Sexual Deviance

Sexual deviance in relationship to marriage differs in a number of ways from sexual deviance as seen in the individual (Chapter 7). First a paradox: it must not be assumed that a degree of sexual deviance is incompatible with a good marital relationship. This applies not only with the commonest sexual deviance, homosexuality, but also with other deviant sexual behaviour such as transvestism and exhibitionism. While it is perfectly true that in most cases a good relationship under these circumstances depends on a certain degree of acquiescence and connivance on the part of the wife, it is important to approach the situation with care; certainly not to assume a need for change. A number of women, for example, are aware that their husband's fantasy life during sexual intercourse excludes them. Fantasy may, for example, be narcissistic as when a man thinks of

making love to himself; or fantasy may be homosexual when the wife
is experienced as a man. While wives might be disappointed or sad
about this they may prefer to achieve orgasmic release rather than
try to change the fantasy life of the husband with the risk of producing
a lesser degree of sexual potency. The marriage therapist must, therefore, approach the problem of sexual deviance in marriage with
circumspection.

Secondly sexual deviance as it presents in marriage is a less severe
aberration than sexual deviance presenting in the unattached individual. This is because a measure of attachment to the opposite sex is
almost certain to be or to have been present; without this it is most
unlikely that all except the most self-punishing woman would agree to
set up a permanent relationship. Thus in marriage there is usually a
degree of bisexuality (see Chapter 7 pp. 214—216), of ability to make
sexual relationships with both sexes. It is often possible, therefore, to
make surprising therapeutic advances. It would be a mistake to assume
by this that one is changing a person's basic or preferred sexual align-
ment. There may, however, be very good reasons for changing a person's sexual behaviour if he wishes for this; for example a person of
predominantly homosexual orientation who wants a wife, a home
and children. He may relinquish homosexual behaviour but possibly
not, or not always, relinquish homosexual fantasy. It is an individual
matter how far couples wish to communicate on this or how far there
is an actual or tacit acceptance of the less-than-perfect for the sake
of a workable sexual or marital adjustment.

Homosexuality

Homosexuality presenting in marriage is usually as bisexuality. This
presentation may take one of the more exotic forms of marital problem
as for example in the homosexual who wishes to set up a household of
three persons with his wife and man-friend. This arrangement may be
successful but, in my experience, usually at some stage leads to sadness and non-fulfilment on the part of the woman. It may also become clear, in the course of marital psychotherapy, that some degree
of latitude is necessary on the part of the spouse — usually the wife
in that sexual deviance is so overwhelmingly a problem of the male.
It is interesting that I have not seen a marital problem presenting
because of the wife being a lesbian and demanding a degree of flexibility by her husband for her homosexual outlets. As indicated earlier,

it is important in these problems not to make pre-judgments as to the ideal for a given couple. In particular it is necessary to ascertain what degree of commitment to heterosexuality is demanded by the wife of a homosexual man. Does she, for example, demand commitment in fantasy and in behaviour or is she prepared to tolerate commitment in behaviour without either enquiring about, or being too deeply concerned about, a commitment in fantasy?

A further aspect of male homosexuality in marriage is that, perhaps relating to phasic hormonal changes, or to psychological conflicts and pressures, from time to time there is likely to be a recrudescence of homosexual desires. When this happens a homosexual man may be tempted by a casual relationship, as on a bus or tube train, or may, consciously or unconsciously, put himself in a position to make a homosexual contact, for example, impulsively using a public lavatory known to be frequented by homosexuals, going to a homosexual part of a heath near a town and so on. One of the aims of marital psycho-therapy is to help the spouse to tolerate a degree of homosexuality in the partner, perhaps to be able to face up to these unpredictable periods of desire which may be frightening for both partners in threatening the family part of the relationship. The basic philosophy, trite though this may appear, is that life is to some extent a compro-mise and it is not possible to have all possible fulfilments. In pre-marital psychotherapy with a homosexual it is important to under-stand and work through (p. 22) these various points and in particular to allow time for such a person to find a partner whose degree of tolerance is likely to make the relationship a success. The woman who demands total heterosexual commitment is most unlikely to be happy with a homosexual, so that pre-marital experimentation with relation-ships is necessary for a homosexual person who wishes to find a woman to marry.

Positions in intercourse must also be considered. The aim for most couples should be to maintain interest and variety; what is allowable is what is desirable, agreed to and pleasurable for both partners. I know of no evidence whether or not homosexuals married to a woman demand a greater variety of positions in intercourse as for example anal intercourse; in fact it is totally unknown how far anal intercourse takes place in marriages between partners who would regard themselves as heterosexual. It is possible, in an attempt to accommodate sexual deviance on the part of one of the partners, that a particular position or variety of positions demanded by one partner is made acceptable to the other. Or particular methods of stimulation or self-stimulation may be used as when a man stimulates his own breasts or has these stimulated for him. In a particular marriage it may be necessary to discuss positions in intercourse or manipulations or attitudes on the part of the sexually deviant partner if these become increasingly un-acceptable to the more normal partner. This is true throughout the whole range of sexual deviance in marraige.

Transvestism

As a marital problem there are features which differentiate transves-tism from that seen in the individual. The psychoanalytic definition of a sexual perversion is that it replaces the normal sexual outlet; this applies to, so to speak, pure transvestism. Transvestites who achieve marital status however seem to be persons in whom the perverse sexual outlet exists together with the normal sexual outlet. In the marital situation, in fact, it is perhaps appropriate to see the sexual deviation as a passport or ticket for the patient to achieve an approxi-mation to a normal heterosexual adjustment. Thus the transvestite in marriage accepts his transvestism as part of his way of expressing him-self. It seldom consists of full cross-dressing, but takes various forms. Thus it may be a fantasy in which, in reverie, the patient thinks about cross-dressing; it may be that the part-transvestite always wears one undergarment of a female type belonging to his wife or sleeps in one but in the day does without it; or the transvestite outlet may be more subtle still as for example the transvestite who does not cross-dress but dyes his hair blond.

Another way in which transvestism in marriage differs from indivi-dual transvestism is that it often forms part of a collusion between man and wife either tolerated with some amusement or detachment or fully accepted as one of those "kinky things that everyone has", willingly accepted in exchange for a stable family life with a man who in other respects may be sexually normal, loving and a good father. Provided the transvestism is a part-deviance and provided that it is accepted within the marriage by the spouse this should not lead to a psychosexual problem. Problems may arise when the wife does not know about this facet of her husband's activities either in the present or in the past. Past transvestite activity, particularly if it has involved any semi-public investigation as by a psychiatrist, or by the law, can be a source of fear and guilt on the part of a patient terrified that his wife may be made aware of what may be a long-past misdemeanour.

From a therapeutic point of view behavioural modification may be the most appropriate way of dealing with the problem as it presents in marriage. Either individual psychotherapy or conjoint marital therapy may also be appropriate. In individual therapy the aim (particularly where the transvestism is a guilty secret) is to bring the patient more to terms with his feelings about his problem and to help him to a better general adjustment including a better establishment of his own identity and his psychosexual identity. Conjoint marital therapy will be used where the wife is aware of the situation and may be perturbed to find that it remains a problem with the husband despite not being a problem with her. Joint discussions will then help to clarify the situation and to allow the partners to settle for what may otherwise be an excellent relationship both between themselves and also between them and their children.

Transsexualism

Gender dysphoria (p. 231) with the identification with the female so powerful that a sex change operation is requested, presents not infrequently as an individual problem, less frequently as a marital problem. If the latter, it may be compounded with transvestism. I saw a couple in whom cross-dressing by the husband had been accepted for some time, reluctantly, by the wife as an acceptable outlet for the husband's gender dysphoria. When the frequency and elaborateness of his cross-dressing became increased, the children were involved, being disturbed by, and making fun of, their father. The wife's attempts to suppress the cross-dressing led to depression and overt desire for a sex-change operation. These desires were held in check "because of the children". While cross-dressing was, to a certain level, tolerated by the wife, it was made clear that, with family and extra-family pressures, a sex-change was unacceptable and would mean a break-up of the family.

In this type of agonizing, and fortunately rare, situation an ongoing psychotherapeutic relationship may be established with both partners. From this it is hoped that an appropriate solution might emerge. Unsympathetic handling of a transsexual can result in depression, suicide attempts or attempts at auto-castration (*British Medical Journal*, 1966).

Fetishism

Fetishism resembles transvestism except that sexual attention is aroused and satisfied in relation to a particular garment. In marriage this usually presents in one of two ways: either the problem is a mild one, possibly even a secret, as for example when a man becomes stimulated by leather jackets or high-laced boots worn by strangers in the street and fantasies these objects during sexual intercourse without telling his wife; or problems may arise because the wife is taken into his confidence in an attempt to make her take part in the fetishistic behaviour. Thus the fetishist may ask his wife to dress up in a particular way, e.g. in a nurse's uniform, in order that sexual arousal is achieved. Again there usually seems to be a spectrum of what behaviour is tolerated in marriage so that wives may allow a certain amount of fetishistic behaviour. Thus she may agree to pretend to be a prostitute both partners calling this their "game". The wife may, however, draw the line when the demands of the husband become greater, for example, demanding particular sorts of day clothes to be worn before intercourse such as fur coats or particular types of undergarments such as pants which are translucent across the vulva. Another example would be where a middle-aged or elderly man demands that his wife wears clothes, particularly underclothes, suggesting an age group to which she does not belong. The absurdity and lack of dignity of this situation may arouse her anxiety, resentment, anger, refusal and seeking outside help.

In my experience this type of problem is more difficult to deal with than the problems of homosexuality and transvestism in marriage discussed previously. Fetishism is more likely to be a complete deviance, in the sense that it entirely replaces a normal sexual outlet, rather than a part-deviance as discussed previously in which it can take place together with a normal sexuality. It also tends to develop in that increasing demands are made of the spouse and there seems no compromise. I have never successfully treated a fetishistic problem by marital therapy and this compares unfavourably with the problems previously discussed. One of two things happens: either the man, possibly sensing his imperative needs, refuses to attend therapy because he cannot or will not moderate his sexual demands; or else he does attend and it becomes clear that there is not likely to be any change.

I have implied that psychodynamic marital therapy is unlikely to be effective here; no series of cases has been reported, so far as I know, where this particular problem has been treated by behaviour therapy

for the individual or by marital contract therapy. Such research
would be welcome.

Sadomasochism

As with other sexual deviations sadomasochism forms a spectrum of
behaviour in marriage. At one extreme is the fully developed clinical
picture in which normal sexual adjustment is impossible as it is replaced by cruel acts on the part of the man or his need for punishment (whipping, beating, or other forms of flagellation). Another
expression of the extreme end of the spectrum is the solitary masochist (who may of course be married) who combines an addiction to
pornographic literature with practices which are life-threatening, for
example partial self-strangulation. This is mainly a forensic problem
and is a not uncommon cause of self-destruction.

In marriage, however, the situation presents differently. A sadist or
a masochist may get married and then find later that his sexual deviance
is more powerful than he thought so that he cannot sustain the marital
sexual relationship. More commonly the expression of sadomasochism
consists of behaviour which is on the borderline of what is acceptable
to the spouse. Thus one partner may become verbally aggressive and
the other verbally submissive. A collusive behaviour pattern is frequent:
thus, if a man's potency depends upon masochistic fantasies, his wife
may be willing to help him achieve sexual fulfilment at a price rather
than to risk removing this deviant behaviour therapeutically with the
uncertain possibility of achieving a "normal" sexual adjustment. An
interesting variant is when the sadomasochistic behaviour is placed on
a conditioning basis as when the wife merely has to raise her hand as
if to beat her husband for him to gain penile erection; or even on a
verbal conditioning basis when she has merely to utter certain threatening words to stimulate his erection.

These patterns of collusive behaviour can become extremely complex, successful within limits, and frequently reduce the possibility of
a marital sexual problem. Problems may arise if the playful pattern
becomes more serious the male partner needing actually to beat his
wife; or when, even if remaining on a playful level, the man begins to
feel depressed or guilty about his need when he may present either
with or without his wife in order to alleviate the problem. As with
fetishism my experience is that this problem must be approached
very carefully; any attempt at modification by prolonged psycho-

therapy is unlikely to be successful. It is better to attempt, using conjoint marital therapy, to get the couple to accept and settle for some form of compromise as for example the playful behaviour described above. As with fetishism I do not know of reports of a sadomasochistic marital series treated with behavioural modification techniques. Such an experiment would be informative.

Exhibitionism

The exhibitionists who come to the attention of the marital therapist are somewhat different from the individual exhibitionist described by Hertoft (p. 204). This sexual deviation is compatible with an excellent marital adjustment and the deviant behaviour may not only occur relatively rarely but is done in situations which would be unlikely to lead to disclosure. Exhibitionists can achieve a remarkably good adjustment in all areas of marriage both sexual and loving. Possibly the most difficult cases to deal with and potentially the sadest are those who achieve an excellent sexual and family adjustment but get arrested from time to time so that family and professional ruin is a constant threat as when a report appears in a local newspaper.

Therapeutically with this group both psychodynamic and behavioural psychotherapy has been tried (Rooth, 1971). Both methods achieve some success but this is unpredictable. Although I have seen a number of exhibitionists it has not been possible for any of them to accept the possibility of conjoint marital therapy with the wife knowing about the husband's difficulty and both coming to terms with this. Possibly it is because of the nature of the act this is found unacceptable to a wife however admirable she feels her husband to be in other respects.

In summary, the most important points about sexual deviance as it presents in marriage is that in most cases the patients probably come from the more normal end of the deviance spectrum so that they may have a good marriage relationship outside the sexual area and may also be capable of heterosexual arousal and successful heterosexual performance. The most appropriate therapeutic intervention is to aim for modification of the guilt, depression, anxiety and general misery surrounding the act and to get both partners involved. This may not always be possible or allowed by the sexually deviant person in which case individual dynamic psychotherapy may be of help either in modifying the strength of the need or in helping the patient to become

more to terms both with himself and with this particular aspect of his
personality.

Relationship Problems in Marriage

Sexual problems may present in marriage and there may be no other
problems. On the other hand a couple may present apparently with a
sexual problem when in fact the underlying problem is connected with
their relationship. Thus a couple presented with a "frigidity" problem
of the woman. It transpired that she was aware when she married her
husband that she had difficulties relating to sexuality. What she was not
aware of was that her husband was marrying her, despite not being
especially attracted to her sexually, because he wished for a platonic
relationship. What was soon revealed was that both partners shared as
an underlying problem an unresolved, over-close relationship with
parental figures. This led both of them to adapt in marriage to a
comfortable, non-sexual, relationship. It was hardly logical, in this
situation, to attempt to treat the individual sexual problem without
attempting to help with the shared underlying relationship problem.
If relationship problems underly sexual problems, for any chance of
therapeutic success these need to be examined before the sexual
problems as such are tackled. It is of course up to the couple whether
or not they want to see the situation in this light or whether they wish
to take it elsewhere as, for example, to a behavioural psychotherapist
who might be persuaded (although this is much less likely with the
increasing psychological sophistication of behaviour therapists) to
tackle the problem at a level of pure sexual behaviour.

Sexual Problems Secondary to Psychiatric Disturbance

Research on marital interaction by Kreitman and his colleagues
(Kreitman *et al.*, 1970) has shown that psychiatric disturbance in the
man may relate to marital tension. Measures of neurosis in the spouse
increase with length of marriage which they call a "convergence"
phenomenon. This research was not however aimed at psychosexual
problems in marriage. It is of course true that psychosexual problems
in one partner do sometimes appear as secondary to, or in reaction to,
identifiable psychiatric disturbance on the part of the spouse. This

situation is however relatively rare as a cause of marital tension compared to the situation in which broad areas of difficulty in the relationship lead, directly or indirectly, to sexual difficulty. These difficulties will now be considered in relation to the phases of a marriage, dominance, affection and decision-making.

Phases of Marriage

The statistics of marital breakdown (Fletcher, 1973) show clearly that this is most likely early in marriage and considerably later, around 17 years after marriage. It is obvious that problems of establishing a marriage are likely to be involved in the first group of problems and the second group is likely to be related to children growing up, leaving home, the marriage partners being thrown back again on their own company and resources which may be severely strained. Marriages pass through developmental phases which are not quantifiable. In assessing a marriage it is important to be aware of the possibility that the relationship was, at one time or another, more stable or less stable than it appears at the time of examination. Clues may be sought where children are involved by noting that one child is more psychologically damaged than the others. In this case enquiries should be made about how the relationship was at the time of conception or early childhood of the disturbed child. As an example, a number of men are in professions which, when children are young, demand a great deal of time away from home. Such separations may be a source of stress which may reflect on the child or children. Alternatively, situations can arise at a later stage of marriage as in the elderly in relation to retirement, the presence of the man around his wife all day being a source of stress which may lead to sexual dysfunction.

Dominance and Affection

Many attempts to describe marital interaction include the parameters of dominance and affection (Ryle, 1966). In the assessment of any relationship it is important to enquire about these two areas of interaction. They should also be assessed directly by observation of the couple in the joint interview. As with other aspects of marriage, it is important not to make pre-judgments as to what is "normal". A dominance-submissiveness relationship only becomes a dominance-submissiveness conflict or problem if it is felt as such, or complained of, by one of the partners, or if it expresses itself in the psychosexual areas as a cause of sexual dysfunction.

With affection the same caution applies: differences are not necessarily problematic. In sexuality, however, they may present as a difference in the ability to become totally preoccupied with love-making as opposed to being able to carry out the mechanics of sex without emotional envolvement. Perhaps because of differing relationship needs of men and women, mechanical sex, if a problem, is more usually seen as such by the woman than by the man. She may complain that her husband is an efficient and effective lover but un-committed in the way that she is and would like him to be.

Decision-making

A detailed consideration of decision-making is a useful and easily available way of assessing marital interaction. Are decisions made by one or the other partner or are they taken jointly? Common areas of assessment include family planning; plans for child-upbringing as for example education or religious upbringing; financial decisions; decisions as to holidays and spare-time entertainments. At the joint interview particularly, it will soon be clear whether or not there is agreement or disagreement and, if disagreement, whether this has been recognized. Also, whether if there is disagreement this has spilled over as resentment to disturb sexuality.

Assuming that sexuality and relationships have been assessed along these lines, it is then possible to decide whether the sexual problem is paramount or the relationship or, so far as can be determined, there is a combination of both sexual and relationship problems. It is probably true whatever psychotherapeutic technique is adopted that sexual problems presenting within an otherwise good relationship have a basically good prognosis but psychosexual problems embedded in a bad relationship have a much more uncertain outlook.

Conjoint Marital Therapy

Counselling (Chapter 2), group psychotherapy (Chapter 3), individual psychotherapy (Chapter 1) and behavioural psychotherapy (Chapter

4) in relation to marital problems have been described. The technique of psychodynamic conjoint marital therapy will be briefly noted here. It is described in more detail elsewhere (Crown, 1976).

Following the tripartite assessment the therapeutic alliance is established exactly as with individual psychotherapy. The major difference arises in deciding whether or not there should be one therapist or two. I have suggested that until there is convincing evidence of differential affectiveness the emphasis should be on the use of one therapist because this allows psychotherapy to be spread more widely among those who need it. The third important decision is whether or not every session should be a joint session or whether there should be a combination of joint sessions and individual psychotherapy sessions with one spouse. In my experience this arrangement should be entirely flexible. It is helpful for the couple to decide themselves what they need and also to alter this from time to time without prior notice to the therapist so that they may appear at the consulting room saying that, having discussed it, one or the other or both decided to come. Another difference from individual psychotherapy is that marital psychotherapy sessions may be more widely spaced. While Dicks (1967) seems to imply that once-weekly sessions are necessary, and this may be the most usual spacing, in my experience certain couples do better with more widely spaced sessions the emphasis for the effectiveness of treatment being put on what they do between sessions. Thus three-weekly spacing seems helpful with some couples; even less frequently with others. Marital psychotherapy is essentially short-term therapy. It usually becomes clear within a few sessions whether or not there is likely to be useful therapeutic progress and goals are usually then attained within a few months. Three to six months is perhaps the length of the majority of treatments.

Psychotherapeutic interventions in marital therapy may follow the lines of those in individual psychotherapy, for example, linking past and present, present and present and present and future. Psychological defences against anxiety may also be interpreted as appropriate. A major difference is that transference interpretations, because of the presence of the third person, do not usually form an important part of marital psychotherapy. On the other hand aspects of the here-and-now particularly ways in which the relationship may be modified, take a central place. Unlike individual psychotherapy, experiments may be carried out by the partners between sessions and reported upon, refined and re-practised. Successful readjustments provide considerable impetus for further adjustment and further reward. A num-

ber of the technicalities noted in this section are discussed in more
detail in the chapter on individual psychotherapy.

It should not be forgotten that a combination of therapies, for
example, behavioural contract therapy and psychodynamic marital
therapy may be appropriate for the individual marriage.

Summary

This chapter describes how psychosexual problems present in marriage
and their evaluation. Psychosexual problems may be of sexual dysfunction or sexual deviance. Sexual deviance in the marital setting may
be successfully combined with a reasonable or even a good heterosexual adjustment. Relationship problems in marriage may be
secondary to psychiatric disturbance but more usually relate to broad
areas of malfunctioning such as differences in dominance, affection
or decision-making. Marital assessment is done with each spouse
separately followed by a joint interview in which the couple are observed and relevant techniques of marital therapy (psychodynamic,
behavioural, etc.) are decided. Marital therapy is not necessarily aimed
at preserving relationships. Separation or divorce may turn out to be
the appropriate course for a particular marriage and this possibility
must be faced in planning treatment.

References

British Medical Journal (1966). Transsexuality. April, 873–874
Crowe, M. (1976). Behavioural treatments in psychiatry. *In* "Recent Advances in
    Clinical Psychiatry." (Granville-Grossman, K. Ed.), Churchill Livingstone:
    Edinburgh.
Crown, S. (1976). Marital breakdown: epidemiology and psychotherapy. *In*
    "Recent Advances in Clinical Psychiatry." (Granville-Grossman, K. Ed.),
    Churchill Livingstone: Edinburgh.
Dicks, H. V. (1967). "Marital Tensions." Routledge and Kegan Paul: London.
Divorce Reform Act (1969). HMSO: London.
Fisher, S. (1973). "Understanding the Female Orgasm." Penguin Books:
    Harmondsworth.
Fletcher, R. (1973). "The Family and Marriage in Britain." Penguin Books:
    Harmondsworth.

Kreitman, N., Collins, J., Nelson, B. and Troop, J. (1970). Neurosis and marital interaction: I. Personality and symptoms. *British Journal of Psychiatry* 117, 33 46.

Masters, W. H. and Johnson, V. E. (1966). "Human Sexual Response." Little, Brown and Co: Boston, Mass., USA.

Masters, W. H. and Johnson, V. E. (1970). "Human Sexual Inadequacy." Churchill Livingstone: Edinburgh.

Rooth, F. G. (1971). Indecent exposure and exhibitionism. *British Journal of Hospital Medicine.* April, 521—533.

Ryle, A. (1966). A marital patterns test for use in Psychiatric research. *British Journal of Psychiatry,* 112, 285—293.

9 | *Psychosexual Problems in A Religious Setting*

IRENE BLOOMFIELD and LOUIS MARTEAU

Statement of Position

In this chapter we are examining two groups of people whose former or present religious beliefs are directly related to current sexual difficulties.

One group of such people presented at a Health Service psychiatric clinic and the other at a Christian counselling centre. Since the survey was carried out retrospectively figures were not kept in a manner which was necessarily comparable. We have each examined those people who came to us and are presenting our findings. This means that the two groups differ from each other in certain respects but are sufficiently representative to draw some general conclusions.

The reason for examining these two groups is to see what difference the setting may make to the presentation of the problem, method of treatment and outcome.

While the term "therapy" has been applied to the medical setting and "counselling" to the pastoral, the process and techniques do not really differ.

General Introduction

Attitudes to Sex in Religion and Mythology

Religious beliefs have been used from time immemorial as man's means of coming to terms with his physical environment and with the society in which he lives. They have been a way of making sense and order out of what would otherwise have been incomprehensible, terrifying or overwhelming.

In ancient religions or mythology they gave man the feeling that he had ways of influencing and controlling these awesome forces of nature. This is illustrated by one of the fundamental beliefs of ancient religions which was that the union of trees and plants could not be fertile without the actual union of humans. Our forefathers tried to hasten the growth of trees and plants by the symbolical marriages of deities or other exalted figures like the King and Queen of the May.

This principle of sympathetic magic underlies many religious beliefs concerned with fertility and initiation rites.

Hinduism, Buddhism, Yoga

The leitmotif of most Eastern religions, i.e. Hinduism and Buddhism is to deliver man from pain. Human suffering is seen to be rooted in illusion because of man's confusion between spirit and nature. Illumination is thought to be achieved through knowledge and meditation or through techniques like yoga.

The Yogi practises sexual abstinence in order to conserve nervous energy. Yoga attaches great importance to these secret forces of the generative faculty which is thought to dissipate precious nervous energy unless carefully preserved.

This idea is reflected in the intense fear of some Hindu and Moslem patients seen by I.B. who expressed great anxiety about the loss of life force through any form of sexual activity, but particularly through masturbating or "wet dreams".

In many of the ancient Indian religions sexuality has two ritual functions:

1. to procure universal fecundity, and
2. to symbolize the conjunction of opposites.

The ceremonial union between priest and prostitute expressed a desire to effect the reintegration of opposites. The ritual significance of sexual union in Indian religions has affected the attitude of believers towards the value of sexuality. (This is illustrated in the Kamasutra.)

Judaism

In Judasim sexual relationships in marriage are sanctified by law. "Be fruitful and multiply" is a commandment to the orthodox. It is unlawful to use contraceptives.

It is a mizvah (a religious duty) to have sexual relationships in marriage but not outside the marital union. "Thou shalt not covet thy neighbour's wife". (When King David sent his captain Uriah to certain death because he wanted to take his wife Bathshebah for himself, the prophet Nathan reproached him as much for his adultery as for the murder.)

Christianity

Attitudes towards sex in Christianity are illustrated in many of the examples throughout this chapter. Some of the effects of the puritan element in Protestantism are still very much a part of the English culture even in this permissive society.

Religion and the Use of Symbolism

Psychotherapy and religion are both concerned with the basic themes of human life and endeavour. All the major religions have made great use of symbolism, and the dynamic systems of psychology have made us even more aware of the power of the symbol. As Anthony Storr (1960) remarks:

> "Psychotherapy is by its very nature concerned with the basic themes of human life. Love and hate, birth and death, sexuality and power: all the vast complexities of the emotions which stir and sway the hearts of men are the daily concern of the psychotherapist. Even if he wishes to, it would be impossible for him to avoid having some views as to the meaning and significance of the momentous themes with which he is concerned."

It would not seem surprising therefore that both psychology and religious teaching should be concerned with sexuality and that both should have their own symbolic form of expression. Both are also concerned with the paradox of human life. Love can be experienced as tender and nurturing or as restricting and killing. Every gain which the infant makes towards independence and maturity must also involve a loss in closeness as the child moves from its first symbiotic relationship into final independence and on to the time when the parents will become dependent on the child. In every new beginning there is a little death. Man is faced with an infinity of desires in a very finite body. Some of his greatest powers also become some of his greatest dangers.

The greater the power, the greater become the moral imperatives in the religious field, It is therefore no surprise that many of the religious faiths surround sexuality with moral imperatives, just as many civilizations surrounded it with taboos.

At the same time Harry Guntrip (1964) reminds us in his interpretation of guilt and fear that:

> "Much ill-informed religious teaching in the past has fostered pathological guilt and made for depression. The prople who take home to themselves condemnatory preaching are usually those to whom it least of all applies."

The moral theologian is concerned with guilt, and takes as his premise that the individual is acting totally freely. In psychotherapy we are concerned with the appropriateness of a particular emotion. It may be just as pathological to be overtaxed by guilt as to have none.

Symbolism is a normal way in which man tends to express the deeper emotions which he cannot himself define or put into words. For this reason the symbols which he has already taken to himself in a religious setting may be of great value as vehicles to express these deeper human conflicts. They are however also imbued with their own symbolic meaning and the two may often be confused.

> Mary who was dying of cancer and in great pain was treated by a hypnotist. During this process it was discovered that she had very deep and angry feelings about her mother. The hypnotist asked her to take a rose into her hand and pull out the petals one by one, in so doing to express symbolically the feelings that she had against her mother in order to release them. When Mary came round from the hypnotic state she felt released from some of the anger which had been pent up inside her but unfortunately this process had also become associated with the rosary on her bedside table. In this single act the rosary and her mother had become entwined and she found herself now faced with death without that living faith which had hitherto been her consolation.

Norms and Conflict

Social Conflict

It is clear that religious beliefs have a significant influence on man's attitude towards sexuality. Different cultures put very different emphases on what they regard as desirable and acceptable sexual behaviour. The breaking of codes of sexual conduct still cause guilt, anxiety and paranoid feelings, whereas the inability to achieve the standards of sexual performance laid down by our society will cause feelings of shame and inadequacy in those who do not attain them.

Difficulties arise for the individual who wants to conform to the code of his society and to gain its approval, but whose impulses and desires are in conflict with this code.

He can deal with this conflict in a number of ways depending on whether he is aware of the source of his unease or whether the possibility of going against the code is experienced as too dangerous and too painful so that such a possibility cannot even be acknowledged and has to be pushed underground and repressed.

Many of the people who come to see a psychotherapist have come to grief because they have not been able to reconcile the conflicting needs of their impulses and their value system.

Others are suffering because they have not achieved satisfactory relationships. They feel that they have not measured up to society's norms of attaining adult sexual relations, marriage and parenthood. They feel that they have failed.

Religious Conflict

There are some social groupings which share a common belief to such a degree that the laws of the country and the people's mores support each other. In such a grouping an individual may find himself in conflict not only with the norms of society but also with his own religious beliefs. In other social groupings the individual may find himself and his religious faith in the minority. But besides being one who has a specific faith he is also part of his cultural group. The conflict may be externalized but at a deeper level will be found within his very self.

In a Christian culture many human emotions have been labelled "bad". Anger, aggression and sometimes even sexuality are required to be suppressed both by culture and religion. The Victorian mother's advice to her daughter on the eve of marriage was "Close your eyes and think of the British Empire".

Jung has pointed out that:

"One of the main difficulties lies in the fact that both theologians and psychotherapists appear to use the same language, but this language calls

up in their minds two totally different fields of association. Both can
apparently use the same concepts, and then are bound to acknowledge, to
their amazement, that they are speaking about two different things."

This is certainly true of these so-called "bad" feelings.

Sister Grace's young brother was shot during an episode in Northern
Ireland. She is faced with the need to repress all her feelings of anger
while those around her are expressing them volubly. To the psychologist, this is a bad repression of aggressive feelings, while to her
it is a temptation to sin. But aggression and anger are not exactly
the same thing. Aggression is fundamentally that inner power
which enables an individual to cope with critical developmental
periods of life and the individual stresses of their situation. The
feelings experienced by Sister Grace are real feelings which she
needs to acknowledge and accept. Once she has accepted them and
been able to forgive she will cease feeling "tempted to sin" and
see herself called to an act of "heroic virtue". Deadening herself to
these feelings can only lead to grave depression.

In considering the social and religious norms and the conflict they
evoke, it is interesting to note the difference between men and women
which appeared from the research of Kinsey (1948, 1953). He noted
that men were more influenced by social and cultural norms than by
any other factor, while for women there was no factor which was as
vital as their religious fervour, irrespective of the religious observance
they followed.

These findings however, as all the religious factors investigated by
Kinsey, suffer from a major deficiency. They are related to the current
religious status of the individuals investigated at the time of the
research. Our finding has been that this is by no means as relevant as
the religious status of their childhood and family background. Many
of our cases reported here were not at all committed to their religion
at the onset of their problems but were still reacting to childhood
experience.

The Two Groups

The Hospital Setting

Of 57 patients in therapy either individually or in groups with I.B., 28
have some form of religious background. They are either priests,

rabbis, monks, nuns or theological students, or people who are practising their religion now. A few people are included who have lost their
faith but had a religious upbringing either from parents or schools.

This means that over 50% of the people seen have some sort of
religious background. Of the 28, 6 are Anglicans, 6 Roman Catholics,
3 Jews, 1 Baptist, 5 nuns, 4 ministers and 3 went to convent schools
but are not practising their religion now.

The total number of patients seen by I.B. during 1974 was 104 but
this included people seen only for assessment and follow-up. The proportions of those with and without religious backgrounds were much
the same.

Fifty per cent of people with a religious background in a clinical
setting is a relatively high proportion. The reason for this is that I.B.s
interest in this field is known to her colleagues in the Department and
to referring agencies outside.

Christian Counselling Setting

Over a period of three years, 200 clients, an average of 66 per annum,
sought help at the counselling centre directed by L.M. Most of them
saw their problems in religious terms but their psychological condition might be classified as follows:

Table 1

Two hundred clients presenting at a centre with a religious setting

Presenting problems

42 With Depression which covered major feelings of anger which they were
    unable to express about their family parental relationships.
    This led into their problems of personal identity and the manner in
    which it had been affected by these feelings.
    From here to an examination of their feelings about their own identity —
    and thus sexuality.
    Two of these presented directly with sexual problems which they
    related to such experiences.
35 With anxiety about the manner in which they were relating with others.
    They felt guilty at the manner in which they handled their inter-personal
    relationships.
    This led to an examination of their own identity and parental relation-
    ships.
23 Psychotic episodes.
19 For general advice of a superficial nature

17 With marital problems
17 With homosexual problems (5 lesbian)
12 With problems about their inappropriate reactions to persons of the same
      or opposite sex — over sensitivity, jealousy, relationships with clergy,
      inability to accept the humanity of Christ.
 5 With masturbatory problems
 4 With addictions
 4 With scrupulosity and obsessional behaviour
 3 With sexual promiscuity
 2 Phobic
10 Problems with their vocation; not followed up dynamically
 7 Assessments before entering religious life

Reasons for Referral and Problems

The Hospital Clinic

The examples listed are only of religious patients in whom sexual difficulties were present.

1. A proportion of people came because they thought that there was something physically wrong with them. They saw themselves as sick — like Francis whose migraine attacks virtually knocked him out for two days at a time. He was certain that this terrible pain must be caused by a tumour. Nigel was convinced that there must be a hormone treatment to increase the size of his sex organs and Ian wanted some physical treatment to make him heterosexual.

2. Another group saw themselves as psychiatrically ill or were seen in this way by their doctors. They were afraid that they might be "going mad", and might need a safe place to contain them, like Cathy who was suddenly unable to remember who she was or who her husband was and who felt that the world was a terribly threatening place. There was Elaine whose voices told her that she was better dead and Sandra whose misinterpretations of reality caused havoc in her community.

3. Group 3 consisted of those patients who were regarded as suicide risks and in several cases had made previous suicide attempts like Anita who became suicidal every time she saw her mother, because mother's rejecting attitude re-emphasized her feelings of worthlessness, and Ronald who could not face the breakdown of his first stable homosexual relationship.

4. People in this group came because they felt that they had not

been able to get the help they needed from their ministers or were afraid that they might be misunderstood and judged by representatives of the Church, like Valerie who felt that she could not tell her priest that she wanted to do away with herself since this was a mortal sin, and Catherine who was convinced that the priest she consulted had made advances to her after she told him about her father's sexual approaches to her.

5. People in this group came because they had lost their faith but their religion still affected their attitudes and emotional lives, like Jennifer who hated the God of her strict Baptist background but still spent most of her life defending herself from His wrath.

6. There were a few people who had got into a collusive discussion about theological matters with their pastoral counsellors and could not resolve this impasse in the religious setting, like Norma who was convinced that she had offended against the Holy Ghost and who was determined to involve her counsellor, whom she knew to be a priest, in a theological discussion about the Holy Ghost, or like Margaret who had become converted during a psychotic episode and could not distinguish between the symbolic and the factual, so that the Eucharist took on a sinister meaning for her.

7. A few patients were referred to the hospital by their pastoral counsellors when these found themselves out of their depth as with Jonathan a curate, who should feel loving towards members of his congregation but in fact had intensely violent and even murderous feelings towards the young men in his congregation whom he saw as having so much more of everything than he had himself.

Jean's counsellor became worried about the counselling relationship because she was an active member of his congregation and therefore met the minister in a variety of contexts. She had asked to see him because she felt that she was possessed but he did not believe that exorcism would help her accept her feelings of rage and come to grips with them.

The priest who offers warmth to the emotionally deprived woman can easily be misunderstood and Jean interpreted her pastoral counsellor's acceptance and warmth as an offer of physical love and did her utmost to seduce him.

Disadvantages of the Clinical Setting

There were a number of patients who expressed great concern about coming to the hospital because they feared that their religious beliefs would not be understood by non-religious psychotherapists and that they might even be ridiculed.

Another fear was that the process of psychotherapy would rob them of their faith, that it would be analysed away and that they would be left with nothing.

Being labelled a psychiatric patient undoubtedly has disadvantages however much we in the profession may protest about this. It frequently militates against obtaining employment or further training. It makes it impossible to emigrate to certain countries or even to get temporary posts abroad. It affects the premium of life insurance and in some cases makes it virtually impossible to obtain insurance cover.

The whole clinical setting was off-putting to many people because of the inevitably lengthy procedure of doctor's referral, waiting for the initial interview, a further wait for therapy but without certainty of treatment at the end of this period because of the shortage of therapists in the Health Service.

Religion can also be used as a defence.

Noreen, referred to I.B., expressed her resistance to therapy in this form. Whenever the time for her annual breakdown approached, she became unwilling to look at herself. She would say "There is no point in coming to see you, because you will not be able to understand my religious feelings. I prefer to take my problems to my spiritual director. He will give me the guidance I need."

Playing the spiritual director off against the therapist was also a popular technique with Cathy who was very adept at this game and whenever her negative feelings about the therapist got the upper hand she would say with great glee: "I went to see Fr John. He is kind." The implication was that the therapist was unkind and unhelpful.

The Christian Counselling Centre

Since the majority of these presenting problems would seem to be the same as those presenting in any psychiatric out-patients, one might first ask, what brought them to a Christian counselling centre. About 50% had in fact been referred either by doctors, psychiatrists or psychiatric units in hospitals while the other 50% had been referred by clergy or other religious organizations.

Of those who presented their problems to the Counselling centre
there were a number of reasons for referral.

There were those who saw their problem as a purely religious one.
Since the matter presented had moral overtones the whole problem
was seen as religious. This is particularly true in the field of sexuality.

Brigid had for many years lived a promiscuous sexual life and since
the death of her mother had wished to return to the practice of her
religion. But she was torn between this and her constant need for
indiscriminate sexual relationships. John had taken part in a Black
Mass and forms of devil worship and sought to be exorcized.

There were those whose expression of emotional disturbance was
so strongly couched in religious symbolic terminology and whose
attitude to life so steeped in a particular religious frame that they
found it difficult, if not impossible, to work with anyone who could
not communicate in their terms of reference.

David was steadily starving himself to death both as an act of
penance for his past sexual misdemeanours and as the only way he
had discovered which now enabled him to control them. He had
been a monk whose terms of reference were bound up with the
sayings of the fathers in the desert. Joseph had obscene religious
thoughts and was unable to pass down a street which contained a
church. He has no religious background but was terrified of hell
and desperately wanted to be reassured that he was not destined
for it.

There was a group which had failed to find effective help in a
medical or psychiatric field and now wondered if they could find it in
a religious setting.

Joan had been sexually assaulted over a long period of time by her
father and having recently been converted to a fundamentalist
group of Christians became acutely aware of herself as sexually evil.
She went into a depression. Her need was more for the acceptance
and forgiveness of God, at least at the symbolic level through acceptance by a pastoral counsellor once she had been able to uncover
the pleasure she had gained from this experience.

Quite a large group were emotionally disturbed but did not wish to
have themselves labelled as "mentally sick". They felt that they were
in need of help to cope with their emotional problems.

Elizabeth had reached the top of her profession and was living quite a satisfying life, but at the same time felt that in some way she was still not reaching her full potential. Though her early relationships with her parents had been broadly satisfactory there were still areas of conflict through which she needed to work.

Disadvantages of a Christian Counselling Centre

There can be some difficulties which may arise purely from the setting of a Christian counselling centre.

1. There is danger that the counsellor may collude with the religious feelings, and in so doing be unable to see the underlying emotional problem.

2. The clients themselves may block all psychological insight and be unable to see anything but a religious problem.

3. There is a danger that the counsellor may become too closely identified with the client, especially where there is a conflict between religious and cultural norms, e.g. Abortion and Euthenasia.

4. Both client and counsellor may be in danger of accepting the God fantasy in too personal a form. The client may really be wanting God to remove the problem and see the counsellor as God's agent, and the counsellor may collude with this fantasy.

5. The client may be blocked with a medical label which he uses as a defence against any examination of his problem. Thus if I am suffering from "depression" I do not have to question what is depressing me. The use of such labels, especially by a client who has experienced many years of psychiatric treatment may be very difficult for the pastoral counsellor.

Presenting Problems

Overt Sexual Problems

Homosexuality

The emphasis on sexual behaviour in some Christian faiths added to a highly moralistic upbringing may lead to a sense of utter despair and even suicide for the homosexual person. The heroic battle which the individual may fight with his own sexual problems against the background of disapproval and condemnation leads to a feeling of rejection.

John, fifty-four years, (referred to L.M.) suffering from an over
sensitive conscience in every field of life, was also sexually attracted
to other men. He had battled with this throughout his life with
some success and also with the occasional failures. He found himself
faced with a dilemma. Since the cause of his pain was in his feeling
of guilt brought about by his religious faith, this would be solved by
giving up that faith. But he was then faced with the pain of guilt and
despair. His overwhelming need was to feel accepted, and accepted
by his church. Yet his church seemed to find it difficult to give him
that acceptance. This made it even more difficult for him to accept
himself. He searched around to try and discover a priest in whose
eyes he could find acceptance since the acceptance by a psychiatrist
or therapist could not fulfil his overwhelming need to find himself
symbolically accepted by God. His feeling of guilt in the homosexual sphere had generalized into every sphere of life. Seeing a
pebble in the street he felt obliged to remove it in case a cyclist fell
off his bicycle, diverted a lorry, which ran into a bus queue; in no
time at all John had become a mass murderer.

Jane (referred to L.M.) on the other hand wanted to become a boy.
She felt that somehow even from the age of four she had always
been a boy. She did not want "treatment", she did not wish to be
"cured", but she came to a Christan counselling centre for "permission". Her parents were conscientious Christians who felt that
such a change was an attack upon the very principles of their faith.
They were unable to see that this was also an attack upon them,
nor were they able to work through the difficulties presented by
this situation since the whole matter had now become a "moral
issue". Each would try to line up clergy on their side and engage in
a battle. Their religious setting had become the symbolic battleground.

Impotence

Daniel (referred to I.B.) was an orthodox Jew, fifty years old at the
time of his referral. It seemed that he had become impotent during
the past eighteen months and this was causing him great distress.
He had come to England two years before having divorced his wife
after twenty-seven years of marriage. All through his marriage he had
never had any problems over potency although there had been
other problem areas between the couple.

When he came to England he had to live in a furnished room and
found this humiliating and very lonely. He did not know how to find
companionship but unable to bear the isolation and loneliness he
went to social clubs and even discotheques to find female company.
He felt that the girls he met at these establishments expected him
to take them home and "to have sex".

It came as a great additional shock to all his other troubles
that he found himself unable to perform the sexual act when he
did what he felt was expected of him by these girls. He had lost his
family, his home, his circle of friends and his status in society and
the loss of his potency seemed like the last straw.

In therapy we looked at his feelings about himself and about casual
sexual relationships and he was surprised to discover how deeply
ingrained the injunctions about sex outside the marital relationship
were still within him.

He thought that he had liberated himself from the Jewish laws
relating to sexual relations and had accepted that this was a different
age with different values from those with which he had grown up.
But in his heart he despised the young women whom he took home
to beat the feelings of loneliness.

When during his treatment he established a stable relationship with
a woman whom he respected and thought he could marry, all the
sexual difficulties vanished and he was once more able to have a full
and satisfying sexual relationship.

It seemed that what had turned a downward spiral into an upward
one for him was the possiblity of looking at his sexuality and sexual
attitudes as part of his total value system. When he achieved a
measure of reconciliation between the two his potency was
restored.

Gerard an Anglican Priest (referred to L.M.) presented his problem
as one of depression brought about by the impossibility of his parish
setting where he felt absolutely ineffective. Only incidentally did
he also complain of 15 years of impotence. All his feelings about the
physical impotence had been transferred into feelings about his
pastoral life.

The total sense of "impotence" had to be examined in the light of
his feelings about himself.

In the hospital setting impotence was seen by Daniel as a biological
dysfunction with psychological overtones and thus correct for presentation, although his work was possibly more relevant. In the Centre

Gerard could present the way in which his work was making him feel impotent but did not present his impotence as a major factor.

Frigidity

Noreen (referred to I.B.) had come jointly with her husband because of marital difficulties.

In joint talks with the husband we looked at the interaction between her husband Ernie and herself and it was quite surprising to see this normally timid, anxious and devout young woman behave in an extraordinarily domineering, hurtful and even cruel fashion towards her husband.

One session stands out in my mind when she yelled at him "I don't know why I married you. I have never loved you. I cannot make love to you because I am so angry with you. I do not really want to give you anything." It was then that I learned that she was totally frigid and had never achieved an orgasm in her ten years of marriage.

In a confused sort of way she seemed to regard it as almost a virtue to "suffer" sex rather than enjoy it. She had picked up attitudes to sex from her mother who hated "the whole nasty business". Carefully selected texts from the Scriptures, especially from the writings of St Paul, had contributed to her self-image as a pure, virginal, Christian woman.

Frances (referred to L.M.) was referred for pastoral support while her husband was in treatment. She was suffering from religious scrupulosity, which had been a dominating factor throughout her life, and which was most severe in her sexual life. These feelings however were in contradiction to her religious beliefs, in so far as she held that sex in marriage was good and to be enjoyed. She also experienced any "good" feelings as in some way sinful. Her life had been almost dedicated to killing any feelings. Her real problem was concerned with her sexual identity.

Both had been referred because their husbands were in therapy though Noreen was being seen as involved in a marital problem and Frances as one who needed pastoral support. For Noreen, religion was used as a defense against sexuality, while for Frances it had failed to give her the reassurance which she needed to overcome her problem of sexual identity.

Masturbation

Jennifer (referred to I.B.) presented with an inability to communicate and make relationships with people. (She is typical of a small group of people who enjoyed the discovery of masturbation until they learned that adults disapproved.) From then on pleasure and pain become closely associated especially in the sexual sphere, and as soon as there is any hint of pleasure, they are beset by feelings of guilt and fear and something has to be done to change the enjoyment into punishment before greater punishment can befall them. Jennifer said:

> "Before I was thirteen my sister reported that Miss R. had told them about self-abuse and how it was a sin. I had always masturbated for as long as I could remember but I thought I was the only person in the world who did it, so some time after that I went to the priest and said 'Father I have committed impure acts.' The priest told me to say three Hail Marys, but that did not make me feel any better. I have always had the feeling that some terrible doom or punishment will befall me and that there is nothing I can do about it. Sooner or later I will be found out and that will be it. That will be the end of me."

Masturbation is still the only form of sexual activity from which she gets any satisfaction at all although she has slept with many men, but there is no real pleasure for her in anything to do with sex or with anything else, because pleasure means pain and pain must be avoided at any price, but every move for Jennifer contains the threat of pain; so she masturbates to comfort herself, and this starts the whole never ending cycle all over again.

Gloria (referred to L.M.) also presented with difficulties in making relationships, although her anxiety about masturbatory habits were high on her list of problems. It had begun as a child when she identified more with the boys in the neighbourhood than the girls. She was always able to climb trees higher than the boys and competed with them in all their games. She began to masturbate while imagining she had a penis. She was now disturbed that she had actually deformed herself and feared to have sexual intercourse since her deformity would then become visible. Added to this was the guilt which she now felt about the habit, and that the deformity must in some way be her punishment.

A medical examination revealed that in fact she was well within the bounds of normality. Her real problem seemed to be in her inability to accept her own femininity and it was this area that was explored with some success.

Both cases presented with an inability to communicate and a sense of isolation, but Jennifer is an example of one whose earlier experience of religious support had been one of failure, so she turned to the Hospital Clinic. On the other hand Gloria did not see herself as in need of psychiatric help as such but was seeking forgiveness and was concerned about her presumed punishment.

Promiscuity

Promiscuity is frequently not due to an insatiable sexual appetite, but may have very different causes.

Sally (referred to I.B.) came from a strict Catholic background but she was apt to go to bed with anyone who asked her. She obtained little sexual pleasure from these casual contacts but felt that she could not refuse anybody.

She connected this with feelings which began when she was seven:

"I was carefree until the age of seven. One day Mother asked me 'Do you want to go to Confession?' I did not really want to go but I could not say so. I hated that dark box and the priest who could not see me and having to confess when I did not even know what I had done wrong. But I did not say any of this. When I saw the priest I did not tell him that I had not wanted to come to Confession, so I sinned again and then I went to Communion still not having confessed. From then on it all built up and got worse and worse and nothing was ever right again. I knew that I was doomed.

Since I am already doomed I do not feel that it is worthwhile trying to be good. I go to bed with lots and lots of men but I never get any satisfaction out of it. I have never yet had an orgasm.

She was in fact unable to make any contacts with people except at a very infantile level which required physical contact. Her sexual exploits were a search for the only satisfaction she had known in the early physical contact with her mother.

Josephine (referred to L.M.) was concerned that she had led a very promiscuous life and now wished to return to the practice of her faith. At the same time she felt that she would never be able to live a life without sexual relationships. She wanted support and reassurance from her pastoral counsellor as well as seeking the forgiveness of God. Gradually it became clear that her recourse to sexual intercourse had been a defence against full interpersonal relationships. Nothing prevented the relationship from progressing as effectively as getting into bed. She began to see her problem as one of difficulty in interpersonal relationships and the connection this had with her childhood.

Guilt played a part in both cases. Sally's earlier experiences had made it impossible for her to feel that the Church had anything to offer her. Josephine had come to L.M. as a representative of the Church from which she sought forgiveness but found that she needed counselling.

Underlying Sexual Problems

Sexual problems are often not presented at the outset either in the Hospital or in the Religious Counselling settings.

Some patients are not sure that it is legitimate to bring sexual problems into a medical setting. The religious taboos in sexuality account for the way in which so many good Christians cannot acknowledge their sexual problems even in the pastoral setting, which they might be expected to regard as appropriate.

It is much more common for people to present with depression, anxiety, psychosomatic symptoms or character disorder, and it is only in the course of therapy that they bring out their sexual difficulties. Sometimes it is because they do not see these difficulties as the most important ones, or in a few cases they find it hard to talk about sex.

The Religious or celibate priest who presents with depression cannot in a sense be said to suffer from sexual problems, but it is his or her inability to come to terms with celibacy which can produce a whole range of psychological disturbance which includes depression, anxiety states, psychosomatic illness, or psychotic episodes.

Depression

Ronald (referred to I.B.) was a final-year theological student and a more than usually gifted person, but he could not give his mind to studying because he had grave doubts about himself as a future minister and even as a human being. He was in a state of acute and often disabling depression with all the symptoms of early waking,

apathy withdrawal, loss of appetite, general malaise, and uncontrollable weeping. He was first seen after a serious suicide attempt.
When he first came he said bitterly:

> "I did not ask to be homosexual but what is to become of me? I am
> not fit to be a priest. If I cannot cope with my own feelings how will I
> cope with those of other people?"

Ronald was able to look at himself in the therapeutic situation, to face conflicts and tolerate the inevitable pain in quite an extraordinary manner. In the process he discovered strengths and resources within himself which he never knew he possessed. He learnt to use these, to make a very full life for himself with many different kinds of relationship. This made him less dependent on a single person. He is now a very successful priest who has been able to enrich the lives of the many people with whom he comes into contact.

Anita (referred to I.B.) had been a nun for fourteen years. She came because for half of that time she had suffered from acute bouts of depression.

At nineteen she was an attractive lively young girl engaged to marry a fellow student but before the date of the marriage could be finalized she felt a call to join a religious order. She fought this for a long time because her love for her fiance was very real but she felt that she had to give the religious life a chance.

She still believed in the value of the religious life but her longing for the kind of closeness she had with John her fiance was overwhelming and she could see no way of finding this kind of relationship within the present structure of the religious life. Yet to leave the order was equally unthinkable because of the loyalty she felt towards it.

Anita is still struggling with her dilemma, her loyalty to the religious life is still a powerful force but her need for a loving relationship which includes physical affection and possibly sex is at times overwhelming.

When that happens she becomes deeply and severely depressed and cannot see any way out and I fear for her.

Anita is one of many in this same predicament. There is no universal solution, the answer must be different for every individual and has to be appropriate to each in his or her particular situation.

Sister Susan (referred to L.M.) taught young children in a school where for many years she was happy in her work and her vocation. Then she began to become depressed. This occurred when the school had begun to make rapid strides in teacher/parent relationships. There seems to be no conflict with parents, in fact quite the contrary. She enjoyed meeting the parents who were pleased with what she was doing for their children and yet after an evening spent with the parents she found herself depressed. She could identify with the children but not with their mothers.

The basic problem was that she could not accept herself as a potential mother since she had never been able to face her own sexuality.

David (referred to L.M.) was very depressed and unable to cope with his daily life. He had been engaged to a girl of his choice for some time and was in the process of arranging the details for his marriage, which included preparing the new flat. In talking about his relationships with his fiancee David mentioned that they had never petted, still less had any thoughts of intercourse — "I am a good Catholic and do not believe in sex before marriage". When asked "Do you mean 'I am a good Catholic and therefore have no desire to have intercourse' or 'I would like to have intercourse with my fiancee but because I am a good Catholic I do not'?" He saw that he really meant the first. The real problem was his underlying homosexuality.

Janet (referred to L.M.) presented in a very depressed state, saying that her mother and father were such wonderful people. Gradually she was able to talk about the family rows that had occurred in the house, and how these had somehow been connected with something her father had done. For one period in her early childhood her father had been away for quite a while. In reality the mother had been driven to alcohol by the father's criminal activities which had eventually led him into prison. While such a terrifying background might well lead to denial in a small child, this had been heightened by her religious upbringing and her need to "honour father and mother". Only when she was really able to accept the feelings that she had about her mother and father was she able to forgive them. Having done this she was then able to examine her own feelings about men and women, her own femininity and sexuality. The difficulty for Janet was that she could not really reach her sexual problems until she could accept the anger which was forbidden by her religious attitude; depression was the only feeling she could bring.

Anxiety

Anxiety and the guilt which often seems to accompany it are often linked in the believer with an overwhelming need to be good and perfect. Feelings of anxiety and agitation about accomplishing their duty, and relating with others at work or in the community are aroused by the demand for full Christian love and involvement. This driving need to be perfect "as our heavenly Father is perfect" produces a strain which can lead to total breakdown.

This striving for perfection may sometimes be a cloak for an underlying inability to accept human weakness and sexuality.

Eileen (referred to L.M.) a nurse who had risen to a senior post found herself more and more anxious about her professional responsibilities. Small failures in herself and in others acquired enormous proportions. She worked hard throughout the day and into the late hours without any sense of satisfaction. She felt driven by a need for Christian perfection. She could remember nothing of her childhood before the age of ten.

After a period of counselling she was able to recall her earlier years and became aware of some of the negative feelings in her relationship with her parents. She was then able to recognize her ambivalent feelings about her own sexuality and the way in which this problem had been hidden behind her work and her need for spiritual perfection.

Jonathan (referred to I.B.) presented with an anxiety state. He was an Anglican curate in his early thirties who had tried two other professions before he started his career in the ministry.

He suffered from extreme attacks of anxiety and panic as well as depression and feelings of unworthiness. He had had three previous admissions to psychiatric hospitals during which he had been treated with drugs and ECT. He had also made two suicide attempts.

In his first interview he said:

"I feel that I am the most loathsome creature on God's earth, a miserable worm that should be trodden underfoot. I am ugly and disgusting. Everyone turns away from me. I am sure that you will do the same. All women do. There is no place for me on this earth".

This was all the more frightening because of the need to be the good priest. Though he was bisexual and longed for a relationship with a man or woman he kept everyone at bay because he felt so unworthy and loathsome. In his childhood he read and studied instead of engaging in "proper boys" activities like football and tinkering with cars as his brothers did. No matter how hard he tried he could not gain his father's approval and therefore decided to find a more appreciative parent by devoting his life to the "Heavenly Father". Unfortunately the earthly representatives of the Heavenly Father were not as accepting and loving as Jonathan had hoped and he felt let down and disappointed.

He generally wore scruffy clothes, sported an unkempt beard and went around as if carrying a banner which said "I am disgusting but you ought to love me all the same". At the same time he was also saying "No-one could love me. There is no point in making myself look better" and so he was always bringing about rejection and disapproval.

When he began to recognize his intense resentment towards all authority figures and his envy of all the young men he saw around him who seemed to have all that he had missed (the brothers who gained father's approval), his panic attacks ceased and he could begin to look at the way in which he brought about disapproval and what he could do to change this. He could look at the assets he had in himself and how these could be used and increased.

Within four months of starting therapy he had changed his appearance. He no longer felt ugly and loathsome and managed to find a girlfriend. This had been unthinkable before, because he always presented himself as unacceptable to women. From that time onwards he no longer felt murderous either towards "fathers" who despised him or envious of "brothers" who deprived him. He now felt that he could get approval and love from others and he was therefore able to give some to the parishioners, who previously had appeared to him persecuting, demanding and hostile.

Both examples illustrate how the injunction to be good may interfere with the acceptance of bad feelings which can be sexual, as in Eileen, or envious and aggressive, as in Jonathan. They also show the two classic neurotic reactions to "goodness" — "I cannot be good" as in Jonathan, and "I need to be good" as in Eileen.

Schizophrenic Episodes

If good and evil are experienced as forces acting upon the individual from outside, such as hearing voices and a sense of being possessed, this may be described in religious language. Religious language does in fact lend itself particularly well to such descriptions. The believer can justifiably refer to the occasions on which God and the Saints spoke to those now canonized by the Church. "If the Spirit spoke to them, why should He not speak to me?" The "Faust Syndrome" is one which often occurs, at least in some form, during the adolescent period.

Peter (referred to L.M.) aged fourteen years began to feel that two old ladies across the road were looking at him, watching his every movement. He was frightened to get undressed in case they were watching through the window. He cursed them and wished them dead. Within a week the first had died, aged eighty-five years. Her death was followed two weeks later by the second aged eighty-seven years.

Peter was also having difficulty with his school work and being unable to discover a quotation he needed for an essay, he offered his soul to the Devil and dropped a volume of Shakespeare on the floor. It fell open at the right page. His imagined power to kill and to find the right quotation convinced him that he had indeed sold his soul to the Devil. Peter's problem had in fact started before these events. He had been anxious about achieving eternal life in heaven and salvation. He had felt himself unable to be "good". He resolved the problem by giving up the struggle selling himself to the Devil. His problems were linked with the onset of his sexuality in adolescence, gradually overwhelming him until he escaped into a psychotic world of his own.

There are schizophrenics for whom some aspect of religious symbolism becomes concrete and factual.

Elaine (referred to I.B.) came from a strict Baptist background. Her main problem as she experienced it was her love for another woman.

When her mother discovered this she was horrified and said "It would have been better that you had died than that you should bring such disgrace on the family".

When Elaine's lesbian feelings were aroused, that part of her which shared her mother's feelings seemed to take over and shouted at her, "You are a disgrace. You should be dead". The voices which seemed to come from outside were very powerful and frightening and sounded like the voice of God. Elaine tried desperately to get away from them. She rushed to the window to escape and the fact that she was three storeys up did not register. She just had to get out. She never recovered from her injuries.

Paranoid Reaction

People can feel very isolated in a Religious Community even though they are constantly in the company of others. Some find it hard to acknowledge their own critical, hostile feelings and therefore project them onto others.

Sandra (referred to I.B.) had been a nun for thirty years when she came into therapy. In all this time she had never felt accepted by her order. She was in her late fifties and had no way of living outside a Religious Community but she was constantly misinterpreting what other members of the Community were saying to her and felt accused, criticized and unwanted. Sandra's reasons for joining the Community had been very confused.

She was the middle child in her own family and felt out of it. Her elder sister was regarded as special because she was first and her younger brother because he was the only boy, but no-one thought of Sandra as special.

At the age of twelve she told herself

"Men will not be interested in me because I am so shy. Marriage is really very ordinary and fraught with problems. I do not think it is for me. I do not really want the same as everyone else. I want something more exalted. I want to be special. I shall give my life to God. I shall be the bride of Christ."

Unfortunately the order she joined did not see it in that way and right from the start made it clear to her that she was just an ordinary member of the Community and very lucky to be accepted at all. They did not see her as special.

This meant to her a total rejection of what she was offering and set up the vicious circle of feeling hurt and resentful but being unable to acknowledge these "un-Christian" feelings they were projected onto others.

She also found sexual feelings unacceptable and these too had to be denied and projected.

Problems of Sexual Identity

There was a group which presented with problems over their sexual identity: the woman who could not accept her female role and wanted what men have, and the man who envied women (especially their child-bearing capacity). A number of men and women both inside and outside Religious Communities felt like children in an adult world.

The affirmation of sexual identity which occurs in the married state may help to breach whatever minor problems have occurred during the period of childhood growth and development. Such affirmation is naturally missing from those whose Religious life is bound up with a vow of celibacy. Not only is their sexuality not affirmed, but it has to be played down. Many living the celibate life, and feeling that they have left all "that" behind, may still be left with problems which arise from their identity as male or female. In this sense sexuality is not confined to genitality, but relates to their whole personality. Several people were referred to the Hospital Clinic who illustrated the feelings of being a child in an adult world.

Marjorie (referred to I.B.) was a sixty-year-old nun who liked to sit on the floor and huddle in a corner like a little girl. She did this even when the sisters in her Community were discussing Community affairs. She nevertheless resented the fact that others treated her as a child and had not resolved her conflicting feelings.

Gareth (referred to I.B.) was a monk and a university chaplain but when he entered the staff room he felt like a child in a grown up world. This made him feel inadequate and unable to establish the contacts which were necessary in his work.

Bill (referred to I.B.) had a wife ten years older than himself and three children. His wife treated him as one of the children. He resented this but felt so worthless that he could not allow himself to acknowledge such feelings. In his childhood his mother had said to him "I don't know why the Good Lord put you on this earth". Since that time he had felt so bad that he had no right to exist nor to be part of the human race. He was not too sure what the wicked things were that he had done at the age of six but felt that it must be because of his sadistic fantasies to do with sexual organs and defaecation. His sexual and emotional development were arrested at this point in spite of being a husband and a father.

Paul (referred to I.B.) illustrated the group of people who find it difficult to make relationships at all because of their family background. Like a number of other theological students, Paul decided that he was going to find a more satisfactory mother than his own in Mother Church and a more satisfactory father in God the Father. His own mother was a very dominant woman who criticized and

rejected him most of the time but at other times was exceedingly
seductive towards the growing boy. His father was weak and inadequate and despised by mother. Paul was disappointed by his
father because he seemed unable to stand up to his powerful wife.

Mother had great expectations of Paul; she could not accept him as
an ordinary child but would either make him into a confidante
complaining to him about father's inadequacies or reduce him to a
feeling of utter uselessness and total failure because he seemed
unable to meet her expectations of being a better husband than
his father. She was also extremely inconsistent in her behaviour
towards him. He never knew whether he was going to be praised
or punished for the same behaviour. At first he felt a sense of outrage about the unfairness of mother's behaviour towards him but
any expression of such feelings brought about such a torrent of
abuse and vilification that he could only protect himself by cutting
himself off from all his feelings. Soon he was no longer even aware
of anger, resentment or hatred towards his mother.

When he came into therapy he seemed to have only one response
to every situation and this was a vacuous smile which remained
fixed on his face no matter what drama was being played out
around him. The members of the psychotherapy group which Paul
attended called it his Cheshire Cat smile because he himself seemed
absent and only his smile was present. They tried in various ways
to get close to him but eventually became exasperated because no-
one and nothing seemed to pierce the thick brick wall with which he
he had protected the vulnerable inner core of his being. Paul did not
actually have any sexual problems. He was simply terrified of
women and kept away from any contact with them.

He was like a latency boy in his sexual development and had
managed to hold his own so long as he was in the college situation,
but the prospect of qualifying and having to deal with women in a
parish setting terrified him and he was unable to work for his final
examinations. He described it as "a shutter coming down every time
I attempt to read a book".

It was a very long and arduous journey that Paul had to undertake
before he rediscovered the intense and conflicting feelings of hatred
and excitement aroused in him by his mother's attitude towards
the growing boy.

Sister Joan (referred to L.M.) illustrates the importance of remembering that even a celibate nun is still a woman. Sister Joan under-

went hysterectomy at the age of thirty-six, just at the time when her brother was getting married, and her younger sister was producing her first child. At this point she went into acute depression. Since her mother had died only three months prior to this event the depression became focused on grief and mourning.

The temptation in the therapy was to look at the relationship of Sister Joan with her mother, whereas in fact the more dramatic problem for her was her own sexual identity. It might be felt that a nun is hardly likely to miss what she never intended to use. This is to overlook the fundamental point that she is a woman, and a woman whose creative powers have never been confirmed in the production of a child. The removal of her creative organ is a powerfully symbolic act, bringing to life many of the feminine and maternal feelings of which she may have been unaware and which may then be experienced in vague anxiety or depression.

By the same token prostatectomy may be experienced by the celibate man as a symbolic attack on his unconfirmed virility and lead to acute depression.

Therapeutic Principles and Management

Stafford Clark (1970) reminds us that:

> "The doctor and the priest are concerned each in his own way, with man's needs. One of these is the need to believe. Man is not, and cannot be, content to accept life as meaningless . . . but they are not only concerned with man's needs, they are pledged to minister to them, though in essentially different ways. These ways are complementary, in just the same sort of way that the inter-relationship of the spirit, mind and body is a complementary one."

The unity of individual personality and the manner in which any one of his "parts" will have an effect on the whole make the need for co-operative work even more necessary when we are faced with the breakdown of a human personality. There are certain areas of man's function which can properly be regarded as being within the sole concern of one particular profession at a given time, although even then that particular specialist may co-operate with other professions upon which the individual also relies. There are various ways in which we may understand the disintegration of the human personality; as one of organic or chemical nature; in terms of bad learning; as unconscious reaction to early childhood experience; as a loss of meaningfulness in life; or as the result of the present spiritual disaster of mankind.

It may be more important to consider how the individual himself experiences the problem and how he seeks to answer it.

It was found that the people quoted in this chapter who had some form of religious background saw their problems in two ways. There were those who saw their difficulties as being religious or moral ones which therefore had to be taken to the minister. The second group saw themselves as suffering from some form of emotional disturbance or mental illness which they felt it more appropriate to take to their doctor. It would be as unwise for the minister to neglect the underlying psychological stresses and personality problems which are expressed in purely religious terms as it would be for the doctor to ignore the religious dimensions and the power of the symbols within which these psychological problems are contained.

While the ideal situation, as far as the patient is concerned, might be to find a minister who is also a psychotherapist, or a psychotherapist who is also theologically aware, this may not always be possible.

It is a general principle that the therapist should be able to accept the client as he is. This should include his basic beliefs and way of life, even though the therapist may not share these. The client however may find it difficult to accept this principle either intellectually or emotionally. This may result in his playing down the religious context in these areas of his conflicts because he feels that they may not be understood or accepted. It may also result in his dismissing or intellectualizing any insights which bear upon his religious life or beliefs. Such problems are usually not present if the therapist is known to share the clients' beliefs or if he has been "canonized" by a reputable religious figure. Thus if his minister has recommended the therapist who is known to be sympathetic to the clients' religious beliefs, even though he does not share them, there is a "halo" effect which may be all that is necessary. A Catholic or Jew might feel happy with a therapist who was known to be an Anglican. Much of the work described in this chapter by the therapist in a hospital setting is of this nature. The religious problems could be discussed freely and examined without fear of ridicule or rejection.

However the therapist who does not share, or fully understand the religious symbols, may also have problems in working with and through them. Some might feel that they should not be worked with in any case, although this may be more a question of the school of thought of therapy than a question of religion. The process of therapy could be considered as either teaching the client our frame of reference or of trying to learn his language. In the latter case problems may arise for the therapist. There would then be three alternatives: *a.* the client could be transferred to another therapist; *b.* he could be referred to a suitable minister for some discussion in the religious field; or *c.* the therapist might consult with a minister with whom he could discuss the symbolic implications. This last possibility would seem to be the best.

> Angela, referred to I.B., blocked the process of therapy by challenging her therapist saying that she could not understand her spiritual conflict. "You wouldn't understand about Catholicism." She felt that she needed someone to mediate between her and God. I.B. referred her to L.M. where she resisted examining her conflicts blaming all her difficulties with religion onto the changes in the Church. "Nothing is the same — they've changed it all." She was helped to see that the problem was more in her own emotional reactions to the changes, reactions which she experienced about any change. She was then able to return to I.B. and continue her therapy. As she was enabled to come to terms with her own emotions she was also more able to meet her religious needs.
>
> Cooperation here was helpful to Angela because she was able to express her anger with the Church to the priest who symbolized the Church, which her therapist could never do.

If the client and the religious therapist have a common belief what difference is this likely to make to the therapy? At one end of the spectrum there may be little difference between the religious therapist's approach and any other form of therapy; at the other it may more closely resemble a full spiritual exorcism. Between these two possibilities there are a vast number of intermediate possibilities. The manner in which the religious content may be utilized will depend on the religious therapist's attitude and training. Such a variety of psychological approach may make referral difficult and confusing. However it is often equally difficult for a minister or doctor to choose a psychiatric setting for someone in need, bearing in mind the variety of approaches which exist.

In the last decade ministers of all religious denominations have come to recognize their need for deeper psychological understanding in their work of pastoral care. Some have managed to train themselves as therapists while others attend supervisory groups. The Association for

Pastoral Care and Counselling has been set up in Great Britain as a national organization with particular concern for the development of training in pastoral skills which would take into account not only theological insights and commitment but also the contribution of the Social Sciences to the understanding of man. It is especially concerned with setting up standards of training in Pastoral Counselling.

In the majority of cases where the approach to the patient would call for a team approach the Association have suitably trained members who are prepared to cooperate in management and consultation. There are also a large number of religious-based Counselling Centres which provide a suitable resource.

As far as outcome in therapy is concerned we are again faced with the fundamental attitude of the therapist, or his philosophy of therapy. Is it a process of cure from a mental disease, or is it a process of helping individuals to come to terms with and accept what is painful? How can the person be asked to make sense of his total life with its frustrations? Where can he find the strength for sublimation, forgiveness, acceptance, meaningfulness and purpose in living? What do we answer one who asks for a reason to live?

It may be that every form of therapy which looks at the whole person will also need to examine these existential questions.

There may well be a more positive outcome in therapy for the individual who has religious beliefs which enable him to answer some of these questions than for the person who has no faith.

While examining the problem of those who present in religious terms, or whose defences have been built around a religious framework, it is also important to see in what way religious faith may itself provide some major contributions towards healing.

The Judeo-Christian tradition presents us with some of the major paradoxes of life, and many of those who seek help appear to have swung towards one side of the paradox while denying the other. Thus the whole paradox of life itself might be summed up in the text:

> "Anyone who finds his life will lose it; anyone who loses his life for my sake will find it." Matth. 10,39.

It is implicit in the Christian faith that this life is not everything; it is meant to be a valley of tears and we are meant to carry some cross. These ideas are more fully exemplified in the writings of Wilson (1973) and Williams (1968).

The purpose of counselling in such a Christian setting is not to remove the cross but to enable individuals to carry it more effectively, to make positive use of their frustrations, and to become aware of their own personal challenge in life. These concepts must enter the contract which the counsellor will make with the client. Religious faith is sometimes seen as reinforcing the root of the individual's neurotic difficulties. This causes some therapists to equate the faith with the individual's neurosis, and ignores the therapeutic potential of religious faith. The religious counsellor may use his own vocabulary of religious terms, enter into a dialogue about faith and enable the client to meet God through prayer. Religious therapists who work with the techniques of creative imagination, fantasy and Gestalt have an opportunity to integrate these techniques with the life of prayer and meditation.

This is particularly true for those who express their religion in more emotional terms, while for those whose religion is expressed in a more ritualistic form the religious symbols themselves may work as a positive force.

Writers such as Maslow (1962) and May (1975) have drawn attention to man's need for values and meaning. It may not be possible to remove suffering but authors like Frankl (1962) and Heimler (1975), both survivors of concentration camps, re-affirm in their work the principle of Nietche:

> "A man can live any how as long as he has a why to live."

References

Belliveau, F. and Richter, L. (1974). "Understanding Human Sexual Inadequacy." Coronet Books, Hodder: London.

Dominion, J. (1968). "Marital Breakdown." (Pelican), Penguin: Harmondsworth.

Douglas, M. (1970). "Natural Symbols." The Cresset Press (Barrie and Jenkins): London.

Egenter, R. and Matussek, P. (1967), "Moral Problems and Mental Health." Alba House: New York.

Fairbairn, W. R. (1966). "Psychoanalytic Studies of the Personality." Tavistock Publications: London.

Frankl, V. (1962). "Man's Search for Meaning." Hodder and Stoughton: London.

Group for the Advancement of Psychiatry (1968). Report No.68. "The Psychic Function of Religion in Mental Illness and Health." New York.

Guntrip, H. (1964). "Healing the Sick Mind." Allen and Unwin: London.

Hagmaier, G. and Gleason, R. (1959). "Counselling the Catholic." Sheed and Ward: London.

Heimler, E. (1975). "Survival in Society." Weidenfeld and Nicolson: London.

Hiltner, S. and Colston L. (1962). "The Context of Pastoral Counselling." Abingdon Press: Nashville, Tennessee.

Kinsey, A., Pomeroy, W. and Martin, C. (1948). "Sexual Behaviour in the Human Male." Saunders: Philadelphia.

Kinsey, A., Pomeroy, W., Martin, C. and Gebhard, P. (1953). "Sexual Behaviour in the Human Female." Saunders: Philadelphia.

Maslow, A. H. (1962). "Towards a Psychology of Being." Insight Books.

O'Doherty, E. F. (1965). Religion and Personality Problems." Burns and Oates.

O'Doherty, E. F. (1974). Religious therapy, *In* "Psychotherapy Today." (Varma, V. Ed., Constable: London.

May, R. (1975). "Man's Search for Himself." Souvenir Press: London.

Stafford-Clark, D. (1970). "Five Questions in Search of an Answer." Nelson: London.

Storr, A. (1960). "The Integrity of the Personality." Penguin: Harmondsworth.

Williams, H. A. (1968). "The True Wilderness." Constable: London.

Wilson, M. (1973). "The Temptations of Jesus, Religion and Medicine." (Melinsky, H., Ed.), Student Christian Movement Press: London.

10 | *Sexual Behaviour in the Elderly*

BRICE PITT

In my last four years of psychiatric practice with patients aged 65 and over, I can recall only three referrals on the grounds of sexual disturbance. One was a man in Brixton Prison for writing an obscene letter to a sixteen-year-old girl, and stealing underwear from a women's hostel; he was libidinous (or "oversexed") because of an episode of hypomania. Another was a man in an Old Peoples Home who was reported to be exposing himself to children in the park; he was suffering from dementia. The third was a woman of 70 who feared venereal disease as a result of sexual contact with a lover aged 90! Problems of impotence or "orgasmic" dysfunction (frigidity) have never been presented. Such sexual difficulties obviously occur in old age, but they seem to be accepted, or not disclosed, with resignation or diffidence.

Many people find the ideas of sexual activity in later life distasteful. The phrase "dirty old man" is eloquent. The lack of physical attraction by the elderly, the inability of post-menopausal women to procreate and the "incest taboo" which renders most children reluctant to consider their parents' sexual needs, probably all contribute to this distaste. Old people themselves, brought up at a time when sex was not a subject to be spoken of, are very slow to talk of their needs, especially to professional workers like doctors and social workers whom by tradition, they hold in some awe (Felstein, 1970).

Past Studies

The Kinsey reports (1948, 1953), included a very small proportion
of the elderly. Only 106 of the 14,084 men studied, and 56 of 5,940
females, were over 60. At 60, only one in four of the men was no
longer capable of intercourse. By 80, the proportion was three out of
four, a very steep decline, though the frequency of other outlets
(masturbation, nocturnal emissions) had fallen off at no greater a rate
than between the ages of 30 and 60.

Finkle and others (1959) interviewed 101 male patients aged between 55 and 86 whose presenting complaints did not *per se* contribute impediments to sexual activity. Of 51 patients 69 years or less
of age, 33 (65%) were potent in the sense of having copulated at least
once in the previous year. Of 50 over 70, only 17 (34%) were potent.
However, individual differences were marked, and two men over 80
were active to the extent of 10 copulations a year.

Masters and Johnson (1966) found that men over 60 were slower
to develop erection, penetrate and to ejaculate than younger men.
From interviewing 123 men over 60 (71 in their 60s, 37 in their 70s
and 15 in their 80s) they found that the most important factor in
maintaining effective sexuality in ageing males was consistent sexual
activity. High sexual output in the formative years, sustained in the
thirties, correlated with evidence of regularly recurring sexual activity
in middle age and later.

From the Duke longitudinal studies (Pfeiffer, 1975) first of a group
of 260 volunteers, men and women over 60, and secondly of 502
men and women aged 45–69, it was found (Pfeiffer and others, 1969)
that 80% of 20 men over 60, whose health, intellect and social
functioning were not significantly impaired, reported continuing
sexual *interest*, and 70 per cent regular sexual *activity* at the start of
the study, but that ten years later while the proportion of those
interested was unchanged, the proportion of those *active* had declined
to 25%.

Newman and Nichols (1960) assessed sexual activities and attitudes
of 250 volunteers aged 60–93 (average 70), and found that of 101
subjects without a sexual partner only 7% were sexually active, whereas of 149 still married and living with their spouse 54% were still
active, frequency of intercourse ranging from three times a week to
once in two months. Every subject rated strength of current sexual
urge as less than in youth, but whereas those with strongest youthful
urges now rated them as moderate, those with weak to moderate

hout sexual feeling at all. Sexual activity only
g age in those over 75, the age at which signs
me obvious. Women's lesser sexual activity may
ha.   being regulated by husbands who are older.

Kinse,   d that there is little evidence of any ageing in
sexual capacitu.   f the female till late in life. Females' frequency of
maturbation, sexual dreams and orgasm in intercourse rise gradually
with age to a maximum and stay more or less level till after 55 or 60.
Diminution of sexual intercourse is largely due to decline in spouse's
performance. One woman of 90 was recorded as still responding
regularly in coitus. The effect of the menopause was uncertain. Of 173
women who had gone through the change 46% had had no orgasms
for a year or two beforehand, and did not change, and of the remainder, 39% felt unchanged, 13% believed responses had increased, and
48% decreased.

Masters and Johnson found a definite diminution in the duration
of physiological response to sexual stimulation in females over 60,
but capacity for orgasm was not diminished. They interviewed 54
women of 60 − 37 between 61 and 70, 17 between 71 and 80, and
found that a large part of the post-menopausal sex drive in women
relates directly to sexual habits established during the procreative
years. In the Duke studies, men always reported greater sexual
interest and activity than women of like age. The determining factor
for continuity or cessation of sexual activity in marriage was generally
the husband, and in the study group aged over 60 only 39% of the
women but 82% of the men still had intact marriages. Women outlive
men and tend to marry men who are a year or two older, so are likely
to be deprived of a sexual partner for seven years or so at the end of
their lives. The studies confirmed Masters and Johnson's findings
that a high level of sexual interest and activity in youth was highly
correlated with continued interest and activity in later life. This was
true of both sexes, but more so in men. Interestingly, the oldest age
group studied were more sexually involved than the next to the oldest
age groups, perhaps comprising an elite of survivors from whose midst
less highly advantaged individuals had already been removed by death.

The conclusions from the literature are then:

1. there is a general decline in sexual *activity* throughout adult life,
with a sharp decline in those over 75;
2. the decline in sexual *interest* is much less marked, at least in men;
3. female sexual activity reaches a peak in early middle life, and any

subsequent decline is largely secondary to masculine decline or widowhood;

4. the presence of a sexual partner, an active early sex life and good physical health all conduce to sexual activity in old age;

5. there is immense individual variation.

Clinical Disorders

Depression

Depression could be one of the many ills contributing to the decline of sexual activity in the senium. Depression is more common at this age than at any other, yet whereas in younger people its effects on the libido are well known, it seems that too often elderly patients are not asked the relevant questions because of embarrassment or the assumption that at that age sexual activity will have ceased. Among the many crosses which the elderly have to bear is the youthfulness of those who treat them, none of whom have ever experienced old age! It is certainly possible that the effective treatment of depression with one of the anti-depressive drugs may also improve sexual interest and performance.

Mania and Hypomania

Mania and hypomania may lead to sexual misbehaviour, as in the example at the beginning of this chapter. Men become bold and old ladies frisky, though actual extra-marital intercourse as a result of mood elevation is almost unknown, and the evident disturbance of other forms of behaviour than sexual means that the patient is eventually recognized as ill and tolerated after suitable (tranquillizing) treatment.

Sexual Misbehaviour

Sexual misbehaviour usually taking the form of exhibitionism or interference with children, is not common but accounts for a relatively high proportion of the acts of delinquency with which old men are charged. Surprisingly, the basis is very rarely dementia. Dementia prevails in at least 10% of those aged 65 and over, yet sexual misbehaviour as a result of disinhibition (by excessive loss of cells from the brains cortex) is an exceedingly rare presenting sign. More often, the elderly deviant is intellectually intact but has a past history of potency problems. Children are, unhappily, much more available to him than young women, who would be repulsed by sexual advances from an old man. Children on the other hand may be attracted by his "grandfatherly" qualities and thus exploited. Whether they are also corrupted or endangered is highly questionable, but though Hirschmann (1962) has claimed good results for psychotherapy in elderly sexual offenders there are enormous difficulties in settling them back into their own communities because of public outrage (Pitt, 1974).

Counselling

Counselling the elderly requires tact and humility. All too often it is assumed that there's little to be done "at their age", and that simple environmental manipulation, such as arranging a Home Help or attendance at a Club, will suffice. Patient listening, however, allows a more considered assessment. An occasional comment to check irrelevancy or show continuing interest may be all that is required to produce a very clear statement of the old person's thoughts and feelings. Further questioning to fill gaps and clarify uncertainties is based upon the counsellor's experience of the elderly and their problems, and judgement about what may be important to this person at this time. Some very old people tire quickly, and it may be necessary to see them several times to piece the story together, but most are very glad to talk and will gain confidence from the tacit acceptance of what they have to say by a sympathetic listener. The counsellor, should recognize that sexual activity, like any other intellectual physical or social activity, may be continued well into the senium by those who are fit and interested, and even where there is small capacity for sexual performance there may still be considerable interest. This is an important argument against sexual segregation of the elderly in institutions, with staffs of the same sex. Most "dirty old men" are normal old men whose feelings younger people are too embarrassed or disturbed to recognize. The counsellor should appreciate that while many old people accept their waning sexuality with resignation, others with continuing needs may not speak of them because of shame and embarrassment at having feelings past the supposedly appropriate age. Help to do so may give considerable relief and release to continue sexual activity for as long as it can be enjoyed.

Summary

The assumption that the elderly are neither interested nor active in sex arises from their own diffidence in talking about sexual matters and the prejudices of the young. However, studies have shown that there is only a sharp decline in sexual activity in those over 75, and that where there has been an active early sex life and where health is good and a partner available, sex is enjoyed well past the age of retirement.

Depression is a common disorder in the elderly, and its treatment may increase sexual interest and performance. Sexual misbehaviour in old age may be symptomatic of mania or hypomania, or be a form of deviation in those with previous potency problems. It rarely indicates dementia.

Counselling involves a readiness to listen to old people without prejudice or impatience, and an awareness that some may have sexual needs about which they wish to talk. They may either feel encouraged to gratify their desires with their sexual partner, if available, or may come to terms with what they have lost.

References

Felstein, I. (1970). "Sex and the Longer Life." Allen Lane: The Penguin Press: Harmondsworth.

Finkle, A. L., Moyers, T. G., Robenkin, M. I. and Karg, S. J. (1959). Sexual potency in ageing males, *Journal of the American Medical Association* 170, 1391–1393.

Hirschmann, J. (1962). Sur Kriminologie der Sexualdelikte des alterden Mannes, *Gerontologia Clinica* A115–119.

Kinsey, A. D., Pomeroy. W. B. and Martin, C. R. (1948). "Sexual Behaviour in the Human Male." Saunders: Philadelphia.

Kinsey, A. D., Pomeroy, W. B., Martin, C. R. and Gebhard, P. H. (1953). "Sexual Behaviour in the Human Female." Saunders: Philadelphia.

Masters, W. H. and Johnson, B. E. (1966). "Human Sexual Response". Little Brown: Boston.

Newman, G. and Nichols, C. R. (1960). Sexual activities and attitudes in older persons, *Journal of the American Medical Association*, 173, 33–35.

Pfeiffer, E. (1975). Sexual behaviour. *In* "Modern Perspectives in Psychogeriatrics." (Howell, J. G. Ed.), Churchill Livingstone: Edinburgh.

Pfeiffer, E., Verwoerdt, A. and Wang, H. S. (1969). The natural history of sexual behaviour in a biologically advantaged group of aged individuals, *Journal of Gerontology* 24, 193–198.

Pitt, B. (1974). *In* "Psychogeriatrics." pp. 97–98. Churchill Livingstone: Edinburgh.

III | Psychosexual Problems in Medicine and Surgery

11 | *Psychosexual Problems Seen in General Practice*

J. S. NORELL

Medical men, accustomed to looking for abnormalities, encounter peculiar difficulties in examining the psychosexual area because of the absence of universal standards of normality. Sexuality is so obviously a personal attribute, and so much influenced by family, tribal, class, racial and other cultural factors that one might despair at attempting to set out norms that have any meaning. Moreover we are here considering not only disorders of behaviour but of thoughts and of feelings, the ineffable nature of which strikingly complicates the task.

In general practice the difficulties are compounded by several other factors. In the first place, psychosexual disorders are not encountered in a pure form — if indeed they exist anywhere. It is not merely that they are diluted by so much else that comes the general practitioner's way, but that they inevitably contaminate and are contaminated by other aspects of the person's functioning, and it is these latter that may clamour for the doctor's attention. In other words, the psychosexual component may be real enough but it may be overshadowed by the clinical or social situation which exists as the cause or effect of the sexual disorder. Nor is it always easy to distinguish cause from effect.

Undifferentiated Clinical Material

An additional complication for the general practitioner is the diversity in the ways the disorder may present. Colleagues practising in other branches of medicine enjoy the advantage of some degree of previous selection in their case material. This filtering may be undertaken professionally as by the general practitioner or case-worker; or patients may be self-selected as in VD departments, or walk-in clinics catering for the emotionally distraught. By thus identifying the trouble boundaries are set on the area in which a search for the probable cause is to be made. The generalist however completely lacks this pre-sorting, his material is undifferentiated. He is available to all inhabitants in the neighbourhood who may consult him on any matter they choose, and one of his first tasks is to identify the area in which the trouble lies.

The difficulty over definition remains. Substituting the word "problem" for "disorder" goes some way towards resolving it for now our concern is with whatever is perceived by the patient as a problem; we are no longer harrassed by the need to make objective measures of the problem nor beset by doubts as to what constitutes a "genuine" psychosexual problem. But this still leaves open the question, "A problem to whom?" Any patient who has a problem may become a problem to others but this is especially true in the area of psychosexual functioning. A person with a psychosexual disorder may not see himself as possessing a problem, that is to say, he is not the sufferer. Instead, the spouse may suffer and may be the one who complains; evidently the spouse has a problem. Does this make the spouse the patient?

All doctors encounter this sort of tangle but those practising family medicine are peculiarly vulnerable to being enmeshed in the complexities of family psychodynamics. The psychosexual problem may be a source of private misery and as such may be taken to the general practitioner for advice and treatment. More usually the problem is one which affects or is shared by two people; the couple may present together, or one or other may attend; but in the vast majority of cases it is the woman who does so.

Even at this point however it is uncommon for the subject of psychosexual malfunctioning to be made explicit, and since it may manifest itself in a variety of ways its presentation to the doctor may be accordingly diverse, with psychological or somatic symptoms or a mixture of the two. Sometimes the problem may have its expression in a social, or more correctly anti-social, situation; and quite often it is transferred to a third person as when a child is brought along as the bearer of symptoms. Since the general practitioner is a generalist and a doctor to the whole family the opportunities for symptom-substitution by the patient are very great. But the overt symptoms are not always mere token introductions to the underlying sexual problem, not just a way of gaining the doctor's ear. The symptoms may for the time being represent the problem; may be as far as the patient wishes to go just then.

Here then is another difficulty for the general practitioner; the need to negotiate an agreement with the patient over the true nature of the problem and the allocation of responsibility as between the partners. In other specialities this necessary prelude to a "contract" can be assumed or very readily established. No such assumption is possible in general practice: diagnosis and treatment within the family may have to proceed while gradually reaching agreement about the problem with all concerned. In the face of the patient's resistance to the recognition of a psychosexual problem the general practitioner must work with whatever the patient allows him, with whichever member of the family is accessible; trying to avoid in the one case a series of futile investigations, and in the other collusion over scapegoating.

The manifestations of psychosexual disorders may be very numerous but the underlying factors seem to be few. No doubt faulty child-rearing is the remote cause in a great many cases but more immediate causes include immaturity, a sense of deprivation, failure — real or imagined, resentment towards the partner, and depression. Traditional psychiatric diagnoses are unhelpful in the management of most sexual problems; so too are conventional labels of personality types, though of course patients do display these various traits, sometimes in such an extreme form as to represent a caricature. Mostly, in both sexes and in all ages depression is the common feature, the term subsuming inadequacy, low self-esteem, or defeat. Anxiety as such is not so prominent though it may be present as a fear of pain, of failure to be adequate sexually, of getting pregnant, or of infertility. The status of guilt is likewise uncertain: many patients duly report the single childhood trauma but its relevance seems doubtful.

Problems in Men

Males are less frequent attenders than females in general practice and the disparity is most marked in early and middle adulthood; the number of men reporting sexual problems directly or indirectly is correspondingly low. This may be related to opportunities which men have for other outlets, including alcoholism, gambling, promiscuity and criminality; while not male preserves, these particular vices attract men far more than women.

Men reporting sexual difficulties fall into two groups: those in their twenties, and those in their forties and fifties. They complain of impotence of some degree, occasionally attributing the trouble to their spouse or partner. Inability to obtain or sustain an erection, or premature ejaculation with failure to penetrate may be of relatively recent onset; the impotence may be related to an imminent or recent marriage, or may come on after years of apparently satisfactory family life. Generally, reassurance is sought from the doctor about the normality of the genitalia, but a brooding introspection about alleged defects in the penis may be pronounced and border on a delusion.

Overt physical disease is relatively infrequently associated with psychosexual problems; it is remarkable how couples cope with, or are resigned to, gross obesity, severe arthritis of the spine or hips, or the presence of an ileostomy. A history however of a previous coronary thrombosis or stroke may certainly cast its shadow over the couple's sexual life, but the apprehension is not always volunteered and the doctor may need to take the initiative in raising the issue. Alcoholism is in a special category. Chronic alcoholic abuse undoubtedly reduces sexual potency in the male but may not be apparent to the doctor, and even when he suspects it it may be denied. By the time it becomes obvious it may be difficult to decide which has come first, and whether drinking has been resorted to as a consolation for sexual inadequacy. Drugs used in the treatment of some illnesses are themselves increasingly a cause of impotence, especially anti-depressants and anti-hypertensives.

The man's own expectations obviously play a major part in bringing him to his doctor, and in this cultural factors may be important. This is vividly illustrated in a general practice which contains communities of different races and religions; for instance, Irish Catholics, Jamaicans, Turks and Pakistanis may have differing expectations of normal sexual activity and will therefore show different thresholds for reporting sexual problems, for example, a declining potency with age: a Turk may begin to have serious doubts about his manhood if coital frequency drops below once nightly.

Men complaining of impaired potency often relate this to social stresses or those arising from their particular situation; for instance, business or financial worries, redundancy or other threat to a career, shift work; the stress associated with impending examinations; over-crowding at home, housing stress concerning neighbours, in-laws or tenants; illness in the family, especially a child; a feeling of boredom with a settled married existence.

Case Histories

The following short case histories will illustrate the sort of psychosexual problems presented by men in an urban general practice.

A 24-year-old clerk working in a city office; he had a cockney accent but was well-groomed. He wanted advice about his penis which he thought was now excessively bowed as a result of frequent masturbation in his teens. There had been an unsuccessful attempt at intercourse a couple of years before; he had no girlfriend now but was in any case unwilling to try again until the defect had been put right. Examination revealed normal genitalia but reassurance and explanation repeated over several interviews failed to satisfy him and he insisted on referral to a surgeon. He gave the impression that this fixed belief in a damaged penis was a sort of alibi through which he could avoid being exposed to the humiliation of failing in sexual intercourse.

A 26-year-old Irish plasterer complaining of gradually lessening potency over the last two years, with failure to satisfy his wife. They had been married seven years, and had two children aged six and two. For two months he had been completely impotent with premature ejaculation. He seemed depressed and his only satisfaction came from "boozing with friends" on a Saturday night.

A school-keeper aged 43 years, but looking older, with premature ejaculation for five years. He was now impotent and attributed this to the fact that his wife, aged 42 and with four children aged 13 to 2 years, was on the "pill" and therefore not at risk for pregnancy.

An accountant aged 29, with non-consummation of his 4-month marriage. He attributed this to a "virus illness' contracted on his honeymoon abroad. His wife was aged 31 and described as "pure, a virgin". He was able to have successful intercourse with experienced, "paid" women but was shy with "pure" girls. In the course of four interviews at weekly intervals he was able to express his uncertainty about getting married and to ventilate his anger with his

in-laws as well as his frustration at work. He reported satisfactory
coitus with his wife, there was more "harmony" in the marriage,
and he had been given more authority at his work.

A manager aged 45 with two grown up children had been impotent
for a year. His wife aged 49 he described as fat, menopausal and
possessing a strong libido and no longer satisfied by him. He had
tried extra-marital experiments unsuccessfully and had even pur-
chased a patent "stimulator". He had been highly sexed in youth
and feared being "burnt out too soon". He was depressed and considered the stimulator was like "flogging a tired horse". He seemed
apprehensive about the physical examination and urine tests and
felt relieved to hear they were normal.

An unemployed orderly aged 61, divorced for 30 years, one daughter aged 33, and now living with a home help aged 51. He was worried about declining potency: he could get erections but no climax.
He wondered if he was getting "past it". He was short of breath
because of chronic bronchitis and was afraid of getting a heart
attack during coitus. In two further interviews he discussed his
sexual frustration and masturbatory fantasies, and began to look
less depressed. He seemed to accept a brother—sister relationship
with his friend.

A security officer aged 34, his wife of the same age, with four children. He wanted to discuss vasectomy. His wife was depressed on the
"pill" and was having no sexual satisfaction because of his premature ejaculation. There was a suggestion that the operation might
be seen as a cure for his partial impotence.

A printer aged 30 attended with his wife, a clerk aged 23. They had
been married six months but there had been no consummation.
His erections were poor and infrequent and he blamed her for not
being warm and responsive. She had been on anti-depressants since
her father's death five years before; her mother was a retired sales-
lady; sex was never mentioned in the home. She was disappointed
on the honeymoon; the husband said she was inhibited but that he
"did not press the point". Examination of the wife revealed no
vaginismus (her husband remarked on her readiness to have a physical examination); she could be inert and sullen but also lively; she
laughed at his ineffectualness. He emerged as inadequate, effeminate
and passive, and irritatingly evasive over the question of having
children, which she strongly wanted. There was little movement in

three months of weekly interviews, some jointly, some singly. They argued about having children, and blamed each other. He persisted in depicting her as a repressed worrier; she lapsed into a state of empty, unfulfilled depression.

A showroom representative aged 42 came with his second wife aged 40. He had a son aged 20 by his first wife whom he divorced; he had remarried two years before. The problem was unsatisfactory intercourse, attributed by him to his wife's inadequate vaginal musculature. He needed a good deal of active stimulation and had a preference for anal intercourse. She on the other hand was resentful of his preoccupation with the mechanical aspects of lovemaking, feeling that the romantic element was missing. She had what he described as a "puritanical" view of his interest in pornography. During further interviews incompatibility in sexual outlook was shown and there was mutual projection of bad qualities, but some improvement was achieved. There were fewer recriminations, they were more tolerant of each other; and they reported successful weekends of "love-ins".

A caretaker aged 52 complained of impotence of nine months' duration. He had read about hormone treatment and wanted a course of this because he was afraid of losing his wife, who was eight years younger. (She had in fact referred to his impotence and her frustration six years before.) He was given to bouts of depression, had a poor work record, and often smelled of alcohol at a morning consultation, but both he and his wife denied that he drank more than an occasional pint of beer. His wife had undergone hysterectomy for fibroids two years before, and suffered from backaches. He was prescribed a course of male hormones by mouth without improvement. He was not then overtly depressed but he felt inadequate as a husband and asked to see a psychiatrist to demonstrate to his wife that he had done all he could. The psychiatrist recommended anti-depressants. The wife came for "something to buck her up". A year later the husband demanded hormones by injection for his impotence; his wife was distressed by his obsession with his potency and by his paranoid accusations which had now made her frigid. He was referred to an endocrine specialist who found no hormone lack but definite evidence of chronic alcoholism affecting the liver. Shortly afterwards he was admitted to a medical ward in delirium tremens, and on his discharge was given a stern warning against taking any alcohol. He continued to request treatment for impotence, "for the wife's sake"; sexual activity seems to have returned but marital relations remain turbulent.

A clerk aged 51 attended with his wife of 48, a secretary. They had two daughters aged 25 and 18 still living at home in a three-bedroomed Council flat. The husband had had a stroke three years before and was found to have a raised blood pressure. He had made a full recovery and had been prescribed medication to lower his blood pressure. Initially this had made him depressed; other tablets were substituted which made him feel drowsy and interfered with ejaculation. The medication was changed once more and he was now unable to get an erection, and it was this that the couple had come about. He appeared "stick-in-the-mud", while she was jolly, extrovert and sociable. Previously placid, the husband was becoming increasingly depressed about his impotence which he ascribed either to his raised blood pressure or the medication. He used to take pride in his sexual prowess and still had undiminished libido, but he was discouraged over his "useless member". He affected unconcern over the possible seriousness of his blood pressure but referred to a friend with a similar condition as "poor chap". The wife thought him reckless for missing his tablets and was apprehensive about his heart condition. Once, before his stroke, she had become frightened when during intercourse he stopped breathing and went scarlet in the face. She was now afraid of his blood pressure "going sky-high".

The husband felt puzzled, frustrated, and angry with himself; he thought he might as well be dead. But it seemed possible that the wife was contributing to the impotence in some way, fearing that sexual activity posed a danger to her husband and preferring him to stay alive, if impotent. In discussion with her separately it was suggested that perhaps she related her husband's erection to his blood pressure going "sky-high"; and she was encouraged to see that his sexual frustration might be at least as detrimental to him in the long run as the small risk of another stroke during coitus. Meanwhile changes were made in his medication in case the anti-hypertensive drug was one of the factors in his impotence.

Male homosexuality does not figure as a sexual problem in the general practice setting. Occasionally a distraught parent may try to enlist the doctor's help to correct their teenage son's homosexual orientation, or a wife may hint darkly that this is the explanation for her husband's lack of sexual interest in her; but it is unusual for homosexuals themselves to feel dissatisfied and to approach their family doctor on this account.

Complaints of lack of energy may sometimes be an allusion to loss of potency especially amongst Asian immigrants, for whom "weakness" is an equivalent. *Pruritus ani,* which is said to have sexual connotations, is certainly common in men displaying tension states but seems not to be a particularly good pointer to psychosexual problems as judged by the psychotherapeutic techniques available in general practice.

Problems in Women

Amongst women, the occurrence and the expression of sexual problems is very much bound up with social and cultural pressures. The notion of wifely duty prevails through all classes and most races; sexual pleasure is not a commodity all women have felt they had a right to. There is evidence that this may be changing, and certainly women are expecting more from their sexual lives than pregnancies and child-rearing. Hence they are more inclined now to consult their general practitioners over frigidity or loss of libido, rather than merely be complained about by their husbands, as formerly.

There seem to be fewer women now with primary frigidity, presumably because of less repressive upbringing and the opportunities for experimentation provided by the "pill" and by our looser social structure. Occasionally a despairing husband will bring along his wife with whom intercourse has proved difficult or impossible. Painful intercourse may be associated with local inflammatory states or an uncommonly resistant hymen but it is remarkable how rarely in general practice this is found to be the explanation. Occasionally the woman conforms to the classic hysteric personality type and has a suitably gentle and considerate spouse quite unable to take on a forceful role. Where indicated a discussion takes place on the techniques and practical measures such as lubrication, but it can happen that a striking improvement follows on the doctor's physical examination of the woman. It is as if he had exercised "droite-de-seigneur", a symbolic initiation, but sufficient to make the husband now acceptable.

Other women may display a flirtatious teasing and lure the doctor on to greater and greater efforts in an attempt to effect a cure. These efforts are generally unavailing but the doctor, now challenged and on his mettle, may doggedly pursue his quarry. Or the woman may arouse her doctor's protective feelings and by posing as a damsel in distress cause him to fly about in all directions, slaying her dragons. One of these will be her husband, depicted as a monster of depravity; or a difficult mother-in-law, demanding child, unsympathetic housing department — the list may be long. Sexual problems in women so easily spill over into other areas of their lives but often, at the root, there is uncertainty about their functioning as females stemming in very many cases from improverished mother—daughter relationships.

Secondary frigidity is very much more common and is often traced back to a childbirth, not necessarily the first. Lesser degrees may occur with tiredness and depression as features; these symptoms are understandable considering the stresses imposed on women bringing up a family in crowded living conditions, and perhaps working as well. A clue to the probable course of events is sometimes given at the post-natal examination, usually six weeks after the confinement. When the woman indicates that they have waited for the examination before resuming intercourse this suggests nowadays that she may be very glad of the respite.

A common expression of sexual difficulty is through the problems associated with contraception. The woman may find fault with a succession of oral contraceptives or devices, or allege that her husband is unhappy about them, so that it is difficult to institute effective and reliable birth control in her case. When menstrual irregularity or pain is added, as it often is, or profuse vaginal discharge which recurs in spite of treatment, the opportunities for intercourse dwindle. Fear of pregnancy may certainly interfere with normal sexual performance in women, but that same fear may be employed by them, unconsciously, as a form of coitus control. Behind this may be feelings of resentment towards the husband, or depression, or low self-esteem. One may make more headway by considering the relationship aspects of the situation rather than pondering the causes within the woman herself. The couple may seem incompatible, as if they have diverged, the woman continuing to grow and leave the husband behind, or vice versa; as if the contract has now changed and their needs of each other are no longer the same. In these cases, perhaps they are in the great majority, the sexual problem is an indicator of a more general marital pathology requiring from the general practitioner a wider approach than a genital-orientated one.

More profound psychosexual disturbance is expressed through a variety of destructive, sometimes self-destructive, manoeuvres. Reckless exposure to venereal disease, promiscuous sexual behaviour, a disregard of birth control, repeated induced abortions, demand for sterilization or hysterectomy are some of the ways in which women may act out degrading and self-punitive impulses. Into this category may also come requests for surgery to reduce the size of the breasts.

Case Histories

The following short case-histories illustrate the range of sexual problems amongst women, as seen in general practice.

A girl in her early twenties, recently married and living in one room in her parent's house. She had headaches and abdominal pain and displayed much nervous tension, but had big, childlike eyes. Enquiry revealed that they were not having intercourse because, as she explained, it would be embarrassing if her mother were to walk into their room. The doctor completely accepted this explanation until when relating it at a seminar case discussion he was asked, had it occurred to him to enquire why they had not thought to put a lock on their door?

A West Indian woman aged 32, with three children here and two more "back home", still single and waiting for her man to "name the day". She had menorrhagia and was making heavy weather of her birth control. She expressed resentment towards the children's father and was impatient to become married. Her situation was not an abnormal one in her culture but contact with English women and a different style of home life had made her dissatisfied with her lot.

A 25-year-old with two children, the husband an actor. She was attractive, vain, and self-centred. She complained mainly of vaginal discharge and of absence of sexual feeling. Parental relationships were poor: at odds with her father, superficial contact only with her mother. She became more depressed as she got in touch with her feelings. Later she rebelled, became an emancipated women's libber, and a prominent member of a local action group. She installed a lover in the marital home (which she owned jointly) and had a child by him which she breast fed for nearly twelve months.

A single woman of 30 was attending a hospital psychotherapy group because of depression. She was extremely unhappy and had had four induced abortions abroad. She had no existing relationships, described her previous general practitioner as having no time for her (he had in fact done a lot), felt her psychiatrist to be very unsympathetic, and was unable to talk in her group.

A Turkish woman, single, 31 years old had just had her third abortion. She had been depressed since childhood; at the age of ten had wanted to die. Herself illegitimate she had to pretend to be her mother's sister so as not to spoil her mother's chances of marriage. The mother had insisted on the patient's first abortion. She cried over her lack of mothering; she still bought herself toys and dolls.

A secretary, single, aged 41, with a married man friend. Six months after her father died she became pregnant, but then had the pregnancy terminated. She wept when talking of her father, and was shattered by the abortion; she realised she had needed the baby as a tangible expression of her relationship with her friend. She made a joke about "snatching babies from their prams". Asked if it was a boy she replied, "Yes", and gave the names she had chosen, those of her father and her friend.

A working class girl of 22, unmarried but living with her Maltese boy friend in his mother's home. He did no work but she had part time employment outside as a domestic. Their baby was always being brought to the doctor on account of very minor upsets, difficulty with feeding, and allegations of lack of robustness. She seemed overwrought on one occasion and admitted that their sexual life was virtually nil now, though normal formerly. "I can't bear him to touch me"; she was unconcerned whether he found another woman or not. It was only after the marital relationship had improved with the prospect of finding their own home that she revealed to the doctor her intense resentment of her mother-in-law who continually undermined her by making adverse comments on the baby's state of health. This resentment was readily transferred to the husband who would not take his wife's part, and she said this led to the extinguishing of all sexual feeling in her.

A woman, widowed at the age of 34 when her husband aged 40 died of a coronary thrombosis, and with two young daughters; she attended regularly to obtain prescriptions for hypnotics without which she said she could not sleep. She began to complain of vulval irritation, and later of urinary difficulty and vaginal discharge, for which no physical cause was found. She denied she had any sexual feeling and was not interested in meeting any men. It was several years before she took a man friend and had intercourse, whereupon she developed a "honeymoon" cystitis.

In general practice many of the children's problems that are presented prove to be manifestations of the parents' sexual difficulties. Even more frequently however the symptoms in the child serve as a "ticket of entry" to the doctor. It is for this reason presumably that otherwise sensible and level-headed mothers repeatedly attend the doctor for minor departures from health in their offspring, or for its alleged restlessness at night, or for failure to consume a certain quota of nourishment. It is usually possible for the doctor to satisfy himself fairly rapidly on the child's wellbeing and to then turn his attention to possible underlying problems in the marriage or in one or other of the parents. In this he may receive very little help from them: the child may well be the "presenting symptom" but the substitution is generally at an unconscious level and his probing may be met with resistance rather than with relief.

The continuity of care available in general practice confers considerable advantages in this sort of work because the doctor is afforded repeated opportunities; if the penny does not drop with him, or if he meets undue resistance, he can await a more favourable occasion. The informality of the general practice setting is also a help, and so too is the fact that presenting clinical material is completely undifferentiated for this allows patients to express their problems in the way that seems most natural, even if it is a way that is is not most direct; it is the doctor's responsibility to understand the meaning of the patient's behaviour, including the behaviour in the consulting room. This gives the patient a freedom which contrasts with the framework into which he must fit in the setting of specialist practice, and may make it possible for work to be done at an early stage rather than on late pathology when a vicious circle may exist and the parties have consolidated their positions. It also means that help can be proffered before the nature of the problem is explicitly stated; even before agreement is reached with the patient on the area to be studied.

Referrals

The practitioner may decide that he needs specialist help with some of his patients with psychosexual problems, but the decision is rarely a simple or automatic one; the referral is usually the resultant of a complex equation. On the one side he will consider the possible seriousness or obscurity of the condition presenting; the availability of specialist help and the range of services offered; and his expectation of any good coming from it. Pressure from the patient or spouse for specialist referral may be the determining factor in his decision to seek outside help.

On the other side of the equation are the practitioner's resources; not only adequate time, which is obviously a vital resource, but the requisite skills for the work, and aptitude — quite simply, whether he has the stomach for it. He may take the view that being the family doctor strengthens his position, or that it compromises it. His practice facilities will be a factor, especially the extent to which he can call on the support of interested colleagues, not just his partners, but paramedical staff such as nurse, health visitor, or social worker; they may be able to help either in separate or in joint interviews with patient and spouse. An increasing number of general practices have attached para-medical staff, though only a few are from social work departments.

In a few instances practices have regular visits from the staff of neighbouring psychiatric departments. These visits may be once a week or once a month and may involve the consultant psychiatrist, his registrar, a case-worker, psychotherapist, or clinical psychologist. This arrangement offers a number of advantages over the conventional out-patient referral, not least because it allows a more accurate definition of the doctor's problem in the course of informal contacts with him. Also the familiarity of the practice setting may encourage some patients to see a "specialist" who would otherwise be reluctant to do so. But the help given by psychiatric colleagues in these circumstances is not limited to those patients actually seen by them; the practitioner is able to discuss many more cases and receive both support and direction. In this way his professional skills can be enhanced and he retains responsibility for the management of the case (Brook and Temperley, 1976).

But this begs the question as to what is wanted by the practitioner in making a specialist referral. Not all his patients with similar problems are so referred, so evidently he exercises some selection. Just who gets referred? For what? And to whom? Some of the factors involved have been mentioned above but the basis on which the choice appears to be made is not always clear, and there may be other, perhaps unconscious, factors at work. Amongst these may be a need for respite on the part of the doctor; collusion over the "label" for the problem; scapegoating; the doctor's pessimism about the outcome; or even his possessiveness. The criteria for referral may be in part unconscious but this is not to say they are irrational; it is only that the motivation may be obscure and this must increase the difficulty for the specialist who is being consulted.

As to which specialist is consulted, the choice for most practitioners is wide, and patients with similar presentations may find themselves referred to a gynaecologist, a urologist, an endocrinologist, or to a psychiatrist of any one of a number of persuasions. The choice is determined largely by how the practitioner sees the problem, and this implies some initial sorting-out of the material presented; but it must also reflect his own orientation to the management of psychosexual problems. In turn this will influence the way in which the patient is prepared for the referral; whether the problem is seen as something the matter with the sexual apparatus, or as affecting the patient in his totality as a person. Inevitably the doctor's own philosophy will come over to the patient. Apart from this, work may have to be done with the patient to bring him to see the need for outside help, and this may require several consultations.

For the practitioner, the referral may not be the end of the matter but may present him with a fresh set of problems. He may have a role in supporting spouse or relatives and in interpreting to them what is going on in the specialist department. The patient himself may continue to consult him even though under specialist care, and the practitioner may need to redefine his relationship; if the specialist approach is mechanistic, the patient may be in need of a "personal" doctor; if psychotherapeutic, then the practitioner may limit himself to issuing prescriptions. In this three-cornered relationship there are many opportunities for confusion and competition, and even conflict. This points the need for special attention to be paid to the relationship between practitioner and specialist; ideally there would be good lines of communication and a spirit of openness so that each could feel adequately briefed about the situation as the other saw it.

Whole-person Medicine

The general practice approach to psychosexual problems may seem casual, ad hoc, opportunist; but it offers unique advantages to the doctor giving primary care (which includes preventive measure and

surveillance) to his defined list of patients. The special features of
general practice may prove however to be double-edged weapons. For
instance, the comparatively easy-going atmosphere in the practice may
preclude the patient from feeling a serious commitment to treatment.
He may prefer the anonymity of an agency beyond his neighbourhood.
Or the practitioner may be non grata because of an assumed closer
relationship with the spouse. The biggest drawback is the expectation
on the part of the patient that his doctor will provide solutions to the
problem based on his traditional medical role; that is to say, either a
medicine to help make life tolerable for the sufferer, or pressure on
the spouse to make him (or her) change.

The practitioner who wishes to be more than a body-technician,
but a doctor to the total person, will encounter difficulties in assuming the dual roles. He may be dealing with sensitive and emotionally-
charged material, and employ transference in its resolution; his style
may be counselling, "non-directive and non-judgemental". At the same
time he is physician to the body, touches his patient, makes physical
intrusions, prescribes medicines and gives direct advice — even
"doctor's orders". The situation is potentially embarrassing to both
parties and is capable of being exploited by the patient or the spouse.
The doctor may feel harried by provocation or testing out, and may
feel uncomfortable in straddling the separate fields of body and mind,
and his response may be to lurch from one to the other; or to be the
"psychological doctor" for a few of his patients while to the remainder
he is the "body doctor". Even with the former he may become de-
moralized, perhaps from getting his fingers burned (or knuckles
rapped) and retreat by reverting to what he sees as the traditional
medical role.

This is an unsatisfactory state of affairs which has its root in the
very notion of the duality of mind and body. The real challenge
facing the practitioner is genuinely to integrate these two aspects of
his work until he feels he can pass easily and naturally from one
approach to the other; to renounce the "either/or" principle in
favour of a comprehensive one. The idea of one role contaminating
the other is behind the argument for specialization in psychosexual
work within the primary care setting. The opposing philosophy
seeks to combine the requisite qualities in "a proper doctor" (Balint
and Norell, 1973). There is growing support for a holistic approach
in the giving of primary care, and for those practitioners wishing to
undertake further training there are seminars available run under the
aegis of The Balint Society, The Tavistock Institute, and The Institute

for Psychosexual Medicine.*

The general practitioner and his patients might have more to lose if he were to give up his whole-person orientation, ceased to "formulate his diagnoses in physical, psychological and social terms", and abdicated from his task to "intervene educationally, preventively and therapeutically to promote his patient's health" (*Royal College of General Practioners*, 1972).

References

Balint, E. and Norell, J. S. (Eds.) (1973). "Six Minutes for the Patient: Interactions in General Practice Consultation." Tavistock Publications: London.

Brook, A. and Temperley, J. (1976). *Journal of the Royal College of General Practioners*, 26, 86—94.

Royal College of General Practioners (1972). "The Future General Practitioner: Learning and Teaching." British Medical Journal: London.

*The Balint Society, 11 Briardale Gdns., London, N.W.3.
The Tavistock Institute of Human Relations, Belsize Lane, London, N.W.3.
The Institute for Psychosexual Medicine, The Cassel Hospital, Richmond, Surrey.

12 | *Untoward Effects of Drugs on Sexuality*

G. BEAUMONT

Although much attention has been paid in recent years to the unwanted effects of therapeutically active drugs, relatively little of this has been given to their adverse effects on sexual behaviour. It is known that many drugs can affect sexuality, but few serious attempts have been made to assess the severity or the size of the problem. Although it is known that there are a number of important drug groups whose effect on sexual function is clearly understood, information on the majority of therapeutic substances is limited to occasional individual reports of adverse reaction. Since the problem of sexual impotence is probably more common than supposed and frequently under reported, the evaluation of occasional individual reports of drug-induced sexual side effects is difficult and often inconclusive.

Drugs may have unwanted sexual effects in both males and females. For reasons that are obvious, those affecting the male have been more definitely identified and substantiated. Untoward effects in the male include inhibition or abolition of ejaculation, erectile impotence, failure to achieve orgasm and loss of libido. In addition, hormonal and gonadal changes have been demonstrated in animals following the administration of large doses of certain drugs. There is evidence that these changes may also occur in man.

Much confusion has been created in reports of unwanted sexual side effects because of a frequent failure to identify the precise nature of the disturbance. For instance, impotence in the male is often reported as a drug induced side effect without the specific nature of the disturbance being made clear. The nature and incidence of drug induced side effects is less easy to demonstrate in the female than it is in the male, although there seems to be evidence of both drug induced orgasmic impotence and loss of libido.

Drugs may act adversely on sexual behaviour both peripherally and centrally. They may also adversely affect sexuality by their action on endocrine pathways and hormonal secretions. Peripheral effects are usually brought about by drugs whose known pharmacological action is to alter or block biogenic amine-uptake mechanisms. In the male, such peripheral effects are clearly understood. They most commonly lead to ejaculatory disorders although where their effect is less specific, total impotence, with failure to achieve erection, may ensue. The possible role of peripheral mechanisms in the female is less clearly understood and probably less important. Central effects of drugs on sexuality are thought to be brought about by their action on the limbic system and perhaps by hypothalamic endocrine disturbance.

The majority of unwanted effects of drugs concern the inhibition of sexual responsiveness. However, a few drugs have been considered, under certain conditions, to cause enhancement of sexual drive. Nevertheless, there is no evidence that the recent therapeutic revolution has provided any agent which might give encouragement to mankind in its centuries old search for effective aphrodisiacs.

Adverse Effects of Drugs on Ejaculation

Drugs most likely to interfere with ejaculation are those which have peripheral alpha adrenergic blocking properties. Perhaps the best known are those used in the treatment of hypertension.

One of the earliest reports of drug induced failure of ejaculation was that concerning dibenzyline by Green and Berman in 1954. Dibenzyline acts at the neuroeffector junction and is specifically sympatholytic not affecting the parasympathetic. Because of its adrenergic blocking action the drug was used in the management of hypertension. Green and Berman observed that four male patients out of seven treated with dibenzyline experienced failure of seminal emission during intercourse. They commented that the mode of action of dibenzyline in producing the effect of failure of ejaculation was the same phenomenon as that occasionally observed as an untoward effect of bilateral thoraco lumbar sympathectomy. They pointed out that in the:

> "complex physiology of ejaculation, the musculature of the epididymes, vasa deferentia, seminal vesicles, ejaculatory ducts, prostate, perineum and penis all must act in coordination. The peristalsis of the vasa deferentia, seminal vesicles and ejaculatory ducts which discharge semen into the urethra as well as the contraction of the internal vesical sphincter which prevents reflux of the semen into the bladder are induced by efferent impulses from the hypogastric plexuses which derive from the thoracolumbar (sympathetic) outflow".

Dibenzyline, they thought produced failure of ejaculation by blocking these adrenergic impulses at the neuroeffector junction.

One patient in the series reported by Green and Berman reported the passage, after coitus, of "pure white urine". It was suggested that with drug induced failure of ejaculation such semen as did reach the urethra might reflux through the relaxed internal sphincter of the bladder and be later voided in the urine.

Subsequently, failure to ejaculate has been reported as a troublesome side effect of a number of anti-hypertensive agents — guanethidine, guanoclor, bethanidine, bretylium, debrisoquine, clonidine and methyldopa. Another group of drugs likely to cause interference with ejaculatory function are the psychotropic drugs. Tricyclic antidepressants like imipramine, desipramine, amitriptyline and clomipramine will cause it. Ejaculatory problems are perhaps most commonly seen with clomipramine.

Some of the earliest reports of inhibition of ejaculation by psychotropic drugs concerned the neuroleptic agent thioridizine. It has been suggested that the incidence of this untoward effect may be as high as 30% on this compound. Failure to ejaculate has also been reported as a side effect of chlorpromazine, chlorprothixine, chlordiazepoxide, perphenazine, tri-fluoperazine and butaperazine. It has also been reported on drugs of the butyrophenone and monoamine oxidase inhibitor types.

From the reports available it is quite impossible to estimate reliably the true incidence of ejaculatory disturbances on both anti-hypertensive and psychotropic drugs. Undoubtedly the size of the problem is under estimated. Patients have a natural reticence to admit to problems of this type and physicians do not always deliberately enquire of them. There is evidence that the effect is dose related and that also tolerance may develop. Small doses of psychotropic agents may have no effect or simply delay ejaculation, whereas larger doses bring about complete failure. This fact can be turned to advantage in the management of patients with premature ejaculation.

The possible consequences of drug induced failure of ejaculation may be considerable. It has been suggested that it is one of the causes never discussed between patient and physician, of failure to take prescribed medication. There are also considerable personal and marital consequences in both psychiatric patients and those suffering from hypertension. For the hypertensive, concern about failure to achieve proper sexual relationships introduces an additional stress into an already anxious and perhaps limited life. For the psychiatric patient failure to achieve satisfactory marital relationships may further undermine confidence and increase anxiety and depression. Very often depressed patients experience a loss of libido and sexual drive in the early stages of their illness. As the symptoms improve and sexual interest is restored patients may find that the satisfactory performance of coitus is limited by inhibition of ejaculation. Under these circumstances, which are regarded by some as rare, but whose incidence is really quite unknown, a change of medication may be required. Alternatively, reduction in dosage, if the psychiatric condition permits, might allow satisfactory sexual relationships. Some patients have discovered that it is possible to enjoy full relationships for a few days if medication is discontinued and then later recommenced. In view of the long half life and tissue retention of many psychotropic agents this may not be harmful or seriously reduce steady state drug levels in patients on maintenance therapy. Obviously some marital counselling in order to avoid possible interpersonal difficulties may be required in patients on large doses of psychotropic agents.

Adverse Effects on Erection

Whereas it is relatively easy to understand what is happening in supposed drug induced ejaculatory disorders, it is not quite so easy to appreciate the situation in suspected drug induced erectile impotence. In ejaculation the mechanism is clear and under sympathetic control. The probability is that all drugs which interfere with ejaculation are exerting a peripheral effect. It is significant that the same problems with ejaculation have been observed in masturbation, as in coitus. The situation is obviously more complicated as far as erection is concerned. Although there clearly exists a peripheral mechanism central factors are probably of much greater importance.

The physiological process by which erection is achieved is controlled by the parasympathetic system. It has been reported that the drug methanthiline bromide may produce erectile impotence. This effect is presumably brought about by an anti-cholinergic effect on parasympathetic pathways. There have also been reports of erectile impotence occurring on agents like propantheline. It would seem, therefore, worthwhile to look for unwanted sexual side effects amongst patients receiving anti-spasmodic, anti-cholinergic preparations.

Non-specific ganglion blocking drugs like hexamethonium, mecamylamine, pentolinium and pempidine formerly used in the management of severe hypertension produce total impotence in the male the drugs appearing to act unselectively on both sympathetic and parasympathetic pathways.

It is interesting that there is an apparently dose related effect on erection of a number of psychotropic agents. Tricyclic anti-depressants like imipramine, desipramine and protriptyline and monoamine oxidase inhibitors such as mebanazine have been reported to cause erectile impotence. Presumably these drugs are exerting an anti-cholinergic effect in this situation. Interestingly small doses of these drugs have no effect on sexual performance, larger doses may inhibit ejaculation and still larger doses prevent satisfactory erection.

In attributing erectile impotence to ingested drugs great care must be taken in establishing a clear cause and effect relationship. It is essential to ensure that patients were normally potent before treatment and able to achieve full erection regularly. Since central factors have such a profound effect in achieving and maintaining erection many psychological and maturational influences may interfere with the achievement of satisfactory erection. In depressive and anxiety states failure to achieve erection may be a symptom of the disease rather than a consequence of its therapy. Since the true incidence of erectile impotence is unknown and since for reasons of modesty and personal pride patients may not readily admit to having such a problem, the opportunity to attribute it to drug therapy is a considerable temptation. It therefore follows that as in the case of all supposed drug induced adverse effects but especially those which involve sexual behaviour great care must be taken to exclude pretreatment abnormality and disease induced abnormalities.

Adverse Effects on the Female

Very little is known about the possible adverse effects of drugs on female sexual behaviour. There have, however, been reports of orgasmic impotence occurring in patients receiving psychotropic drugs and in a few instances there seems to be strong evidence favouring a cause and effect relationship.

The relationship between central and peripheral components in the female is less understood than it is the male where ejaculation is under sympathetic control and erection under parasympathetic. Sympathetic mechanisms do not appear to be as important in the female. It may be that anti-cholinergic parasympathetic effects can disturb female responsiveness. It could be conjected that the psychotropic drugs reported to have caused orgasmic impotence in the female affect clitoral responsiveness. The whole subject is almost totally unexplored and warrants further investigation. As in the case of abnormalities of erection in the male, great care has to be taken in attributing failure to achieve satisfactory orgasm in the female to ingested drugs since many other factors in the patient's personal history and disease state may be playing a role.

Drug Effects on Libido

Loss of libido has been claimed to be a side effect of many forms of medication. Again the side effect is extremely difficult to confirm without reservation. The effect has been particularly claimed with a number of psychotropic drugs. Certainly central depressant drugs appear to reduce libidinous desire and it is likely that it is through a central depressant effect that the adverse effects attributed to psychotropic drugs have been produced. However, in psychological disease loss of libido is frequently a symptom of the illness for which psychotropic drugs are being administered. In physical illness, too, libido may be readily impaired. Again careful history-taking is required to assess predrug levels of sexual desire and to eliminate disease induced effects.

Hormone levels, particularly of progesterone can influence interest in sex. Marked changes of libido have been observed in women premenstrually. Studies in both psychiatric and gynaecological patients, as well as in experimental animals have suggested that progesterone can decrease interest in and the frequency of the enjoyment of sex.

Much controversy has centred around the possible anti-libidinous effect of oral contraceptives. Some oral contraceptives have been accused of causing a reduction in sexual appetite. It has also been suggested that these agents may cause depression — in itself a likely cause of loss of libido. Conflicting claims have been made for both increased and reduced coital rates. Unfortunately, any studies into the effects of oral contraceptives are complicated by other contaminating factors. Relief of "the fear of pregnancy" may overide pharmacological effect and produce increased sexual drive and activity. Alternatively, feelings of guilt about taking oral contraceptives may have an opposite effect. Patients may well have previously sheltered behind the "fear of pregnancy" statement in the past and used it as a justification for relative abstinence from sex.

The survey on "Oral Contraceptives and Health" conducted by the Royal College of General Practitioners (1974) concludes that oral contraceptive users certainly complain of loss of libido more than non-users, but they point out that "they have many reasons and opportunities to do so which are unconnected with the pharmacological action of the "pill". Clearly, they say it is much easier for a woman to discuss sexual feelings at the same time as she is discussing contraception with her doctor than at other times. This may partly explain the increased rate of complaint of loss of libido by oral contraceptive takers. The rate of complaint in patients on the pill apparently showed no relationship to the dose of steriod administered. Reporting is highest in the first twelve months of use. One factor that is suggested is that pill takers have greater expectations of sexual satisfaction than non-takers. Certainly oral contraceptives produce greater sexual activity.

In certain interesting placebo controlled trials of oral contraceptives no difference was found in the incidence of loss of libido on the two treatment regimes and in another the incidence of loss of libido on placebo was reported to be 30%.

According to the Royal College of General Practitioners "there is no evidence that oral contraceptive users have more severe depression than non users". The survey suggests that depression due to oral contraceptives may be a less important problem than had been previously assumed. However, there have been studies which have demonstrated an increase in depression associated with pill usage and an association with the progesterone content.

The issues of loss of libido and depression on oral contraceptives, two conditions which may of course be related, do not as yet appear to be fully resolved.

Hormonal Effects of Drugs

Through their action on the hypothalamic pituitary gonadal axis some drugs may affect levels of pituitary hormones. Probably the most widely studied compounds in this respect are reserpine and chlorpromazine. Experiments in a variety of animal species have indicated that both reserpine and chlorpromazine inhibit or suppress hypothalamic or pituitary function with a resulting increase in prolactin production and a decrease in the secretion of FSH and LH or ICSH. Other phenothiazines have been found to have similar effects. In man phenothiazines and reserpine have also been found to stimulate prolactin secretion as have methyldopa, butyrophenones, tricyclic anti-depressants, oestrogens and TRH. Prolactin suppressants have also been found. They include L-dopa, monoamine oxidase inhibitors and certain ergot derivatives.

A variety of changes have been shown in male animals following the administration of phenothiazines, varying from no effect to oligospermia and atrophic changes in the testicle. The degenerative changes observed were degeneration of the seminiferous tubules and impaired spermatogenesis. In pigeons and ring doves an increase in prolactin secretion and a decrease in FSH and LH/ICSH production has been shown to lead to rapid and extensive testicular atrophy. Reserpine has also been shown to produce similar effects in rats, mice and chickens. Though not studied as extensively as reserpine phenothiazines have been shown to produce similar changes in animals. Chlorpromazine, perphenazine and mepazine all have similar gonadal effects to those of reserpine. In animals chlorpromazine administration in high dosage leads to reduction in the motility of sperm and reduced fertility. Concentrations of chlorpromazine greater than 200 mg/ml are spermicidal to dog sperm.

It should be emphasized that all the gonadal changes observed in animals are produced by high, relatively toxic, drug doses. Little is known about the effect of compounds in normal therapeutic doses, on fertility in man. It is known, however, that these and other compounds affect prolactin production and increase urinary FSH production in both males and females. The possible sexual effects of these changes remain largely unexplored.

The question of fertility in schizophrenia has been controversial for many years. In this condition therefore there is some difficulty in distinguishing drug effects from possible features of the disease since reserpine or phenothiazines are likely to have been used. There have been suggestions that in schizophrenia fertility is lowered and that in male schizophrenics oligospermia may occur. Before the advent of phenothiazines testicular atrophy was reported to occur in some schizophrenics and in fact pregnant mares serum gonadotrophic hormone was thought to bring about regeneration of the tubules and was therefore advocated as a treatment for schizophrenia.

Few systematic studies have been performed to examine the possible gonadal effects of therapeutically administered drugs both from the point of view of gonadotrophin production and sperm production. Reduction in urinary gonadotrophin production has been reported on a few patients on long term chlorprothixene administration and polyspermia with associated necrospermia in some cases receiving butyrophenones. Other patients on the same agents displayed lowered motility. Patients receiving tricyclic antidepressants have been found to have aspermia or reduced sperm count and semen volume. By contrast, the mono-amine oxidase inhibitor phenelzine was found to produce increased spermatogenesis in depressed males. There are obvious difficulties in performing routine seminal analyses on patients receiving psychotropic drugs. The possible effects of such agents on spermatogenesis are therefore difficult to evaluate. Nevertheless, the subject would benefit from further study.

Drugs Which Increase Sexual Desire

The possible effects of drugs increasing sexual drive, appetite and performance is a vexed one. Small amounts of alcohol have always been regarded as being capable of increasing sexual desire, but decreasing performance. Sexual impotence resulting from prolonged alcohol abuse has been reported to persist for years after the achievement of sobriety.

There have been some reports of enhanced sexual behaviour in patients receiving L-dopa for Parkinsons Disease. Some reports suggested that this agent uniformly and specifically stimulated sexual drive. Others felt that enhanced sexual drive was merely an expression of the overall increase in function and well being that results from the treatment of Parkinson's disease with L-dopa. Some studies have shown increased drive in some patients but not in others. There is as yet insufficient evidence to suggest that L-dopa possesses aphrodisiac properties.

There are experimental drugs like p-chlorophenylalanine (PCPA) which produce compulsive sexual activity in animals. This drug inhibits the synthesis of 5-hydroxytryptamine without affecting that of catecholamines. The key to central sexual effects of certain drugs may be this 5HT effect. It is of considerable interest that like L-dopa, serotonin antagonists such as methysergide have been observed to increase sexual behaviour.

Mankind has always sought after aphrodisiacs. Despite claims that a variety of drugs might produce enhanced sexual desire and activity as a side effect — drugs such as yohimbine, amphetamines, caffeine, nicotine, opiates, psychostimulants, hallucinogens, marihuana and amyl nitrite — none of them have been convincingly demonstrated to possess aphrodisiac qualities. This however could hardly be described as an untoward effect of drugs on sexuality.

The whole subject of drug induced sexual side effects is very much in its infancy. Effects on desire, performance and fertility require much further investigation. Such research may not only provide information on the true incidence of untoward drug induced effects, but might also throw some light on the amine and hormone pathways, both central and peripheral, involved in sexual behaviour.

References

Bartholomew, A. A. (1968). A long-acting phenothiazine as a possible agent to control deviant sexual behaviour. *American Journal of Psychiatry*, 124, 7, 917—923.

Beaumont, G. (1974). Sexual side-effects of drugs. *British Journal of Sexual Medicine*, 1, 5, 10—12.

Blair, J. H. and Simpson, G. M. (1966). Effect of antipsychotic drugs on reproductive functions. *Diseases of the Nervous System*, 27, 645—647.

Bowers, M. B. Jr., Waert, van M. and Davis, L. (1971). Sexual behaviour during L-dopa treatment for Parkinsonism. *American Journal of Psychiatry*. 127, 12, 1691—1693.

Carlson, B. E., Sadoff, R. L. (1971). Thioridazine in schizophrenia. *Journal of American Medical Association*, 217, 12, 1705.

Ditman, K. S. (1964). Inhibition of ejaculation by chlorprothixene. *American Journal of Psychiatry*. 120, 1004—1005.

Freyhan, F. A. (1961). Loss of ejaculation during mellaril treatment. *American Journal of Psychiatry*, 118, 171—172.

Green, M. (1961). Inhibition of ejaculation as a side-effect of mellaril. *American Journal of Psychiatry*, 118, 172—173.

Green, M. and Berman, S. (1954). Failure of ejaculation produced by dibenzyline. *Connecticut State Medical Journal*, 18, 30—33.

Greenberg, H. R. (1965). Erectile impotence during the course of Tofranil therapy. *American Journal of Psychiatry*, 121, 1021.

Greenberg, H. R. (1971). Inhibition of ejaculation by Chlorpromazine. *Journal of Nervous and Mental Disease*, 152, 5, 364—366.

Greenberg, H. R. and Carrillo, C. (1968). Thioridazine-induced inhibition of masturbatory ejaculation in an adolescent. *American Journal of Psychiatry*, 124, 7, 991—993.

Haider, I. (1966). Thioridazine and sexual dysfunctions. *International Journal of Neuropsychiatry*, 2, 255—257.

Heiler, J. (1961). Another case of inhibition of ejaculation as a side effect of mellaril. *American Journal of Psychiatry*, 118, 173.

Hodge, J. V. (1966). Guanoclor as an antihypertensive drug. *British Medical Journal*, 2, 981—984.

Horrobin, D. F. (1974)."Prolactin 1974." Eden Press: Montreal.

Horwitz, D., Pettinger, W. A. Orvis, H., Thomas, R. E., and Sjoerdsma, A. (1967). Effects of methyldopa in fifty hypertensive patients. *Clinical Pharmacology and Therapeutics*, 8, 2, 224—234.

Hughes, J. M. (1964). Failure to ejaculate with chlordiazepoxide. *American Journal of Psychiatry*, 121, 610—611.

Johnson, P., Kitchin, A. H., Lowther, C. P., Turner, R. W. D. (1966). Treatment of hypertension with methyldopa. *British Medical Journal*, 1, 133—137.

Khan, A., Camel, G., Perry, H. M. (1970). Clonidine (Catapres): A new anti-hypertensive agent. *Current Therapeutic Research*, 12, 1, 10—18.

Lemere, F. and Smith, J. W. (1973). Alcohol-induced sexual impotence. *American Journal of Psychiatry*, 130, 2, 212—213.

Royal College of General Practitioners (1974). "Oral Contraceptives and Health." An interim report. Pitman Medical: London.

Seedat, Y. K. and Pillay, V. K. G. (1966). Further experiences with guanethidine — a clinical assessment of 103 patients. *South African Medical Journal*, 40, 140—143.

Shader, R. I. (1964). Sexual dysfunction associated with thioridazine hydro-chloride. *Journal of American Medical Association*, 188, 11, 175—177.

Shader, R. I. (Ed.). (1972). "Psychiatric complications of medical drugs." Raven Press.

Shader, R. I. and DiMascio, A. (1970). "Psychotropic Drug Side Effects: Clinical and Theoretical perspectives." Williams and Wilkins: Baltimore.

Simpson, G. M., Blair, J. H. and Amuso, D. (1965). Effects of anti-depressants on genito-urinary function. *Diseases of the Nervous System*, 26, 787—789.

Taubel, D. E. (1962). Melleril: Ejaculation disorders. *American Journal of Psychiatry*, 119, 87.

13 | Sexual Problems of Disabled People

DUNCAN GUTHRIE

In 1973 the National Fund for Research into Crippling Diseases established a committee on the sexual problems of disabled people, SPOD. At the time virtually no steps had been taken to help disabled adolescents or adults in an area in which the National Fund's impression was that disabled people were likely to have considerable problems, in their personal and sexual relationships. I personally put it no stronger than this because up until then no research had been carried out and no scientific assessments made. When SPOD started holding meetings and contact was made with disabled people, their sponsors and their families, as well as with professionals working with the disabled, it soon became very clear that the problems were much more numerous and diverse than had been thought. Fortunately this coincided with an increased freedom to discuss sexual matters which would have been quite impossible even a few years previously and matters which had until recently only been sniggered at in male company could now be discussed openly and calmly.

The need to help disabled people was very obvious indeed; the way to help them was not so clear, although some kind of counselling service certainly seemed to be suggested. There were, however, two aspects which offered clear contra-indications for establishing an immediate counselling service. The first was that there were few, if indeed any, counsellors trained or experienced in counselling disabled people in this area, a situation that could be remedied. The second and more important one was that a special SPOD counselling service

would run contrary to all new thought about the integration of
handicapped people into the community. To set up a new, selective
counselling service would constitute a ghetto attitude as much as
congregating housing for the disabled in a single area, and apart
from the rest of the community.

Investigation

First, however it was clearly necessary to undertake an investigation
with a view to identifying and quantifying the problems. SPOD com-
missioned the Research Institute for Consumer Affairs (a) to establish
the nature and incidence of sexual problems among physically disabled people as engendered or exacerbated by the nature of their disability and (b) to attempt identification of measures for the solution
or alleviation of such problems: in particular to explore the need for
and feasibility of a counselling service to this end.

The study was to be conducted in relation to persons within the
range 16—64 years, permanently or long-term impaired in physical
function or activity to an extent which limits mobility, dexterity,
self-care or relationship with others. It would not take into account
the purely mentally or sensory disabled who it was felt would probably be the subjects of other studies later.

It was decided that the study should be conducted by means of
(a) a survey to be carried out among disabled people living within the
community at large (b) a less numerically-based but still intensive
study of the problems of disabled people who live in residential establishments and (c) a review of the previous study of the subject (sparse
in this country but more plentiful in certain others).

The City of Coventry (population 335,000) was chosen for the
survey. Its population accorded with the national pattern, including a
typical spread of social classes and a substantial immigrant minority
characteristics of Midland cities. By means of postal contacts and
questionnaire, about one eighth of the adults (between 16 and 64)
were approached and, if disabled, asked if they would afford interviews. From these a "survey population" of 212 was obtained.

Findings

The main findings of the study were based on this survey: the
"sample" (about one-sixth of the known disabled people in Coventry

who fell within the survey's ambit) was sufficient to be taken as
representative, and there is no reason to believe that the situation is
different in other parts of the country. The range of disorders involved
was, again, typical.

It was found that more than half (54%) of the 212 people interviewed had current sexual problems, regardless of the degree of their
disability. As general handicap increased, so did the incidence of
sexual problems, until among those most severely disabled sexual
difficulties were found to exist for nine in every ten. In addition to
these, almost a fifth had been subject to sexual problems since dis-
ablement which had been overcome by personal effort or which had
faded into insignificance only with time or increasing age.

One can never be certain about "what might have been", but every
indication was that this incidence was at least double that likely to
have arisen had the people concerned not been or become disabled.
Certainly, the problems arising could undoubtably be associated
directly with the illness or disability of the persons concerned in 70%
of these cases, while in another 20% the disability played some part,
at least, in causing them.

Men tended to be subject to such sexual difficulties significantly
more often than women, and had less often been able to overcome
them. This probably reflects the customarily more active role demanded of men in sexual activity. Problems were most frequent among
the middle-aged: here the menopause, difficulties of middle age
among males in general, and the greater number of married people in
this group (obviously, sexual problems tend to come more to the fore
in marriage than in the single state) play a part.

Problems could be broadly grouped into those of potency and
sexual capacity; of physical comfort; physical safety; difficulties of
sexual movements and postures; emotional/psychological considerations; and of sexual relationships. The number of separate problems
which could be defined was almost double that of the persons subject
to them — disability can be multi-problematical.

The incidence of sexual difficulty was, understandably, higher in
relation to some disabilities — (notably those connected with the
central nervous system or skeleto-muscular apparatus) — than in
others. Yet problems of one kind or another were found in relation
to almost every type of disability encountered, in some persons, at
least, in all these groups.

Marriage, or the achievement of any satisfactory sexual relationship, was less frequent among our disabled subjects than among the

population in general; its frequency decreased as severity of handicap increased. There were indications (supported by other studies) that breakdown of marriage was more frequent.

In the residential study, much the same range of sexual problems was encountered among residents of the various institutions visited as among people in the population at large. Here, however, the people concerned were subject to the extra restrictions and frustrations brought about in a situation where neither opportunity nor encouragement for any free development of sexual relationships exists. Indeed, one of the major conclusions of the SPOD study was that the whole question of sex and sexual problems in the residential setting urgently needs consideration and discussion toward achieving a more satisfactory situation.

Counselling

In conjunction with the study — in particular with the survey — arrangements were made whereby those people encountered who had sexual problems could be offered advice or counsel — where this could effectively be given — concerning them. Not all were willing to avail themselves of the offer — too often the reply was met, "It's too late," or, "I'm too old now". Nevertheless, among those who were advised or counselled in such problems — about three quarters of those concerned — the assistance can be claimed as effective in the majority of cases. In some it was remarkably effective, and the unhappiness of many years was dispelled.

Yet comparatively few people interviewed had received this kind of help previously, and among these the assistance had been effective in less than half the cases in which it had been received. Only a minority of respondents had any realistic idea as to where advice might be sought and the tremendous majority felt that some service to this end was urgently needed.

Some proof that SPOD is already proving its value are the grateful letters which I have received from the disabled and their families. One such letter comes from a mother whose daughter had no clear sexual organs and who had to be provided with an exterior apparatus for controlling excretion.

> "I have just been reading in a Magazine all about you and it gave me a lot
> of comfort to know someone cares about sex for the disabled. I have
> known for nearly fifteen years that there would be a time when I would

need help: but who could I turn to? The family doctor — no he doesn't know — and then he has such a lot of work with all his other patients. It is not for myself I am writing this, but for my very lovely daughter Molly, who looks so very perfect to me, and nobody would ever really understand. She has asked me to write this letter for her, as we are very close and have shared everything together . . . She has started getting asked out by boys, and I am so very pleased for her — but also frightened. I do not want her to get hurt. Molly and I have talked about everything and she knows she cannot have children and a normal relationship in married life because they will have to see her body which from the waist down is scarred so much it is unbelievable, and the new bladder, which is an ileal bladder, is on the outer wall of her tummy. I just want her to be happy, we are so lucky really, we have fun. I have no family only Father, he is nearly 82 Bless him, I couldn't talk to him its difficult without a mother. But I have needed someone else to talk to beside Molly and this is the first time I have been able to. I help other handicapped and can cope. I love to help other people, because I know how lonely it can be. But Molly and I have always hoped that there would be some organization somewhere some day. Molly has developed quite well with a nice little bust and gets more wolf whistles than I ever did. She is a very loving girl always wanting to help around the home and I let her — especially with my son. I have been lucky. Ten years after Molly I got Mark and she adores him. Everything I have written Molly knows. I have a super husband, and he reads the magazine with me. I hope that SPOD will become really known, as it has helped me just writing it down, and its a beginning.''

Future Action

It will be SPOD's aim, over the next two or three years, to make the provision of information, advice or counsel more readily available to those disabled people requiring it in their sexual difficulties. Other necessary tasks are to try to improve the training of doctors, social workers and occupational therapists; better sex education for physically handicapped children, particularly those in institutions; and appropriate preparation for marriage, like the courses run by the Spastics Society.

14 Sexual Problems Seen by the Obstetrician and Gynaecologist

H. A. BRANT

The Obstetrician and Gynaecologist has unrivalled opportunities not only for assisting his patients to achieve or maintain healthy psychosexual functioning but also for detecting psychosexual disorders and managing them either personally or by referral. As his specialty focuses on the female genital tract around which sexual and reproductive functions centre, patients tend to take particular note of his advice and to regard him as the expert most qualified to manage sexual problems. Unfortunately he is not always able to fulfil this expectation. In his training and experience, orientation has often been almost exclusively directed towards the structural and physical aspects of physiology and pathology while scant attention has been given to psychology and the emotions and practically none to the intimate personal details of sexuality. This is not surprising for the organic aspects of Obstetric and Gynaecological practice have been expanding rapidly and becoming increasingly more effective. Sound practice in this area must hold a high priority in training but it can so easily occupy most of the available time. Knowledge of human sexuality has been developing more slowly. There had been a tendency to regard many sexual dysfunctions as manifestations of deeply rooted serious psychopathology which is expected to be relatively unresponsive to even prolonged and intensive psychoanalytical management. The relative simplicity and essentially reflex nature of

the basic sexual response which is intricately and reciprocally influenced by all levels of the brain was not clearly appreciated until
the recent extensive studies of Masters and Johnson (1966, 1970).

Many people have been subject during their development to the
imposition either actively or passively of inhibitions and the negative
contingencies which follow erotic impulses and expressions so that
there has been selective suppression of the sexual response. People
who function well in other areas of their lives often have sexual
problems with relatively immediate causes such as lack of knowledge
and understanding of sexual response and function, anxiety about
performance and fear of rejection or ridicule by the partner. The
many reports by behaviour therapists and others have confirmed that
response to explanation, education and reassurance and the newer
approaches to treatment often lead to relatively rapid resolution of
these sexual problems. In her monograph Kaplan (1974) gives a lucid
and comprehensive account of these new approaches to treatment.
They conceptualize management around the simple sexual reflexes
which are essentially involuntary in nature. The emphasis is on
enabling couples to minimize the impact of the many acquired inhibitory influences which modify this reflex function. There is progressive facilitation of sexual responses as the two people learn to create
a loving atmosphere which maximizes sensuousness and the pursuit of
erotic pleasure in their relationship.

The gynaecologist, like so many others, has until recently been
limited in his outlook on the problems of sexuality by the scarce and
often poorly founded literature, by his own experience, by what he
has gleaned from patients and by anecdotal knowledge from the
community of which he is a part. He has not received formal training
in his medical school and has been offered very little by his senior
colleagues as he has advanced in his specialty. He has been subject
even if less rigorously to the same cultural taboos and evasions as his
patients. He has not, therefore, found it easy to enable them to
discuss intimate sexual matters and has probably not known what
advice or guidance to give even when he has understood the problem.

Recent developments in sexology are providing the gynaecologist
with more specific knowledge and new insights which when blended
with all aspects of his practice can add a new dimension to it. Irrespective of the extent to which he personally undertakes therapy for
sexual problems the gynaecologist is developing his awareness and
broadening his understanding of sexual matters so that his therapeutic
potential is increasing.

Practical Intervention

The gynaecologist in seeing a patient referred to him may merely be
serving as the meeting point between the patient and possible help.
Contact is made between patient and gynaecologist for a wide variety
of reasons many of which would not at first sight seem to involve
psychosexual function. It is only acceptance of the all pervasive relevance of psychosexual function in gynaecology and obstetrics which
leads him to recognize aberrations which may be partly disguised and
to identify opportunities for prophylactic intervention. By being
alert to the possible psychosexual consequences of social circumstances, phases of life, illnesses and operations, the gynaecologist can
by appropriate explanation, interpretation and reassurance be highly
effective in preventing or modifying the development of problems.
All doctors in clinical practice should try to recognize sexual disorders in their patients. For the gynaecologist, questions about sexual
function should be a part of routine interrogation and an awareness
of sexual function should accompany observation and physical examination of the patient. The difficulty arises in developing the sensitivity
and judgement necessary to know when further exploration of sexual
function is likely to help in resolving the patient's problem or to
know when it can be helpful to the patient in a more general way not
necessarily related to the presenting problem. It could well be that
all patients would benefit from discussion in this field but many
would resent probing and such simple practicalities as the time available and the eptness of the interviewer must dictate a practical compromise. Sexual function is still a matter of privacy and is not easily
discussed by the majority of women so that it is necessary to create
an atmosphere in which intimate confidences can be divulged. A
major factor in the creation of this atmosphere is a genuine interest
by the gynaecologist in the sexual welfare of his patient and a desire
and competence to promote his patients interests in this area. This
competence includes an ability to listen attentively and sympathetically and with the detachment which will accept possibly unfore-
seen revelations without shock, embarrassment, judgement or
censure.

The first reaction of the doctor from whom a patient seeks advice
can be critical in determining the further course of the interview. It
can greatly facilitate or completely negate development of the quality
of professional relationship needed for therapeutic discussion in this
area. In gynaecological outpatient clinics with limited time available

it can be difficult to give the patient the impression that her problem
is considered important and worthy of full consideration.

The way in which to introduce the idea that a further more extensive interview or perhaps referral to a colleague is needed calls for
some delicacy and judgement. A patient who as the result of a considerable personal effort has launched into discussion of her sexuality
should if possible be allowed to unburden herself. If referred to a
colleague too soon she may baulk at the thought of seeing another
stranger and is quite likely to default the appointment unless time
is taken to build up the image of the colleague and to give an outline
of the probable course and benefits of the proposed interview or
treatment. She cannot be coerced and must be a willing participant.
If the colleague is working in an adjacent area, personal introduction
can greatly facilitate acceptance. Even when referral is intended,
another more leisurely personal interview to probe further and build
up confidence can be the more certain way of ensuring continued
attendance.

The proportion of work undertaken by the gynaecologist with each
patient depends on his abilities, inclinations, available time and on
the facilities for referral or collaborative management at his disposal.
It is quite clearly his function to at least recognize or suspect sexual
problems in patients in his care.

Opportunities for education and positive reinforcement are constantly present. Whenever the possibility of an operation involving the
genital tract arises, comment and reassurance about the effects on
sexual function should be made early and subsequently reinforced by
further comment and discussion. The importance of repetition cannot
be overemphasized. Most patients, because of anxiety and pre-
occupations, grasp very little of the significance of advice given in
relation to a projected operation. If there is a concensus of advice
from all staff involved with the patient's care she is more likely to be
left with clear concepts which will help her in adjusting to her altered
state.

Sexuality during and subsequent to pregnancy needs to be positively introduced at the antenatal and postnatal visits without waiting for a question while discussion of the impact of the organ or function loss of hysterectomy, ovariectomy or sterilization is mandatory.
Approval and reinforcement of the patient's self regard which is so
vital for effective interpersonal functioning is conveyed in many verbal
and non-verbal ways in the communication between gynaecologist
and patient.

Psychosexual Problems are Often Relationship Problems

Many patients who present to the gynaecologist particularly when complaints are not clearly circumscribed or persist despite apparently adequate treatment — are seeking a way to discuss and ask for help about unhappy relationships (Hebb, 1974).

Psychosexual problems are usually problems of sexual communion (Gusberg, 1973). Difficulties in interpersonal relationships are more often responsible for sexual dysfunction than genital failure. The patient who feels confused or bad about her genitals or genital function is likely to present to her doctor complaining about this area and is therefore referred to a gynaecologist. The reason behind the feeling may well be inadequacy, hurt, guilt or uncertainty in the field of relationships rather than physical disorder of this part of the body. Unhappiness in relationships is presented as illness. The interpersonal problem is seen in a certain light by the complainant but her assessment may be biased or incomplete. Gynaecologists need to suspect the psychosomatic nature of complaints and to be able to accept the inherent distress or despair and view them with understanding and tolerance. It is so easy for him to stifle the patient by interpreting the problem in his own way rather than in hers.

In the partners of a marriage relationship there are whole worlds of attitudes, feelings, prejudices and habits which have been developed through the past and are constantly undergoing modification. Sexual function must be seen in perspective as a part of the total relationship.

As gynaecologists, we usually have the woman with her problems before us but it is essential for us to remember that she represents only half of the interacting couple. The effort required to interview the man involved can be most rewarding and revealing. Perhaps even more valuable is to arrange to see the couple together. It is often only in the presence of the third person that the couple are able to communicate directly to each other their feelings, hopes and fears. When the woman is seen alone she may not volunteer the information that the problem is principally on the man's side in the form of lack of libido, impotence or premature ejaculation. She may not, have suspected this. Discussions of the sexual implications of sterilization or operations such as hysterectomy directly with the couple minimizes later problems. On the other hand the husband whose information comes only indirectly through his wife often has only a vague understanding and tends to retain fantasies and unjustified fears. Women repeatedly comment that it is only after the first fathers' class in the antenatal education programme when discussion is with husbands and wives together that communication with each other about the pregnancy really gets under way and they start to appreciate the implications for their relationship.

It is also wise to think one stage further and to remember that the couple is interacting with a much larger intimate and more remote circle of friends, relations and acquaintances. In discussing hysterectomy with a woman it can be most helpful to enquire whether she knows anyone who has had the operation and what effect the operation has had on the friend's sexual life. If this has been favourable there is often little need for further comment. Such an influence from the wider circle provides a situation with which the patient readily identifies. It is concrete and real and may have had its influence over a long time. When the influence has been unfavourable the task of reassurance and education is so much more difficult.

Body Image

Essential to an ability to relate effectively to another and to accept the differences in a partner is a healthy feeling of self acceptance and self worth. If a woman has had parents who value and respect each other in their roles of man and woman she is likely to be able to adjust to and accept the world of the person she marries. By genuinely valuing herself she can value the differences in her partner (Hebb 1974). The same principle applies to the parts of her body and their functions. Women need to feel comfortable with their femininity and with their sexual feelings and genital organs.

Many women need reassurance about their general image of themselves as being capable of normal sexual function. They may have more specific anxieties. Many don't seem to know that greater or lesser differences between the two sides of the body are common and normal. Frequently questions relate to relative sizes of the breasts, labia or of the two sides of the abdomen. Such apparently trivial questions may reflect the extent of anxiety but may really be the clue to a much more extensive anatomical and functional self doubt — a few appropriate questions are usually sufficient to indicate an underlying problem.

In early pregnancy women often ask whether the breasts or nipples

are too small for breast feeding and they are anxious to know
whether there is enough room "down there" for the baby to be born.
Whether or not these questions are asked they should be anticipated.
A full history and physical examination form an essential basis for
appropriate reassurance. It is a frequent task of the gynaecologist to
reassure women about their physical attributes and functional capacity
in relation to sex and reproductive functions. The need for this reassurance is so nearly universal that it is a necessary part of all gynaecological and obstetric practice to be incorporated as an essential
prophylactic and therapeutic measure. In our system of nurture the
genital tract and the presumption of sexual and reproductive functions are not adequately recognized. They are omitted from the
schedule of generous praise and acceptance which is aimed at en-
hancing self confidence and enabling the growing child to feel comfortable about herself and her abilities. Rather than with praise and
acceptance it is usual to greet expressions of developing sexuality
such as curiosity, display or self stimulation with displeasure and inhibitory action.

No doubt these strictures are intended to regulate and civilize the
developing sexual impulses and desires but if over emphasized the
result can be to stifle the ability to respond with the freedom and
spontaneity which facilitates sexual expression under appropriate
circumstances.

It is not at all surprising that the sexual problems seen by the gynaecologist often revolve around fear, anxiety, under-confidence and an
inability to behave with the unselfconscious abandonment which is
so much a part of free sexual communion.

Expectation Versus Reality

Although some of today's young women have grown up with more
favourable influences and have developed more outgoing attitudes to
sexuality, they have also come to expect of themselves more exacting
standards in sexual performance. These expectations are encouraged
by idealized pictures of sexuality sometimes suggested in the popular
press and in the more serious sex literature and by implication in
social conversation. A woman may set her standards of sexual performance at a level which is not realistic for her.

A further difficulty is that some of the traditional standards of

sexual morality have, in the interests of so called freedom, been swept
aside without being replaced by identifiable new standards. A vacuum
may be present in which women are uncertain, bewildered and vulnerable. In wishing to conform to supposed popular norms they can
be in danger of exploitation. For the woman, greater sexual freedom
can imply greater anxiety and insecurity in her sexual role. It can be
a factor in the stress responsible for some of her symptoms.

The Gynaecologist as Educator

An important function of the gynaecologist is to listen with interest
sympathy and emotional detachment. He has also to act as an
educator in putting before the woman the facts of sexuality as they
are currently known while at the same time interpreting them to her.
The concept of normality in sexual function must be judged by different standards for different individuals. Constant ecstasy with
orgasms anytime anywhere with anyone may be the poetic ideal of
the truly liberated woman but such a standard has no relevance for
the average patient. The gynaecologist can help her to a standard of
normality which is in keeping with her own unique biological endow-
ment, background and marital and emotional circumstances. She
should not necessarily feel guilty if she does not experience orgasm
every time or has no interest in fellatio, cunnilingus or anal intercourse.

In his role as an educator the gynaecologist can try to teach each
woman to stop generalizing from the sexual manuals and the "how
to do" books and take an honest look at her sexual desires, her
sexual partner and their relationship (Jorgensen 1973). She has to
work out her own norm and not pitch her expectations for emotional
and sexual happiness at an unrealistic level.

Reproduction

Pregnancy, birth and the early months with the first baby are accompanied by considerable physical, emotional and social changes. The
associated stresses can have far reaching implications for the relationship and psychosexual functioning of the couple. This whole area is a
fertile field for the educative and supportive function of the obstetrician and his team.

Many of the reactions of the couple are characterized by ambivalence. A deepening of emotional attachment accompanies the joy and fulfilment felt with the arrival of the first baby but there is a counterbalancing threat to the relationship from the many stresses to be endured and the adjustments and self-sacrifices to be made in accommodating the demands of the baby. Sensitive handling by all those who take part in the management of all phases of pregnancy and labour can assist the woman and her husband to come to terms with their experiences and their emotional reactions to them.

Antenatal Education

Education of the patient and her husband should be a feature of all contacts between staff and the patient during pregnancy and labour but this effort can be intensified and amplified when a programme of antenatal classes becomes a recognized part of patient care. Ideally these classes take the form of group discussions which range over considerable areas of emotional and physical functioning. They include pregnancy, labour, delivery, the puerperium, sexual function and parenting. The possible disasters such as malformations and stillbirth, obstetric operations, episiotomies and tears of the perineum are also covered. These discussions need to be led by an antenatal educator well versed in the practical physical aspects of obstetrics as well as the psychology of it so that patients can develop a realistic picture of the experiences which lie ahead. An accepting attitude is built up through an understanding of the wide spectrum of possible forms these experiences may take.

Pregnant women in the community can become over conscious of being different from other women and can resent their physical changes as unattractive and grotesque. In the group setting they are reassured by seeing other women in a similar state, some at least of whom are very happy with and proud of their pregnant state. They gain from discussion and by sharing anxieties and fears with the other members of the group.

Pregnancy

There are many misconceptions and much ill-founded information. Many couples are concerned for instance that coitus may adversely affect the pregnancy. They are worried that the developing foetus may be harmed or that abortion or premature labour may be induced, especially by orgasm. In the absence of clear evidence that miscarriage can be so induced it seems reasonable to be reassuring and to advise couples to follow their inclinations. Restrictive advice may not be heeded and as the spontaneous abortion rate is around 20%, many couples could have unnecessary guilt and anxiety from attributing a chance abortion to coital indulgence a few hours or a few days beforehand. Although one emphasizes that there is no real supportive evidence, it seems reasonable to advise those with a history of abortion or with significant bleeding in the current pregnancy to avoid coitus during the first 16 weeks if only for their own peace of mind should a further abortion occur. Advice to avoid coitus and particularly orgasm in late pregnancy when there is a history of premature labour is probably more firmly based. Uterine contractions which are accentuated at orgasm may continue and lead into labour. If at either of these times coitus is avoided, other expressions of affection and love making not leading to orgasm are in order. Discussion of the pelvic anatomy and of the protective pressure equalizing influence of the liquor reassures that the foetus cannot be harmed by coitus.

Libido may be increased or decreased during pregnancy with wide variations in patterns of change between individuals. Reduction of libido may be a reflection of anxiety. A woman may have gained the impression that professional advisers are against coitus in pregnancy or she may consider sex dirty and therefore harmful to the pregnancy. Occasional couples have come to believe that once the pregnancy is established, feelings of mutual love and affection should be channelled into maternal and paternal preparations rather than dissipated in mutual sexual indulgence. It seems clear, however, that for many couples the free expression of tenderness and love through coitus in pregnancy brings them closer together emotionally. This increases their sense of fulfilment, well being and personal and mutual regard in such a way that they have an increased ability to relate to the foetus and their baby.

Many women experience brief or prolonged phases of relative frigidity during pregnancy. There may be merely a diminution in sexual responsiveness with insufficient lubrication. Defective lubrication may often be partly due to the different hormonal stimulus in pregnancy altering the quality of secretions as seems to occur in some women when they are taking the contraceptive pill. The temporary use of a simple lubricant may be all that is required. The lack of sexual responsiveness may, however, represent the emergence of a relationship problem requiring counselling. Orgasmic capacity or desire may be heightened or diminished. As with similar problems in the non-pregnant, women are encouraged to discuss their desires and feelings with their husbands so that misunderstandings are avoided and mutual solutions found. Coital technique may need reviewing. The male superior position is usually less satisfactory as pregnancy progresses for the breasts are more tender and sensitive and pressure on the enlarging abdomen can be uncomfortable. The couple can be reassured that the liquor redistributes any such pressure so that the baby cannot be harmed. The deeper penetration which occurs in this position can be uncomfortable when the presenting part is low in the pelvis in late pregnancy. The couple is encouraged to experiment with gentler coitus with less deep penetration and with changes such as to the lateral or rear entry positions.

Labour

The emotional impact of labour which can so much influence subsequent psychosexual functioning is partly determined by what the woman expects of labour. The woman who has come to expect an easily managed joyful experience may react with disappointment, anger or resentment and may feel the loss of personal integration and self respect. On the other hand, the same experiences can be accepted without these negative reactions when such a patient has been led to more realistic expectations and to more accepting attitudes. The effects of the labour experience on a woman's future emotional functioning are considerably influenced by the labour situation and by her perception of the attitudes and intentions of the people with whom she is in contact. The effects of what she perceives as a warm, kindly, concerned and supporting ambience are quite different from those of what she perceives as indifference, disapproval, rejection or hostility on the part of attending staff.

Reaction to Obstetric Trauma

Women can have quite grotesque fantasies about the damage and distortion which have resulted from the birth. These are exaggerated when forceps have been used or when haemorrhage and extensive lacerations have occurred. When general anaesthesia has been necessary there is likely to be increased difficulty in coming to terms with the physical implications of the birth. When, however, general or effective regional anaesthesia have not been given when indicated so that the patient has found a procedure unacceptably frightening or painful, the outlook for satisfactory compensation is even worse.

Women need a frank description of any procedure which has been carried out during or after the birth process so that they are not unnecessarily shocked if they decide to look under the dressing on an abdominal wound or to view the perineum with a mirror. They need a chance to ask questions and need reassurance about the efficiency of the repair and involutional processes and advice on resuming coitus.

At the postnatal examination four to six weeks after the birth the woman is given a careful physical examination then is reassured, advised on coitus and contraception and told about pelvic floor strengthening exercises. Granulation tissue may need cauterization and the patient may be given vaginal dilators or advised on manually stretching a scarred area. The considerable initial pain and swelling of the sutured perineum pass after a few days but pain and tenderness during coitus can persist for weeks or several months. It is so important that women are encouraged and given the opportunity to return for further check examinations and possible treatment when symptoms persist. One commonly finds a woman as much as 30 years removed from the birth of her first child who on direct questioning gives a story of dyspareunia and unsatisfactory coitus dating from the birth of this child. Often she has not sought advice or has felt discouraged when she has. In some of these women the physical problem seems to have been aggravated by unresolved body image problems resulting from the birth experience.

Husbands at Delivery

Encouraging the involvement of husbands in the pregnancy and labour processes and in child nurture is a further recognition of the mutual cooperation which is the essential feature of sexual communion and reproduction. The suggestion that has been made that to have a man at his wife's delivery is liable to inhibit their future sensuous relationship seems to reflect a limited view of psychosexuality and the dynamics of the couple. It is uncommon for a woman to find second stage sensations similar to those of sexual stimulation while those who liken the sensations at delivery to orgasm are quite exceptional. The affinity between husband and wife during the second stage and at delivery is an extension of their emotional relationship. When coitus is accepted as mutual communion, the exclusion from a husband's knowledge of a traumatic situation which may deeply affect his wife's sexual response is more likely to result in misunderstanding and a deterioration of the relationship.

Undoubtedly there is plenty of room for good management by the attendants to ensure that the experience is positive rather than traumatic for the couple and to ensure that the man is incorporated and enabled to feel a part of the process. There should be no coercion or obligation and clearly both wife and husband should desire his presence. His role is essentially to be with his wife at the top of the delivery bed sharing with her the experience of the birth and helping by comforting her in minor ways and sharing concern. There seems little doubt that all parties involved — husband, wife and attendants — need preparation for this situation so that relationships and roles are established. Rather than being devisive or interfering with mutual attachment this sharing under reasonable circumstances of a high point in their emotional relationship brings couples closer together emotionally and helps in furthering the subsequent bonding with their child. The occasional instances in which the influence of the husband's presence at delivery seems to be unfavourable for the relationship are better managed by helping the couple to come to terms with the experience and with any other problems they have through discussion rather than by an edict to exclude all husbands.

Usually the possibility of the husband's presence through part or all of the first stage of labour is considered separately from his presence at delivery but similar considerations apply. The influence on the relationship of his presence or absence is determined to no small extent by expectations based on community attitudes and those of friends, relatives and professional advisers and attendants. Both husband and wife need education and support in their roles. They also need support in the informed decision they make about whether or not the husband will come to labour or delivery. Nowadays women more often want their husbands with them in labour. If in this circumstance a husband elects not to come the relationship of the couple can be adversely affected. If the woman finds labour traumatic and thinks her husband is insufficiently concerned and perhaps having a few drinks with friends she can feel bitterly disappointed and harbour resentment against him. The problem is compounded when he seems to have little concept of what she has gone through in having their baby. It is not surprising that coital relationships may subsequently be unsatisfactory or in abeyance.

Post-Delivery Interviews

The importance of making additional efforts to encourage women and often their husbands to ventilate anxieties, anger, uncertainties and disappointments about pregnancy and labour is beginning to be recognized. The aim is to rationalize experiences to date and to minimize the retention of emotions and fears which could interfere with future function. At the same time an outline of any implications for future child bearing or sexual function is given. Every effort is made to cultivate the woman's image of her femininity and to reinforce her feelings of worth and fulfilment. If she has borne a small-for-dates or premature baby she may see this as evidence of her inferiority as a woman until she realizes that the mechanisms producing these problems are beyond her control. Enabling women to come to terms with the past in this way allows them to grow into the future with a minimum of sequelae likely to inhibit emotional expression. For some women or for their husbands experiences have been so traumatic that without this additional help the possibility that coitus may lead to another pregnancy, labour and delivery is quite sufficient to suppress sexual responsiveness.

Some people are more vulnerable to long-term disturbance. It is particularly those whose prepregnancy emotional stability was precarious or those couples with unsatisfactory relationships. They can sometimes be identified and given extra help during and following pregnancy and birth so that they may be encouraged to grow emotionally through these experiences.

The need for the opportunity to work through experiences and reactions is even more pressing when there has been a stillbirth, neonatal death or birth of a deformed baby. Women and their husbands automatically delve into the past for aetiological factors and so often wonder again about the possible part which has been played by not having wanted the child, by having contemplated or attempted to induce abortion or by having had coitus during pregnancy. They need

reassurance on these and other points and warning about the relative
depression and sadness which follow these catastrophies. Follow-up
management can be most helpful.

Abortion

The negative experience of abortion is normally followed by mild to
moderate depression of varying duration and accompanied by reduction in libido and sometimes aversion to coitus. The impact is conditioned to a large extent by the way in which the woman had regarded
her pregnancy. Spontaneous abortion of a wanted pregnancy, particularly when it is not the first abortion, can be associated with a
marked reaction which is exaggerated by the possibility of having
to face in the future another similar disappointment. Provided that
this reaction is anticipated by the woman and particularly by her
husband and that both are able and encouraged to work through the
grieving reaction by a discussion with each other, with friends and
with professional advisors, then a satisfactory resolution can be expected within a few months. If a husband is not aware of this emotional impact he can interpret his wife's disinclination for coitus as
a rejection of him.

When an unwanted pregnancy is terminated legally or illegally, the
emotional consequences tend to be more complex as many factors
are involved. Whereas a spontaneous abortion can be regarded as
unavoidable, the decision to end a pregnancy involves an intellectual
decision by the woman. No matter how pressing the social indications
put forward they tend to be in conflict with the woman's developing
maternal instincts. There is inevitably ambivalence. The more advanced the pregnancy, the greater the potential for emotional conflict,
regret and depressive reaction. There can be feelings of guilt and of
inadequacy and unworthiness in the feminine role.

Many additional factors influence the impact of termination. Of
paramount importance is the woman's life situation and the way she
has felt about the pregnancy. With unmarried women the pregnancy
has often resulted not from a deep desire to have a baby or from a
devious plan to trap her lover into marriage but simply as a result of
having coitus without adequate contraception — a by-product of
coitus.

The inadequacy of contraception practice may have been due to an "it won't happen to me" attitude or "just this once without it will be allright." The contraception method chosen may have failed. Contraception may not have been considered or if so may have been rejected. There may have been laziness, lack of organization or carelessness with contraception or the subtle alterations of intellectual responsibility associated with sexual arousal may have predominated. Most of these considerations apply also to married women.

A woman can feel deeply hurt when the pregnancy is rejected by her lover or when knowledge of the pregnancy leads to an abrupt ending of the relationship. The woman's social situation may be one in which she might quite reasonably conclude that termination will be the best solution for her. She has made an intellectual decision. Even so her future relationships and psychosexual responsiveness may be adversely affected in an unpredictable way by many factors which operate at an emotional or partly subconscious level. These include her social, family and religious background, her general outlook on life and her more specific attitudes to reproduction.

Whether or not a woman seeks termination will be influenced by its availability and by the attitudes to it of family, friends, acquaintances and professional attendants. They also influence the way she will feel about herself subsequently.

Ideally abortion services would be freely available and women with unwanted or possibly unwanted pregnancies would report early. A woman and preferably her husband or consort would be helped to come to a decision about the pregnancy by counselling with one or several professional advisors such as family doctor, gynaecologist, social worker or other assistant and would be referred to a psychiatrist when indicated.

When a decision had been made both would be generously supported in it and would provide support for each other. Unfortunately the situation is often managed in a less than ideal way especially when the abortion is illegal. As a consequence the psychosexual sequelae can be prominent and can sometimes operate for many years.

The crisis surrounding abortion can be used in a positive way for reappraisal of life situations and attitudes. Associated problems such as unsatisfactory sexual functioning or contraception, unsatisfactory interpersonal relationships, or unsatisfactory social situations can be uncovered and an attempt made to resolve them. Counselling, support and the opportunity for the patient to come for follow-up discussions if desired can be the most important influences deciding the ultimate effects of the abortion on emotional maturation and subsequent psychosexual functioning.

The possible psychosexual sequelae of abortion have to be set against those which may have resulted had the particular pregnancy not been aborted. In our complicated present day society the relatively short lived problems which may follow a reasonably well managed abortion can be of little consequence when compared with the great socially and personally triggered problems which can result when an unwanted pregnancy continues. Here again support systems if available can mitigate the problems.

The process of coming to terms with the emotional difficulties stemming from unwanted conception can result in emotional growth and maturation but the risks involved undoubtedly favour avoidance of unwanted pregnancies.

Surgical Procedures

As gynaecological operations involve the organs of sexual expression it is not surprising that there are psychosexual implications. These should be given due prominence in planning surgical procedures, explaining them and their implications for the future to a woman and her husband and in giving appropriate advice and reassurance. It is essential to repeat explanations and advice several times and by follow-up to provide further opportunities, for when in a state of anxiety or distress people often fail to grasp an explanation or it may be forgotten or become distorted or confused with the passage of time or by conflicting information from others. Ill-planned, distorting or prominent scars on the lower abdomen can interfere with a woman's image of her bodily attractiveness so that cosmetic considerations should be given due weight.

Hysterectomy

This common major operation of women is most often performed for benign conditions and has considerable potential for improving the quality of sexual relationships and of the general pattern of life. The woman with menorrhagia is freed of the restrictions, social embarrassment and general discomfort of continual excessive and irregular bleeding and can assume a new vitality. The women with the chronic pain of endometriosis can change from the life of a semi-invalid to full vigour and freedom without the increasing dyspareunia which had for years made coitus all but impossible.

However, because of the central place the uterus has occupied in the woman's image of her femininity, its removal without adequate concomitant psychological care, reassurance and education can on occasions lead to a collapse of effective sexuality. Reactions to the operation vary widely and are influenced by many factors. These include the woman's emotional maturity, her age, marital situation, the quality of her sexual functioning and the quality of her inter-personal relationships, her psychological status, her knowledge of the implications of the operation and not least by the opinions about the operation held by relatives, friends and acquaintances. The way in which the woman has been prepared for the operation and supported through it and the quality of the physical care she receives are further factors with far-reaching implications.

Women need specific reassurance about the effects of the operation and the associated loss of menstrual function — that it does not lead to loss of feminity or to obesity, headache, mental disturbance or the development of male characteristics and features such as growth of hair. It is not the end of sex life. Provided there is not too much vigour until tenderness settles and confidence returns, it can be resumed four to six weeks after operation. The tissues are initially less supple and there may be some pain, slight bleeding and the need for a lubricant but as coitus tends to prevent the vault of the vagina becoming distorted as scar tissue retracts it is better in the long term interest to accept these minor difficulties than to delay coitus longer. As with all operations, follow-up physical examinations add to re-assurance.

Single women tend to experience more emotional difficulties after hysterectomy. Although the need for it may be accepted on the intellectual level, post-operative depression and a sense of loss can be quite prominent. Although such a woman may be approaching 50 years of age and be without any immediate prospect of marriage and without any conscious wish for children, hysterectomy can strike a death blow to a secretly cherished belief that some day she would have a baby. Without adequate explanation and discussion her femininity can be deeply wounded. Particularly if she is still virginal such a woman appreciates an opportunity to discuss her sexuality or potential for future sexuality.

The use of technical jargon in talking to her can inadvertently give a patient a false concept. To speak of "total" hysterectomy rather than just hysterectomy or the removal of the womb conjures up the image of "total" extirpation with nothing remaining — an end to sexual life and the onset of premature senility. In the technical sense "total" is a remnant from the days when it was necessary to make the distinction from the now almost outmoded sub-total hysterectomy in which the cervix was left in the hope that its retention would improve the quality of sexual response.

Oophorectomy

The ovaries are not usually removed at the time of hysterectomy in menstruating women but may be when there is chronic inflammatory disease or endometriosis and will be when there is malignant disease of the uterus or probable malignant disease of the ovaries. Except in some malignancies and unless the patient's condition contra-indicates it, a regular oral dose of oestrogen, once adjusted to needs, eliminates the symptoms which would be associated with the abrupt surgical menopause. With oophorectomy, as with hysterectomy, there is the possibility of a serious disturbance of a woman's feeling of feminine well-being with a consequent loss of confidence in sexuality. As the regular taking of the oestrogen pill serves as a reminder of her loss, the woman needs full explanations and reassurance as well as discussion of the implications of not taking oestrogen tablets.

Operations for Prolapse and Urinary Stress Incontinence

Coital capacity and function after vaginal surgical procedures is considerably influenced by the skill and judgement of the operator who aims to leave satisfactory vaginal length and diameters without tender scar tissue after taking due note of the patient's age, her expectations with regard to coitus and of pre-operation involutional changes and tendencies. If resumption of coitus with the aid of a lubricant is not delayed much beyond six weeks post-operation, contraction of scar tissue is minimized. Both partners need encouragement, explanation and follow-up interviews for anxiety about possible damage particularly when tenderness and slight bleeding persist can undermine confidence.

Procedures to Assist Unsatisfactory Coital Function

The management of non-consumation is essentially behavioural
rather than surgical even when the problem appears to be principally
on the female side. Anxieties and misconceptions need ventilation
and discussion. Permission and encouragement in digital dilatation of
the introitus and exploration of the vagina by the woman herself or
by her partner are an important aspect of the programme for establishing sexual responsiveness. In almost all cases they make a far more
effective contribution to solving this interpersonal problem than .
would surgical incision of the perineum to enlarge the introitus. So
often problems remain after this latter management.

Pain or difficulty on coitus because of developmental defects in
the form of partial or complete vaginal septa may settle after progressive dilatation but as the tissues may be thick and unyielding excision
may be required because of continuing dyspareunia.

Vaginal adhesions and contractures which have followed surgical
procedures usually yield to progressive dilatation and coitus. In post-
menopausal women vaginal instillation of oestrogen cream is required
as a first step to soften the tissues. It is then followed by a maintenance
dose of oral oestrogen. Sometimes minor surgical intervention or
plastic reconstruction is required. Vaginal dilators and digital dilatation may be necessary over a relatively long period particularly when
coitus is infrequent.

When the vagina is congenitably absent, the Williams operation
(Williams, 1964) in which an external vagina is constructed from vulval
tissue is now more favoured than attempts to construct an internal
vagina. This operation is also useful following surgical ablation of the
vagina or its extensive obliteration after radiation therapy for carcinoma. Vaginal stenosis after radiation can be minimized only by
persistant dilatation over a relatively long period.

For dyspareunia due to retroversion of the uterus in association with
endometriosis or adhesions of previous inflammatory disease of the
pelvis, there is a clear indication for surgical intervention. Sometimes
normal ovaries lying deeply in the pelvis as a result of retroversion can
be the cause of collision type dyspareunia which is corrected by
surgical ventrosuspension. The identification of such women with
retroversion for whom ventrosuspension is likely to be helpful requires
close questioning and observation. More often this type of episodic
dyspareunia provoked by deep penetration reflects insufficient
development of the congestion lubrication phase of sexual response.

There is inadequate dilatation of the vagina and inadequate relaxation of its musculature and of the uterine supports. As with superficial dyspareunia associated with insufficient lubrication, management is directed towards improving the quality of sexual communion.

Ovarian agenesis

Where ovarian development has failed the neuter-type female form develops. As such a person is reared as a girl she secures female psycho-social sexual development so that even in the absence of ovarian hormones there is no confusion of sexual identity. The administration of oral oestrogens improves secondary sexual characteristics. Local oestrogens and oestrogen tablets are essential for improving the thickness and suppleness of the vaginal walls so that coitus is not traumatic. Oestrogen also facilitates the congestion lubrication response to sexual arousal. The addition of a progestogen enables cycling of vaginal bleeding. These regular "periods" are reassuring as they reenforce a feeling of being feminine. Although not capable of reproduction, these girls can marry and have happy secure relationships.

Lower Abdominal and Pelvic Pain

A woman's complaint of pain may be due to an organic disorder in the pelvis or to a dysfunction of bowel or ovary. It may, however, reflect a sexual problem. The complaint is not uncommon in late adolescence and during the engagement period when there may be considerable sexual stimulation without adequate emotional release. There may be no identifiable relationship to stimulation or it may follow coitus. The symptom may represent a vague or poorly formulated dissatisfaction with genital function — as the sex organs are "down there," the dissatisfaction is experienced as lower abdominal or pelvic discomfort of a rather vague type. The gynaecologist should not conclude that he has failed when he is not able to explain such pain in organic terms. Help with a problem found by a general review of the woman's sexual function may well be followed by resolution of the symptoms.

Vaginal discharge, Vulval Odour

Lack of understanding of normal physiology may, particularly during
adolescence, be the principal basis of these complaints. An increase in
the amount of vaginal discharge may be due to infection but may be
associated with increasing sexual stimulation. A complaint of discharge or odour which persists without apparent cause and which is
not convincingly evident on examination may well, like lower abdominal pain, reflect a psychosexual problem.

Disorders of Menstruation

The relationship between problems in psychosexual functioning and
disorders of menstruation — amenorrhoea, oligomenorrhoea, menor-
thagia, irregular vaginal bleeding and dysmenorrhoea — is difficult to
define and quantify in individual cases. There is good theoretical and
considerable anecdotal evidence of association. Undoubtedly psychosexual problems can be identified in many women with these complaints but it is unwise to be too ready to conclude a cause and effect
relationship. Relevant organic disorders are identified and treated as a
first move. In other women, although symptoms may not disappear
during the course of or as a result of help with psychosexual problems,
these women are sometimes enabled to come to terms with and
improve their tolerance of symptoms. The improvement in psychosexual functioning which can result from appropriate management
fully justifies attempts to identify psychosexual problems in patients
with these symptoms. Sometimes a patient who has adjusted to a
psychosexual problem or who has no desire for change is better left
with it. To consider treating a problem identified in a patient has
quite different implications from treating a problem with which the
woman presents.

The Menopause and Climacteric

In correct usage the term menopause applies only to cessation of
menstruation and the climacteric is the period which precedes and
follows it but the term menopause is often synonymous with climac-

teric in common usage. Many women pass through this phase with little disturbance but for many others it is a time of crisis and turmoil. There are complaints of hot flushing, sweats, loss of libido, irritability, lethargy, depression, headaches, vaginal discharge, vulval itching and soreness, dyspareunia, frequency and dysuria, all of which may place a considerable strain on emotional and sexual relationships.

How much these symptoms are due to withdrawal of oestrogen and how much due to complex emotional and social factors is uncertain. Some respond to oestrogen replacement therapy. All the self doubts and anxieties about attractiveness, sexuality, femininity and marriage stability which come up at this time have insidious psychosexual repercussions. Provided confidence is maintained, and oestrogen supplements are given when indicated, sexual function can continue and is often enriched through this phase of life. The trend towards using oestrogens as prophylaxis in the absence of the above mentioned symptoms to reduce the rate of involution of the genital tract and of secondary sexual characteristics and to maintain a more youthful appearance is growing. Only careful follow-up and controlled studies will establish whether or not this approach to management will prove of sufficient value for more universal application.

Conclusions

It is indeed a reflection of our society that love-making which is the central emotional and physical expression of the love relationship which binds couples together has been, until recently, so little studied and understood by professionals and by people in general. It is small wonder that doctors specializing in reproduction and the female genital tract can so often encounter problems in psychosexual functioning. There is increasing scope for therapy and almost unlimited opportunities for prophylactic measures. Undoubtedly the attention given to these psychosexual aspects of the work of the gynaecologist, as an individual or member of a team, will increase considerably in future practice.

References

Bandry, F. and Wiener, A. (1974). *American Journal of Obstetrics and Gynecology*, 119, 705–711.

Gusberg, S. (1973). *Obstetrics and Gynecology*, **42**, 136.

Hebb, B. (1974). *Proceedings of the Royal Society of Medicine*, **67**, 773–776.

Jorgensen, V. (1973). *Obstetrics and Gynecology*, **42**, 607–610.

Kaplan, H. S. (1974). "The New Sex Therapy." Bailliere Tindall: London.

Masters, W. H. and Johnson, V. E. (1966). "Human Sexual Response." Little, Brown and Co: Boston, Mass. USA.

Masters, W. H. and Johnson, V. E. (1970). "Human Sexual Inadequacy." Churchill: Edinburgh.

Williams, E. A. (1964). *Journal of Obstetrics and Gynaecology of the British Commonwealth*, **71**, 511–512.

15 Sexual Problems in Urology

JOHN BLANDY

His aptitude and training makes the urologist despise anything savour-
ing of non-organic disease, and he is usually as ignorant as he is afraid
of anything to do with psychiatry. Yet many common disorders bring
him patients whose problem is in the mind, or whose treatment has
important psychological overtones. Many of his investigations involve
manipulation of the genitalia. Many of the symptoms which concern
his patients arise from the sexual taboos of religion: others arise from
misunderstanding about ordinary physiological processes or the range
of normal anatomical variation. Serious difficulties stem from infertility, or from its investigation. Others concern pathological processes,
or the operations which are done to attempt to correct them.

Sexual Taboos

Since both surgeon and patient are caught up in a certain socio-
religious context, neither can escape his heritage of prevailing taboos.
Of these, the universal preoccupation of man with his foreskin brings
a steady quota of patients to the urological clinic.

Circumcision

Circumcision dates from the stone age where it originated along with

other ritual mutilations, many of which survive. To judge by contemporary aboriginal Australians, circumcision was only the first of
a progressive series of ritual mutilations which culminated in sub-
incision of the urethra back to the scrotum, and removal of the foreskin was only the first feature of the ceremony of initiation at
puberty. In most cultures circumcision remains a puberty rite, and is
purposely painful, so that the boy's brave disregard of the pain can
earn him admission to the secrets and mysteries of manhood. In some
tribes scarification, amputation of digits, tattooing, the removal of
incisor teeth, and infibulation are added to or substituted for circumcision. An interesting anomaly in many of these initiation rites is
their transposition to infancy with the settling and progressive urban-
ization of the tribe. So circumcision, which in Biblical times was an
initiation ceremony at puberty, as it had been in Moses' Egypt,
developed into a neonatal ceremony: so too the Nuer of the Sudan
were obliged to extract the unerupted incisor tooth buds from the
infant mandible: and in more recent times, the custom of infant
baptism (Ghalioungui, 1963: Remondino, 1891).

One disturbing feature common to many of these ceremonies is that
the tribesmen have forgotten their original meaning, and will explain
the ceremony on grounds either of health or beauty: e.g. circumcized
women are cleaner, circumcized men less prone to syphilis, boys look
so ugly with those great front teeth, and so on. Even today in the
West the statistics of the incidence of penile cancer in Africa are
strained to justify infant circumcision in Europe (Blandy, 1976a).

There are certain limited surgical indications for circumcision. The
natural cleavage plane between prepuce and glans is not developed
until the age of 18 months or 2 years (Gairdner, 1949), and the un-
reduced prepuce probably serves a useful role in protecting the glans
from ammoniacal dermatitis and meatal ulceration. Later on however,
if the prepuce cannot be drawn back, the glans cannot be washed,
and smegma accumulates which in time leads to bacterial balanitis,
and ultimately, in a very small proportion, to carcinoma. So in societies where soap and water are in short supply, circumcision is an alternative prophylaxis. In the West, where both are available, circumcision
should be performed if the prepuce still cannot be retracted by the
age of 3 years or so — an age at which only a small number of operations are needed, and the procedure is much more safe for the child
than when performed in infancy. The common demand for neonatal
circumcision in some countries of the West reflects a most interesting
survival of a Stone Age practice.

Taboo Against Playing with the Penis

Even today many men are brought up to regard handling the penis as
wicked and sinful, and it is not only the Irish who share this super-
stition which was once adduced as evidence of original Sin. It is still a
commonplace to encounter middle-aged men made miserable by
recurrent balanitis because they have never been taught to keep their
penises clean, and their evident shame at having to mention such a
distasteful subject to their doctor speaks volumes for the efficacy of
the indoctrination of pulpit and confessional, though the taboo must
surely antedate any of our contemporary religions by millenia.

Masturbation

The etymology of the word, signifying "defile with the hand", still
echoes in school and seminary where, in the past, discovery might
lead to drastic punishment. Even today grown men come to the
urological surgeon with symptoms attributed to this innocuous
physiological activity, conscious of the risks of blindness, testicular
atrophy, weakness and epilepsy about which they were warned as
boys.

Wet Dreams

In the Orient the same taboo is extended to include nocturnal emissions, which are no less unhealthy, wicked, and weakening. It took a
few years before the Separated Pakistani Syndrome (SPS) was widely
recognized in English Casualty departments. Typically the patient is
separated from his wife, who has remained at home until he can earn
the money for her fare. Denied licit sexual outlet he has nocturnal
emissions, and knowing their serious consequences, he turns to his
doctor complaining of pain in the abdomen, head, back, front, arms,
legs, and private parts, together with overwhelming weakness. Failure
to recognize the aetiology of this condition may betray the doctor
into ordering a succession of investigations one or more of which will
inevitably (by chance) turn out to deviate from the norm, and so
appear to justify some form of treatment. The mere fact that treatment has been prescribed confirms the patient's own diagnosis of the

aetiology and of the seriousness of his plight. Since the cause continues, the symptoms do not improve.

Coitus in Menses

Several religions forbid coitus during the menses reflecting ancient taboos against contamination with menstrual blood, which in many societies led to the seclusion and punishment of women for their recurring anti-social activity. Since lovemaking is apt to continue conflict arises, and the worried male may bring his penis to the surgeon with all those symptoms which are likely to follow contact with such a dangerous effluent. Again, the unwary though careful surgeon may commence a series of investigations which will inevitably, if pursued with sufficient diligence, disclose some minor disorder.

Misunderstood Physiology and Anatomy

Prostatic Congestion and Semen Overflow

Most men who notice a little glairy fluid at the end of the penis after passing a constipated bowel action will think no more of it: but to the unfortunate who has experienced gonorrhoea in the past, or who has a guilty conscience, this may signify late relapse, or the beginning of some dreadful complication.

Even without any such memories to trouble them, many middle-aged men notice discomfort in the perineum, which may be referred to the penis, and cause some slight discomfort on urination. A common underlying feature is a sedentary occupation, and rather infrequent coitus. Rectal examination may disclose a slight bogginess of the prostate gland, whose gentle massage causes a flow of prostatic fluid from the meatus. Leukocytes in this fluid may easily be taken to signify infection, as may the culture of those innocent commensal organisms which contaminate the fluid as it traverses the anterior urethra. If these features — a few pus cells and some innocent organisms are taken to signify infection, then the unfortunate patient is assigned the diagnostic label *prostatitis* (Oates, 1976). If in turn the patient is particularly anxious and introspective, and displays his discomfort in terms of excessive pain, he may be led to demand treatment.

Traditionally the treatment for such prostatitis is forcible massage of the gland to express the evil fluid which has accumulated there. Nowadays no other inflammatory lesion in the body is treated by being squeezed, since this contradicts every known precept of pathology, and the persistence of this form of treatment raises interesting questions about the nature of the relationship which has grown up between the patient and his surgeon. It would be wrong to give the impression that there is no such entity as prostatitis: acute infection does occur in this gland, as it may in any other part of the body, but when it does, it gives rise to heat, swelling, and tenderness in the gland, and to elevation of temperature and malaise in the rest of the patient. Pathogenic organisms can be recovered from the urethra or the urine, and the condition either responds to chemotherapy, or, like other inflammations, forms an abscess which either bursts or has to be drained. But unlike the patient described above, none of these patients with acute prostatitis go on to develop the features of "chronic prostatitis".

An even more serious pitfall attends the surgeon who is cajoled by his patient into carrying out a radical removal of the offending organ. This always makes the patient worse, and the unhappy surgeon now discovers that the patient has manipulated him into performing an operation whose sequelae in terms of a painful scar, incontinence, impotence or stricture, provide him with endless and sometimes justifiable grounds for complaint.

Nux Amatoris

A young man is often seen in the casualty department in the midnight hours with pain in the groin and testicle which has come on after an evening of unrelieved sexual stimulation. There are no specific signs but the casualty officer will admit him on the suspicion of appendicitis, and the registrar on duty will remove the appendix, being justifiably wary of missing a gangrenous appendix in a fit young man — a notorious surgical pitfall. If diagnosed, the condition is relieved by recumbency, a warm bath, and ejaculation.

Normal Anatomy Discovered

The introspective spotty adolescent makes many discoveries about his marvellous physiology and his rapidly changing anatomy. Often he

becomes worried by the pearly penile papules which sometimes frill
the edge of the corona glandis, and become prominent in erection to
the alarm of the young man fascinated by the astonishing performance
of his penis. Others notice a varicocele, hydrocele, or the presence of
the normal epididymis behind the testis. Many of these young men
need but reassurance to go away happy: but the odd one does not.
He knows there is something wrong, if not here, then somewhere else,
and will draw your attention to the normal valleculae on the back of
his tongue, or the follicles on his scrotum. A common symptom is
that he smells, and his friends are talking about him. Any chance
remark which savours of ideas of persecution or reference should
caution the surgeon to refer the patient to an expert in this field, and
the worst thing he can do is to commence a series of investigations,
for these will at once confirm the patient's conviction that he does
indeed stink.

Sexual Dysfunction

Lack of Libido

Patients who suffer from a true hormonal deficiency seldom complain of a want of libido, perhaps because they do not know what
they are missing. Hormonal disorders may be detected by other stig-
mata of endocrine imbalance e.g. Klinefelter's syndrome, and one
may confirm them by measurement of FSH, LH, and prolactin in
serum and urine (Blandy, 1976b). Such cases are the exception. So
too are patients who are taking stilboestrol for cancer of the prostate,
or drugs for their hypertension, which depress their libido. Most men
with this complaint have a psychosomatic basis for it.

In many the disorder is one of misplaced rather than missing desire:
the secret homosexual may be active in his club though impotent at
home. The executive may lust for his secretary, but not his obese and
bossy wife. The unfortunate young man may discover that he has
married a substitute for his mother.

In several men the disorder is but one feature of depression. Surgeons ought to be better at recognizing depression than they are: it
masquerades as prostatism and may present with impotence.

Curiously, the most common form of impotence to present to the
surgeon as a symptom is "barrister's impotence", though barristers

are by no means the only thrusting young men to whom success in their profession comes before their marital obligations. Fatigue and inattention is common in all walks of life where the husband works too hard, takes work home, and retires to bed to sleep. The diagnostic investigation and the remedy are simple. A holiday away from the telephone and the children will restore libido and performance. But the aetiology is more complex: the man who is killing himself with overwork is often enjoying the martyrdom — but it is difficult to know why. The doctor is often the last person to offer useful advice.

Disordered Erection

Organic deficiency of erection is not common. Any condition which interrupts the blood or nerve supply to the penis will disturb erection. It is a complication of fractures of the pelvis, which involve both nerves and blood vessels, and of thrombosis of the bifurcation of the aorta in Lériche's syndrome. Since erection begins with stimulation of the pelvic parasympathetic nerves, it is prevented by radical removal of the tissues on the lateral wall of the pelvis for carcinoma of the rectum, bladder or prostate, and the same nerves may be affected by amyloid, or the peripheral neuropathies, of which perhaps diabetes is the most tragic, since it affects otherwise fit young men.

Several drugs act so as to block the parasympathetic nerves, and interfere with erection. Many of these are used in treatment of hypertension, but several, including lithium are employed in depression.

A bent erection is a common and legitimate complaint and may be accompanied by pain (Blandy, 1976a). It is due to the development of hard white plaques of fibrous tissue in and around the corpora cavernosa and spongiosum. These prevent the blood from filling the spongy tissue of the corpora, and so the penis is bizarrely twisted or bent. The most common symptoms are caused by the anxiety which the patient feels upon noticing his deformity or the lump of fibrous tissue in the flaccid penis. But in some the problem is one of pain, either from the erect organ, or during intercourse when it may be so bent as to fail to enter the vagina. Nothing is known of the aetiology of this condition, indeed, little more is known now than when it was first described by Peyronie, court physician to Louis XIV, in 1743.

A rare but serious emergency follows the failure of an erection to subside. Priapism is a painful and distressing condition. It occurs out of the blue in connection with the sickle cell trait, in treatment with heparin, and in leukaemia. It may follow coitus, and is usually attributed to excessive lovemaking by its reporters who generally do not define the limits of normality in this regard. The pathology is still uncertain: there is no clotting of blood, and the erection only involves the corpora cavernosa, never the glans penis or corpus spongiosum. Left alone, the erection is painful and protracted over about a week, and then slowly subsides, leaving a flaccid organ which never erects again. If a by-pass operation is performed as an emergency, and the blood shunted into the corpus spongiosum or the saphenous vein of the thigh, the erection is allowed to subside, and the patient is given his only chance of a return to normal potency.

Unwanted erections disturbing sleep are rare but real, and in my experience I have never found a convincing cause for them. It may be necessary to provide the patient with a small dose of stilboestrol to control an otherwise distressing and unwelcome symptom.

Disordered Ejaculation

Ejaculatio praecox occurs in domestic animals and in those in the zoo, and is probably purely physiological. Those who complain of it have two symptoms: the ejaculation may shame them by taking place before penetration — a common symptom in the very young and virile. Or they may complain that they cannot defer ejaculation long enough to provide their wives with an orgasm.

In the first instance all that is necessary is a explanation of the physiology concerned, and reassurance, combined with some flattering suggestion that not all men are so highly sexed, and not all have such a hair-trigger mechanism, will often alleviate the patient's fear. The remedy is to repeat the exercise a little later, when the mechanism is not so delicately primed.

In the second situation the problem is more complex, since it reflects not so much a disturbance of physiology as an interesting aberration of social mores. Most of these patients are kindly intelligent young men who have gone to some trouble to study the available handbooks on lovemaking, from which they have gleaned the misleading information that persistence and friction will in time be rewarded with an orgasm on the part of their wife. Few of these handbooks describe the proper role of the clitoris and the attention owed to it, and few couples find the penis an adequate means of stimulating it. To some extent this is a symptom of the West, where women are conditioned to expect orgasm unlike their Oriental sisters, or their simian cousins.

Inhibited ejaculation may be caused by many factors. The creaking bed, the thin partition, or the toddler wandering about in search of a glass of water, are all powerful inhibitors of orgasm as most couples will testify from their experience. Pain may be an equally inhibitory experience: and there are a number of minor anomalies of the penis which may become very painful at the critical moment. A prepuce which retracts easily in the flaccid state may become painfully stretched over the erect one. A tight fraenum may rupture. In either event the surgical remedy is simple, and the tragedy is that so many young men have had to have their first experience of making love inhibited and frustrated by these minor, but painful lesions.

Retrograde ejaculation may occur if the internal sphincter fails to contract during orgasm. The internal sphincter is stimulated through the sympathetic nerves, which may be injured during operations to replace an aneurysm of the aorta, or the excision of pelvic cancer, or they may be blocked by drugs given for hypertension. Dissection of the retroperitoneal nodes for cancer of the testis may interrupt the sympathetic chain higher up in the abdominal posterior wall, and deliberate sympathectomy for arterial disease may also be followed by impaired ejaculation. In some of these patients in addition to failure of contraction of the neck of the bladder there is failure of contraction of the seminal vesicles and vasa deferentia in which are stored the semen. In a few cases the retrograde ejaculation follows the surgical removal of a bladder neck which was preventing the urine from leaving the bladder, either in congenital bladder neck obstruction or in the course of prostatectomy (Blandy, 1976b).

Blood sometimes appears in the ejaculate and gives rise to much concern. It is very seldom of any significance and in the only cases where I have found any pathological process associated with this symptom, it could very well have been by coincidence.

Sexual Connotation of Common Urological Disorders

Stricture

In Africa today urethral stricture is one of the most common and important surgical diseases, accounting with its complications for

more surgical admissions than any other single pathology. Even in
the West where gonorrhoea is less rife and more promptly and effectively treated, it is still a common urological condition. It seldom
gives rise to impotence, though an old woody stricture of long standing may cause contracture and chordee from shortening of the corpus
spongiosum. Hold-up of the ejaculate behind a stricture may give rise
to discomfort and to infertility.

Urethritis

Gonorrhoea usually causes a profuse and characteristic yellow discharge with burning discomfort on voiding as the urine passes down
the acutely inflamed urethra. In some 10 to 15% of cases the gonorrhoea is symptomless. In an equal number of cases a urethral discharge
is caused by some other organism, perhaps belonging to the *Chlamydia*
group, perhaps related to *Trichomonas vaginalis,* and perhaps without
any identifiable pathogenic cause. Treatment of non-gonococcal
urethritis is often somewhat empirical and relapse is frequent. The
important thing in the management of these patients is that they
should be seen and treated by a specialist venereologist from the
start, since the penalty for missing associated syphilis or for not effectively tracing the appropriate contact may be very dangerous. The
urologist is more often pestered by patients who in the past may have
had gonorrhoea or non-specific urethritis, and have been properly
treated and cured, but who remain with the symptoms of "Chronic
prostatitis", and will accept no reassurance. The aftermath of treated
gonorrhoea or non-gonococcal urethritis has no effect on sexual performance, but its effects on the patient's feelings of guilt and self
criticism are often very important. One has to be continually on guard
against submitting these patients to too many investigations, and in
particular, to refrain from applying the label prostatitis to them without good evidence (Oates, 1976).

Benign Enlargement of the Prostate

No male can escape the changes which take place in his prostate gland
as he gets older. In youth, the prostate surrounds the urethra like a
doughnut, and is made up of numbers of tube-like glands whose
secretion contributes a small proportion — perhaps as much as 0.5 ml —

to the ejaculate. Each tube is surrounded with a muscular sleeve which is believed to expel the contents during ejaculation. In the mid-forties age changes can be detected in the prostate gland consisting of small knobs of white tissue formed by whorls of fibrous and smooth muscle fibres with a certain degree of hypertrophy of the glandular acini. Gradually enlarging and coalescing, these nodules cause the gland to swell, pushing up the base of the bladder, and pinching the urethra from side to side. In nine cases out of ten the distortion of the prostate causes no bother, but in the tenth, it leads to obstruction to the outflow of urine from the bladder. As time goes by the bladder compensates for the increased outflow resistance by an increase in the thickness and coarseness of the muscle of its wall. Eventually this hypertrophy no longer compensates for the increased resistance and the urine is no longer completely expelled. The patient notices a diminished force in his urinary stream, and the presence of a small quantity of unemptied urine makes him constantly want to void. If things are allowed to continue unchecked he may eventually reach a state where the bladder wall becomes atonic and inert, and back pressure begins to damage the kidneys. None of these changes has any effect upon the patient's sexual desires or performance — until the very last stages when renal failure is making the patient very ill, and I can find no support for the popular belief that the enlarging prostate makes the old man behave like a satyr. Once only in some three thousand patients has this suggestion been raised, in an unfortunate man whose poor stream and excessive frequency made him repeatedly go in and out of a public lavatory where he was arrested for loitering with intent to commit an immoral offence (Chapter 10).

One of the major concerns of the urologist is to make sure that he does not mistake symptoms caused by enlargement of the prostate from those due to depression. Many an elderly widower wakes at 3 a.m. with nobody to share his grief with, and has nothing better to do than pass his water and perhaps make himself a cup of tea. Since at this age his prostate will be enlarged anyway, it is all too easy to label him as suffering from enlargement of the prostate, and to put him down for an operation.

The size of the prostate gland on rectal examination is remarkably difficult to judge, even with experience, and even when the patient is fully anaesthetized, and in any event it has nothing whatever to do with the existence of outflow obstruction or not, since the worst obstructions may occur with the smallest glands and vice versa. If the operation is only performed for the presence of radiological evidence

of outflow obstruction (and this should now be routine practice)
then this error will not occur.

With modern techniques of prostatectomy the patient's sexual
activity should not be disturbed provided that it was in order beforehand. Removing the bladder neck, which is usually part of the operation means that ejaculated semen may run back into the bladder, but
this is only of importance to the patient who secretly fears that
retention of the taboo fluid semen will do him harm. It is as well to
discuss this aspect of the procedure with every patient put down for
prostatectomy since to many men it is feared as bringing the end of
love-making.

Undescended Testicle

Although it is likely that there is a slightly greater incidence of
infertility among men with a single undescended testicle, the difference is not great, and there is no reason why these men should not
lead a perfectly normal life. A few are deeply concerned about the
condition, and need reassurance, and in such patients it is usual to
learn that they have had endless courses of injections in childhood in
order to attempt to bring down the testis. There is no evidence that
injections of gonadotrophins ever bring down an undescended testis
which is not a "low retractile" gonad and therefore going to settle
of its own accord in the scrotum. For other children with high retractile or ectopic testicles orchidopexy should be carried out around the
age of six without further ado (Whitaker, 1975). The operation should
never be delayed until puberty when it raises all kinds of doubts in the
child's mind as to his true gender and sexuality.

Orchidectomy

Often it is necessary to remove a testicle for tumour or inflammation,
or because it is lodged so high in the groin that it cannot be brought
down to the scrotum, and runs a risk of subsequent malignancy if not
removed. Most healthy young men are satisfied with the explanation
that a man is not blind with one eye, and in Britain at any rate it is
not usual to offer the patient a false testicle made of silastic. The
patient who insists upon such a prosthesis usually has serious under-

lying psychological problems, and will be unsatisfied with the feel of the plastic gonad. A few men are concerned about the effect of uni- lateral orchidectomy upon their manhood, and need tactful reassur- ance that all will be well. Even in those rare and unfortunate cases where the testis has to be removed for malignancy, and the patient is irradiated afterwards, intercourse, potency and ejaculation remain unimpaired, as indeed does fertility, provided the contralateral testicle is protected throughout treatment (which is the usual practice).

Removal of both testicles after puberty seldom makes any differ- ence to the patient's appetite or enjoyment of intercourse. Such an operation is seldom necessary except in the course of treatment of carcinoma of the prostate with advanced and widespread metastases when in any event the patient has often undergone treatment with stilboestrol. For the exceptional patient with carcinoma of the pros- tate who is still sexually active most urologists will now attempt to treat the growth with radiotherapy and put off, as long as possible, the administration of stilboestrol. Orchidectomy is for these men less likely to give rise to impotence than hormones.

Operations for Bladder Cancer

It is necessary to remove the bladder and urethra in some patients in whom radiotherapy has failed to control a bladder tumour, or where the growths are so widespread and so numerous that radiotherapy is known to be ineffective. The operation necessarily removes the nerves and vessels upon which potency depend, and the patient is rendered unable to achieve erection or ejaculation.

In addition to this severe penalty, the method of urinary diversion advised nowadays is usually by way of an ileal conduit, which means that the patient must wear a bag on his abdominal wall in which the urine is collected. When urinary diversion is performed for non- malignant conditions, it seems curiously seldom to pose a serious threat to the married life of the young patient. Many girls live happily married lives in spite of their abdominal stomas, though at the outset they will need considerable help, and in the first year after they begin their new life with a urinary diversion it is of considerable help for them to have the support and comradeship of others in the same boat, so that they should always be put into touch with the local ileostomy club.

Infertility

A recurring cause of mutual recrimination and sadness is the sad
theme "dayspring mishandled cometh not again" — so common today
when couples postpone the decision to try to start a family until it is
too late. Often the only available target for pent-up hostility is the
doctor in the infertility clinic. The stresses engendered in such a clinic
are quite severe and have a considerable effect upon the staff as well
as the patients, particularly when artificial insemination is embarked
upon: almost no other procedure is so fraught with recurrent disappointment. It is important before embarking upon any attempt to
use AIH that the odds are fully explained — that each couple knows
that it takes (on average) 10 inseminations — i.e. a year of trying —
before success is achieved (Usherwood *et al*, 1975).

Problems also arise from the unwillingness of some doctors to tell
the truth, or to make a decision, though it is usually the most important part of the work of the clinic to arrive at a diagnosis, and tell the
couple if all is hopeless, as soon as possible. Surgeons who do not
shrink from telling a patient that he is to die from his metastases,
often draw back from telling a man he cannot become a father. To
many patients, particularly those from Arab countries, such a diagnosis is absolutely unacceptable, and even in Europe it is the rule to
find couples making the rounds from one infertility clinic to another.

Vasectomy

Volumes have been written about the psychological aspects of vasectomy though there is only a small corpus of knowledge to act as a
guide. There is little doubt that a bungled or complicated operation
which is followed by pain and prolonged sickness gives rise to a
severe psychological aftermath. In the study of Wig and Singh (1972)
where up to a third of the operations were followed by local sepsis
or haematoma, there was a high rate of psychological sequelae. In the
first thousand vasectomies studied at the Margaret Pyke Centre only
5 in the 271 who answered the questionary wished they had not had
the operation done, and these had all had surgical complications, or
had had to wait an inordinate time before being told that the operation was successful (Barnes *et al.*, 1973). This rather low rate of
psychological complications may have reflected the special care which
was taken in the preliminary counselling of these patients, for it is

now generally realized that vasectomy leads to disaster if used in the attempt to float a sinking marriage, or to punish an erring husband.

One interesting feature has emerged from the follow up of these cases. Occasionally one finds an intelligent and well motivated man who suddenly declares himself to be impotent some months after the operation, just when he is told that his semen has been cleared of all sperm. This seems to be related to the element of risk-taking which appears to be an important factor in some relationships. The same reaction is described after tubal ligation.

Dialysis and Transplantation

One might not expect to find an important field for concern over sexual relationships among those who are condemned to death from renal failure, and temporarily reprieved by dialysis or transplantation, and yet it is among these usually young and always brave people that impotence and infertility pose some of the most important difficulties. As things stand today, the survival rate of patients on intermittent dialysis, whether at home or in a hospital unit, is better than the survival after transplantation — in terms of head-counting. Many of these men and women are able to lead active useful and happy lives at the cost of twice or thrice-weekly dialysis. But they are usually impotent and generally infertile. In many centres transplantation is offered as a rule only to those patients who cannot get on with dialysis, or who are developing serious complications involving the joints or cardiovascular system. But one important benefit of a successful transplant is that the patient returns to an active and satisfying sexual life. Knowledge of this makes the dilemma of the doctor who must choose when to offer a transplant to his patient even more difficult.

The Urologist's Role

In dealing with the problems of sexual difficulty which come to his clinic, the urological surgeon has but a small role to play. Largely his work consists of *not* doing anything: a hard part for a surgeon to play. He must refrain from offering useless hormone pills to men who think themselves impotent: he must refrain from diagnosing prostatitis for the patient whose anxiety has been centred upon his perineum: he must be sure he does not carry out vasectomy without the most careful preliminary counselling (a role he does well to delegate to someone trained in the art). Much can be done by recognizing common but trivial anomalies, and by offering firm reassurance. Referral to a psychiatrist, if necessary, should be clear and unambiguous. Only if it is done in this way is the patient likely to carry through the referral and to retain his motivation for treatment. And when the surgeon must remove the testicles or the genitalia for cancer, it is no less important that he should concern himself as much with the patient's fears and imaginings, as with his soft tissues.

References

Barnes, M. N. *et al.* (1973). One thousand vasectomies. *British Medical Journal*, 4, 216–221.

Blandy, J. P. (1976a). Penis and scrotum. *In* "Urology." (Blandy, J. P. ed.), Ch. 40. Blackwell Scientific Publications: Oxford.

Blandy, J. P. (1976b). Infertility and impotence. *In* "Scientific Foundations of Urology." (Innes Williams, D. and Chisholm, G. C. Eds), Heinemann Medical Books: London.

Gairdner, D. (1949). The fate of the foreskin. *British Medical Journal*, 2, 1433–1437.

Ghalioungui, P. (1963). "Magic and Medical Science in Ancient Egypt." Hodder and Stoughton: London.

Oates, J. K. (1976). Prostatitis. *In* "Urology." (Blandy, J. P. Ed.), Ch. 34. Blackwell Scientific Publications: Oxford.

Remondino, P. C. (1891). "History of Circumcision." Davis: Philadelphia and London.

Usherwood, M. and Halim, A. (1975). Artificial insemination. (in press).

Whitaker, R. H. (1975). Orchidopexy and orchidectomy. *British Journal of Hospital Medicine*, 14, 282–294.

Wig, N. N. and Singh, S. (1972). Psychosomatic symptoms following male sterilisation. *Indian Journal of Medical Research*, 60, 1386–1392.

16 | *Sexual Problems Related to Contraception and Family Planning*

S. J. STEELE

Introduction

The professional working in family planning or involved with the investigation and treatment of infertility will be asked about sexual problems. Men and women sometimes come to such clinics hoping that they will receive help over a sexual problem or that they can be reassured about something which they fear is abnormal. Sexual problems may be severe enough to prevent satisfactory intercourse and therefore cause infertility, while they may also be vitally important in the choice and acceptability of a contraceptive method. The fear of pregnancy can be very strong and may in itself lead to a wide variety of difficulties, while bad advice and injudicious investigation or treatment by the doctor sometimes create problems for the patient or couple concerned when they did not exist before.

The patients who go to obtain advice about contraception or infertility generally anticipate that they will meet doctors and nurses with special knowledge in this field and an understanding of sexual function and difficulty. It is usually the female who goes to the family planning clinic though her husband, fiancé or boy friend sometimes accompanies her and there seems to be an increasing acceptance of the joint responsibility of the partners. She knows that she is very likely to be subjected to an intimate examination involving her genitalia, although she often finds the prospect worrying and embarrassing, but she will tend to approach the doctor with less embarrassment than she would otherwise do because she knows these examinations are a normal part of the doctor's work. Greater distress and embarrassment may be related to sexual problems since it is difficult to obtain a sympathetic hearing or helpful advice from many doctors because they are themselves embarrassed about, and relatively ignorant of this area of medicine.

The Presentation and Identification of Problems

The patient may go to see the doctor prepared to voice her anxiety or she may hope that the doctor will "sense" the problem, give her a suitable opening to express it, or detect or solve it during pelvic examination. Doctors and nurses who do family planning work should be well aware of this but vary greatly in their sensitivity to the signals of distress from such patients. As in all branches of medicine time for consultation is limited and an atmosphere of urgency will deter the patient from unburdening herself and reduce the impression of sympathy and willingness to listen, which for most patients are essential qualifications of a good doctor. Lack of privacy, the presence of a nurse, trainee or observer, noise or the divided attention of a doctor may severely inhibit the patient; if there is a third person present the doctor may be alert for the patient who looks uncomfortable or indicates a wish to be seen on her own and grant this right to the patient who needs it. The behaviour of the patient at the time of the examination may suggest a problem or the patient may choose this moment to reveal one.

There is an increasing awareness of the frequency of psychosexual problems and the distress and social disturbance they produce and the first duty of the doctor in general practice, family planning or gynaecological clinics is to be able to identify them and to avoid treatment which may create problems or exacerbate those which already exist. There are dangers in probing unnecessarily or uninvited into the marital and sexual lives of our patients and doctors and nurses must recognize the difference between enquiries relative to treatment or invited by the patient, and those pursued without any indication. The doctor undertaking family planning work should be equipped to help with some of the sexual problems or if they are too complex to recognize this and refer the patient to another doctor or clinic where appropriate help can be given. Credit must be given to those in the Family Planning Association who first recognized the need to help with sexual and marital problems. The study which ten doctors started with Dr Michael Balint led to the publication of Virgin Wives (Friedman, 1962) and the momentum increased when other doctors joined in seminars, some of their work being reported in Contraception and Sexual Life (Tunnadine, 1970). Training courses in family planning for doctors and nurses now include instruction and/or seminars on the subjects of sexual function and problems.

The psychological aspect of sexual problems can involve the counsellor as well as the patient. The danger of the doctor having failed to come to terms with his or her own sexuality and seeking to do so by treating patients, or being unable to do so because of his own problems should be obvious but needs to be stated forcibly in relation to an area of medicine where patience, experience and understanding are needed to achieve success and where it is all too easy to do harm. The doctor giving advice about family planning, whether as general practitioner, family planning clinic doctor or gynaecologist must be aware of the dangers, ready to hear revelations from patients without surprise or embarrassment and able to help the patient without allowing his own moral views, as distinct from his professional ethical code, to intrude.

The Variety of Problems which may be Encountered

The whole range of psychosexual and marital problems may be encountered in family planning clinics. Adolescents, single patients, married couples, those involved in extra marital relationships or with guilt about previous sexual activities or pregnancy will be seen in the course of clinics for contraception and infertility. As the public become increasingly aware that the doctors at these clinics may be able and willing to help more will almost certainly make their way to the clinics. Where there is sexual deviation or a woman is worried about her husband's behaviour the problem may be mentioned, particularly if she knows the doctor in the clinic, while men occasionally go to clinics on their own in search of assistance or reassurance and may also be seen in the course of investigating a couple for infertility. Although this chapter is written for the professional worker in clinics and surgeries, lay workers should be aware of the likelihood of men or women coming in to seek support with a psychosexual problem and should know where or to whom to refer them.

Infertility

Patients with infertility often find difficulty in obtaining satisfactory help. A complaint of such emotional significance cannot be evaluated at a brief consultation and there are relatively few good infertility clinics and experienced doctors with an interest in this field. In general patients are well justified in seeking advice if they have not achieved a pregnancy after trying for a year; they may justifiably seek advice earlier if they are particularly worried or if they know that there is some factor, be it a sexual problem or physical disorder, which is likely to prevent conception. There is a tendency for general practitioners and hospital doctors to rebuff these patients in the early years seeing them briefly and advising them to continue trying for a longer period, sometimes years, after which investigations may be considered. Only a patient, sympathetic consultation will reveal the couple's or patient's anxieties or any psychosexual problems.

The Sexual History

The history of a couple complaining of infertility should include specific enquiry about the frequency of intercourse, enjoyment and any problems associated with it. This necessitates interview of the partners separately since one may not be aware that the other has a problem or there may be something in the past such as a previous pregnancy or extra marital liaison which the patient has not confided to his or her partner. I always put direct questions about intercourse and sexual difficulty to each patient at the end of the history by which time they have usually relaxed and are encouraged to talk freely. After the history and examination the couple are seen together and there can be further joint discussion of any sexual problem if this is appropriate.

Assessment of the Sexual Problem

Sexual problems once identified must be assessed in relation to their effect on the chances of conception and the damage they are inflicting on the marital life and general happiness of the couple. Major sexual problems which prevent intercourse are sometimes missed and I have seen women who have undergone extensive investigation and even been admitted to hospital when intercourse has not taken place for some months and in at least two cases where it has never occurred. If infertile patients are to be treated properly these difficulties should be identified when the history is taken but if they are missed a pelvic examination of the woman, a negative post-coital test or failure of the husband to produce a specimen of semen may indicate their existence to the alert doctor.

Although Jeffcoate (1975, p. 586) states that 5% of women seeking advice on sterility have not consummated their marriage there is little recognition of the frequent occurrence of sexual problems between infertile couples and their significance in contributing to infertility. In a recent prospective study (Steele, 1976) of 500 couples complaining of infertility and seen at the Margaret Pyke Centre I found 165 (37%) with sexual or marital problems. Some of the couples had more than one difficulty and I have classified these in Table I. This high figure suggests that psychosexual problems are relatively common, at least among infertile patients, and they frequently pass undetected during investigation and treatment.

TABLE I

Sexual problems in 500 couples complaining of infertility

Dyspareunia (female)	65
No orgasm (female)	40
Infrequent orgasm (female)	38
Impotence	30
Loss of libido	20
Infrequent intercourse	18
Apareunia	12
Iatrogenic	11
Premature ejaculation	9

A vital factor influencing these problems and in their treatment is satisfactory communication between the marital partners. It is important to discover whether there is communication or not and this is usually determined by interviewing the couple separately and then together. If the husband is not seen or the couple is interviewed by different doctors there is a high risk of the problem and the state of communication not being revealed.

Problems Affecting Fertility Directly

If intercourse has never taken place (apareunia) or is infrequent this may be the cause of the infertility. In most, but not all cases dyspareunia is not sufficient to stop intercourse although it may mar its enjoyment in varying degree. Peterson (1961) stressed the dangers of compulsive adherence by patients to doctors' advice marring sexual pleasure. This can occur because of advice about the frequency of intercourse or undue emphasis on a particular day in the cycle, "instruction" to use one position, insemination with the husband's semen, repeated post-coital tests or simply as a result of increased anxiety engendered by investigation and treatment. While many patients tolerate this interference with their normal sexual life others find the loss of spontaneous activity and the clinical intrusion more than they can bear. It is important for doctors involved in the investigation of infertility to appreciate the dangers of undue interference, directly or indirectly in marital relationships. If they do not do this loss of libido, infrequent intercourse, impotence or marital disharmony may be the result particularly when the husband and wife are not equally motivated.

In some cases of sexual difficulty, including those of severe physical handicap and specific problems preventing intercourse (an example was a very happily married couple where the husband needed a circumcision but could not face the prospect or even its discussion) artificial insemination using the husband's semen may be welcomed or even sought by a couple; if there is no other bar to conception there is a good chance of success. In general, however, help with the specific problem is an essential prerequisite to further investigation or treatment and may be the only measure required.

Problems not Preventing Conception

Many sexual difficulties do not prevent conception although they may reduce the chances and harm sexual enjoyment and marital harmony.

Dyspareunia was the commonest finding in my own series (Table I) and it varies greatly in amount from mild or temporary discomfort to intolerable pain sufficient to stimulate the woman to avoid intercourse altogether. Because dyspareunia with a recognizable cause such as vaginal pathology or a prolapsed ovary in the Pouch of Douglas was the only sexual problem of which most doctors and medical students were aware for a long time there is now a tendency to minimize the significance of organic causes and look solely for a psychological aetiology. Vaginismus often increases dyspareunia as the fear of pain produces tension and apprehension with reduction of libido and sexual satisfaction. Organic causes of dyspareunia include:

fibroid, ovarian cysts, prolapsed ovaries;
pelvic inflammatory disease;
vaginal or uterine prolapse;
vaginal septa, rigid hymen;
perineal or vulval infection and inflammation;
tender perineum

Lack of secretion due to inadequate sexual response will also cause dyspareunia.

Marital Problems

Associated with, or causing psychosexual problems may be marital difficulties or events in the past which are painful to the patient. A pregnancy or termination before marriage may be a potent source of guilt, particularly if the knowledge has not been shared, leading to sexual inhibitions and dysfunction while a termination within the marriage can affect both partners.

Delicacy in handling psychosexual problems is essential or serious damage may result. The need for this is exemplified by a couple without a child after more than ten years of married life. Satisfactory intercourse had never taken place because the wife apparently had vaginismus and the husband was impotent. Each partner, unknown to the other, had had satisfactory extra-marital intercourse.

Some women come to the infertility clinic seeking a child as a solution to marital disharmony or even incompatibility. The social, emotional and sexual background may be extremely complicated and it is generally unlikely that a pregnancy will solve problems of this sort. Sometimes the woman is not even sure she wants a child but comes

because of pressure from husband, family or even friends. It is important also to recognize the racial pressures where husbands expect their
wives to prove their fertility before marriage or may desert apparently
infertile wives after marriage.

Artificial Insemination by Donor

The difficulties of adoption in the United Kingdom have led many
couples to seek and obtain A.I.D. Jeffcoate (1975, p. 606) condemns
this measure unreservedly and there is clearly a situation in which the
marital relationship may be strained and the husband in particular feel
inadequate sexually when he produces no spermatozoa. Many of the
patients who seek A.I.D., however, have very happy stable marriages
and this enables the wife to carry her own child while there is less
doubt about the genetic background than there would be with adoption. There is no evidence of serious consequences provided that there
is adequate counselling and consideration beforehand. Behrman
(1968) found only one divorce among 800 couples who had accepted
A.I.D. compared with the American average of 1 in 5 marriages and
Cory (1948) reviewed 400 cases in which the results were as satisfactory as with adoption.

The Selection and Acceptability of Contraceptives

There is a wide choice of contraceptive methods and none of these
is ideal, i.e. completely reliable, without side effects and non-
permanent. The choice of contraceptive may be made precipitately or
after consideration, with or without consultation with husband or
partner and with or without medical or expert advice.

    If the choice is made at leisure and in consultation many factors
will affect it.

    1. Previous experience with contraception, if any.
    2. The patient's assessment or knowledge of the reliability of
    methods (influenced by information or opinions expressed in
    the press, books, on radio or television and by expert advisers).
    3. The "appeal" or otherwise of a method e.g. the advantages
    of regular, lighter periods without dysmenorrhoea for the pill

or revulsion at a "messy" method such as the diaphragm involving genital handling.

4. Cultural, racial or religious influences.

5. The experience of friends or relatives — a failure with a method experienced by a next door neighbour may have a quite understandable but illogical effect on the patient.

6. Convenience in relation to domestic and social factors such as the domicile of the patient, the accommodation, privacy and washing facilities where intercourse takes place.

7. Relation to sexuality: e.g. variation of libido in the menstrual cycle or any sexual difficulty already experienced.

8. The anticipated effect of the method on gynaecological, medical or psychological problems.

9. Direct expert advice to use a particular method.

10. Acceptability or non acceptability of the method to the partner.

(11. Cost and availability of the method chosen.)

The selection of a method represents a compromise in the acceptance of the advantages and disadvantages of any method and experience may lead to its rejection. Conflict or stress may occur between partners where one has anxieties about a method which is acceptable or even apparently beneficial to the other, a situation seen most often with the pill. The final choice of contraceptive may well be one about which the patient, the partner, or both have misgivings. It is unfortunate that the majority of wives go to a family planning clinic on their own (Cartwright 1970, p. 156) although joint counselling is clearly important and disputes may lead to, or be the result of marital discord (Runciman, 1974).

The difficulties associated with specific methods of contraception will be discussed later but before a psychosexual problem can be attributed to a specific method there are other potent influences to consider.

Fear of Failure

For many women and families and for some men pregnancy would be an absolute disaster and for many of these fear of conception is always present to some degree. With all methods showing statistical failure rates and some women unsure of their ability to use a method properly (e.g. forgetting to take the pill) or unsure of their boyfriend's integrity this should be easily understood. A recent failure of a contraceptive method for the patient or for a friend or relative may increase this fear.

Fear of Side Effects

The knowledge that the patient may suffer other effects, whether major or minor, may worry the patient and the partner and this concern is often increased by the experience of others and publicity about untoward effects in the media.

Guilt about Sex

A man or woman may have been brought up in such a way that she feels it is wrong to want or enjoy sex or that these feelings are a betrayal of parents or their upbringing (Tunnadine 1970, pp. 44—46). This, or ignorance or insensitivity by the male partner may be responsible for a feeling that sex should not be enjoyed, is dirty or abnormal. A recent termination of pregnancy may produce guilt as well as adding to the subsequent fear of pregnancy.

Desire for a Child

A man or woman may want a child greatly although for "logical" social or medical reasons pregnancy must, at least temporarily, be prevented. The woman may be using contraception because of social circumstances or because of encouragement or pressure by husband, boyfriend, doctor or even relatives and so may become depressed and perhaps frigid, while the husband occasionally becomes depressed or frustrated with consequent impotence or even an extra-marital affair to prove his fertility.

Previous Psychosexual Problems

A careful history will sometimes reveal that the problem preceded the use of the incriminated method. In some cases the use of a specific

contraceptive may exacerbate or complicate a sexual problem. In
others the patient may only have experienced intercourse while
using one form of contraception and it may not be the contraceptive
which is at fault. The vast literature and controversy surrounding
experience with oral contraceptives has encouraged doctors and
patients to be precipitate in attributing untoward symptoms or events
to the pill.

Coincidental Disease or Depression

The patient may become depressed for other reasons such as the desire
for a child, marital difficulty or bereavement. It is important to recognize this and not to attribute it, for example, to oral contraceptives.

Practical Policy

The professional asked to advise about contraception should discuss
fully with the patient or couple their views on individual methods
and use his expert knowledge to inform or reassure where possible. If
the patient or her partner is still unhappy or worried about one method
after reassurance then it is generally better to avoid using this and to
seek a more acceptable alternative. A knowledge of the difficulties
which may be associated with the various techniques will help the
adviser to avoid methods which may create anxiety or exacerbate pre-
existing problems (for example encouraging a man with some
degree of impotence to use sheaths). It is important to remember that
some methods must interfere with the enjoyment of intercourse either
because they involve interruption to the preliminary sex-play (vaginal
diaphragm insertion, sheath or chemical spermicide), prevent free
and normal coitus (rhythm method, coitus interruptus, or interfermora)
or involve disturbance after coitus (sheath, post-coital douching).

Problems with Specific Methods of Contraception

Oral Contraceptives

The combined oestrogen-progestogen pill is the most effective reversible contraceptive available and the confidence of patients in it is

generally high. The considerable medical literature and the attention of the media mean that men and women are well aware of the possible side effects and often apprehensive about them. Fear of side effects and the efficiency of the method, which can be unwelcome to those who strongly desire pregnancy, may be potent factors in producing sexual difficulties (see. p. 391). Cartwright (1970, pp. 34—36) found that 1 in 4 women taking the pill had symptoms, including being "off" sex and only 1 in 10 thought the pill had no effect on health. The incidence of serious side effects is less with the lower dose pills but anxiety and problems increase whenever there is adverse publicity in the media. When there is a fear sufficient to cause problems explanation and reassurance may be sufficient but if they are not a change to an alternative method is logical, though it may not be an easy decision if the patient or couple are unhappy with the loss of reliability or the available alternatives. Older women who have been on the pill for many years seem sometimes to become increasingly concerned about the long-term effects if they continue on it for a further period of 10 years or more; sterilization is a very satisfactory solution for some of these patients if they can obtain it. Any consideration of stopping the pill must also take into account the relief of dysmenorrhoea and the decreased menstrual loss which are beneficial side effects.

There is no doubt that some women lose their libido when they take oral contraceptives. In addition to the factors already mentioned this may be associated with depression, whether due to the pill or not. The cyclical variation in feminine sexual desire and responsiveness is well recognized and is discussed by Singer and Singer (1972) and Kaplan (1974). There is disagreement about the timing or variation of the peaks of sexual desire but the pill would tend to suppress a peak associated with the follicular or oestrogenic phase of the cycle, to level out the normal changes in steroid levels and to reduce the ovarian production of androgen. Hertzberg (1969) found that 27% of 52 women who discontinued the pill did so because of decreased libido and Hertzberg (1971) suggested that although there is an increase in sexual activity after starting to use a safe method the increased libido is not maintained in women taking oral contraceptives. The Royal College of General Practitioners (1974) suggested that there might be a considerable bias when they reported that pill takers complained four times as often of diminished libido as non-users, and the variety of causes makes assessment difficult. A change of preparation may be helpful in relieving other problems and thereby help to restore libido. Sometimes vaginal dryness is associated with taking oral contraceptives and leads to dyspareunia and loss of libido. A lubricant, change of pill or change of contraceptive may provide the solution and only patient and sympathetic discussion and advice will help the patient to make the best choice. If a patient really fears the pill it is unwise for her to take it unless her fears can be resolved.

The progestogen pill offers less security without suppression of ovarian steroid production. Loss of libido may occur for the same psychological reasons and the progestagen may adversely affect any peak in the follicular phase of the cycle.

Intra-Uterine Contraceptive Devices

Unlike other methods this requires no effort on the part of the woman and no disturbance during pre-coital activity. It does, however, sometimes produce longer, heavier periods and discharge which may have a "putting off" effect on either partner and, by limiting intercourse produce frustration and dissatisfaction. If the general psychological factors, such as disapointment that pregnancy will not follow sexual activity, do not reduce libido (Fleck, 1972) it is unlikely that a device if it is generally acceptable to the patient will have any specific adverse effect on sexual life and it will in many cases improve marital and sexual life (Kieszkiewicz *et al.*, 1972). The onset of dyspareunia after insertion of a device may be due to pelvic inflammatory disease which must be excluded.

Chemical and Mechanical Methods used in the Vagina

The mechanical devices and spermicides have few side effects but they demand anticipation of, and preparation for intercourse which goes against the inclination of many women (Diamond *et al.*, 1973) or interruption of sexual activity. The disturbance particularly on a cold night is likely to lower the woman's "sexual temperature" and to give the tired or reluctant male an interval during which he may lose the effect of arousal and want to go to sleep. Occasionally pressure from the male partner to stay in bed and do without the contraceptive "this time" may cause a little discord or if successful an unplanned pregnancy. Rarely allergy to the mechanical device or chemical may produce dyspareunia. This method demands strong motivation in the female and is reliable if it is well used. The necessary

preparation and genital manipulation and the messiness of the method
are distasteful to many women and also to some men (Cartwright,
1970, pp.144–145).

The Rhythm Method

This method which is declining in popularity (Population Report,
1974) but acceptable to Roman Catholics has low acceptance rates
and relatively high failure rates (Tolor *et al.*, 1973). It does not permit
regular spontaneous sexual activity and demands a degree of abstinence while not really providing security against pregnancy. For those
for whom no other method is acceptable it is far better than nothing
but otherwise it must be regarded as insufficiently effective as a
contraceptive method and a barrier to a full and satisfying sex life.

The Sheath

This method is under the control of the male. It involves a brief pause
before coitus while it is put on the penis. Cartwright (1970, p. 32)
found that half the mothers commenting on the sheath remarked on
its unpleasantness. The idea of a "barrier" between penis and vagina
may not be liked by male or female and means that intercourse is not
the complete union which some women in particular seek. The loss of
sensation to the man is appreciable and may interfere with erection in
an older man or one with a tendency to impotence. It may occasionally
help a man with a tendency to ejaculate too quickly. If withdrawal
does not occur before loss of erection the sheath may come off and
semen spill dangerously in the vagina so that there should be withdrawal immediately after orgasm which prevents a couple enjoying
the pleasure and relaxation of the resolution phase. Some women
complain of burning or discomfort when a sheath is used – this may
be due to clumsiness on the part of the male, penetration before the
female is excited or discomfort from an unlubricated sheath. An understanding of sexual responsiveness, the use of lubricated sheaths, a
chemical spermicide or an additional lubricant such as KY Jelly (even
saliva if nothing better is available) will help to overcome these difficulties.

Coitus Interruptus (Withdrawal)

This method prevents completion of sexual intercourse. The male must control himself and withdraw immediately before ejaculation, directing the semen away from the vagina. The method has become less popular as more reliable methods which interfere less with coitus, have become available. It is a method which may worry the woman, since it is out of her control, and she may not reach orgasm. Her partner may bring her to orgasm by direct stimulation of the clitoris digitally or orally but if the woman has experienced satisfactory uninterrupted intercourse before she may be less than satisfied with coitus interruptus. If she does not reach orgasm she may be disappointed, perhaps resentful and Masters and Johnson (1966) have demonstrated that excitement without orgasm can produce pelvic vasocongestion and emotional disturbance. This method is useful in an emergency but as an elective method of family planning it is not satisfactory.

Sterilization

Sterilization implies permanent and generally irreversible contraception. There is a crucial decision for the couple in deciding whether husband or wife should be sterilized and proper counselling is essential to ensure that both understand the nature and effects of the operation and accept the implications. The view of sterilization as castration (Erikson, 1954) is a serious example of the misleading ideas which many people have about it and one which can lead to grave psychosexual complications if not corrected. Sterilization under duress has been frequently condemned and Barnes and Zuspan (1958) showed that women sterilized in the puerperium at their own request were more satisfied subsequently than those to whom it was suggested for medical reasons. Younger patients, not surprisingly, seem more likely to have regrets or problems (Barnes and Zuspan 1958; Campanella and Wolff, 1975) and dissatisfied patients sometimes show poor knowledge of the operation. Di Musto *et al.* (1974) found 95 satisfied women out of 100 who had been sterilized and attributed this to proper counselling.

Sterilization is of most benefit psychosexually where fear of pregnancy has caused problems such as avoidance of intercourse, frigidity or impotence and where previous contraceptive methods have been unacceptable or poorly tolerated through fear of side effects (as with the pill) or because of direct interference with sexual pleasure (examples are the cap which is distasteful to one or both partners and the sheath which interferes with sensation). The "sacrifice" of the partner who undergoes sterilization may be genuinely appreciated by the other in a stable marriage and be a contribution to it. In a less stable marriage conflict may occur because the sterilized partner does not receive the expected recognition. Some patients seek sterilization as a solution to frigidity or marital problems while some women hope that vasectomy will help them by reducing their husband's sexual appetite or enjoyment. Where there is instability in the marriage or disturbance due to extra-marital affairs sterilization may lead to greater insecurity and conflict with increased suspicion of infidelity. There is also a risk that increased sexual freedom consequent on the relief from fear of pregnancy may lead one or other partner to worry about their sexual performance, particularly if their sexual "appetites" are unequal. A concern to prove their masculinity or femininity may lead husband or wife respectively to pursue more frequent intercourse. Wolfers (1973) writing about vasectomy advises that pre-existing marital, sexual or psychological instability should be taken as contra-indications. This is clearly wise advice and well justified on the evidence but these are only relative contra-indications and each case must be judged on its merits and in the knowledge that some of these problems are solved or lessened by sterilization, male or female.

Assessment of the results of sterilization is difficult because the lives of two people are involved (Edey 1972), the time interval before assessment may be crucial and pre-existing problems may not have been recognized (Wolfers, 1973).

Vasectomy

The Simon Population Trust (1969) in a follow-up of 1000 cases found 57.5% of marriages were more harmonious, 0.5% less harmonious and the remainder unchanged while 73.1% of men and 79.4% of women found that their sex lives had improved. Landis and Poffenberger (1965) studied 330 couples who had chosen vasectomy as their method of birth control and reported that 38% had increased sexual desire and 70% greater enjoyment. It is interesting, however, that Rodgers and Ziegler (1968) found no difference in sexual behaviour between a group of couples taking oral contraceptives and another where the men had undergone vasectomy. In general, fears of infidelity, anxiety and castration associations have not been confirmed and it is noteworthy that in the Simon Population Report (1969) 99% of the men would recommend the operation to others.

Female Sterilization

There is generally stronger motivation for a wife to seek sterilization than for her husband since it is she who suffers the direct results of unwanted pregnancy. Timing in relation to the last pregnancy, the reasons for seeking or accepting sterilization, age, previous marital and sexual problems whether recognized or not, previous contraceptive experience and the time spent in hospital and away from her family will all influence the patient's reaction to the sterilization. The increased likelihood of problems in the young and the need for counselling have already been described. Association with abortion may account for the 22% adverse response reported by Ekblad (1961) and the performance of sterilization with termination is generally better avoided. Whitehouse (1971) reporting 25% of 95 women who claimed loss of libido emphasized the need for proper counselling. Thompson and Baird (1968), Cox (1973), and Sim *et al.* (1973) report good results and these include patients sterilized in the puerperium. Though good counselling should lead to satisfactory results in most cases, many problems may be found in the course of this and new problems may still emerge after the operation while the subsequent loss of a child or a change in the marriage may lead to regret, guilt and secondary sexual problems.

Summary

Those who advise patients about contraception and infertility must be aware of the sexual problems which their patients may have and those which may occur as a result of investigation and specific forms of contraception or treatment. Because of the association of family planning and sexuality patients expect doctors in the appropriate clinics to be able to help them with their problems. Doctors, and to some degree nurses also, undertaking this work must have come to terms with their own sexuality and be alert to identify patients with difficulties, and in need of help, without probing uninvited or inappropriately into patients' sexual and marital activities and relationships. The significance of sexual problems in infertility and the complex factors which may influence the choice, use and acceptability of a contraceptive method are described. The problems which may be associated with particular contraceptives are indicated but the relationship is complicated by the efficiency of the contraceptive, the reasons for its use, fear of side effects and many other influences acting on the patient to accept, tolerate or reject a method.

References

Barnes, A. C. and Zuspan, F. P. (1958). *American Journal of Obstetrics and Gynecology*, 45, 331–334.

Behrman, S. J. (1968). *In* "Progress in Infertility." (S. J. Behrman and R. W. Kistner, Eds), p. 720. Little Brown and Co: Boston, Mass., USA.

Campanella R. and Wolff, J. R. (1975). *Obstetrics and Gynecology*, 45, 331–334.

Cartwright, A. (1970). "Parents and Family Planning Services." Routledge and Kegan Paul: London.

Cory, W. H. (1948). *Obstetrics and Gynaecology*, 56, 727.

Cox, M. L. (1973). *British Medical Journal*, 2, 419.

Diamond, M., Steinhoff, P. G., Palmore, J. A. and Smith, R. G. (1973). *Journal of Biosocial Science*, 5, 347–361.

Di Musto, J. C., Owens, E. B. and Klomparens, K. A. (1974). *Journal of Reproductive Medicine*, 12, 112–116.

Edey, H. (1972). *Medical Counterpoint*, 4, 19–25.

Ekblad, M. (1961). *Acta Psychiatrica Scandinavia, Supplement*, 161, 156.

Erikson, H. M. (1954). *In* "Therapeutic Abortion." (Rosen, H. Ed.), p. 57. Julian Press: New York.

Fleck, S. (1972). *In* "Psychosomatic Medicine in Obstetrics and Gynaecology." 3rd International Congress, London 1971 (Morris, N. Ed.). pp. 517–519, Karger: Basel.

Friedman, L. J. (1962). "Virgin Wives." Tavistock Publications: London.

Hertzberg, B. N. (1969). *Clinical Trials Journal* 6, 203–204.

Hertzberg, B. N. (1971). *British Medical Journal*, 3, 495–500.

Jeffcoate, N. (1975). "Principles of Gynaecology." Butterworth: London.

Kaplan, H. S. (1974). "The New Sex Therapy." p. 54. Ballière Tindal: London.

Kieszkiewicz, T., Spychowa, V. and Kieszkiewicz, J. (1972). *In* "Psychosomatic Medicine in Obstetrics and Gynaecology." 3rd International Congress. London 1971 (Morris, N. Ed.), pp. 521–522. Karger: Basel.

Landis, J. T. and Poffenberger, T. (1965). *Marriage and the Family*, 27, 57–58.

Masters, W. H. and Johnson, V. E. (1966). "Human Sexual Response." pp. 119–120. Little Brown and Co: Boston, Mass., USA.

Peterson, J. A. (1961). *In* "Office Management of the Infertile Couple." (Tyler, E. T. Ed.), pp. 298–299. McGraw Hill: London.

Population Report (1974). 1, 1, 14.

Rodgers, D. A. and Ziegler, F. J. (1968). *Psychosomatic Medicine*, 30, 495–505.

Royal College of General Practitioners (1974). "Oral Contraceptives and Health." p. 20. Pitman Medical: London.

Runciman, A. P. (1974). *Journal of Reproductive Medicine*, 13, 6, 216–218.

Sim, M., Emens, J. M. and Jordan, J. A. (1973). *British Medical Journal*, 3, 220–222.

Simon Population Trust (1969). "Vasectomy: Follow-Up of a Thousand Cases." p. 15. Simon Population Trust, Cambridge.

Singer, A. and Singer, J. (1972). *Journal of Biosocial Science*, 4, 471–481.

Steele, S. J. (1976). To be published.

Thompson, B. and Baird, D. (1968). *Lancet*, 1, 1023–1027.

Tolor, A., Rice, F. M. and Lanctôt, C. A. (1973). *In* "Proceedings of the 81st Annual Convention of the American Psychological Association, Montreal 1973." pp. 353–354. American Psychological Association, Washington, DC.

Tunnadine, L. P. D. (1970). "Contraception and Sexual Life." Tavistock Publications: London.

Whitehouse, D. B. (1971). *British Medical Journal*, 2, 707.

Wolfers, D. (1973). *In* "Vasectomy." (Ziegler, F. J. Ed.), p. 81. Information Corporation: New York.

17 Sexual Problems Seen by Venereologists

P. RODIN and DAVID GOLDMEIER

Introduction

At first sight it might seem that, apart from any discomfort of the disease, people who come to VD clinics should not have sexual problems. On closer inspection, however, it becomes obvious that these most certainly exist, either at the patient's first attendance or arising later for various reasons. For example, a married man may have sought other sexual outlets because of an unsatisfactory sexual relationship with his wife; if he acquires an infection as a result of this and passes it on to his wife, this can only make matters worse. If the underlying psychosexual problem is not dealt with the whole process is likely to be repeated. Perhaps even more disturbing is when a moment of weakness results in the same course of events in someone who primarily had a satisfactory relationship with his wife. In some cases the wife's pregnancy may have resulted in a transient loss of attraction, or restriction of sexual intercourse may have been advised by the obstetrician. Although in the past long periods of abstinence were required before cure of many of the sexually-transmitted diseases could be demonstrated, with modern treatment the periods required are much shorter, so that in general fewer problems arise from this.

As will be seen, physical and psychological conditions are often closely interwoven, but for clarity the problems are classified into those primarily associated with a physical condition and those in which the primary problem is psychological.

Sexual Problems Associated With Physical Conditions

A lesion may cause pain or discomfort during intercourse or it may remove the desire for intercourse by the fear or shame that it produces, particularly when it is thought the condition might be venereal in origin and that the regular sexual partner might become affected. Those lesions which are persistent or recurrent put most strain on a sexual relationship, especially when there is a fear (justified or not) that intercourse will produce a relapse.

Sexually-transmitted Diseases

These may be grouped into those that are legally defined as "Venereal Diseases", and other sexually-transmitted diseases.

It is self-evident that promiscuous persons are more likely to acquire a sexually-transmitted disease. Those who for various reasons are unable to form lasting psychosexual relationships may become promiscuous and thus become frequently infected. Male homosexuals seem to make a relatively large contribution to this group.

In most cases reassurance can be given that treatment of the particular sexually-transmitted infection is effective. The patient is also assured, where necessary, that confidentiality is strictly observed. Sexual partners will generally need to be examined, and only when this has been done, appropriate treatment given, and subsequent tests of cure completed, can intercourse be resumed. Obviously delay in seeing the sexual contacts is also likely to result in delay in resumption of intercourse. Great tact is required in handling the situation so as to avoid recrimination between the regular sexual partners.

The Legally-defined Venereal Diseases

These comprise syphilis, gonorrhoea and chancroid.

Syphilis

Because the incubation period of this disease can be as long as three months, it is often difficult to know what advice to give when asked how long a person should wait before resuming intercourse with a regular partner after a casual exposure with someone about whose health nothing is known. However, most infections declare themselves within a month, but waiting even this long is liable to result in awkward questions being asked by the regular sexual partner. One can only advise the patient that the longer he waits the better, but he must be the judge of the danger to the relationship in this respect. There should also be no genital contact whatsoever, and this is even more difficult to observe than avoidance of intercourse. The use of a sheath will also lessen the risk of transmitting infection, but where this has not been used before by the couple it is likely to arouse suspicion. Fortunately, apart from among male homosexuals, the incidence of syphilis in the United Kingdom is low.

Although the genital lesions in syphilis are usually painless, the patient will often cease to have intercourse for the reasons already stated. Patients with late manifestations of syphilis, and adults with congenital syphilis, should be reassured that even if untreated they are not infectious through sexual or other contact. Though neurosyphilis may result in impotence, the latter can also result from fear of the disease or fear of transmitting it to the sexual partner.

Modern treatment of syphilis with penicillin renders patients with infectious syphilis non-infectious very rapidly, and some venereologists allow patients to resume intercourse as soon as their treatment and that of all the infected traceable sexual contacts are completed. However, because of the small risk of infectious relapse, the more cautious advise against sexual intercourse for a further minimum period of six months. It is best not to have any fixed rule but to judge each case according to the various social as well as medical factors prevailing. Thus, the advice given to someone whose regular sexual partner is already known to be infected will be different from that given to someone who has not yet started sexual relations with his fiancée. Again with homosexuals the main aim should be to impress on the patient the importance of not resuming intercourse until his contacts have been examined and either been treated or completed surveillance showing them to be uninfected. To ask for more from many homosexuals seen in clinics is likely to achieve little, but of course each case should be assessed individually.

There is much controversy as to whether contacts of patients with infectious syphilis should be treated when there is no evidence of disease when they are first seen. Obviously if this is not done, but surveillance for three months undertaken, then intercourse should be prohibited to avoid "ping-pong" reinfections.

Formerly, because of the long courses of arsenical and bismuth preparations that were required, and the greater risk of infectious relapse in pre-penicillin days, patients were advised to refrain from intercourse for two years or more after the diagnosis of infectious syphilis was made. It is doubtful if many patients followed this advice, but those that did must often have suffered from severe psychosexual problems.

Gonorrhoea

After a short incubation period (a matter of days) males, apart from passive homosexuals, usually develop urethral discharge, and often pain on passing urine. Once this is noticed intercourse is generally avoided. However, there are individuals who continue to have intercourse at this stage, and so continue to transmit the infection to others. This may be because they are ignorant of or unconcerned about the fact that such a discharge may be a manifestation of a sexually-transmitted disease, or because of an overpoweringly strong sexual desire. There are a small but perhaps increasing number of men who are asymptomatic carriers of gonorrhoea. Such people will obviously continue to have intercourse, as will women with an un-complicated gonococcal infection who are usually asymptomatic.

The local complications of gonococcal urethritis in the male are now uncommon in the United Kingdom, and other developed countries, because rapidly effective treatment is given at an early stage. When they do occur, intercourse is likely to be painful or impossible. Local complications in the female are commoner than in the male. An acute gonococcal Bartholin's abscess makes intercourse too painful to attempt. Acute salpingitis is the commonest local complication and is likely to cause deep dyspareunia. If an innocently infected woman were to become sterile as a result of the infection, the husband may suffer guilt feelings and the sexual relationship be impaired. If she knows her husband's infidelity to be the cause of her sterility this will very likely make matters worse. All doctors concerned with such patients must take care not to inject their own moral attitudes; a few careless or misguided words spoken to the wife could wreck a marriage which may otherwise have survived. Some argue that if the marriage cannot survive such knowledge, it is doomed anyway, but such a cynical attitude is unworthy of doctors. The situation has to be faced more often in relation to uncomplicated gonorrhoea in an innocently infected woman who is asymptomatic. Many experienced venereologists avoid the use of the word gonorrhoea in such a situation; however, if she asks point blank "is it gonorrhoea?" and the diagnosis has been proven by culture tests, then one cannot answer "no".

The practice of orogenital intercourse is apparently becoming increasingly popular. This is reflected in the prevalence of gonococcal pharyngeal infection. A study in Denmark (Bro-Jørgensen and Jensen, 1973) showed that 7% of heterosexual men, 10% of women, and 25% of homosexual men with gonorrhoea had pharyngeal infection. Although pharyngeal infection was usually associated with urogenital or rectal infection, in a small number of cases the pharynx was the only site of gonococcal infection. Infection of the pharynx does not usually produce any symptoms, but febrile tonsillitis and remote complications can occur. Rather surprisingly the frequency of pharyngeal gonorrhoea seems to be much lower in the United Kingdom, even amongst homosexuals, most of whom admit to practising orogenital sex.

Modern treatment of uncomplicated urogenital and rectal gonorrhoea is simple, generally one injection or oral dose of an appropriate antibiotic being all that is necessary. However, problems exist in relation to pharyngeal gonorrhoea which is more difficult to eradicate. How long should patients, treated for gonorrhoea, be asked to abstain from sexual intercourse? In general, this should be as long as it takes to prove cure, and three examinations at roughly weekly intervals should be adequate. During this time it is hoped that the accessible contacts will also have been examined, but delays in this must be added to the period of abstinence if the patient intends to continue the relationship with the individual concerned. Further delays may be added owing to the development of post-gonococcal non-specific urethritis which quite frequently develops in the ensuing weeks after treatment of gonorrhoea. It is also inadvisable to masturbate or drink alcohol soon after treatment of urethritis from any cause, as this might delay healing.

Although most cases of gonococcal vulvovaginitis in children are contracted non-venereally in the United Kingdom, in some instances sexual assault may have taken place. In either case those managing such cases should be careful to avoid adding to the potential for future psychosexual problems.

Chancroid

This is now so rare in this country that it will not be considered
further.

Other sexually-transmitted Diseases

Only the more commonly seen conditions will be considered.

Non-specific Urethritis (NSU)

This is now the commonest problem that venereologists have to deal
with. As NSU is usually a milder disease than gonococcal urethritis,
more patients are likely to continue to have sexual intercourse in
spite of it and quite often men with this condition are completely
asymptomatic. Furthermore, in women non-specific genital infection
is usually asymptomatic and difficult to diagnose with the routine
tests presently used. Treatment of men with NSU is not as simple as
that of gonorrhoea, requiring prolonged courses of tetracycline for
up to three weeks. Even then a proportion of patients relapse, particularly if they resume intercourse immediately after the course of
treatment, so that the period of advised abstention from intercourse
and masturbation is likely to be at least four or five weeks after starting treatment. Most venereologists treat the contacts with a similar
course of tetracycline, and, as with gonorrhoea, delays in seeing the
contacts will prolong the period of abstinence.

A common reason for recurrence of NSU after treatment is premature resumption of intercourse, but in some unfortunate patients
the condition persists or relapses in spite of their obeying all instructions. In others all evidence of disease disappears but the patients
have persistent symptoms for which there seems to be no organic
basis. It is all too easy to attribute the symptoms in some cases to
"chronic non-specific prostatitis" as judged by examination of the
prostatic fluid, but as the changes indicating chronic non-specific
prostatitis can be found in a third of healthy men it is very difficult
to interpret the findings in the individual case.

The management of NSU requires a close observation of the
patient's psychological reaction to his condition, particularly when
there is difficulty in eradicating it or when the patient believes he is

not better although there is no evidence of disease. The latter often has a fear of infecting others together with guilt over having acquired the disease in the first place, so it is easy to see how sexual problems can arise. It may require much reassurance and persuasion to get these patients to resume intercourse; they may feel happier if they use a condom for the first few weeks, which they can dispense with after further examination again shows no evidence of disease. Where practicable, this temporary use of the condom on resumption of intercourse can be advised in all cases, because if used carefully (without prior genital contact, with care in removal and washing of hands and penis afterwards) it can help in the difficult decision of deciding whether a recurrence of NSU is a relapse or a reinfection.

Where there has been difficulty in eradicating the infection, it is often of value to see both sexual partners together. NSU is more likely to throw great strain on a marriage than gonorrhoea, which, although a legally-defined venereal disease, can be more easily and rapidly eradicated. Even though most married men who get NSU do so as a result of extra-marital intercourse, this is not always the case, and it can be helpful to point out to a suspicious wife or fiancée that the disease is not "VD". It is obviously helpful to be able to see such contacts in clinics held apart from the VD clinic; if this cannot be done the patients must be told that so-called VD clinics also deal with other conditions. If psychosexual problems are to be avoided, tactful and sympathetic handling of patients with NSU is essential. All too often repeated courses of antibiotics are given, sometimes on doubtful evidence of NSU, with scant attention being paid to the patient's increasing anxiety and sometimes depression, which may result in impotence or premature ejaculation and consequent damage to present and future relationships. There are some patients, however, who latch on to a recurrent, often mild, NSU, as an excuse not to have sexual intercourse for extended periods, if at all. They commonly have added symptoms, obviously unrelated to their NSU but attributed by them to it. These patients are difficult to help and should be seen by a psychiatrist.

Non-specific genital infection in women may be complicated by salpingitis. Such women often complain of deep dyspareunia. As with NSU in men non-specific salpingitis may run a relapsing course and thus seriously interfere with sexual activity. The male partner might be asymptomatic so that the cause of the women's pelvic pain and tenderness could easily be missed and a less effective antibiotic given. Non-specific salpingitis, like gonorrhoea, may also result in sterility.

Polyarthritis due to Reiter's disease occurs in about 1% of men who have NSU. These patients should be reassured that the arthritis itself is not transmissible, but while the urethritis persists intercourse should be prohibited. The disease is much less common in women, and those affected rarely have affected consorts.

Herpes simplex virus infections

Herpetic lesions of the penis or vulva are usually painful and will preclude intercourse taking place. When all the lesions have healed the patient is less likely to transmit the infection, although the virus persists between overt attacks and may be recovered from a normal looking cervix. However, intercourse itself may be a provoking factor causing a fresh crop of lesions to appear, especially when there is inadequate lubrication and consequently more trauma. Using a lubricant may help in the latter cases, but there is no proven method of preventing recurrences.

Oral herpes simplex infections may be transferred to the genital area by cunnilingus or fellatio, so that orogenital contact should be avoided when the partner has a "cold sore". Finding the same virus type in the oral and genital lesions will give added support for this mode of infection. Explanation by the physician concerning such a mode of spread may help to remove suspicions of infidelity that one or both partners may have harboured.

There are some unfortunate men who develop genital herpetic lesions with great frequency, and hence with great disruption of their sex lives. Unfortunately, there is no effective way of preventing these recurrences, but the immediate application of idoxuridine in high concentration may cut short the duration of the lesions.

A woman with genital herpetic lesions in late pregnancy is liable to pass the infection to her child at birth, particularly if she has a primary infection. The resulting neonatal illness is often serious with a high mortality. With this in mind, if a man has had extra-marital intercourse and has acquired herpes genitalis, he should be advised about the possible sexual transmission of the infection and its consequences to mother and child. The final decision as to whether intercourse should take place is obviously difficult. Certainly, as a minimum there should be no sexual contact until the lesions are well healed, and if his wife is near term there should be none at all until after delivery. If intercourse has already taken place, careful observation of the wife is necessary, with frequent cultures for herpes, even in the absence of lesions, as well as serological tests for herpes. The presence of herpes virus in the genital tract near term would be an indication for Caesarian section.

Male homosexuals are not immune to the effects of this virus. Herpetic ano-proctitis leading to intestinal obstruction and urinary retention in a homosexual seen at the Whitechapel Clinic (Goldmeier *et al.*, 1975) was associated with so much pain that he has not attempted passive intercourse since.

Candidiasis

In females *Candida* infection is the commonest infection reported by VD clinics (Department of Health and Social Security, 1974). Its increasing prevalence might, in part, be related to the increased use of oral contraceptives, users of which have been shown to harbour the organisms more frequently (Catterall, 1966). Other common predisposing factors are pregnancy and broad-spectrum antibiotics. Whether sexual transmission is the commonest mode of acquiring genital *Candida* infection is uncertain, but the sexual contacts are commonly found to harbour the organism. Although a less common infection in men, the incidence of *Candida* balanitis has also been increasing in recent years (Department of Health and Social Security, 1974). Women often harbour *Candida* in the vagina, and men on the penis, without symptoms, so that host factors seem to be of importance for proliferation of the organism and production of the disease.

There is a great variation in the severity of symptoms due to *Candida* infection, but itching and burning, rather than vaginal discharge, are likely to be the prominent symptoms. The itching can be intolerable, especially at night, and in these patients sexual intercourse is unlikely to be desired and may exacerbate the symptoms. Dyspareunia is thus a likely complaint in those more severely affected, especially when dryness and fissuring are present. Fortunately, rapid improvement is obtainable with nystatin and several other anticandidal preparations, but some women suffer frequent recurrences with correspondingly serious marital discord. Careful assessment is required so that all possible sites (especially oral and rectal) from which auto-reinfections can occur are treated. The male partner may carry the organism without symptoms and be the source of reinfection. Predisposing factors should be dealt with as far as possible, but stopping an oral contraceptive should only be considered when all other measures have failed.

There are a number of women who have covert psychosexual problems who come to sexually-transmitted diseases clinics complaining of dyspareunia. *Candida* may well be found by chance and be offered as the cause of the dyspareunia; but the symptoms are out of all proportion to the physical signs, and persist after the *Candida* infection has been eradicated. These patients often go from hospital to hospital before the underlying psychosexual problem is recognized and investigated.

Males with *Candida* balanitis may have severe itching and soreness and sometimes tightening of the foreskin with inability to retract it. The urine should always be tested for glucose, as diabetes is occasionally found as a predisposing cause. The symptoms will obviously lead to sexual difficulties. Although the condition generally clears up rapidly with nystatin cream, the patient may get repeated recurrences after sexual intercourse which may make him less keen to partake of it. His sexual partner should be examined even though she may have no symptoms, as she will usually be found to be harbouring the organism. Concurrent treatment is important, but if all measures fail to eradicate the infection permanently in her case, then washing of the penis and the use of nystatin cream after intercourse should prevent his recurrent balanitis. Occasionally the male contact of a female with *Candida* infection develops balanitis in which *Candida* cannot be found. This may be due to an allergic response to *Candida*, and, if so, will cease when the organism has been eradicated from the sexual partner.

Trichomonas vaginalis Infection

This is a common cause of foul-smelling vaginal discharge which may make the affected woman ashamed, and be off-putting to her partner. The associated inflammation may be severe and lead to dyspareunia. Before the discovery of a rapidly effective cure (metronidazole) in 1959, many women's lives were made miserable by what was then a very intractable condition.

Although it can cause non-gonococcal urethritis, the organism is most often carried asymptomatically by males, and its presence can be difficult to demonstrate. It is thus often necessary to treat the male partner to prevent reinfection. Although considered to be a sexually-transmitted disease, women may harbour the organism for years, so that its detection at a particular time does not necessarily indicate recent infidelity. Patients should be told this, so that unnecessary marital disharmony is avoided.

Genital Warts

Small genital warts may be ignored by the patient, but in other cases fear of a more serious cause for the lesions will result in considerable anxiety. Warts can also occasionally become so massive that they result in mechanical interference with intercourse. Difficulty in clearing the warts and persistent soreness due to treatment may place restrictions on sexual activity. What may seem a minor condition to the doctor could well have serious psychosexual effects on the patient.

Scabies

The itching of scabies tends to be worse at night. This, together with an unsightly rash and the frequent presence of penile lesions, may affect sexual desire. Unfortunately, scabies is often misdiagnosed so that patients suffer needless discomfort for long periods.

Pediculosis pubis

The discovery of pubic lice ("crabs") by an individual is likely to result in distaste and diminished libido.

Chemical Agents

Balanoposthitis and vulvovaginitis may result from primary irritation or sensitization by locally applied chemical agents. Such agents may have been used because of fear of having acquired venereal disease after a casual sexual exposure. Patients may use strong solutions of Dettol or other antiseptics, and may mistake the consequent inflammation for a manifestation of a sexually-transmitted disease. Condom sensitivity is also seen occasionally and can obviously place restraints on intercourse when it is the chosen method of contraception. Such patients are generally referred to a dermatologist for detailed patch testing against the various components of the condom. Sometimes another brand may be found which lacks the offending agent and Durex market a "Special Allergy Formulation Protective". Also worth bearing in mind are possible sensitizing agents in the various creams sold as sexual aids for impotence and premature ejaculation; when such patients attend VD clinics the underlying psychosexual problems should not be forgotten.

Vaginal deodorants and some soaps can also cause vulvovaginitis with associated dyspareunia. They may have been used in an attempt to mask an offensive vaginal discharge, perhaps resulting from a trichomonal infection.

Dermatological Conditions

Apart from those mentioned above patients are sometimes seen in VD clinics with other non-venereal dermatological conditions affecting the genitalia. It may have been fear of venereal disease which brought the patient or referral by a general practitioner for exclusion of a venereological cause. Findings of no significance, such as prominent coronal papillae (hirsutes papillaris penis) or ectopic sebaceous glands (Fordyce spots) may, nevertheless, greatly worry some persons when first noticed, and appropriate reassurance should be given. The non-venereal nature of conditions such as balanitis xerotica obliterans, psoriasis, lichen planus, Behcet's disease, Stevens-Johnson syndrome, and fixed drug eruptions affecting the genitalia, should be explained to the patient to avoid needless additional anxiety and possible psychosexual problems.

Urological Conditions

Similarly, patients with non-venereal urological conditions may find their way to VD clinics. Although recurrences of bacterial cystitis in women may follow sexual intercourse, this is not usually on the basis of sexual transmission of the organism concerned. Great distress may be suffered by women with the "urethral syndrome" but up to now the venereologist has been able to add little to the elucidation of this condition. Again, men with conditions such as torn fraenum, paraphimosis, Peyronie's disease, etc. should be reassured about the non-venereal nature of their complaint.

Ano-rectal Conditions in Homosexuals

In large cities — particularly London — male homosexuals make up a disproportionately large part of the VD clinic attenders (in relation to their supposed number in the community). Homosexual promiscuity is said largely to account for this situation. Female homosexuals rarely present to VD clinics.

Primary psychosexual problems will be mentioned later. Physical conditions in passive homosexuals likely to be particularly troublesome and restricting sexual intercourse are massive ano-rectal warts and ano-rectal herpes (see p. 409). Painful anal fissures may be produced by traumatic intercourse and even when due to other causes prolonged periods of abstinence may be necessary before healing occurs. It is also not unknown for patients with primary syphilis of the anal region to have had the lesion diagnosed as an anal fissure and excised before the true diagnosis was discovered.

Sexual Problems as Seen by the Venereologist where the Cause is Primarily Psychological

The "Bangladeshi Syndrome"

This may be defined as a chronic psychosexual problem arising in Bangladeshi men living in the East End of London. Language, cultural and socio-economic factors are implicated. A similar syndrome has been described in Indian immigrants in Southall (Clyne, 1964).

Most of the men are in their twenties and thirties and are Muslims. They are generally married but leave their wives and children in Bangladesh while they come to this country for several years to earn money by doing semi-skilled or unskilled work. These men often live together in overcrowded all-male communities. One of the many problems they face is that of lack of a satisfactory sexual outlet. Because of their limited English and lack of social poise such outlets are mainly with prostitutes. Some thus acquire sexually-transmitted diseases. However, a complaint of urethral discharge and penile pain may bring the patient to the clinic, but no evidence of sexually-transmitted disease is found. Careful questioning reveals that the urethral discharge mostly occurs at the end of micturition, or whilst straining at stool. This picture points to prostato-vesicular overflow and is physiological, being a consequence of sexual continence. These men often insist they have gonorrhoea but they do so only in the original sense of the word, i.e. running of the sperm! Another complaint may be of "weakness" which is regarded as due to "too much night pollution" (nocturnal emission). Sometimes the genital symptoms are subordinate to various others such as chest or abdominal pain, so that the patients may attend various other departments before the underlying psychosexual problem is discovered. Those men who have had sexual experience with prostitutes may be no better off. This is generally too infrequent to act as a satisfactory outlet, and when attempted is often unsuccessful with premature emission or impotence. Cultural and religious taboos seem to dictate that masturbation, like frequent nocturnal emissions, is harmful. It is therefore not practised.

Treatment of this complex problem is difficult. The patient has little insight into his conflict. At the root of the problem is his sexual continence. This could be resolved by his rejoining his wife, but by so doing he will have to abandon his money-raising enterprise and failure in this would have its own psychological repercussions. Bengali-speaking doctors in the area will be an obvious asset by rooting out depressive or other treatable psychiatric problems in the patient's illness. It is difficult to get the patients to accept that their symptoms are functional; they are loathe to use masturbation as a sexual outlet so that nocturnal emissions are likely to continue. Treatment, especially by injections, is often requested by the patient for his supposed illness and sometimes a placebo does seem to help when simple explanation and reassurance have failed.

Venereophobia

Venereologists commonly see patients who have a fear of venereal disease. In most cases this is transient, being relieved by examination and reassurance. The term venereophobia is used only for those patients who persist in this mistaken belief, which is really more of a delusion than a phobia. They may attend several hospitals insisting that their belief will eventually be shown to be true. In some cases the patient has, in fact, had a venereal disease but cannot accept that he has been cured.

Not surprisingly, the condition is associated with impaired sexual function, and most of these patients have infrequent or no sexual intercourse and do not enjoy it when they do. The venereophobia might have arisen during a period of sexual inadequacy and serve as an excuse for curtailing further sexual activity. If there is obvious anxiety or depression, then tranquillizers or anti-depressants may help. Unhappily the condition is often intractable but the patient may learn to live with his myth which he presumably needs to maintain.

Because NSU is now so common it may trigger the condition, and a relapsing NSU may well confirm in the patient's mind that he has an organic cause for what are quite unrelated symptoms. Fortunately very few patients with relapsing NSU develop full-blown venereophobia, although, as already mentioned, anxiety is common and depression may occur.

Symptoms Used as an Excuse to Avoid Sexual Intercourse

Some patients are seen in VD clinics who complain of symptoms which, after careful assessment and full investigation, cannot be explained on any physical basis. Certain of these patients (particularly males) will fall into the category of venereophobia, but others have no worries about venereal disease and seem to need their symptoms as a reason for not having sexual intercourse. Although seen in both sexes, it is more often come across in women, and most of these patients find their way to gynaecologists rather than venereologists. However, if the underlying psychosexual problem is not recognized by the doctor or not accepted as being significant by the patient, she may attend several hospitals and different departments, including the VD clinic, with symptoms such as vulval soreness and irritation, or abdominal pain, made worse by intercourse.

Ignorance about Sex and Sexual Problems Presenting as Such to the Venereologist

Apart from men with the "Bangladeshi Syndrome" few patients are either sent to, or attend VD clinics of their own accord, primarily because of overt sexual difficulties such as impotence or premature ejaculation. Sadly, these complaints are not always dealt with sympathetically elsewhere, and much more needs to be done to help couples with psychosexual problems. Unfortunately, this is not easy to do in hard-pressed VD clinics, but it is important to lend a sympathetic ear and to examine the patients thoroughly so that they can be reassured regarding the absence of general illness or venereal disease as a cause of their problem. If prolonged counselling is required, and the time or expertise of the venereologist too limited to provide this, then arrangements can be made for the couple to be seen elsewhere.

Men with sexual problems may well increase in number because of the greater demands of and greater proficiency expected by their now more sexually aware partners. The ready availability of most VD clinics may prompt some of these men to attend there rather than elsewhere. In some cases they may have previously attended a VD clinic for other reasons and may relate their present problem to past sexually-transmitted disease. Some patients are embarrassed to discuss the matter with their general practitioner, and prefer to do so with someone they do not know.

Homosexuals may, of course, also suffer from premature ejaculation and impotence. Most of those seen in clinics have accepted their homosexuality, but occasionally a homosexual asks to be "changed". Others, whilst not wanting to change, become anxious or depressed about their orientation. Complicated psychosexual problems are likely to arise when a previously repressed homosexuality asserts itself in someone who has married, particularly when homosexually acquired disease is subsequently transmitted to the spouse.

The following two case histories are examples of problems related to ignorance about sex which we were able to help at the Whitechapel Clinic:

Case 1: A 45-year-old moderately intelligent man was being followed up at the Whitechapel Clinic because of recurrent NSU. A psychosexual history was taken when he complained of mild, vague, persistent perineal pain. There was, at this time, no evidence of NSU or prostatitis.

He had been married for 23 years and had two grown up children who lived away from home. Both he and his wife denied either pre-marital or extra-marital intercourse. He complained that he wanted intercourse about twice a week, but his wife was uninterested and "a television addict". On closer questioning, he had little knowledge of sexual foreplay which amounted to only brief fondling of the breasts; he did not know of the existence of, and had never felt, the clitoris. Conversation about intercourse was taboo. On speaking to the wife, she complained that her mother had never talked about intercourse, and she had got the impression "it was dirty". Intercourse with her husband was a shock to her at first, and she had never subsequently enjoyed it. She therefore "took no interest".

Sex education and supportive psychotherapy have eased the tense home situation somewhat, and have made intercourse more enjoyable than was hitherto possible.

Case 2: A 19-year-old dairy farmer's son complained of penile soreness on attempted intercourse with his wife. They had been married for one year; neither had had sexual intercourse before marriage. She had intended to use a cap and foam as contraception, but the marriage had not been consummated. The pain on attempted intercourse had rendered him impotent. He and his wife were examined. No physical abnormality was found in her case. He had a slightly phimotic foreskin and a taut fraenum that split on attempted intercourse. He had never retracted his foreskin, and was surprised when this was done by the doctor. All the problems were resolved by frenulectomy.

In both these cases, sex education was lacking. In Case 1 it was never given. In Case 2 it was given but not understood. Both patients presented of their own accord to the clinic.

Who Should Attend Clinics?

Individuals who develop symptoms after sexual intercourse outside of a regular relationship are likely to think of the possibility of sexually-transmitted disease and most will attend a clinic or their own doctor, who will probably refer them to a clinic. It is not sufficiently recognized, however, that infection might exist in the absence of symptoms. This is commonly the case in females and passive homosexuals. Thus, anyone who has been exposed to risk of infection or suspects this possibility for any reason (e.g. suspicion of infidelity of the regular partner) should attend a clinic for examination and advice.

Patients attending for so-called "check-ups" are welcomed by clinics and more ready attendance by such persons, particularly women and passive homosexuals, would lessen the burden of the contact-tracer. Clinics are also happy to see patients with genital conditions apparently arising in the absence of sexual contact other than with the regular partner. For example, many women with *Candida* infection are seen in whom the mechanism of infection is uncertain and who may have harboured the organism for long periods before symptoms arise; genital herpes can arise from orogenital contact which may not have been practised by the couple until the relationship has existed for some time; NSU sometimes occurs in married men when neither they nor their wives have been unfaithful. It is hoped that the general public will realize that attendance at a clinic does not automatically imply promiscuity and infidelity; nor do the staff of clinics attempt to pass moral judgement on those who do behave in this way.

Summary

The fact that a patient has, or thinks he may have, a sexually-transmitted disease, generally implies that he is capable of sexual intercourse. It does not, however, mean that his sex life is necessarily a happy one. The reverse might be the reason for a married patient's infidelity. The various problems that may arise in relation to sexually-transmitted diseases and other conditions seen in VD clinics are outlined. Those conditions that can be difficult to eradicate or are prone to recur (e.g. non-specific urethritis, genital herpes, genital warts) will be more likely to have psychosexual repercussions. It is incumbent on the venereologist in his management of these patients to do his best to avoid adding iatrogenic sexual problems.

Primary psychosexual illness presenting to the venereologist is usually chronic, complex and difficult to treat. Various symptoms might be used as an excuse to avoid sexual intercourse and the underlying psychosexual problem may not be recognized. Certain groups of immigrants having no regular sexual outlet may have special problems. Fortunately frank venereophobia is rarely seen. Difficulties resulting from ignorance of the anatomy and physiology of sex are not commonly seen, but may be effectively dealt with by the venereologist.

References

Bro-Jørgensen, A. and Jensen, T. (1973). Gonococcal pharyngeal infections. *British Journal of Venereal Diseases*, 49, 491–499.

Catterall, R. D. (1966). *Candida albicans* and the contraceptive pill. *Lancet*, 2, 830–831.

Clyne, M. B. (1964). Indian patients. *Practitioner*, 193, 195–199.

Department of Health and Social Security (1974). "Annual Report of the Chief Medical Officer for 1973." pp. 48–58. HMSO: London.

Goldmeier, D., Bateman, J. R. M. and Rodin, P. (1975). Urinary retention and intestinal obstruction associated with ano-rectal *Herpes simplex* virus infection. *British Medical Journal*, 2, 425–426.

18 Sexual Problems Following Major Abdominal Surgery

G. T. WATTS

The surgeon involved in major abdominal operations is usually concerned with pathology which, even if not life-threatening, must
inevitably take pride of place over all other considerations. Unless
therefore the patient makes an explicit comment on sexual matters
the subject is not likely to be given any attention by the average
surgeon. A few patients will ask when normal marital relationships
may be resumed but this is unusual and in any case is merely a question of return of strength in scars. Most patients recommence coitus
as wound discomfort goes. Others of course may use the operation as
an excuse for abandonment or change in marital pattern but here the
issue is not in effect connected directly with the surgery. On the other
hand there are patients where there is a desire to resume coitus but
when the attempt is made it is found to be impossible for either
organic or emotional reasons. These patients have often lost contact
with the surgeon by the time the trouble is recognized or admitted
and hence the surgeon is unaware of its existence.

Sexual problems after surgery may affect either sex and may be
caused directly or arise indirectly from effect on the partner. This
latter point is very little recognized. It is most obviously seen after
breast surgery. Many women who have had mastectomy, either volun-
tarily or involuntarily leave the marital bed and sleep alone. Many of
their husbands seek sexual satisfaction elsewhere and divorce is much

more frequent in women who have had mastectomy than in the rest
of the population — a situation which may perhaps be ameliorated
now that reconstruction of the breast after its removal has become
a sound and regular practice, even in cancer.

   Inability to have intercourse normally may arise either by organic
blocks or by psychological ones. The first may be simply mechanical
or it may be patho-physiological whereby the normal mechanisms of
erection, secretion, muscular contraction etc. cannot occur.

"Mechanical" Problems

The most obvious mechanical barrier to coitus is one affecting a scar.
Inevitably a tender or weak scar will interfere with sexual activity. The
usual and incorrect answer given to a patient who asks when coitus
may be resumed is three months. This is an arbitrary figure based on
the usual of concept of healing time in wounds and the assumption
that the scar will be subject to maximum strain in what is seen as a
violent form of activity. Even were either of these premises inevitable
and, even were the patient unable to vary the coital position, such
caution is unnecessary and most patients are able to return to a satisfactory relationship at the end of 3—4 weeks if the hazards are explained. Most do not wish to start much earlier after major surgery,
but if they know that it will be possible, then the anxiety, frustration
and emotional damage which would otherwise ensue is avoided.
Often too the use of mild analgesics such as aspirin can be recommended with advantage, especially if there is tenderness of scars in crucial
areas.

   The other type of mechanical hazard to which patients are exposed
is when some deformity is produced which actively interferes with
coitus, either on its own or because of other effects such as the need
to wear appliances. The most frequent is some form of intestinal stoma
and these merit consideration separately later. There is a certain
cavalier-like attitude to these still widely extant amongst surgeons,
especially of the rather out-dated "wide excision cures cancer" school.
Since they tend to adopt the "You're lucky to be alive" attitude the
patient often departs with gratitude, accepting the limitations imposed
without complaint or comment. Even if this attitude is to be adopted
by the surgeon, however, it still behoves him ill not to consider the
fact that the site or method of his operation can often be modified
without hazard to his principles and to attempt to make life more

tolerable to a victim who has after all already suffered emotionally from the disease itself and the need for surgery.

Other mechanical problems ensue from such complications as herniae in scars. Sexual satisfaction is difficult to achieve if a restraining hand or belt is needed to contain the surge of bowel, omentum or other organs into a sac. Modern anaesthesia, in this country at least, is now such that it is fair to say that anyone fit enough to perform the sexual act is fit enough to tolerate an anaesthetic and operation to correct such a problem. Admittedly, large defects may pose a problem but synthetic material for closing defects and suturing wounds now available are easy and safe to insert even in these cases and the reticence one felt in the days of fascial grafts or kangaroo-tendon repair is out of date.

As a side-comment it is perhaps appropriate here to remark on what is perhaps a sexual problem in reverse, namely excessive obesity which cannot be controlled by dietary or medical measures. Here the mechanical difficulty posed by the great weight and deformity of the excess fat can be resolved by an operation. The jejuno-ileostomy operation propularized by Baddeley (Baddeley, 1973; Brewer *et al.*, 1974) is highly successful in these patients and is often successful in other ways in that when the obesity has been overcome the patient is able to solve the psychological or sexual problems which precipitated the onset of the trouble.

Pathologico/Physiological Interference with Coitus

This type of problem may affect both sexes. Both men and women may suffer from severe and widespread dissemination of disease or infection but when this occurs the patient's overall state is usually such that there is no desire for coitus by men or women. In other cases, however, the sexes differ greatly. In the female satisfactory relationships may be achieved even in a totally passive role but in the male the necessity to achieve and maintain an erection makes the process more liable to failure, hence this type of problem is more common in the male.

In the female difficulties of this nature only arise following operations on the structures related to the vagina where distortion, narrowing or shortening occur. They are therefore nowadays relatively unusual, for improvement of surgical technique in gynaecology now rarely leaves the short or narrow vagina so frequently created in the

past in an attempt to prevent prolapse or other problems developing
or recurring at a later date. Operations on the rectum do not usually
cause problems directly although when a colostomy is needed other
factors are developed. Rarely does the problem arise now of disturbance of sensation or loss of vagina from wide-sweeping exenteration
operations; the use of better radiotherapy techniques and anti-mitotic
drugs has made them unnecessary.

Despite improved modern methods, however, difficulty can still
occur in the female from complications of abdominal surgery. Remote
complications are not relevant to sexual problems but local ones are
valid in this connection. These take the form of sinuses and fistulae.
These can result from rupture of an abscess, sloughing of tissue,
damage to organs or extension of a still-active process. Fortunately
sinuses from abscesses usually clear up spontaneously unless the infection is of a tuberculous, syphilitic or other similar type. When
disease is still active resolution will not follow and the persistence of
the sinus or fistula may well indicate the presence or reactivation of
such a process and further treatment will be needed. In the young,
Crohn's disease holds first place, followed by ulcerative colitis, while
later in life diverticulitis or cancer are more frequently the offenders.
These patients will need surgery for diversion, or excision of the
disease. Urinary fistulae following surgery result almost always from
damage to the bladder base or ureters in pelvic operations. Needless
to say further surgery is needed although it is amazing that patients
may still enjoy coitus despite the presence of such a lesion. The same
is sometimes true when a fistula occurs between bowel and vagina
although normally most patients naturally find it unacceptable until
the lesion has been corrected.

In the male although fistulae and sinuses may also occur, they do
not usually give rise to sexual problems. The difficulty which the male
experiences is with erection. Here two mechanisms are involved —
maintenance of blood supply and the nervous mechanisms to control
it. Otherwise erection is not possible. It is often said that surgery on
the sympathetic nerve tract will produce impotence in the male. It is
doubtful how true this is for the sympathetic nervous system is
notable for its multitudinous pathways which often make it impossible
to cut off sympathetic supply to a part easily. In the past sympathectomy has been most widely used in patients whose arterial disease has
caused symptoms — mostly in the legs. These patients therefore already
have impairment of blood supply. In the past confusion occurred
because it was not possible to decide easily how much obstruction to

arteries was present nor its site. If there is an obstruction high up the patient will be impotent — the state of affairs usually referred to as the Lériche syndrome. Any operation on the sympathetic system may be blamed for the impotence in these patients but in fact the impotence was pre-ordained or pre-existent. When, however, the obstruction can be removed as in the modern replacement or re-canalizing operations there is a possibility that erection may return. It is, however, important to know whether impotence existed before and to realise that even if the block is cleared the poor blood supply nearer the penis may still prevent re-instatement of erection. Similarly, when, as rarely occurs, an obstruction develops in the blood vessels after an operation, its clearance may not be enough to allow full flow for erection.

Other interference with erection may follow wide clearance of tissues in the pelvis. This in the male is associated with excision of the rectum or less often of the bladder for either malignant or other conditions. At first sight this might also be regarded as due to damage to nervous and vascular mechanisms and in some cases this may be so. Far more often the change is due to emotional factors and this is seen when it is noted that the degree to which impotence occurs depends not on the extent of the operation but on the nature of the condition and the end state of the patient. Those cases who have a colostomy are more likely candidates for impotence. Those who do not, even amongst the older age group can be expected not to be so affected.

The Problems of Colostomy and Other Artificial Openings

We have mentioned earlier the effects on a patient of a fistula into the vagina or elsewhere in the genital area. It is not surprising that one or other sexual partner should find the discharge of faeces, urine or pus in that area distasteful to the point where coitus becomes impossible. Such situations may be unintentional as a result of disease of injury, but what of the case where a planned opening is made in the abdominal wall? This is a not uncommon event in abdominal surgery as, although it is now less necessary for some complaints, new procedures have been developed for others which again need such a measure as part of a life-saving plan in combination with drug and other therapy. Even before the advent of disposable plastic receptacles and adhesive devices it was possible for many of these patients to lead remarkably normal lives but until recently no-one has

considered sexual sequelae. What happened to those already married
and did the un-wed ever reach marriage or sexual life? The result
appears to depend on a very complex combination of factors. The
patients intelligence is important in that, if high, it enables an intellectual over-ride to be achieved or if low it permits the problem to be
ignored. The degree of social development is important too, for those
of fastidious nature will find emotional problems both of their own
and for their partner's reaction and sensitivity. It is significant how
problems disappear and apparent voluntary celibacy is abandoned in
those who are able to be restored to normal after a period with one
of these artificial openings.

There is no doubt that to all except a few, any stoma presents a
major hurdle in sexual life with psychological frigidity or impotence or
lesser degrees of sexual disharmony or inadequacy. This results partly
from revulsion at the possible mishaps from leakage of excrement or
of odour and partly from the feeling of embarrassment at physical
mutilation. Even those who can accept mutilation on their own behalf
are less confident when proferring a deformed body for the close and
tender inspection of others. Only the very sophisticated are regularly
able to be different from the herd with assurance at any time and even
they are disadvantaged where sex is concerned. A mechanical problem
here is less of a hurdle than a deformity. Those with rigid hips or
spines will devise almost unbelievable methods of overcoming the
barriers but a deformity is an intellectual challenge and harder to face.
We have mentioned previously the effect of loss of the breast on
women and the salutary effect of breast reconstruction, but the problem does not apply to one sex or one age. Even the octogenarian male
dislikes the thought of losing a testis but if he knows that he can have
it replaced by a plastic one he accepts the procedure cheerfully! Unfortunately artificial openings of bowel or bladder cannot be so simply
solved but the emotional disaster can be averted by wise planning and
advice.

An excellent example of skill and foresight is shown by the work of
Professor B. Brooke on ileostomy for ulcerative colitis (Brooke 1951,
1952). In this the whole of the colon is removed and the patient has
an opening discharging fluid faeces. The disease occurs in a predominantly youthful, nervous and intelligent group of people and the
emotional implications are enormous. Realising this Professor Brooke
first devised a different opening which allowed easy collection of the
faeces and then developed better collecting bags. He then had a much
more receptive audience to instruct, but they needed confidence.

With his guidance, an association was formed of these people, who met to discuss mutual problems but at a social function. The benefit to patients in relationships was dramatic and with the emotional recovery many of these patients again formed heterosexual relationships and marriage and reproduction both within and outside the group ensued. Without such education there is no doubt that many of these young people would have become frigid or impotent and the operation thought to have damaged vital links in the chain of sexual activity.

Colostomy is a much older procedure than ileostomy and is re-garded by many as simple to manage. Whilst from the solid nature (usually) of the material to be collected this is so, there are also added fears apart from those considerations above – of unexpected diarrhoea or of the escape of unpleasant smelling gas. Both of these are likely under the stress of sexual excitement. Casanova noted that some of his partners had increased bowel noises or passed wind under his hand – how much more likely is this to be a trouble with an unguarded opening! These patients therefore also need education in management of the colostomy by care in choice of foods and in control of the colostomy by this or by drugs. Irrigation of the bowel is a poor method, although at one time popular, for it makes an irritable bowel – much better to have a regular action so that it can be predicted and the colostomy sealed with an unobtrusive adhesive dressing when sexual activity is contemplated.

Odour is an important agent in sexual activity, albeit less in man than in animals. It may have a negative or a positive effect. Although perfume has been in use for centuries it only gained its great popularity when Madame du Barry used it to disguise the foul smell of her royal lover's jaw. Since then it has become more and more widespread at lower and lower social levels and is now at its loudest amongst the working-class male population. For the patient with an artifical opening this is useful although it does not allow the need for clean-liness and local care to be ignored. The smell of any such opening is most often its trademark and this can be better avoided by cleanliness and avoidance of secondary infection than by any counter-odour.

Overall Management of Sexual Problems in Patients Undergoing Major Surgery

Although major surgery in the abdomen whether it be on the blood vessels, the bowel or other organs may directly influence a patient

sexually, in general it should not be isolated from other forms of
stress of an emotional or physical nature that any individual may be
asked to undergo. As in all affairs of life, driving a car, running a bank,
playing a game or exploring a jungle, the secret of avoiding disaster is
anticipation and prevention. For avoidance of the sexual difficulties
in the period following surgery this involves three phases. The first is
to check that there are or have been no antecedent signs of organic
or emotional problems that, aggravated by the surgery, could lead to
later effects. The next is to avoid unnecessarily distressing procedures
which may inhibit the patient sexually and where these are unavoidable to educate the patient in advance and afterwards in the best way
to handle the situations produced. Finally it is vital to be vigilant
without being obtrusive. An over-inquisitive approach makes many
defensive and too direct questioning will be met with the evasive reply
that, "everything is fine", although later the victim or the partner may
reveal the true state of affairs. A casual enquiry after a few weeks or
months whether coitus has been attempted or returned to normal
shows understanding and provides an opportunity for both sides to
broach the subject when necessary.

Organic sexual disorders after abdominal surgery are rare and may
not respond well, if at all, although one never ceases to marvel at the
body's power of recovery, especially where reproduction is concerned.
Emotional disorders on the other hand are a great test of the therapist
as in all other circumstances involving psychosexual disorder. The
greatest danger we have found is to bow to impatience. Modern medicine has led us to expect high speed miracle cures but there are no
antibiotics or operations in this field! Those who treat and those who
are treated must realise this or as a long-term hazard the sexual disturbance may outshine the disease or operation it followed.

Summary

Sexual changes and disturbances following major surgery are most
often emotional in origin although related to the disease process. Less
often they are caused by the disease process itself. The mechanism
in the two sexes is completely different. In the female with organic
changes the disturbance is due almost entirely to mechanical changes
interfering with coitus. In the male, however, the process is a more
complex one in that nervous mechanisms and vascular changes are

involved. Often the processes have been present some considerable time before the surgery and sexual disturbance has been there also, although unrecognised because of the patient's preoccupation with the prime problems.

Emotional sexual problems are by far the most frequent but are usually unrecognized by the surgeon since they are overlooked or do not develop until some time after the operation when the patient has lost contact with the surgeon. All the usual causes of impotence and frigidity apply here although their cause could be missed. The most important factor in predisposition to these problems is some operation which causes either mutilation or aesthetic disability. In both sexes an artificial stoma for bowel content is by far the most important. In the female a voluntary frigidity is often produced by the mutilation of mastectomy. In this type of case it is very important that surgery should be planned to avoid these problems as far as possible and that the patient should be educated so that they may minimize their disability or adjust themselves, or where possible reconstructive surgery should be carried out for the patient to become as normal as possible. When this is done many patients who might have become devoid of a normal sexual life are found to have no problems whatsoever and many procedures which were thought to cause sexual disturbances directly are recognized as emotional phenomena which may be unavoidable.

References

Baddeley, M. (1973). Surgical treatment of obesity. *Proceedings of The Royal Society of Medicine*, 66, 1098–1099.

Brewer, C., White, H. and Baddeley, M. (1974). Beneficial effects of jejunoileostomy on compulsive eating and associated psychiatric symptoms. *British Medical Journal* 4, 314–316.

Brooke, B. N. (1951). The surgery of ulcerative colitis. *Ann. Royal College of Surgeons (England)*. 8, 440–456.

Brooke, B. N. (1952). The management of an ileostomy including its complications. *Lancet*, 2. 102–104.

IV | Sex Education

19 | What About A New Approach to Sex Education ?

MARTIN COLE

Sex Sense or Nonsense

Recent surveys into parents' attitudes about the need for religious instruction in schools has shown that an overwhelming number of these parents want a formal Christian education for their children. These mums and dads are not churchgoers themselves — contemporary Christianity being meaningless to most of them — yet they have a feeling that they ought to "play it safe" and vote for God and the *status quo* — just in case. After all, they argue, christian morality is a good morality and if any brushes off onto our kids so much the better — nothing is lost — so the reasoning goes.

The same kind of complacency seems to prevail when the question of sex education is raised. There are few or no pressure groups in favour of adopting a rationally formulated syllabus in sex education and where such syllabuses exist they are often woefully, indeed negligently, inadequate. The responsibility for the present inaction lies not only with the parents and teachers but particularly on the shoulders of head teachers and local education committees who, being elected representatives, will naturally be the first to "play it safe" in the absence of any constructive ideas of their own. It is this absence of a lead and the absence of a coherent policy for sex education that produces in this instance not a vote for God but a vote for ignorance (which must be bliss) since knowledge about sex means knowledge about VD, abortion, homosexuality, promiscuity and contraception, knowledge of which, of course, must be corrupting.

In discussions about sex passions run high amongst parents and teachers although rarely as high amongst children who, whilst they may have differing needs and hence differing attitudes, tend to co-exist much more readily. Parents cannot afford such a luxury and with vested interest they merrily project their fears and misgivings onto the next generation reliving the conditioning to which they as children were subjected a generation earlier.

I have shown my film (*Growing Up* 1971) to every type of audience imaginable. Two particular instances spring to mind — one was a large audience of biology teachers who were asked by the chairman to indicate whether they felt the film was good or bad for use in schools. A vote was taken after an hour or so of very vigorous discussion about the film and to my surprise the audience split evenly on this question. Half thought it a very good film and, with certain reservations, to be highly commended as a visual aid. The other half thought it appalling and that it should never be shown in schools. What was surprising to me was that one could get this kind of response from an essentially homogeneous middle class audience of professional biology teachers revealing as it did profound and seemingly irreconcileable differences of attitude. The other audience was a sixth form in a London Grammar School. Here the exchange of views was much more restrained and sensible. There was no vote this time and even though there were strong differences of opinion one got the impression that these opinions were based upon experience and reflected their day to day needs. Such a dialogue contrasted very favourably to the heated "academic" exchanges of the audiences of teachers. It seems clear to me that whatever sex education programmes are devised they must be based upon the needs of the consumer. With the best will in the world neither parents nor teachers will necessarily have that critical insight into the diversity of needs of young people. I prefer not to remember a third audience of Head Teachers, who really should have known better. Some of them spent over a quarter of an hour talking about the harmful moral and physiological consequences of masturbation which they were convinced existed — few audiences of adolescents would do that nowadays!

Sex Education "Ends" and "Means"

Sex education is, of course, very important to adults because to them it is something new — few had any when they were young and they are genuinely apprehensive about its consequences. Moreover to many adults sex education is more than simply providing information about sexual behaviour. To them it is about a way of life — about a code of values — indeed it is about how life should be lived — how sex and love must go together — how marriage (heterosexual of course) must provide the vehicle for sexual fidelity and how beautiful (and fun) it all is (or should be). It is to them a way of subjugating young people — of establishing and maintaining pecking orders, of regulating society and maintaining those immutable concepts of the protestant ethic of hard work and the nuclear family. But to most young people it is none of these things. Sex education for them is about contraception and masturbation, menstruation and VD: it is about the positions in intercourse, the hymen and premature ejaculation. Of course values are important to them but since their own are changing rapidly as they grow the second hand sale of a ready made instant morality, a generation stale, is hardly likely to appeal. And they say so time and time again — but even now there are very few sex educators who listen.

If any reliable information about sex is to be transmitted to youngsters it is clearly going to have to be done in school. But the study of sex is not an alternative to R.K. or ethics but a serious subject amenable to the rigours of the scientific method — indeed sexology because it has both academic and applied components would make an ideal O-level subject. It is truly interdisciplinary, not only borrowing from many sciences — biology, psychology, sociology, anthropology — but also from the arts — literature, history and graphic art. The average parent cannot hope to be able to provide up to date reliable information about the subject even if he wanted and, at puberty, even before, there exists a block to "talking sex" in many families — it's far too incestuous a pastime for most. This does not mean that the parent should opt out but his role should be to complement the objective information that the child should be receiving from school from the earliest years. It is worth noting that the regular family doctor may also be sufficiently close to the family to make him also an unsuitable advisor.

There should of course be little argument about what factual information is to be provided — the criterion being that the study of sex should be treated like any other subject and depending upon the child's age and intellectual attainment information should be presented so that a true grasp of the subject becomes possible.

Such an approach is often regarded as over-simplistic by some since they argue that one cannot present facts about, for example, homosexuality and abortion or intercourse and sexual deviation to "emotionally fragile" and immature thirteen year olds. But the evidence is to the contrary since where this is done objectively and sensibly and where visual aids are chosen with care one only detects an insatiable curiosity and a hunger for more information (*Understanding Sex,* 1971; Hunold, 1972; *Sexual Intercourse,* 1973). If it was as straightforward as this there would be few problems — unfortunately all facts, if they are to be made at all interesting, have to be presented in some kind of context. It is almost impossible to teach, especially to children whose interest must be maintained, in an ethical vacuum. Inevitably, therefore, a point of view will be expressed and this is where the trouble starts.

In order to proceed further it might be profitable to attempt to identify the aims and objects of sex education, although the argument very often is not about "ends" but "means". It seems reasonable to adopt a fairly pragmatic approach since much of the distress in adolescence is caused by preventable circumstances. The avoidance of unwanted pregnancy (there were over 50,000 legal abortions in the unmarried in 1974) seems to be near the top of the list. The reduction of the incidence of sexually-transmitted diseases must also be regarded as a problem of high priority although of course it should not be equated in importance to unwanted pregnancy.

A list of objectives to be achieved by a programme in sex education might read like this.

1. The prevention of unwanted pregnancy.
2. The prevention of sexually-transmitted disease.
3. The recognition and acceptance of sexual feelings as being good and desirable for their own sake.
4. The recognition of potentially and mutually damaging relationships.
5. The prevention of unwanted marriages.
6. The development of attitudes and insight which will enable the young person to perceive the role that sexual behaviour plays in the establishment of relationships.

Unwanted Pregnancy

The prevention of unwanted pregnancy involves at least two separate processes. The first is practical and revolves around the availability of contraceptives and the possession of sufficient "know how" by the individuals concerned for them to be used effectively. The second aspect is quite different and is to do with the motivation of those who are likely to be practising unprotected intercourse when they have no wish to begin a family.

The first practical issue need not concern us here in detail although of course much remains to be done to ensure that *all* forms of fertility control are *freely* available to *all* who demand them. The decision by the present Labour government to provide a totally free comprehensive family planning service under the NHS marked a profound step forward. In practice however such a service is far from adequate. Only about half of those women who need abortions are able to obtain them on the NHS and waiting lists for vasectomy on the NHS in some parts of the country are still unnecessarily long.

To provide contraceptives is one thing – to expect people to buy them and use them is quite another. Information gained from questioning patients requesting abortion in London about their contraceptive habits has demonstrated that almost 60% of single women seeking abortion did not even use contraceptives and on the occasion that led to the pregnancy in question nearly 80% were not using any method at all, not even withdrawal or the safe period (Lambert, 1971). Data from Birmingham is almost identical. Clearly then it is not so much a matter of contraceptive failure but failure to contracept. It might be worthwhile to list some of the reasons to account for this risk-taking in the unmarried which in the long term can have such disastrous consequences, although I suppose these risks are taken simply because the short term reward of spontaneous sex is stronger than the long term deterrent of an unwanted child.

1. Financial disincentives.
2. It is "chicken" to use contraceptives since it means conforming to "their" values.
3. It is contrived, artificial, unnatural and interferes with the spontaneity of love-making.
4. The use of birth control is alien to the purpose of sexual intercourse which is to do with making babies.
5. I want to get pregnant – I want something to love.

6. I want to get pregnant to prove I'm not sterile.

7. I couldn't care less and if it's OK with her it's alright with me —girls should look after that kind of thing.

8. If it's alright with him it's OK with me — boys should look after that kind of thing.

9. Hostility of the male towards the female "I'll get her in the club".

10. Hostility of the female towards the male "serve him bloody well right".

11. I can't go on the pill because if I do I shall have to admit to myself that I am sexual which of course I am not because for a woman to be sexy is wrong (that's what I was told at school).

12. I can't go on the pill because boyfriends will think that I am an easy lay (which I am).

13. I can't ask her if she is on the pill because if I do she will think I am only after one thing (which I am).

14. It is much more romantic without the pill — a sign of true love.

15. I want to have an abortion so that I can be punished for what I am doing.

Careful examination of these reasons will show that most of them stem from extremely ambivalent attitudes towards sex. The strong sense of guilt, shame, embarrassment — call it what you will — about adolescent sex leads young people to regard their sexual feelings as being undesirable and therefore such attitudes will inhibit rational and responsible behaviour. The adult society in which these young people have grown up has not encouraged either the boy or the girl to establish good contraceptive habits — indeed it has done just the opposite and fostered a climate of opinion which positively discourages young people from contracepting by regarding adolescent sexual behaviour as being something which is unacceptable. The obvious paradox here is that until sex educationalists can truly "bless" adolescent sexual behaviour so that it becomes completely normalized they will create conflicts and confusion in the minds of young people which will lead to this ambivalence about contraceptive usage.

Boys are still told to "respect" their girl friends and that "nice girls don't". What poppycock! Far too much secrecy still surrounds the subject of sex and many young girls and women learn all they ever know about sex and contraception from their boyfriends or husbands — men who may well have a vested interest in maintaining some form of ignorance in their partners.

Ultimately it is the attitudes of parents and teachers that need to be changed but this is a much more difficult task. After half a life time one has a vested interest in hanging on to one's ideas and it is not easy to change particularly if one seems to be on one's own. The existence of such deeply entrenched attitudes towards sex is clearly illustrated by society's attitude to pornography, attitudes which on examination can be clearly shown to be quite unreasonable. There is not one iota of evidence that either visual or written erotica will modify behaviour adversely — let alone deprave and corrupt — whatever that means. Yet in a succession of trials juries and magistrates up and down the country have found harmless men guilty of a charge of depraving and corrupting — they should be given medals instead, not sentences, since they provide valuable material useful in both sex education and the treatment of sexual problems. And one of the spin-offs of much of the publicity which attaches to these trials is that the young are even more confused since it is clearly seen that pornography is to be condemned yet whatever else pornography is about it is certainly to do with sex. Recently however there have been one or two important acquittals in obscenity trials, notably Rex v. Lindsay in Birmingham this year and I forsee a time when the office of the Director of Public Prosecutions will decide that the *Obscene Publications Acts* are truly unenforceable, that the law is being brought into disrepute and he will cease to waste public funds by sending the heavy boys of the Vice Squad out in their mischievious search for pornography. Is it not surprising that against this sexually punitive background young people find it hard to accept their sexual feelings with confidence? Is it not surprising that they get pregnant? We call it the guilty girl syndrome — or guilty boy syndrome — but why not the guilty mum and dad syndrome! (Cauthery and Cole, 1973).

Talking about contraception in a sex education class therefore involves rather more than displaying the various methods and explaining their mode of action. Careful consideration must be given to the profound reservations that many young people will have about openly obtaining advice. A seventeen-year-old boy attending a talk I gave to a local youth club said to me afterwards, "I know all about contraceptives but what happens if I find I haven't got a Johnnie late one Saturday afternoon when I need it — I can't go into the local chemist because the proprietor knows my Dad — so I'll have to take the risk!" His embarrassment is understandable enough and was presumably similar to that felt by the hero in *A Kind of Loving* who went into a chemist shop to buy some durex but when served by a blonde

instead of the proprietor lost his nerve and came out with a bottle
of lucozade instead!

Adolescents are Sexual

Central to any realistic programme on sex education should be the
idea that the adolescent is sexual. Sex education should at least
therefore create a feeling of benevolence towards sexual activity
instead of ambivalence. So many sex educators are mealy-mouthed
and uptight about sex. It is simply not good enough for them to
say when challenged about some inconsistency like disapproving of
the *Little Red Schoolbook* (Hansen and Jensen, 1971) — one of
the best publications to date in the field — "Don't get me wrong,
I'm in favour of sex, I think it beautiful and such fun *in the right
place of course*." How many times have I heard that! What they
are really saying is, and the message is loud and clear, "God gave
us sex so that deepest feelings between a man and woman can be
communicated in marriage and then and only then can the true
delights be experienced without guilt and shame etc., etc." A
worthy sentiment perhaps but not one which happens to be shared
by many young people these days.

After puberty the development of sexual behaviour commences at
birth, erection in the boy and masturbation to orgasm in both sexes
can be observed from the first year of life, clearly at puberty the
pace quickens and the behaviour becomes more overt. Of course
every sexual activity observable between adults is also observable in
pre-pubertal children and one of the dogmas of sex education
should be *never* to restrain or inhibit sexual activity in a child
whatever its form unless the child is in real physical danger.

After puberty the pattern and rate of sexual exploratory
behaviour becomes much more uniform and accelerates so that by
the age of between 17 and 18 about half the population of male
and female adolescents will have had intercourse. (If it sounds
better it is equally true to say that half haven't.) The proportion
who become sexually experienced after this age increases even more
rapidly when the now young adult leaves school and starts working
and living away from home. The point to be emphasized is that
although the median age of first coitus is about 17.5 years, most
educators do not take this fact into consideration when they design

their syllabus. Since a good half of that sexually experienced
sample are probably not even now contracepting effectively
(Schofield, 1968) the need for assertive education in birth control
is of course essential — but it normally goes by default because of
the moral dilemma that the educators have about condoning and
encouraging sexual activity. Most sex educators that I have met,
and these are sophisticated and experienced people that I am talking about, still have grave reservations about giving a sexual *carte
blanche* to young people. It is however the anxiety-laden reservations that they try to communicate to these young people that
produces the guilt and uncertainty in them and which results in
their ambivalence about their sexualities and hence ambivalence
towards contraception.

Sexually-transmitted Diseases

Nowhere are the uncertainties and fears of adult society more
clearly expressed than in their almost hysterical reaction to the
"epidemic" of sexually-transmitted disease. I shudder when I think
of what is said in the name of sex education when some venereologists visit schools. Some speakers are, I am sure, very good but
others, if their publications are anything to go by, shouldn't be
allowed near a school.

It should be clear to most that there is nothing to be gained in
this day and age by using the threat of VD as a kind of deterrent
to sexual activity but such a punitive approach is still part and
parcel of the programmes of many educators. Once again it is not
so much what is said but how it is said. For example, no good
whatsoever can ever come of showing colour slides of the consequences of tertiary syphilis — the condition is so rare now that
soon it will only be of academic interest. Yet such slides are still
occasionally used with the effect of inducing a considerable amount
of fear in the audience.

An approach which I believe is essential is to try and put the
sexually transmitted diseases in perspective. Compare their incidence
with other infections and stress the *similarities* between *all* infections. In other words, attempt to play down the fact that these are
sexual diseases. It is useful to develop the point that sexually-transmitted diseases are an occupational risk for those who practise sex

just as overeating is an occupational hazard for cooks and that
there is nothing very special about these infections even though
you are treated in a "special clinic". A venereologist friend of mine
puts it neatly when he tells his audiences that the penis or vulva is
an organ of the body like any other. It is subject to infection when
it is used, like any other, and has a right to be cured, like any
other. Such an approach is excellent.

But I hear the cry that sexually-transmitted diseases are not like
other diseases and because the immune reaction of the body is
poorly developed they will not get better without treatment. This
is an important point that must be stressed but at least one can
also stress at the same time that they normally do get better very
quickly when they are treated, which is more than can be said for
some diseases. People catch VD because they make love to other
people who are infected in the same way that mumps or a strep.
throat or glandular fever can be transmitted by kissing. Strictly,
since these can be caught in the "act of venery" they are also
venereal diseases.

There are only four ways of limiting the spread of the sexually-
transmitted diseases: by abstention, by exclusive monogamy, by
immediate diagnosis and cure, or by prevention.

To suggest exclusive monogamy as a means of control is about
as impracticable as recommending abstention yet in the name of
preventive medicine it has long been invoked over and over again
as a most important tool in the control of the sexually-transmitted
diseases. I doubt whether very much human sexual behaviour has
been modified as a result of this injunction — the only consequence
has been the generation of VD phobias which have generalized in
some to inhibit even normal sexual responses. If we are *very* generous and say that only one person out of every two will have more
than one sexual partner then the model exists for the spread of the
disease. *Homo sapiens* is a promiscuous primate and strict sexual
monogamy has never been more than a fond hope for the few by
the few.

Instant diagnosis and cure is again only possible in a minority of
cases because of the ingenious way in which the *Gonococcus* and
the chlamydia, thought to be responsible for some cases of non-
specific urethritis, have developed a largely symptomless way of
life in the female. Contact tracing can of course be very effective
but it is unlikely to do more than limit the spread of these diseases.

Preventive measures are clearly the most important and the ones to which most attention should now be directed. But we hear little of them because, like the provision of contraceptives, it makes it too easy — such an approach is contrary to the punitive antisexual element which still persists in much education about VD. The use of a sheath is of course an extremely effective prophylactic, particularly if the penis is washed before and after coitus with soap and water. For the over-anxious some savlon cream applied to the penis immediately after intercourse is ideal. One should also try to urinate as soon after coitus as possible. Professional call girls who are as experienced as any in this field are usually most meticulous about the hygiene of their clients and themselves. Indeed it is a great pity that the general public could not follow their example — if they did the incidence of gonorrhoea could be reduced to a fraction of its present incidence. Ultimately the most effective method of prevention is by vaccination but because of the body's poor immune reaction several years of research are yet to be completed before effective vaccines will be available. Venereologists in the US are thinking in terms of them being available in about five years. Work in this country is proceeding very slowly and will remain so until fatuous questions like "who shall we vaccinate?" no longer appear in the literature.

Having put the sexually-transmitted diseases in some kind of realistic perspective the dangers must clearly be spelt out — in particular the hazards to the woman if she develops symptomless gonorrhoea and runs a small but significant risk of becoming sterile if she is untreated. It might also be worthwhile reassuring her at the same time by saying that if she regularly sleeps with one or two partners they will certainly provide her with an early warning system enabling her to detect her infection through them.

Attention should also be directed to a correspondingly rare but nevertheless distressing complication of non-specific urethritis to which the male is particularly susceptible. Occasionally this infection will become chronic and can remain for several years. The effects are annoying as much as distressing because very little can be done about them. The symptoms are joint pains, a malaise and sometimes conjunctivitis and prostate pain. Bearing in mind the increasing incidence of non-specific urethritis such complications will also of course become correspondingly more frequent.

The object of sex education in this field therefore is to stress firstly *prevention* and secondly create attitudes which will enable the infected person to feel strongly motivated to take *immediate* steps to get treatment. Anything which will help to achieve these two objectives is good — the induction of shame and terror achieves absolutely nothing. In a nutshell perhaps the sexually transmitted diseases are best regarded as sports injuries.

Success in normalizing sexual behaviour will undoubtedly help adolescents to overcome some of the crises which so often present at this time of life. But such an approach in sex education is also important for its own sake since it will not only create attitudes which will enhance the quality of sexual relationships but it may also well prevent or stem the development of sexual dysfunctions in early adulthood — dysfunctions which may be incipient in the predisposed female or male. In those men suffering from say primary or secondary impotence, premature ejaculation or ejaculatory incompetence and in women who may present with vaginismus, dyspareunia or anorgasmic response there is so often a long history of negative learning rather than single events of traumatic learning. Preventing some of these casualties would be a very welcome consequence of a more compassionate approach to sex in sex education.

Sex and Love

An issue which has bugged sex education for many years is the relationship between "sexing" and "loving". The word sexing is fairly precise and requires no elaboration. Loving probably involves a more complex set of responses which can collectively be described as romantic arousal. These are more difficult to quantify in the way that say Masters and Johnson have analysed human sexual response but there is no doubt that they are quantifiable. Subjectively the feelings experienced are ones of commitment, need, attraction, submission and empathy; such responses being mediated largely by the autonomic nervous system. In most human interactions the arousal experienced involves both sexual and loving responses, nevertheless one or other or both sets of responses can be shut down either partially or almost completely in certain circumstances. For example, high levels of sexual anxiety may inhibit the sexual response and emotional deprivation in childhood the loving response. It is also clear that since experience will modify the expression of this behaviour both an overprotective and overexposed environment could be harmful. Currently however society seems still to be far too overprotective about

sexing with the result that many children and adolescents are exposed
to an unnecessary amount of negative experiences which, leading to
the inhibition of the sexual response, prevent the integration of sexing
and loving in the normal way.

I am thinking of the almost universally accepted idea that relationships which are largely based upon sex are in some sense regarded as
inferior to those where loving feelings predominate. Yet by adopting
these values one denies the growing individual the important freedom
of learning about sex. It is so easy to set up the ideal relationship with
which few would quarrel and yet become so preoccupied with the
ideal that one disregards two essential points. Firstly is the diversity
of need and response of human beings which prevents any realistic
generalizations being made about sexing and loving and secondly
that by becoming preoccupied with "whole" integrated and loving
relationships one inevitably adopts anti-sexual postures which in
time may prevent growth and a possible integration of sex and love
in young people.

Of course at the back of all this is the so called psychoanalytical
ideal. That is a heterosexual relationship between two "mature"
people capable of loving on all planes and sexing as equals, having co-
incident orgasms every time throughout their reproductive lives –
and all with a text above the bed! I doubt if few would argue with
the desirability of such an ideal (as few would about the prospect of
heaven and angels) but as a basis for sex education however it is non-
sense. Sex education must be based upon observable fact, not fantasy
– indeed it is the unreality of sex educators' attitudes to *sex* that
should concern us more than anything.

Of course the situation could be reversed where loving feelings are
denied and sexual responses encouraged and an equally unsatisfactory
situation could prevail. My plea is simply to give sex a chance for
only by a more permissive approach can we expect young people to
recognize and where possible integrate both their loving and sexual
feelings.

Consideration of the conflict between love and sex leads one on to
the *central paradox* of sex behaviour. This is that the establishment
of ideals is often self-defeating since failure to achieve the ideal
creates a sense of inadequacy and anxiety making the ideal even more
elusive. In the love-sex paradigm the greater the denial of sex that
exists, in the hope that this will create a better relationship, the less
the individual is able to achieve a reconciliation of these needs and
hence a good relationship. In part the same paradox applies to homo-

sexuality and masturbation. In a society where homosexuality is condemned the young persons experiencing homosexual feelings will feel
anxious and in so far that it is sexual anxiety that accounts for *some*
types of homosexual behaviour the situation is simply exacerbated by
these negative attitudes. Blessing homosexuality allows the same
adolescents to experience their feelings without shame, normalize
them, and then perhaps learn to cope with the even greater anxiety —
provoking experience of attempting to sex heterosexually. Quite
obviously strict taboos about masturbation have one result only —
they make young people feel guilty about sex which in turn makes
them more inhibited which will mean that they will become more,
not less, dependent upon autosexual rewards. In one instance I found
in the treatment of paedophilia (paederasty) that only by blessing
and hence normalizing such a relationship was one able to suggest
and then actually arrange therapy with a boyish looking girl surrogate
partner.

Thus by proscribing sex and encouraging love one interferes with
the natural morality of the growing adolescent. He becomes confused
because what he is led to believe from his own responses is so often
at variance with what he is told at school. In order to avoid this conflict he should be supported in his personal conviction, where it exists,
that sex is good for its own sake since a denial of these feelings will
result in negative responses in both a sexing and a loving situation.
Such an approach is *not* in support of sexual anarchy indeed such
anarchy is more likely to arise in grossly inhibited communities than
in a society where honesty and reason prevail and where an individual
at least has an opportunity to learn to be responsible for his own
actions, good and bad.

At the risk of being slightly repetitious I think it worthwhile to
attempt to identify again the reasons why sex should be blessed,
approved and normalized in sex education.

In the first place the average adolescent does not have too much
difficulty in "loving". Social pressures are on his side — loving has
always been approved and the need for romantic association is normally quite strong in both sexes unless there has been severe emotional
deprivation earlier in life. Indeed such romanticism is often too
strong, leading to the establishment of unstable and unreal adolescent
pairbonds which if they persist for too long may end in unsatisfactory
marriages — depriving both partners of those essential learning experiences which are so important. The need for such innovatory and
exploratory sexual and loving behaviour patterns cannot be over

emphasized if judgements about long-term pairbonding are to be made with the maximum amount of foresight. Thus, although many young people can love quite well, they often cannot sex at all. This may not matter to them very much at this age — or it may matter a lot and lead to a considerable degree of frustration. However, such "sexual malnutrition" can set them at a considerable disadvantage in later life — simply because of inexperience or predispose to an unstable pairbond as a result of the simple deprivation of experience — the compulsive need to compensate for this providing a threat to the other partner. Men and women who marry and who have never had extra-marital sexual experiences before or during their marriage are really virgins and are behaving in a singularly unbiological manner. Our society may well have succeeded in making a virtue out of such behaviour but the "virtuous" are often paying a high price for their unnatural behaviour as many of us, when we try to heal broken relationships or renew sex lives, which are as dead as dinosaurs, well know.

Promiscuity therefore is good and an adaptive form of behaviour. Of course on occasion it can be a manifestation of a personality disorder but so of course can masturbation and homosexuality, neither of which should be regarded as anything but normal in other circumstances. The great advantage of promiscuous sexing and loving is that such exploratory behaviour allows the individual the opportunity to measure himself against others and acquire the confidence and self-esteem that are so important if effective and adaptive sex behaviour patterns are to be preserved into later life. But in sex education how often do we hear anything in praise of promiscuity. Instead there exists a complete denial of the erotic, the kids only hearing about the rabbit and love — nothing very sexy about them — and of course VD and abortion (but not contraception) because they are punitive. As one girl said, "but they never told us how much we would want to do it". (Morton Williams and Hindell, 1972). If instead, a positive attitude to erotic behaviour is adopted then young people will cease to deny their sexuality and consequently be better prepared to accept realistic warnings in good faith because they could then more readily accept the authority of the teacher (Hill and Lloyd Jones, 1970).

The Princess and the Prostitute

To many young people the antagonistic needs of love and sex are very strong — some are much better at loving and others at sexing

and these differences in personality are probably strongly inherited
(Chilton, 1972). Where this kind of conflict brings an adolescent into
contact with professionals for help and guidance, the rule should be
firstly to normalize their current behaviour pattern to reduce anxiety
and then skilfully to reward those aspects of behaviour which have
been denied. I should guess that in about half the population there is
a complete resolution of this "prostitute-princess syndrome" (the
"cassonova-prince syndrome" in the girl). For the other half it will
persist throughout life although becoming more readily resolved in
advancing years. The sexually inhibited adolescent male may regard
all women as falling into two categories. The princess is the nice girl
whom he sees as an extremely beautiful well-presented person, slim in
build, impeccably dressed, somewhat submissive in manner, who
never smokes and who is everyone's sister and sweetheart but nobody's mistress. Since she is presumed to be so sexually inhibited she
is an ideal partner since she will not be threatening sexually. She will
also be most sought after as a wife and mother since she will be both
faithful and fastidious about the house. The prostitute on the other
hand represents the archetypal fallen woman because in contrast to
the princess she is really sexual. She has a reputation for being a real
flirt and an easy lay. She is quite extrovert, a well built shapely girl
who grew up precociously and "goes out with older men". She is
hardly pretty having rather coarse features and she doesn't think
much of the male sex. She's nobody's sweetheart and everybody's
mistress. Although perhaps she could do with a bath a little more
often, she's an ideal girl to take out for a one night stand. Such stereotypes, even if they did exist once, hardly exist now except in the
minds of some adolescents and adults and particularly in those who
are sexually inhibited. But in a milder form we all know princesses
and prostitutes, cassanovas and princes and the many mixtures in-
between.

    In order that relationships can have some measure of stability it is,
I think, important that a successful resolution of the prostitute-
princess or cassanova-prince syndrome is achieved as far as possible.
Otherwise even short term pairbonding becomes impossible. For
example, many relationships founder because some men and women
simply cannot love and sex with the same person. Investigation always shows that this condition owes its existence, so far as experience goes, to the instillation of negative attitudes about sex. And
even when the relationship persists, because of a sense of obligation
or because of the children, usually sexual activity is only sporadic and

very impoverished. It may be of course that it is not the resolution of say a prostitute-princess conflict that is required for some but a re-evaluation of the idea that sexual fidelity in marriage is a desirable value. My own feelings on this are quite clear, believing as I do that it is quite impossible to renew sexual behaviour between some partners without some extra-marital experience, but I digress. What can be stated with some conviction is that sex educationalists must be on their guard not to imply that there is only one type of relationship, namely, a sexually monogamous heterosexual marriage, however desirable they may regard this. If they do they will lose what little credibility they have in this rapidly changing society.

Design of a Sex Education Programme

It is almost certain that however careful one is, practical problems will arise in any sex education programme. To keep these to a mini-mum it is important to tailor the syllabus and the mode and level of delivery to suit the particular groups one has to teach. Certain re-ligious and social groups may be more sensitive than others and some geographic areas of the British Isles will clearly have more traditional attitudes than others. However tempting it is to blaze a trail and intro-duce a radical programme there is a strong likelihood that one will simply become a martyr to a lost cause. I recall one occasion vividly when many years ago I was asked to give two talks on sex education to a small non-selective secondary school in the heart of the Stafford-shire Black Country. Full of enthusiasm I turned up with my collec-tion of slides and proceeded to talk about the Biology of Sex to the first class. The next morning I received a polite note from the head-master regretting that a change of timetable would make my second visit impossible. Whilst I did not detect any obvious anxiety or hosti-lity amongst the audience I certainly did amongst those teachers who were present and regardless of the rights and wrongs of the matter I had failed because I was perhaps being a little too direct in an area which had very strong traditional values. The same lecture incidentally was very well received in another school in London. Clearly also the age, social class, background and educational status of the children is important and must be taken into consideration when deciding upon what type of approach is to be used.

By and large it is good to mix the sexes in most instances except when one wants to deal with personal feelings and opinions in a group discussion after the more formal teaching period is completed. This separation is particularly important in that period at and around puberty when young people become particularly aware of the sexual feelings. Attempts to start an honest and free-flowing discussion between such youngsters when the sexes are mixed in my experience results either in an extremely inhibited exchange or uncontrollable and non-productive hilarity. It is certainly quite unreasonable to expect a girl or boy to be honest about their own personal sexual feelings amongst peers of the opposite sex.

It is well to remember that just as sex education is a new idea to most parents, so is it to most children and young people. A teacher may have become so familiar with his own teaching aids, slides, films, filmstrips etc., that he may overlook the fact that it is all very new and sometimes strange and embarrassing to his audience. They may well need desensitizing to such an honest and open approach to sex, particularly if they come from backgrounds which by and large will share in common a distaste for an open and frank discussion about sex.

However a teacher should not feel he has failed to communicate to his group if they seem to fail to respond to his efforts in an extroverted manner and ask lots of questions. On many occasions, perhaps seeking my own rewards and having been disappointed that there was no response, I found out later when talking to individuals that they had benefited and enjoyed the class but had been too shy to participate actively.

The use of visual aids is essential in sex education. This is because sex is a visual subject. There are now available for hire a large number of films dealing with most aspects of sex education. The only precaution is to ensure, if it is possible, that the teacher has seen the material beforehand. This is necessary if he and his audience are to obtain the maximum advantage from any visual aid "package". The class may need some preliminary preparation and it is a good idea if he can anticipate some of the questions and discussion that will hopefully arise.

The great advantage of film or indeed any visual or auditory aid which is brought in, so to speak, from the ouside, is that it provides an alternative statement to the one that is being made in the classroom. So far as factual content is concerned there are unlikely to be any major differences. However, values, implicit or otherwise, may differ sharply and it is the conjunction of these differing points of view that provide the essential amalgam needed in a good teaching situation. One cannot teach in an ethical vacuum, nor should one sell a particular point of view. Instead each pupil should have the opportunity to seek out for himself, a point of view which is important and significant for him from a number which may be offered.

Many teachers I know are reluctant to use films which are, in their view, too explicit sexually. Such an approach has been a feature of all our films (see references). For example, if we are dealing with masturbation then we would film it, or if talking about the positions of intercourse these would be portrayed explicitly. The great advantage of such an approach is that it fulfills three important functions. It provides the means of communicating information accurately; if presented properly and in the correct supportive context it reduces shame and anxiety about sex and finally it will help to bring home to the audience that sex is not only about sperms and smegma or the plumbing of the penis but also about erotic feelings. This objective can only be achieved if we allow ourselves the occasional luxury of making sex sexy. Sexual feelings can then be recognized and moreover recognized as being good instead of shameful.

A problem which often concerns those who are actively engaged in sex education is how to overcome communication difficulties when talking to a class of children who although they share the same chronological age are of widely disparate emotional and sexual ages. I believe that this issue is often over-exaggerated. Admittedly there may be boys and girls who, in a class of 14 year olds, have already had extensive sex experience sitting next to those who have not yet reached puberty and are physically and emotionally naive. However, this diversity need not be a deterrent to a realistic treatment of sex since it simply anticipates a similar diversity that they will meet throughout their lives. Those teachers who have reservations about talking to the sexually naive often forget that they may well be projecting their own sexual fears upon a potentially sophisticated group. Above all it should be remembered that these youngsters are preparing to be adults, they are entering a period of development which will culminate in overt sex activity for the majority and it is the teachers' responsibility to establish communication with them if possible *before* their active sex lives begin. This is particularly important in contraceptive education. If the median age of first intercourse amongst the unmarried is between seventeen and eighteen years then clearly the sooner one starts the better.

In conclusion, and perhaps at the risk of an unfair generalization,

I would say that many of the problems associated with sex education stem from the "play it safe", "ignorance is bliss" approach. Many sex educators that I have met who are actively engaged in teaching are often unnecessarily serious-minded, ponderous, turgid, even self-righteous. More tragically they are often simply out of touch with the realities of life. Their values tend to be of the aspirational brand rather than the situational. My final plea therefore is to them. They should remember that sex comes in many colours. It can be beautiful, ugly, serious, fun, aggressive, tender, spiritual, commercial, exciting, boring, joyful or shameful and often sexy and it is that protrait of many, many colours that they have to encompass in their teaching.

Summary

Sex education is a new phenomenon and as such has become an ethical battleground. The simple, pragmatic objectives of providing straightforward and elementary information about the anatomy, physiology and psychology of sex and relating this to the practical issues that normally concern the adolescent, contraception, abortion, VD, facts above love-making and relationships have become lost in an emotive and confused argument. Unfortunately now it is the values, interests and aspirations of the parent, politician and teacher which appear to have taken precedence over those that really count, namely, the values of the consumer — the child and adolescent.

In terms of priority the prevention of unwanted pregnancy and the control of sexually-transmitted diseases must come high in any list of objectives as must also the prevention of unwanted marriages. In practice they do not and the reasons for this are examined in some detail.

Ultimately all the causes of inadequacy in sex educational programmes stem from the sexually repressive and anachronistic values of health educators and others, values which no longer relate to the realities of the society in which we all now live. From whatever source stress and anxiety originates, from the tyranny of unwanted pregnancy, from difficulties in the establishment of meaningful relationships or from the development of specific sexual disorders there can be found a consistent history of negative learning about sex and a denial by the individual of his sexuality. A greater degree of permissiveness must therefore be seen not as an evil spectre eroding the fundamental values of our society but as part of a healthy trend towards providing the individual with greater responsibility for his own actions.

References

Cauthery, P. and Cole, M. (1973). "The Fundamentals of Sex." Corgi: London.
Chilton, B. (1972). Psychosexual development in twins. *Journal of Biosocial Science*, 4, 277.
Growing Up (1971). 16 mm sex education film. Institute for Sex Education and Research, Birmingham.
Hansen, S. and Jensen, J. (1971). "The Little Red Schoolbook." Stage 1.
Hill, M. and Lloyd Jones, M. (1970). "Sex Education — The Erroneous Zone." National Secular Society.
Hunold, G. (1972). "Sexual Knowledge." H. H. Publications Limited: London.
Lambert, J. (1971). Survey of 300 Unwanted Pregnancies. *British Medical Journal* 16th October.
Morton Williams, J. and Hindell, K. (1972). "Abortion and Contraception." P.E.P. Broadsheet Number 356.
Schofield, M. (1968). "The Sexual Behaviour of Young People." Pelican.
Sexual Intercourse (1973). 16 mm sex education film, Institute for Sex Education and Research, Birmingham.
Understanding Sex (1971). Slide talk, Institute for Sex Education and Research, Birmingham.

Conclusion

SIDNEY CROWN

It is appropriate to conclude this book about psychosexual problems by picking general themes from its diversity. The obvious sequence is to consider how psychosexual problems present in a variety of contexts, through management — including but not restricted to sex therapies — and finally to prevention.

Prevalence of Psychosexual Problems

One thing this book has done is to show that the prevalence of psychosexual problems, while quantitatively impossible to determine, is likely to be far greater than suspected from formal surveys. Whether such problems are revealed depends on how a clinical or extra-clinical situation is set up. As doctors, psychotherapists, counsellors and others we merely sample from the total population of sex problems. This sample relates to where we are — in hospital, general practice or community — and who we are — approachable or distant, wanting to know or not wanting to know, to provide help or not, to assist in management or not.

Sexual problems are essentially private and in this they contrast with most other personal problems, for example, psychiatric problems which can be far more easily and willingly shared. Thus when the situation is appropriate for sexual problems to be revealed there is usually a back-log of misery and secrecy. The survey reported by Guthrie (pp. 338–340) illustrates this well. The disabled have not been surveyed previously for sexual problems. When this was done in a la   Midlands town covering a wide age-range and in an appropriately size sample, over half had current sexual problems regardless of their deg e of disability; and of the severely disabled nine out of ten had ps cho-sexual problems.

Prevalence figures vary. However the chapters in this book suggest, whether we classify people according to the stage of their life cycle, or by whether they are seen in hospital medical and surgical departments (and it must be remembered we have only sampled these: there are many other medical and surgical sub-specialities we do not cover) or whether patients are seen in general practice or through community agencies dealing with special interest groups (e.g. r igious groups and pastoral counselling) or with almost forgotten grot s such as the elderly, psychosexual problems are of significance in th all

These problems seem in frequency mainly to be those of se   dysfunction: impotency and ejaculatory problems and, in the female, frigidity. Problems of sexual deviance are however also of importance and interest whether these are considered so-to-speak in pure culture as by Hertoft (Chapter 7) and Mackay (Chapter 4) or whether they present within the context of marriage as by Crown (Chapter 8).

Psychosexual problems can be viewed according to their appearance at various phases of the life-cycle. We have spotlighted three phases: adolescence (Chapter 5) is concerned with the development of identity, including sexual identity; in the young adult (Chapter 6) this identity is rounded and developed and assumes its adult form through experiments in relationships and sexuality. In the elderly (Chapter 10) it is now realised that sexuality remains viable until very late provided sexual adjustment has been good previously. There seem no psychosexual problems unique to the elderly although problems relating to loneliness and death of a partner, and guilt relating to a recrudescence of masturbation are probably of greater prevalance than is recognized.

Presentation of Psychosexual Problems

Psychosexual problems may present directly and to any helping agency or they may present in a number of disguised forms. Direct presentation may be as problems of impotency, ejaculation, frigidity, marital sexual problems or sexual deviation. Important though this is, the recognition of the varieties of indirect presentation is perhaps less

widely appreciated. This type of presentation may occur both within
and outside formal psychiatry. An apparent reason for coming for help
may disguise the underlying sexual problem which reveals itself later.
Within psychiatry patients commonly present with depression or with
anxiety. Anxiety may, in turn, manifest itself in the "free-floating"
form as an anxiety state; as a phobic state where the anxiety is focussed
and specific or as one of a number of possible forms in which the
anxiety finds somatic expression. This may be as conversion hysteria
in which the somatic expression (headache, paralysis, fainting attacks,
pain, etc.) seems to symbolize the underlying conflict not infrequently
a conflict with sexuality. Another somatic expression is in the guise of
a "psychosomatic" disease. These are diseases of complex background
which includes psychological factors. Examples are thyrotoxicosis,
essential hypertension, duodenal ulcer, bronchial asthma, rheumatoid
arthritis, neurodermatitis, ulcerative colitis and others. Although the
precise contribution of the psychological factors is not understood,
despite research work of rapidly progressing sophistication, these illnesses do seem to express underlying stress, tension and conflict in a
massive and undifferentiated way, less obviously symbolic than the
conversion hysterical reaction. While it would be inaccurate to suggest
that sexual conflicts are paramount in psychosomatic disorders, the
importance of sexuality in relationships which are of most significance
means that it is frequently implicated. These points are emphasized
by Norell (Chapter 11). As might be expected it is to the general
practitioner, fulfilling the role of the first contact with medicine for
most people, that sexual problems in one of their disguises often
present.

Psychosexual problems present differently to different specialized
services in hospital and in the community. Detailed examples can be
found throughout the text. Male erectile impotency may be taken as
an example. This might present to the family doctor as a marital
problem; or to a family planning clinic as a contraceptive problem
perhaps as an inability to choose or agree an appropriate method
(Chapter 16). Later it may present to the gynaecologist as a problem
of infertility (Chapter 14). It might present to a urologist as a case of
hypochondriacal fear of abnormality of the penis (Chapter 15) or to
a venereologist relating to an impulsive sexual contact outside marriage
in an effort to bolster confidence in sexuality (Chapter 17). This
hypothetical example could be multiplied throughout the various
chapters of this book. The basic principle, perhaps established more
firmly by the variety of our chapters, is that whatever specialized

service is being offered to clients, the doctor or technical person
involved must read the signs, often heavily disguised signs, that suggest
that what is being talked about is not the obvious and perhaps
"typical" problem of a given clinic but a psychosexual problem.

Physical Factors and Psychosexual Problems

By "physical factor" is meant a medical illness, a drug, an operation,
a disability, something visible and tangible which has an undeniable
effect upon a person's life including sexuality. Many contributors
emphasize that these effects may be direct or they may be indirect.
By direct is meant, for example, the effect on sexuality of a physical
handicap, of a drug which may lead to difficulty with penile erection
(Chapter 12), of the existence of an artificial opening in the abdomen
and of a bag containing faecal matter (Chapter 18), or of a gynaecological condition leading to pain on intercourse (Chapter 14); or the
effect of an inevitably mutilating procedure such as the removal of a
breast or parts of the genitalia. There are many other examples in our
book. No-one can gainsay the importance of these direct causal factors
leading to sexual dysfunction and no physically undamaged person
can predict how they would react to such misfortune.

Almost as important, however, as an actual physical disability or
handicap is the indirect effect on sexuality of physical illness, disability
or a mutilating procedure. Such physical traumata happen to a person
with particular personality strengths and weaknesses; with a personal
life-style; ideosyncratic ways of responding to stress; and with different
forms of emotional investments in his or her body image (pp. 348—349).
Thus, for example, a sensitive woman's reaction to an ileostomy, to any
smell real or feared, or any noise, may be to feel handicapped in sexuality
while a less sensitive, anxious or preoccupied person may merely be
thankful to be fit and alive.

The complex interrelationship between physical, psychological and
social factors is well illustrated from Beaumont's Chapter on unwanted
drug effects. Thus in hypertension a delicate balance has to be attempted between the need for control of blood pressure and the effect on
the individual concerned, and, on the spouse, of sexual dysfunction e.g.
ejaculatory inhibition. The effect of physical factors on sexuality
should not be prejudged. While the stimulus may be, for example, a
relatively standardized surgical operation, responses are those of
individuals and these responses can not be determined by being looked

at through the filters of our own experience and attitudes. This applies to community counsellor, general practitioner or hospital specialist.

Cultural Factors and Psychosexual Problems

If physical and psychosocial factors are relevant to the personal and interpersonal recognition of sexual problems, cultural and sub-cultural factors must not be forgotten. Cross-cultural aspects of psychosexual problems are bound up in the variety of different forms of family and marital structure, social codes, mens' and womens' sexual status, and many other factors. In this book we have only touched on these briefly in relation to venerology (pp. 413–414) and urology (pp. 367–370). This is certainly an understatement of their importance. Cultural factors may be the balancing factors as to whether or not a sexual problem is overtly expressed and, if so, which form this should take — physical or psychological.

One of the important side-issues is the extreme difficulty of getting adequate knowledge in depth from anyone whose culture is markedly different from our own. It is not easy even to know the right questions to ask let alone to know, as in one's own culture, roughly the range of normality of the answers. Useful, straightforward guidance in cross-cultural interviewing techniques is given by Cox (1976).

Management of Psychosexual Problems

The management of a psychosexual problem often involves relatively specialized techniques so that reference to psychiatrists, psychotherapists or to a counselling service is required. Four key phrases seem to spell out the fundamentals of multi-disciplinary cooperation: communication, liaison, mutual trust and shared responsibility.

Communication

Clear communication between doctor and patient is essential particularly when relating to highly personal problems as Brant convincingly underlines for psychosexual problems presenting to the gynaecologist (Chapter 14). The physical findings and conclusions must be spelled out in clear, straightforward, but never condescending,

language. This may be necessary on repeated occasions. Much information is lost in communication between doctor and patient even in
relatively non-emotive areas such as rheumatology (Joyce *et al.*, 1969).
Extra care is vital in dealing with emotionally toned psychosexual
problems.

Liaison and Mutual Trust

If referral is decided upon then liaison and mutual trust are directly
related to whether or not the patient will follow up the referral and
hence whether any treatment will be possible. To establish effective
liaison between specialities in hospital, general practice and the
community services is difficult. A clear, non-ambivalent message must
be conveyed to the patient, the reasons for referral spelled out and the
point made that this is a constructive course of action not a futile
gesture. Norell (Chapter 11) emphasizes this in regard to general
practice; the primary physician sits astride hospital and community
services.

Shared responsibility

Finally the concept of shared responsibility: referral of a patient
should not necessarily mean removal of the patient to someone else's
care with shunted responsibility and loss of interest by the referring
person. Shared responsibility is appropriate to many problems as for
example a marital psychosexual problem in which general practitioner,
gynaecologist and psychiatrist may share responsibility for ongoing
management that may extend over a number of years. The joint interview technique between doctor and both partners in a relationship
(Chapter 8) is often particularly apposite. Once a natural reluctance
to use the joint interview situation is overcome the technique is
remarkably effective in conveying facts accurately, in promoting
communication and ensuring less loss of information.

Sex Therapies

Psychosexual problems may be treated using one of the formal sex
therapies (individual or group psychotherapy; marital therapy; counselling or behavioural modification). In part I of this book we have

tried to outline the different techniques in their essentials and to show the types of problems to which they are suited. All these techniques involve training and this training is becoming more readily available throughout the country in the form of systematic, long-term supervision and case discussion or shorter weekly or week-end courses, lectures and seminars. This book has not dealt in detail with training. The interested reader, medical or non-medical, may most profitably ask the nearest University Department of Psychiatry, University Counselling Service or Regional Post-graduate Medical Centre about available training courses.

Outside the formal sex therapies however it is clear that the bulk of guidance remains likely to be done by doctors working in specialized hospital departments, by general practitioners and by community personnel catering for specialized interest groups — ministers of religion, voluntary workers attached to specialized helping services (epilepsy, multiple sclerosis, the physically handicapped, etc.) and other "lay" or self-help bodies. This emerges clearly from many of our chapters: if all problems were referred to the psychiatrist the psychiatric services would be unable to cope. It seems most likely, however, that persons with no formal training in sex therapy but who are interested and involved will, through sympathetic listening and straightforward advice, help persons with psychosexual problems rather than damage them. What is most important is that persons who find themselves in this role learn how to recognize those psychosexual problems that need more than straightforward counselling so that they can guide the client or patient to one of the available specialized services.

It is supremely important to remember that the attitude and effectiveness of the first person to whom someone with a psychosexual problem turns for guidance is crucial. It is likely to determine whether the patient seeks further help, if that is appropriate, or, on the contrary, turns away hurt and disppointed because of an attitude perhaps of aloofness, disinterest, rejection, hyper-morality or, at the other extreme, emotional over-involvement.

Prevention of Psychosexual Problems

Two approaches to the prevention of psychosexual problems seem to emerge from this book: foresight and anticipation in the individual case; and, for future generations, sex education.

Foresight and Anticipation

The question of prevention through foresight and anticipation is dealt with by many contributors. It involves preparation in advance for possible disabilities that might arise relating to sexuality through some medical or surgical — or even psychiatric or social — intervention. It also involves the unfortunate results of nature or fate as for example the anticipatable consequence of trauma or accident. An area in which this general preventive technique has been particularly successful is in the preparation of partners for pregnancy, labour and childbirth (pp. 350—354). A surgical operation such as for bladder cancer (p. 379) that will inevitably lead to sexual dysfunction through, for example, interference with the nerve supply to the genitals; or to a permanent aesthetic handicap as with an ileostomy (pp. 425—427); or the use of a drug which affects sexual function (Chapter 12), any procedure or manipulation that, directly or indirectly, leads to sexual dysfunction can almost certainly be minimized in its effect by careful preparation for disability. This may also involve later referral to an appropriate helping service such as a club or society containing members who understand a given illness or post-operative disability through direct experience of it.

In all these ways care with communication, preparation, foresight and practical advice and counselling is likely to reduce psychosexual morbidity for the individual patient. Nor should the place of the specialised sexual therapies be forgotten, for example, joint interviews or particular behavioural modification techniques aimed to maximize sexual pleasure even in the case of fairly gross physical handicap.

Sex Education

Our book ends, as surely it should, with a discussion of sex education. As Cole suggests (Chapter 19), sex education programmes that are adapted to the age, intelligence and social-cultural background of the child must surely reduce psychosexual problems both in prevalence and severity. He also makes the point that these courses should pull no punches and must deal with aspects of human sexuality and relationships that young people want to know about. Also, whatever teaching aids are used, visual aids, slides or films, are almost certainly essential.

The sex educator does not himself live in a moral, social or ethical vacuum. His social-cultural milieu will vary both from other sex educators and from those he is trying to educate. A potential sex educator must recognize this so that his or her values and attitudes may be made explicit to those taught; these values can then also be debated. It does not, in principle, matter whether an approach to sex education is presented within the general framework outlined by Cole or another framework as, for example, a religious frame of reference provided this is made clear. The sex educator should be, as far as possible, a reasonably mature and whole person with a thought-through scale of values both within and outside sexuality. Issues broached by Cole, such as the pros and cons of active sexuality in adolescence, should be faced up to and discussed openly; not avoided or swept under the carpet.

Experimentation with different courses of sex education are certainly necessary during the next few years. Courses should vary both in content and teaching methods. Objective evidence should gradually accrue measuring, for example, immediate change in factual knowledge and in attitudes of those taught as well as assessing remote effects in terms of the prevention of psychosexual problems. The methodological problems are considerable but, insofar as the results of any teaching in principle are measurable, it should be possible to make progress. To end with one of Cole's most provocative suggestions, human sexuality, with understanding gained from the arts, sciences, biology, psychology, sociology, ethics and religion, might form an appropriate subject for school-leaving examinations in the future.

References

Cox, J. (1976). Psychiatric assessment and the immigrant patient. *British Journal of Hospital Medicine*, **15**, July.

Joyce, C. R. B., Caple, G., Mason, M., Reynolds, E., and Mathews, J. A. (1969). Quantitative study of doctor-patient communication. *Quarterly Journal of Medicine*, **38**, 183–194.

Subject Index